THE THEORY OF MONEY

JÜRG NIEHANS

The Theory of Money

The Johns Hopkins University Press
Baltimore and London

The Johns Hopkins University Press, Baltimore, Maryland 21218
The Johns Hopkins Press Ltd., London

Originally published, 1978

Johns Hopkins paperback edition, 1980

Library of Congress Catalog Card Number 77–17247
ISBN 0–8018–2055–3 (hardcover)
ISBN 0–8018–2372–2 (paperback)

Library of Congress Cataloging in Publication data will be found on the last printed page
of this book.

CONTENTS

PREFACE

This book is meant to be an introduction into the pure theory of money and monetary policy. Its main topic is the interaction of the money stock with other assets and the flows of goods and services. The book is a "treatise" in the sense of a systematic, comprehensive treatment of the principles of its subject matter. In the monetary field there have appeared no such treatises since Patinkin's *Money, Interest and Prices*, first published in 1956. Since then monetary theory has changed considerably. The present book tries to provide a new synthesis of these developments.

Like other treatises of this sort, this book combines features of both a textbook and a research monograph without claiming to be either. It is similar to a research monograph inasmuch as it includes original contributions that cannot be considered to be "standard analysis." It is similar to a textbook inasmuch as it gives a systematic discussion of the subject, including introductory and expository material and references to the literature.

To achieve a comprehensive treatment in a volume of moderate size, the analysis is limited to fundamental aspects that promise to be of general and lasting significance over a wide range of institutions, countries, and historical periods. In comparison with the two volumes of Keynes' *Treatise on Money*, the present book includes only the "pure theory" and leaves out the "applied theory" of money.

Money is considered in both its microeconomic and macroeconomic aspects. The analysis thus extends from the demand for money by individuals to monetary policy. International aspects, however, are, with a few exceptions, left out, since they would require a separate volume. The theory of monetary growth is also treated only briefly, because after a rapid development in the late 1960s it has progressed little since Stein's *Money and Capacity Growth*. At the microeconomic level the approach is characterized by the decisive role assigned to transaction costs. At the macroeconomic level the main characteristic is the use of a general stock/

flow approach, which includes Keynesian, monetarist, and other positions as special cases.

Chapter 1 reviews the tradition of neoclassical monetary theory by describing how it approached the interrelated issues of the services of money, of its neutrality, and of the integration of monetary and value theory. The subject of chapters 2–4 is the amount of cash balances an individual agent wishes to hold under given market conditions, depending on such factors as real income, commodity prices, interest rates, transaction costs, inflation, and uncertainty. No direct utility of money will be postulated; whatever utility money may have is reflected from the goods money can buy. The key to such an indirect-utility approach is the concept of transaction costs, with factors like speculation and uncertainty appearing as modifying influences.

Chapters 5–7 extend the perspective from individual equilibrium to general equilibrium. It is shown in chapter 5 how market prices and interest rates are determined by the interaction of individual agents, which leads to the problem of the welfare effects of continuing inflation and of the so-called optimal money supply. Chapter 6 raises the fundamental question of the relative advantages of monetary exchange as compared to barter, and of the conditions under which monetary exchange will emerge. While these problems are concerned with money as a medium of exchange, chapter 7 considers the role of money as a medium of account, including the topics of money illusion, deflators, and escalator clauses.

While the first part of the book is mostly about the demand for money, the second part is mostly about the money supply. Commodity money, with the important special case of the gold standard, is analyzed in chapter 8. Chapter 9 investigates the supply of money by commercial banks, developing the argument from the microeconomics of the individual bank to the macroeconomics of the banking system. The following two chapters, covering the traditional subjects of monetary macroeconomics, consider the effect of government-created fiat money on prices, interest rates, employment, and output. While chapter 10 uses a comparative-static approach, describing the adjustments to monetary policy as a sequence of distinct stages, chapter 11 views the adjustment as a dynamic process along a Phillips curve. Chapter 12, finally, discusses the role of the central bank in the economic system and the principles which might guide its monetary policy.

Each chapter opens with a brief nontechnical summary of its content. By perusing these previews, the reader may thus obtain an introduction to the book as a whole.

The main use of the book will probably be at the level of first-year graduate courses, possibly also in advanced undergraduate courses. In fact, the present manuscript has evolved from lecture notes over a period of more than twelve years. The reader is expected to be familiar with the basics of general equilibrium analysis. While mathematics is extensively used, the required tools do not go beyond the elements of multivariate calculus and nonlinear programming. Graphic devices are used whenever possible. The emphasis is on economic substance and not on mathematical rigor.

Having worked on this book for a long time, I owe debts to many colleagues, friends, and helpers that are not reflected in the references. Foremost among these are my former colleagues at Johns Hopkins in the field of macroeconomics and monetary theory, particularly Carl Christ, Louis Maccini, and William Poole. Dermot McAleese, as a research assistant, helped me relate my own thinking to the tradition of monetary theory. For chapter 11, Paul McNelis provided much of the background analysis and all of the computing work; his contribution amounts to coauthorship. The National Science Foundation granted financial support for a limited part of the research on various aspects of the demand for cash balances and on the role of the central bank. Libby Pratt, Becky Ford, Joyce Goldberger, and Susan Donaldson helped me make my manuscript, through its many stages, ready for the printer. My largest, though most intangible, debt is to The Johns Hopkins University, which for eleven years provided the fertile environment for my work.

THE THEORY OF MONEY

One

THE NEOCLASSICAL TRADITION

Introduction

The most fundamental question of monetary theory concerns the services or "functions" of money. Why do people use money? What do they use as money? How much money do they wish to hold? How do they use it? Economists have always found it more difficult to analyze the services of a medium of exchange than those of producer and consumer goods. This is because a medium of exchange derives its usefulness from some sort of imperfection or "friction" in the market, while the essentials of value and allocation can be understood on the assumption of perfect or "frictionless" markets. For about a century, economic thinking about these problems has been dominated by what may be called the "neoclassical" tradition,[1] characterized by an effort to incorporate money into the general equilibrium framework without making the underlying market imperfections explicit. While the verbal discussions of monetary services are full of references to those imperfections, the latter leave no trace in the formal models. In the final analysis, money is typically treated *as if* it were one of those goods whose services does not depend on market imperfections. We may call this a metaphorical approach to monetary theory.

What will gradually develop over the following chapters constitutes a departure from the neoclassical tradition in the sense that it offers an explicit analysis of frictions. At the same time it may be regarded as an extension of the neoclassical tradition in the sense that money and exchange are incorporated into a general equilibrium framework. As a background to this development, the present chapter offers a review, necessarily brief, of what the neoclassical tradition in monetary theory was.

From early times up to the present day, three propositions, though not

---

1. It is remarkable how little Samuelson's account (1968) of what he was taught in the thirties differed from what he could have learned from Walras at the turn of the century or from what is being taught in better colleges today. Few areas of economics have seen so little progress over this period.

universally accepted, have stood in the center of theoretical discussions about money:

1. The use of money increases the efficiency of the economy.

2. Money is neutral in the sense that an exogenous change in its quantity, once all adjustments have run their course, produces a proportional change in all prices, leaving real phenomena unchanged.

3. While money may be different from other goods in important respects, the difference is one in degree rather than in kind; in principle, it should be possible to explain the value of money by the same analytical apparatus that is used to explain the value of other goods.

Since the dawn of economics there has been, in addition, a fourth proposition, accepted by mercantilists and economists, both classical and neoclassical, and reaffirmed by Keynesians, anti-Keynesians, and contemporary theorists. That proposition says that during *transitional* periods a change in the supply of money may have powerful real effects, resulting in fluctuations of output and employment. The discussion of this proposition will be deferred to the second part of this study (see, in particular, chapter 11); the three equilibrium propositions, however, will now be discussed in turn.

1.1. Money and efficiency

Economists (and laymen) have always felt that the use of a medium of exchange increases the efficiency of an economy. The gain was usually considered to be large. It has both qualitative and quantitative aspects. The qualitative aspects appear when monetary exchange is compared with barter. Classical and neoclassical economists were graphic in describing the "double coincidence of wants" of the hungry tailor and the shivering baker which would be necessary for an exchange in a barter economy and the narrow limitations it imposes on the division of labor.[2] The use of money would increase welfare by freeing exchange from the shackles of the double coincidence of wants. It was recognized that the utility of money is due to this increase in welfare, and we can even find the proposition that the supply of money is at the optimum where the marginal cost of an exchange is the same for direct barter and monetary exchange.[3] However, to this day economic theory has never developed an explicit model of multiperson barter.[4] As a consequence, the welfare gain from monetary exchange could

2. A good example is the first chapter of Jevons' *Money and the Mechanism of Exchange* (1875).

3. See Kinley (1904, p. 131).

4. For a recent contribution see Starr (1972). Starr analyzes the (hardly startling) proposition that indirect barter cannot be worse than direct barter and is generally better. The interesting thing is that a century after Jevons such an elementary proposition is still considered to be in need of analytical elucidation—and rightly so.

never be formally analyzed.[5] In particular, it was not clear whether the transition from barter to monetary exchange could be expected to take place spontaneously under the pressure of market forces whenever it promised welfare gains[6] or whether it required an "invention," combined with persuasion, convention, or compulsion.[7] In a vague sense, the inefficiency of barter was often attributed to friction, and money was compared to the lubricant that would reduce that friction. In a frictionless economy, therefore, monetary exchange would have no advantage over barter. An analysis of the role of money in economic equilibrium would thus require a theory of frictions.[8]

Potential elements of such a theory were often mentioned. Thus it was explained that frictions would primarily appear in the form of transaction (or transfer) and storage (or inventory) costs. Writers of neoclassical textbooks seemed to enjoy describing the burdensome inventory and transaction costs in a barter economy. Money, to use Mill's words, thus became a "contrivance for sparing time and labor."[9] The crucial importance of transaction and storage costs is also implied in the recurring discussions of the qualities that make a commodity suitable as a medium of exchange, for if we learn that efficient money should have properties like portability, indestructibility, homogeneity, divisibility, and cognizability,[10] these virtues are easily recognized as some of the numerous determinants of transaction and storage costs. However, up to the present time it was not possible to advance the analysis beyond the collection of plausible suggestions to the construction of contrasting theories of barter and monetary exchange.

The quantitative aspects of the advantages of monetary exchange appear when, in a fully monetized economy, at given commodity prices, an individual is equipped with gradually rising cash balances. The benefit from these balances would have different sources.[11] First, the holder of money

5. What neoclassical economists liked to call a theory of barter was, in fact, something very different, namely a theory of exchange in a world in which it makes no difference who trades with whom and what is exchanged for what. Patinkin's first chapter (1965) illustrates this point. The statement that neoclassical economics was "really" a theory of barter was usually meant to be a severe criticism; it was, in fact, an exaggerated claim. The valid criticism is that neoclassical economics never advanced from a world in which every commodity could serve as a perfect money to the analysis of genuine barter.
6. This was prominently argued by Carl Menger (1871, pp. 253 ff.).
7. For a recent expression of this view see Kurz (1974).
8. See, for example, Hicks (1935).
9. Mill (1857, 2:9).
10. Jevons (1875, chap. 5).
11. For a representative example see Pigou (1917). It is worth noting that the discussion of the familiar transactions, speculative and precautionary motives for holding money did not make much progress from Cantillon to (and including) Keynes.

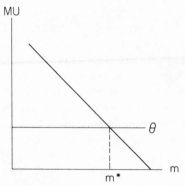

Figure **1.1.1**
The Marginal Utility of Money

would not be constrained to synchronize his purchases and his sales; he could thus schedule his transactions in a more advantageous way. This benefit would, in part, depend on the "payments habits," which were usually regarded as technologically and institutionally determined. Second, cash balances would offer insurance against losses arising either from unexpected needs or from unexpected business opportunities foregone, introducing a precautionary element into the demand for money. Third, the holding of cash might save brokerage and other transaction costs.

The marginal benefit from larger and larger cash balances would presumably decline, ultimately reaching zero where the individual is satiated with money.[12] For given prices, the marginal utility of money can thus be described by a downward-sloping curve (fig. 1.1.1). On the other hand, cash balances might cost something. The cost could be identified as the sacrifice, due to time preference, involved in the holding of wealth instead of consuming it and/or as the income foregone in not holding the wealth in the form of productive capital goods or interest-bearing assets. The individual would try to achieve that level of cash balances which made the marginal utility equal to the marginal cost. If there was indeed a positive marginal cost, the accumulation of cash balances would stop short of satiation.

This argument implies that for given economic conditions each individual has a definite demand for money. In figure 1.1.1 this demand is m^*, which makes the marginal utility of money equal to the marginal cost as expressed (in the absence of capital goods and credit) by the rate of time

12. Pigou quotes Carver: "Some exchanges could scarcely be made at all without the use of money. In these cases the utility of money is very high. . . . Some exchanges could only be made with great difficulty without money, in which cases the utility of money would be considerable. Some exchanges could be made with comparatively little difficulty, in which cases the utility of money would be inconsiderable. And some exchanges could be made as easily without money as with it, in which cases the utility of money will be *nil*" (1917, p. 167).

preference, θ. For given tastes, payments habits, risk, and time preference (but in the absence of credit and capital goods), this demand could be written

$$m = m\,(\bar{x}_1, \cdots \bar{x}_Q; p_1, \cdots p_Q; \theta), \qquad (1.1.1)$$

where $\bar{x}_1, \cdots \bar{x}_Q$ represent the given endowment consisting of goods $1, \cdots Q$, $p_1, \cdots p_Q$ are the market prices of these goods and θ expresses the opportunity cost of cash balances. Demand functions of this type could be added over individuals to give an aggregate demand function of the same form.

The demand function for money was written in many special forms. One of these is

$$m = k \sum_{q=1}^{Q} p_q \bar{x}_q = kp \sum_{q=1}^{Q} \frac{p_q \bar{x}_q}{p} = k\,p\,\bar{x}, \qquad (1.1.2)$$

where p is a suitably chosen price index and $\bar{x} = \sum_{q=1}^{Q} p_q \bar{x}_q / p$ is a measure of aggregate resources.[13] In the "cash balance approach," which this equation summarizes, the so-called Cambridge k indicates what fraction of the money value of resources, on the average, economic agents wish to hold in the form of cash balances.[14] Alternatively, the equation can be written

$$mv = p\bar{x}, \qquad (1.1.3)$$

where $v = 1/k$. In this variant v can be identified as the (income) velocity of money.[15] It is clear that the cash balance approach and the velocity approach are economically equivalent.[16] While such special forms of the

13. Cf. Pigou (1917, p. 165).

14. A comment on the interpretation of (1.1.2) may help to forestall misunderstandings at this point. If k is interpreted not as the desired, but as the actual, cash balance per dollar worth of resources, the equation is transformed from a demand function into an accounting identity, called the equation of exchange. If we add to the equation of exchange the threefold macroeconomic proposition that (1) m can be changed exogenously, (2) an exogenous change in m has no lasting effect on k, and (3) an exogenous change in m has no lasting effect on $\bar{x}$, we obtain the quantity theory of money (or, more accurately, of prices). It states that an exogenous change in m produces an equiproportionate change in p. The same collection of symbols can thus be interpreted as an accounting identity, as a demand function for money, or as a theory of the price level. The recent tendency to identify the quantity theory of money with a rather general form of demand function for money seems to have originated with Friedman (1956); it is not part of the neoclassical tradition.

15. This form, though known since the early nineteenth century, has found its classical elaboration in the work of Irving Fisher (1911). On the history of the quantity equation and the quantity theory see Marget's massive study (1938), a monument to polemic scholarship. Note that k has the dimension time, while v has the dimension $1/\text{time}$ or velocity.

16. In an economy with intermediate transactions the volume of transactions is, of course, larger than final output or income. In this case a choice has to be made between an "income approach" and a "transactions approach." This choice relates to a question of substance, while the choice between a cash-balance approach and a velocity approach is a question of exposition.

demand function for money may be useful expository devices, the substance of the neoclassical approach to monetary theory does not depend on them. Equation (1.1.1) is all that is needed.

The demand function for cash balances can easily be incorporated into a general equilibrium system. There is a demand function for each of the Q commodities,

$$x_q = x_q (\bar{x}_1, \cdots \bar{x}_Q; p_1, \cdots p_Q; \theta). \tag{1.1.4}$$

But the individual can spend no more than he earns, and nothing is thrown away. The aggregate value of commodities demanded thus equals the value of the endowment:

$$\sum_{q=1}^{Q} p_q (x_q - \bar{x}_q) = 0. \tag{1.1.5}$$

This budget constraint was often called "Say's Law" because it formalizes Say's phrase that "commodities are bought with commodities." The constraint implies that there are only $Q - 1$ independent demand functions. If an individual is subject to just this one budget constraint, this means essentially that commodities can be traded costlessly without limit, provided total purchases equal total sales. If this is interpreted literally, there would be no reason for ever using money or otherwise preferring one medium of exchange to another. Of course, neoclassical monetary theorists would have refused to interpret the constraint so literally, but they were not able to formalize what they thought went on "behind the scenes."

In equilibrium, all markets are cleared:

$$x_q = \bar{x}_q. \qquad (q = 1 \cdots Q - 1) \tag{1.1.6}$$

If the market is cleared for all but one of the commodities, it is implicitly cleared for the last commodity, because Say's Law has already made aggregate demand over all commodities equal to aggregate supply. If we assume that the economy is equipped with a certain nominal quantity of money, $\bar{m}$, equilibrium also requires

$$m = \bar{m}. \tag{1.1.7}$$

Disregarding the possibility of multiple solutions and negative prices, these equations determine prices and consumption for all Q commodities and also real cash balances. The quantity of real cash balances in an economy is thus explained jointly with the other variables of the system.

This raises the question whether the quantity of real balances resulting from the interaction of market forces is optimal from the point of view of social welfare. Protagonists of neoclassical theory like Friedman and Samuelson have argued that there is a difference between the private cost of real cash balances and their social cost (for references see chapter 5). The private cost, as perceived by individuals, is equal to the opportunity cost of real balances as represented in the above model by θ. The social cost, how-ever, is zero: Just by maintaining a lower price level, society can raise real cash balances to any desired level, and a lower price level is costless. The implication is that the market economy tends to be undersupplied with real cash balances. This is what Samuelson called the "nonoptimality of money under laissez faire."

The fundamental problem of the neoclassical general equilibrium sys-tem represented by (1.1.1) and (1.1.4) — (1.1.7) is the absence of an explicit account of the factors that make money valuable. Payments habits, risk, and transaction costs do not appear in the system. We do not even know exactly how the marginal utility of cash balances and the demand functions for money are supposed to be derived. While all those picturesque illustrations about the services of money, so dear to the heart of neoclassi-cal writers, are certainly suggestive, they do not amount to analysis.

1.2. The neutrality of money

It is probably the oldest and most familiar proposition of monetary theory that money is demanded not for its own sake but for what it can buy.[17] A neoclassical economist might formalize this statement by saying that the demand function for money (1.1.1) is linear-homogeneous in all prices and can thus be written

$$\frac{m}{p_1} = m\left(\bar{x}_1, \cdots \bar{x}_Q; 1, \cdots \frac{p_Q}{p_1}, \theta\right) \tag{1.2.1}$$

$$= m(\bar{x}_1, \cdots \bar{x}_Q; \pi_1, \cdots \pi_Q, \theta),$$

where p_1 is arbitrarily chosen as numéraire and $\pi_q = p_q/p_1$ are relative prices (with $\pi_1 \equiv 1$). If, for given relative prices, $1/p_1$ is interpreted as the "price of money," the homogeneity postulate can be expressed by saying that the demand curve for nominal cash balances as a function of their "price" is a rectangular hyperbola: The product of m and $1/p_1$ remains constant as p_1 changes.

A neoclassical economist would also argue that the demand for com-modities depends only on relative prices and not on the absolute price level. The demand functions (1.1.4) would thus be homogeneous of degree zero,

$$x_q = x_q(\bar{x}_1, \cdots \bar{x}_Q; \pi_1, \cdots \pi_Q; \theta), \tag{1.2.2}$$

while (1.1.5) can be written

$$\sum_{q=1}^{Q} \pi_q(x_q - \bar{x}_q) = 0. \tag{1.2.3}$$

17. Thus Adam Smith wrote: ". . . money can serve no other purpose besides purchasing goods. . . . It is not for its own sake that men desire money, but for the sake of what they can purchase with it" (1776/1904, 1:405).

As a consequence, money can be shown to be neutral in the sense that a change in its nominal quantity changes only the price level, here measured by p_1, while all quantities and relative prices remain unchanged. The nominal quantity of money thus appears to be of no real significance in economic equilibrium.

The typical neoclassical economist would, in fact, feel that the general equilibrium system can be split into a real part—consisting of (1.2.2), (1.2.3), and (1.1.6)—that determines all quantities and relative prices, and a monetary part—consisting of (1.2.1) and (1.1.7)—that determines the price level and real cash balances. It was thus possible, and perhaps convenient, to discuss value and allocation in the first volume of a treatise, while money and the price level would follow in the second volume.[18] The neutrality proposition implied the quantity theory of prices: For given resources and tastes, equilibrium prices would always change in proportion to the exogenous quantity of money. It should be noted that this proposition does not depend on the use of a special demand function for money like one derived from the equation of exchange.

The precise meaning of the neoclassical neutrality proposition was not always clear. First, neoclassical writers sometimes came close to suggesting that *real* cash balances are neutral. Thus John Stuart Mill stated that "the relations of commodities to one another remain unaltered by money," and "things which by barter would exchange for one another will, if sold for money, sell for an equal amount of it" (1857, 2:9 ff.). Taken literally, this says that the economy is indeed neutral with respect to real cash balances; relative prices are the same in a monetary economy as they would be in the absence of money.

This interpretation poses a dilemma. If money does not affect any real variables it cannot increase efficiency, and if it really increases efficiency it cannot leave relative prices unaffected. Typically, classical and neoclassical economists relied on their metaphors to dispose of this point. Money as a "veil" would not be quite satisfactory, since it does not suggest any real significance, but only obfuscation of the underlying realities. Money as a "lubricant" would be just about right, since oil permits the machine to run without being a part of it.[19] Of course, the strict interpretation of Mill's statement is patently invalid (and Mill perhaps did not mean what he said). Neoclassical economists never seriously maintained that money is a "veil" in the sense that it does not affect the shape of what it is hiding.

18. The order could not be reversed; while relative prices could be discussed independently of the absolute price level, the price level could only be determined once relative prices were known.

19. See Jevons (1875, p. 15), Marshall (1923, p. 38), and Wicksell (1934/35, 2:5). Samuelson updates the metaphor to that of money as a catalyst (1968, p. 3).

Second, the neutrality proposition, strictly speaking, does not apply to commodity money (like gold coins). For gold currency of given weight and fineness the money prices of commodities reflect real factors. On the side of consumption, the money price of wheat reflects the marginal rate of substitution between nonmonetary gold and wheat. On the side of production, it reflects the marginal rate of transformation, through factor reallocation, of gold into wheat. The cost of production theory of the value of money applies. Suppose some new gold discovery, after all adjustments have worked themselves out, turns out to have raised the quantity of gold coins by p percent. In view of the implied shift in the production possibility curve of the economy, it would be a coincidence if the price level had also increased by exactly p percent. The same argument holds, in principle, in the case of a paper money convertible into gold. Neoclassical writers thus tended to be careful in pointing out that the neutrality proposition relates to inconvertible paper currency.[20]

The third point, raised by Lange (1942) and Patinkin (1948, 1965), requires a somewhat longer discussion. Lange and Patinkin argued that the neoclassical dichotomization of the price system, while mathematically consistent, involves an economic inconsistency. Since individuals are subject to the budget constraint, so the argument runs, an excess of aggregate purchases over aggregate sales is reflected in an excess supply of cash balances of equal amount,

$$\sum_{q=1}^{Q} p_q (x_q - \bar{x}_q) = \bar{m} - m, \tag{1.2.4}$$

where $\bar{m}$ is the exogenously given money supply while m is the demand for cash balances. In contrast to Say's Law, (1.2.4) is often called "Walras' Law." The real part of the price system shows that all excess demands for commodities, $x_q - \bar{x}_q$, can be made zero by choosing the appropriate *relative* prices without regard to the absolute price level. This implies that the excess supply of money, appearing on the right-hand side of (1.2.4), is also brought to zero without regard to the price level. But this contradicts (1.2.1), which says that monetary equilibrium requires some particular price level. Patinkin thus concluded that the neoclassical dichotomization of the price system was invalid.

I believe what is invalid is Patinkin's criticism of the neoclassical dichotomy.[21] The worst that can be said about the dichotomy is that its proponents were not quite clear about what they did and thus could not explain it to the satisfaction of scholarly critics. What they, in fact, accomplished was a conceptual partitioning or decomposition of the general

20. Commodity money will be discussed more fully in chapter 8.
21. The following discussion is based on Niehans (1969b).

equilibrium system, logically akin to the Slutsky decomposition of the effect of price on demand and many decompositions in other sciences. Such a decomposition does not occur in the real world; it would require a controlled experiment under artificially imposed conditions. These conditions require that certain things are held constant that, in reality, are variable. In the Slutsky decomposition this artificial constancy relates to real income (in defining the substitution effect) and relative prices (in defining the income effect). In the neoclassical dichotomy it relates to excess demand for money (in the real part) and relative prices (in the monetary part). While Slutsky's substitution effect is "income compensated," the real part of the neoclassical system is "cash compensated." To reject the neoclassical dichotomy on the ground that cash compensation does not take place in the real world[22] is analogous to a rejection of the Slutsky decomposition on the ground that income compensation does not take place in the real world. Microeconomics did not sink so deep.

Formally, the decomposition is achieved as follows.[23] Consider a system consisting of (1.2.1), (1.2.2), (1.2.4), and the equilibrium conditions (1.1.6) and (1.1.7). Suppressing endowments and time preference, it can be rewritten[24]

$$x_q(\pi_1, \cdots \pi_Q) = \bar{x}_q, \tag{1.2.5}$$

$$\sum_{q=1}^{Q} \pi_q(x_{q,} - \bar{x}_q) = \bar{m}/p_1 - m/p_1, \tag{1.2.6}$$

$$m(\pi_1, \cdots \pi_Q) = m/p_1, \tag{1.2.7}$$

$$m = \bar{m}. \tag{1.2.8}$$

It should be noted that Say's Law (1.1.5) does not appear in this system. Instead I use Walras' Law (1.2.4). The real part is now obtained by replacing the actual money supply m by a fictitious money supply $\bar{m}$, where $\bar{m}$ is defined as those "equilibrium balances" which just satisfy the demand for cash balances as described by (1.2.7),

$$\bar{m} = m. \tag{1.2.9}$$

22. Cf. Becker/Baumol (1952), Johnson (1962), Bieri (1963), and Mauer (1966).

23. I interpret Samuelson's interpretation of the dichotomy as being essentially the same as the one given on the following pages (1968, pp. 9 ff.). In the real part of his system, called A, Samuelson regards the quantity of money as variable, unrelated to the actual money supply, while at the same time imposing Say's Law ($A_{\text{III.3}}$). In the monetary part B, the quantity of money is then equalized to the actual money supply. This interpretation is confirmed by Samuelson's reply to Patinkin (1972, p. 292).

24. Patinkin proposed to include real cash balances $\bar{m}/p$ in the demand functions. However, as Archibald and Lipsey (1958) demonstrated, the real balance effect, while potentially important in a dynamic theory of adjustment processes, is irrelevant for full equilibrium. For the neoclassical dichotomy, which is a proposition about the statics of the system, it can thus be omitted. This is recognized in Patinkin (1965).

As a consequence, the right-hand side of (1.2.6) vanishes,

$$\sum \pi_q (x_q - \bar{x}_q) = 0, \tag{1.2.10}$$

resulting in an equation of the same appearance as (1.1.5). It should be noted, however, that the condition (1.2.10) is satisfied through cash compensation, while (1.1.5) is a budget constraint in the absence of cash. (1.2.5) and (1.2.10) are the real part of the dichotomized system, determining relative prices. Once these are known, they can be substituted into (1.2.7) to give the demand for real cash balances. At the same time, the equilibrium money supply $\bar{m}$ is again replaced by the actual money supply m. The resulting monetary part of the system, consisting of (1.2.7) and (1.2.8), then determines the price level p_1.

The economic meaning of this conceptual experiment can be most easily visualized if it is imagined to take place in a Walrasian auction hall. Everybody comes to the marketplace with his tastes, his goods, and his cash balances. Suppose the auctioneer has set his mind on using a dichotomized tâtonnement process. To accomplish his purpose, he first fixes the price of, say, commodity 1 at some arbitrary level.[25] He also makes the following announcement. Whoever at the prices quoted in the subsequent process experiences a shortfall of cash balances relative to the equilibrium cash balance demanded at these prices can get the difference, equal to $\bar{m} - m$, from a compensation fund set up for this purpose. On the other hand, any excess of actual balances relative to equilibrium balances must be paid into that fund. Equilibrium balances are defined as those which give the individual no reason to either decrease his balances by an excess of aggregate purchases over aggregate sales or vice versa.[26] While Walras' Law is thus suspended, Say's Law is made to hold at whatever set of prices is announced.

Having thus established the rules of the game, the auctioneer successively announces various sets of absolute prices for all commodities except p_1. Once he has found the set which clears all markets, we know the set of equilibrium prices for given p_1. *Under the given compensation rule,* any change in the initial level of p_1 would result in a proportionate change in all other prices. The procedure thus determines the equilibrium set of relative prices.

In the second part of the tâtonnement process the auctioneer announces that relative prices are fixed at the equilibrium levels determined in the first stage. He also announces that original cash balances will be

25. Alternatively, he could fix some price index number.
26. Alternatively, whoever at the announced prices wants to sell more than he buys is gradually given additional balances, and whoever wants to buy more than he sells has to give up some balances, until purchases equal sales for everybody. In this way, the compensation mechanism can be operated by trial and error without prior knowledge of the demand functions for money.

restored for everybody. Walras' Law is in force again, while Say's Law is now satisfied only in equilibrium. The auctioneer then calls out various (absolute) levels of p_1, lowering or raising his bid according to whether there is excess demand or supply of money. The equilibrium price level is determined at the point where the money market is in equilibrium.[27] The temporary suspension of Walras' Law, far from making economic non-sense, thus appears as the crucial "trick" by which the tâtonnement process is decomposed into two parts.

This analysis confirms that for a neoclassical general equilibrium system with neutral money there is indeed a consistent decomposition procedure, based on appropriate compensation principles, permitting the determination of real variables in the real sector, while the price level is determined in the monetary sector. However, the amount of intellectual effort which, in the wake of Lange and Patinkin, was devoted to this issue, is entirely out of proportion to its economic significance. The real economic question is not whether a system can be dichotomized, but whether money is neutral. It will later be shown that neutral money is really a limiting case, and perhaps not even a particularly interesting one.

1.3. The integration of money and value theory

Neoclassical economists tended to feel that money and other goods were basically similar. While from certain points of view token money might perhaps be at one extreme of the commodity spectrum, its characteristics could still be measured on the same scale as those of other goods. Even the property of being valued only for what it can be exchanged against may be shared, *for a given individual,* by other goods; groceries for a retailer or real estate for a speculator are cases in point. This basic similarity of money and other things was most clearly expressed by Roscher in his famous dictum that the false definitions of money can be divided into those which regard money as more, and those which regard it as less, than the most marketable good.[28] Others identified the relevant property as "liquidity." The problem was to say exactly what marketability or liquidity are supposed to mean. If this could be done, it should be possible, so it was thought, to analyze monetary phenomena in terms of the same analytical apparatus as other aspects of economic life. To have finally integrated money and value theory was always the proudest boast of monetary theorists.[29]

Such an integration can be sought at different levels. A lower-level

27. Problems of the distribution of cash balances are ignored here.
28. (1880, p. 263). See also Fisher (1930, p. 216).
29. For examples see Walras (1900, ix–x), Hicks (1935), Rosenstein-Rodan (1936), Keynes (1936, p. 292), and Patinkin (1965, p. xxiv, and subtitle).

integration would be confined to demand and supply functions. This may be called the "Cassel Approach" to general equilibrium, since it was Cassel who argued that it was futile to look behind the demand and supply functions. This lower-level integration is accomplished in a general equilibrium system like the one consisting of (1.1.1), (1.1.4), (1.1.6), (1.1.7), and (1.2.4). Money and other goods are treated with perfect formal symmetry by the same analytical apparatus of demand and supply. "The propositions of both theories are derived by applying the same analytical technique to the same demand functions of the same markets."[30] A proper counting of equations and variables and a correct interpretation of the budget constraint and of neutrality are all that is necessary.

However, economic theory has generally not been satisfied with the Cassel approach. In particular, it was thought that it should be possible to reveal the homogeneity properties of (1.2.1) and (1.2.2) as implications of rational behavior instead of just postulating them on the basis of intuition or "introspective evidence." This made it necessary to go behind the demand and supply functions to the underlying optimizing calculus of individuals. The integration issue would thereby be raised to the higher level of utility theory. At this level things turned out to be far more difficult; the lower-level integration was revealed to be more apparent than real, more formal than substantive.

There were, in particular, two difficulties of unequal importance. First, it had to be recognized that the utility of money was crucially dependent on market prices. For consumer goods, indifference curves, constructed without reference to prices, could be confronted with the budget constraint, expressing market conditions. In the case of money, however, the price system was already built into the indifference curves. It was sometimes argued that the endeavor to explain prices by the marginal utility of money while the latter, in turn, depended on prices amounted to a vicious circle. Mises (1924) thought it necessary to break this circle by dynamizing the system. Today's marginal utility of money, determining today's prices, was thus explained by the prices of yesterday, and so forth. In fact, there is no need for such expedients. It is perfectly legitimate (and corresponds to standard operating procedure) to explain the individual demand for money *at any given set of prices* on the basis of the marginal utility calculus, and then to explain the actual set of prices by the interplay of many individual demands and supplies in the market. The problem was not one of logical circularity, but the relatively minor one of recognizing the importance of market prices for the utility of money.

The second problem was more serious. In fact, it caused some outstanding monetary theorists to abandon the integration postulate alto-

30. Patinkin (1965, p. xxiv). For earlier examples see Cannan (1921) and Pigou (1917).

gether.[31] The problem was to understand the economic meaning of the marginal utility of money. The first step was to recognize that the utility of money has a flow aspect and a stock aspect. The flow aspect has to do with the marginal utility of a dollar *spent* on commodities. This presented no problem, for the utility of money in this sense is obviously just a reflection of the utility of the goods money can buy. The stock aspect has to do with the utility of a dollar *held*. It is this stock utility which is the direct motive for demanding cash balances.

The problem was to explain precisely why money stocks are useful. It is clear that, except perhaps for irrational misers, cash balances are not one of the genuine consumer goods appearing in consumer theory. If an individual were assigned specific consumption bundles for every future time period, the addition of cash balances could not make him any better off. It is also clear that money is not one of the genuine producer goods, appearing in an ordinary production function. If a producer were assigned specified inputs for every future time period, additional cash balances could not increase his output. Rather than from direct utility and production, the services of money arise from exchange, being derived from the utility of money spent. The challenge was to make explicit how the utility of cash balances *held* is derived from the utility of cash balances *spent* in the exchange process. This requires a theory of exchange with frictions, which neoclassical theory failed to develop.[32]

Faced with this problem, the typical neoclassical expedient was to treat money *as if* it were a consumer or producer good. This treatment of money was initiated by Walras.[33] He postulated a special "provisioning service" for stocks, both of commodities and of money, arising from the fact that these stocks were necessary to bridge the gaps between incoming and outgoing flows due to the lack of synchronization in the settlement of contracts. Stocks thus appear in the utility function. However, the exact nature of that provisioning service remained unspecified. In particular, Walras did not explain why any stocks are held in the form of money if they could be held in the form of interest-bearing or productive assets. Since Walras assumed away any uncertainty and thus left no motive for precautionary cash balances, the demand for money was presumably due to some sort of transaction costs, but the nature of these was not made explicit.

31. Among them are Wicksell (1936, p. 29; 1935, 2:20), Schumpeter (1934, p. 256), and Hicks (1967, p. 14). Hicks' recent skepticism is particularly noteworthy in view of his earlier call for a "marginal revolution" in monetary theory.

32. Patinkin actually thought, curiously, that there was something inconsistent in identifying the utility of money flows with the utility of the goods they buy while simultaneously postulating some service of money stocks (1965, p. 580). Once again, in the absence of explicit analysis, the intuition of neoclassical economists was sound.

33. It found its definitive expression in the fourth edition of the *Eléments* (1900, pp. 297 ff.). For an excellent summary see Patinkin (1965, pp. 541 ff.).

To illustrate the Walrasian approach, we can use Samuelson's formalization stripped to its bare essentials (1947, p. 117 f.; 1968). Suppose an individual has a utility function including among its arguments the cash balance and, therefore, commodity prices:

$$U = U(x_1, \cdots x_Q; m; p_1, \cdots p_Q). \tag{1.3.1}$$

While the money value of total assets, $\bar{A}$, is assumed to be determined outside the present model and therefore given, the individual can decide the division of assets between interest-bearing assets, b, and cash balances. Interest-bearing assets may be imagined to consist of consols, paying $1 per period, with price p_b and yield $i = 1/p_b$. The return from assets is, therefore,

$$b = i(\bar{A} - m). \tag{1.3.2}$$

The budget constraint can thus be written

$$\sum_{q=1}^{Q} p_q(x_q - \bar{x}_q) - i(\bar{A} - m) = 0. \tag{1.3.3}$$

Maximizing utility subject to the budget constraint yields the $q + 1$ marginal conditions

$$\frac{\frac{\partial U}{\partial x_1}}{p_1} = \cdots = \frac{\frac{\partial U}{\partial x_Q}}{p_Q} = \frac{\frac{\partial U}{\partial m}}{i} = \lambda, \tag{1.3.4}$$

where λ is the marginal utility of income or, equivalently, the marginal utility of money spent on goods. $\partial U/\partial m$ is the marginal utility of the services from money stocks held for one period. The present value of an infinite stream of such services, capitalized at the current rate of interest, must be equal, in equilibrium, to the marginal utility of a dollar spent on any consumer good. This relates the stock utility of money to its flow utility. From the above marginal conditions a demand function for money can be derived simultaneously with the demand functions for commodities. A similar derivation is possible for money as a producer good.[34]

In a formal sense, the theory of money thus seems to be perfectly integrated with the theory of value. From the point of view of economic substance, however, the neoclassical approach still falls short of its integration goal. With respect to consumer goods we know, in principle, how to find out about the properties of the utility functions, namely by inquiring about an individual's tastes. With respect to cash balances and prices this is not

34. On money as a producer good see Friedman (1956, p. 11 ff.; 1969, p. 14), Levhari and Patinkin (1968, p. 737), Harry G. Johnson (1969, pp. 40 ff.), and Fischer (1974).

so. In fact, we only know that the question has nothing to do with individual tastes, but everything with frictions in the exchange system. But since these frictions were not accounted for in the neoclassical system, we do not know what properties we should attribute to the utility function.[35]

This problem is illustrated most clearly in the treatment of homogeneity. That demand functions for commodities are homogeneous of degree zero, and that the demand function for money is homogeneous of degree one, in all prices can be shown to be implied in utility maximization, *provided* the utility function is homogeneous of degree zero in cash balances and all prices.[36] But the zero homogeneity of the utility function has no such rational basis. We are still forced to assume it on the grounds of intuitive plausibility.[37] Propositions we feel are mere implications of optimizing behavior are thus transformed into assumed properties of individual tastes.[38] What we need is a theory that treats money not metaphorically *as if* it were a consumer or producer good, but as what it really is, namely a medium of exchange.[39]

Neoclassical monetary theory offered many suggestions about the possible elements of such a theory. They can all be interpreted as efforts to give analytical content to the frictions in the exchange mechanism. Each concept of friction then implies a corresponding concept of "marketability" or "liquidity" of different goods, measuring their ability to overcome the frictions.

One such element was transaction costs. However, before the advent of modern programming techniques with their inequalities, economic theorists, being restricted to the classical calculus, found it all but impossible to incorporate transaction costs into their optimizing theory.[40] Another element was payments habits. It was easily seen that the demand for cash balances depends on the degree of synchronization of receipts and payments. How much money people want to hold would depend on whether wages, rents, taxes, dividends, and so forth are paid daily, weekly, monthly, quarterly, or annually.[41] If these payments habits were simply an institutional or

35. Cf. Hicks (1935, p. 15): "But merely to call that marginal utility X, and then proceed to draw curves, would not be very helpful."
36. See Samuelson (1947, p. 119 ff.).
37. Patinkin (1965, pp. 80, 96) and Samuelson (1968, p. 8).
38. Closely related is the device of Pesek and Saving, who regard homogeneity as a "special technical property" of money (1967, pp. 59 ff.).
39. Mises (1924, chap. 5), following Knies, argues strongly that money should be classified as neither a consumer nor a producer good, but belonging to a third category of "media of exchange." It should be clear that the real problem is not one of classification but of a better analytical understanding of the functions of a medium of exchange.
40. This point is well illustrated by the example of Marschak (1950), one of the most distinguished and original mathematical economists, working in the field of monetary theory just before the advent of programming.
41. Newlyn (1962) is particularly detailed in this respect.

technical datum, the demand for money—in the absence of other assets—would not depend on an optimizing calculus and would thus not furnish a marginal utility of money. Velocity or the Cambridge k would appear as an institutional constraint—a frequent description in the neoclassical literature. An optimizing calculus could be developed, however, once payments habits were themselves regarded as endogenous results of the exchange process. The individual would then have a choice between more convenient patterns of receipts and payments with higher cash balances and lower cash balances with less convenient payments patterns.

Alternatively, an optimizing calculus might be developed by regarding the dates of receipts and payments as uncertain while every insolvency would expose an individual to some penalty. The individual would then choose between higher cash balances with lower expected penalty costs and higher penalty costs with lower cash balances. This idea was one of the main strands of the "cash balance" tradition with its emphasis on precautionary motives for cash holding. It was this approach Patinkin tried to formalize.[42]

If there were other potential assets besides money, frictions would also be needed to explain why individuals choose to hold some fraction of their wealth in the form of zero-yield money instead of holding all in the form of capital goods or interest-bearing claims. At the time of Hicks' famous paper (1935), this came to be regarded as the central problem of monetary theory. A part of the answer might be found in expected declines in the price of capital goods or bonds with the associated capital losses. This element became the centerpiece of Keynes' speculative motive for liquidity preference and was later generalized by Marschak (1950) and Tobin (1957/58). Another part of the answer might be found in the uncertainty of asset yields. An individual would thus have to choose between a higher proportion of cash balances, promising low risk but also a low expected yield, and a higher proportion of interest-bearing assets, promising a higher expected yield but also higher risk. This approach was initiated by Hicks (1935) and brought to maturity by Tobin (1957/58, 1965) and Markowitz (1952, 1959). Still another part of the answer might again be found in transaction costs. If every conversion of money into bonds and vice versa costs brokerage fees, it does not pay to move from cash balances into bonds for short holding periods. This element, also mentioned prominently by Hicks (1935, p. 19), was developed by Baumol (1952) and Tobin (1956).

Along some of these lines the calculus of individual optimization un-

42. I understand the outline of Patinkin's approach as follows. There is a primary utility function in terms of consumption and the risk of insolvency. Through a stochastic payments mechanism (analyzed in detail by Dvoretzky), this risk is related (inversely) to the amount of cash holdings. This permits the derivation of a secondary utility function in terms of consumption and cash balances. Unfortunately, Patinkin did not spell out the details of this transformation (1965, chap. 5).

der given, if perhaps uncertain, market conditions was developed to a high level of perfection. However, despite brilliant efforts (like Marschak's), neoclassical monetary theory was unable to progress from individual optimization to general equilibrium, where the market conditions in an exchange economy, subject to frictions, would be explained by the interplay of individual actions.

Such a general equilibrium theory will be presented in the following chapters. Of the elements mentioned on the last few pages, it will mainly use two. First, it will spell out the timing of purchases and sales, determined endogenously in a multiperiod model. Second, it will use transaction costs to explain the comparative advantage of different potential media of exchange and the composition of assets. It will be shown that these elements are enough to construct a coherent theory of the services of money, relating the service of money held to the service of money spent.[43]

This implies, negatively, that uncertainty, while indeed important in the world we live in, is not a necessary ingredient of a meaningful general-equilibrium theory of money. In particular, Patinkin's assumption that contracts have randomly distributed settlement dates was not used because, except for financial intermediaries, it does not seem to capture a large part of reality. It is difficult to believe that the demand for money is, for the most part, due to the circumstance that bills are due at randomly determined moments. In fact, contracts over goods and services are typically quite explicit about due dates, and even if the settlement dates were specified precisely in all contracts, we would not expect money to disappear or even to lose much of its importance. The random payments mechanism is indeed a logically conceivable basis for the utility of cash balances, but it is not a particularly persuasive one.[44]

Uncertainty about prices and/or interest rates, on the other hand, may indeed be an important element of a more perfect theory of monetary exchange. It will not be used here beyond the stage of individual optimization

43. This was also the opinion of Marschak (1950, p. 73).
44. Patinkin's random payments mechanism is also unsatisfactory in another respect. If uncertainty about the settlement dates is indeed a serious inconvenience, the market would tend to provide a choice between contracts with different degrees of uncertainty, of course at different prices. (This is illustrated by the banking system where there is a choice between deposits and loans with definite maturities and others—like demand deposits and overdrafts—with more or less indefinite maturities.) It would thus be left to the mechanism of supply and demand to determine the frequency of the various types of contracts. (Thus we find that fixed-maturity deposits predominate in the Eurodollar market, whereas indefinite-maturity deposits play a dominant role in U.S. banks.) In an economy with pronounced risk-aversion, all random elements would be bartered away. As a consequence, money, according to Patinkin's theory, would disappear, paradoxically because of the very risk aversion to which it is supposed to owe its existence! (Characteristically, Eurobanks hold very low reserves.) More generally, Patinkin's money is a substitute for more definite contracts, and this margin of substitution would have to be incorporated into the model.

simply because I am not able to construct a theory of general equilibrium in which the uncertainty about market conditions faced by each individual in his optimizing calculus is derived endogenously by the model. While this simplification will make the analysis less rich than it would otherwise be, it will be shown that it does not go to the heart of monetary theory. While a time dimension and transaction costs are necessary ingredients of a meaningful monetary theory, uncertainty is not.[45]

In recent years, there has been considerable interest in general equilibrium with transaction costs.[46] From the point of view of monetary theory it is of particular importance that the analysis has also been extended to multiperiod models.[47] However, most of these efforts, being in the Debreu tradition of general equilibrium theory, have been preoccupied with existence proofs, usually for economically quite uninteresting and often contrived models. The analysis of efficiency problems has only just begun.[48] It is fair to say that this literature has not progressed to the substantive economic problems that are traditionally regarded as the subject matter of monetary theory. I shall instead take as my point of departure the Walras/Hicks type of general equilibrium theory. Leaving existence proofs to more rigorous minds, I shall try to develop an explicit theory of monetary exchange in close correspondence to the neoclassical theory of value and allocation.

45. There was a time in the thirties when it was fashionable to argue that uncertainty is indeed of the essence of monetary theory (see, for example, Hicks [1933] and Rosenstein-Rodan [1936]). A careful reading of these arguments shows that they are only claimed to be true in the absence of other frictions like transaction costs.

46. See the contributions by Foley (1970), Starr (1970), Sontheimer (1972), and Kurz (1974). About individual optimization with transaction costs see also Karni (1972) and, earlier, Bernholz (1965, 1967).

47. Hahn (1971b, 1973), Starrett (1973), and Heller (1974).

48. As indicated by Hahn (1973) and Starrett (1973).

Two

MONEY STOCKS AND COMMODITY FLOWS

Introduction

This and the following two chapters are about the amount of cash balances an individual agent wishes to hold under given market conditions. The relevant market conditions include such factors as real income, commodity prices, interest rates, transaction costs, inflation, and uncertainty about the future. No direct utility of money will be postulated; whatever utility money may have will be indirect in nature, reflected from the goods money can buy. The discussion will be limited to private nonbank agents; banks will not be introduced until the second part of this study. It should be clear that I am not trying to develop normative models to help individuals and firms in managing their cash balances, nor do I claim to give a descriptive picture of actual cash management. My aim is rather to construct a series of highly simplified models that exhibit certain relationships of potential macroeconomic importance in a particularly clear way. It will be assumed that the economy is fully monetized in the sense that all goods and services are paid for in terms of a universal medium of exchange. The conditions under which such an exchange arrangement may, in fact, emerge will be discussed in chapter 6.

The approach differs from the post-Keynesian tradition in an important respect. While it was always recognized, particularly by Keynes (1936, p. 195), that transactions motives, speculative motives, and precautionary motives are, in principle, joint determinants of the same cash balance, the post-Keynesian monetary theory followed Keynes' suggestion (1936, p. 199) that each of these motives could conveniently be analyzed in isolation *as if* it governed a separate component of the total cash balance. The result was the portfolio approach to the demand for money. As developed by Tobin (1957/58), it treated cash balances as potential investment assets, the demand for which is not related to current transactions needs.

This approach is open to a well-known objection: Since the basic reason for holding speculative and precautionary cash balances is the risk of capital losses on interest-bearing assets, the availability of "money-dominating" assets, which pay interest without involving possible capital losses, would make the speculative and precautionary motives irrelevant for the demand for money. But such assets are, in fact, available in most situations. It seems to follow that the portfolio approach, while perhaps making an important contribution to the analysis of nonmonetary portfolios, has nothing to say about the demand for the medium of exchange.[1] This objection loses its force once it is recognized that speculative and precautionary motives are not independent forces on the same footing as the transactions motives, but secondary factors modifying the basic transactions demand for money. This is the approach used here. It treats money essentially as a transactions asset that would not be held in the absence of current transactions, the demand for which, however, is deeply influenced by the factors isolated in the portfolio approach.

The present chapter is about the interactions between the stock demand for cash balances and the flows of commodities in an individual's plan. It is assumed that money is the only store of value; there are no commodity stocks and no other financial assets. This means that important determinants of the demand for money are temporarily disregarded. Certainly, the choice between cash balances and other assets must have some influence on the demand for money. I believe, however, that the factors discussed in this chapter are the most important. In most economies there exist assets (like time deposits), which bear interest but are practically immune to capital loss. In such cases it is never efficient to hold long-term investment funds in the form of cash.[2] Only short-term funds, related to current transactions, will be held in cash. For most households, however, the pay periods are too short to warrant any temporary investment of transactions funds in interest-bearing assets. It follows that for the bulk of the household sector, the margin of choice between money and other assets is not a major issue: Practically all transactions assets will be held in the form of money, while investment funds will hardly ever be held in the form of money. An explanation of the transactions demand for money in the absence of other assets is virtually all we need in this case. The allocation of transactions balances between money and other assets, important mainly for high-income households and business firms, will be discussed in subsequent chapters.

---

1. An exception would have to be made for an individual who has such a dislike for uncertainty that the mere variability of the yield on interest-bearing assets, even if this yield is always positive, makes him prefer cash balances with a certain yield of zero. This would be an individual who declines a free gift of common stocks because he dislikes the suspense about their price. The fable of the cobbler makes the point that such behavior cannot be dismissed as obviously irrational.

2. Again subject to the exception referred to in the preceding footnote.

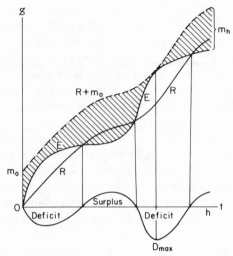

Figure **2.1.1**
Commodity Flows Given

2.1. Commodity flows given

I begin with the elementary case in which all purchases and sales during the period under analysis, say a year of h days, are predetermined.[3] There is an institutional rule stipulating that contracts must be honored, which means that nobody is allowed to go bankrupt. This will be called the "solvency requirement." The question is what cash balance the individual will hold on any day of the year. The answer is simple (see fig. 2.1.1). Cumulate daily receipts R over the year, and do the same for expenditures E. Annual receipts may, of course, be different from annual expenditures; in the graph there is an excess of receipts. The difference between cumulative receipts and expenditures is the cumulative surplus $S = R - E \geqq 0$ or deficit $D = E - R \geqq 0$ for every day of the year. As the graph is drawn, since annual receipts exceed annual expenditures, there is a net cash surplus at the end of the year. This means that the terminal cash balance will be higher than the initial cash balance, whatever their absolute levels.

If the individual began the year without a cash balance, it would immediately become insolvent, expenditures outrunning receipts early in the year. After a period of surpluses in the middle of the year, even larger deficits would appear in the fall. Solvency thus requires that there be an initial cash balance. The minimum initial cash balance, m_0, required to keep the individual solvent throughout the year, is equal to the maximum cumulative deficit $D_{\max}$. In this simple model, any higher initial balance would serve the purpose equally well. It will be assumed, so far without justifica-

3. See Patinkin (1965, pp. 80–81).

tion, that the individual holds, in fact, the minimum initial balance. Once the initial balance is known, the stock demand for money on subsequent days (shaded) is obtained by adding the daily surplus or subtracting the daily deficit; it falls to zero at least once during the year. This model, though trivially simple, is useful to identify some basic forces affecting the demand for cash balances.

2.1.1. SYNCHRONIZATION OF RECEIPTS AND PAYMENTS. Cash balances are held because incoming and outgoing payments are not fully synchronized. All those factors which affect the time profile of receipts and expenditures are thus potential determinants of the demand for money. Money is used because in one period A has excess purchases while B has excess sales, while in another period it is the other way around. Money thus appears basically as a microeconomic phenomenon that owes its existence to the differences between individuals.

In the neoclassical tradition of monetary theory, these determinants of the demand for money were usually grouped under the heading of "payments habits," regarded, at least in a first approximation, as technical and institutional data.[4] It could then be shown that the demand for cash balances depended on two factors, namely (1) the nominal amounts of annual payments and receipts and (2) the payments habits. Strictly speaking, the latter reflect two diverse sets of circumstances. One set consists of the time pattern of commodity flows. Thus groceries are bought every few days, Christmas trees are needed once a year, and the services of an apartment are acquired in a continuous stream. The other set, modifying the first, consists of the terms of payment for given commodity flows. Thus groceries may be paid on delivery, a worker may be paid at the end of each week, and rent may be due at the beginning of each month. It should be noted, however, that with the introduction of terms of payments we have tacitly introduced into the model a second financial asset, consisting of IOUs or trade credit.

2.1.2. THE DEGREE OF MONETIZATION. Direct barter may be interpreted as a case where payments and receipts are so perfectly synchronized that they cancel, thus reducing the need for cash balances. The higher the degree of monetization of the economy, the higher, other things equal, the demand for cash balances. This factor may be important in explaining the demand for money in periods of rapid financial development.[5]

2.1.3. THE PRICE LEVEL. If, with unchanged commodity flows and payments terms, all prices are changed in the same proportion, the demand

4. For representative discussions, spanning more than half a century, see Landry (1905), Angell (1937), and Newlyn (1962, chap. 4).
5. For an empirical study of this factor in the United States, see Selden (1956).

for money on every day of the year will also change in this proportion. No general statement can be made, however, if changes in the price level are accompanied by shifts in relative prices.

This proportionality of the demand for money to the price level could be used to construct a primitive variant of the quantity theory of money. It can be summarized in the proposition that a given change in the money supply results in an equiproportionate change in the price level, *provided* commodity flows, payments terms, and relative prices are unchanged. However, in view of the restrictive proviso, this primitive variant is trivial. The real quantity theory is more interesting, for it maintains that the proviso is unnecessary since commodity flows, payments terms, and relative prices will not, in fact, be permanently affected by a change in the money supply. This proposition will be discussed later.

2.1.4. COMMODITY FLOWS. If, at constant prices, all commodity flows are varied in a given proportion, the demand for money will again change in the same proportion. In this sense, changes in the real variables have the same effect on the demand for money as changes in prices. The difference between the two cases is that prices are exogenously given to the individual, at least in pure competition, while the quantities to be exchanged typically depend on his own decisions. As a consequence, there is no difficulty in imagining an equiproportionate change in all prices, but it may be difficult to specify market conditions under which an individual will indeed wish to vary all his purchases and sales in the same proportion. It will later be found that this is the basic difficulty in extending the quantity theory, originally conceived as a price theory, to real output.

2.1.5. ECONOMIC CONCENTRATION. Suppose two individuals merge their market activities (say, by marriage), while their transactions remain unchanged. The cumulative receipts and payments for the combined household are then obtained by adding the corresponding curves for the separate agents. Unless both individuals had their D_{max} on the same day, the maximum cumulative deficit for the combined household will be smaller than the sum of those deficits for the separate households. As a consequence, the combined household will require *at most* as much cash as the separate individuals and usually less. The same argument can be applied to firms. It suggests that economic concentration, *ceteris paribus*, lowers the demand for cash balances. It should be noted that this argument does not depend on the premerger firms selling anything to each other.

2.2. Variable commodity flows: Initial and terminal balances given

While an elementary model with exogenous commodity flows may help to identify certain basic determinants of the demand for money, its relevance is narrowly limited. The main limitation arises from the fact that the individual can, in fact, vary the quantities he buys and sells. As a consequence he is able to adjust to a range of cash balances just by changing the degree of synchronization of his purchases and sales. If the timing of transactions were indifferent to the individual, he could maintain his solvency with any amount of cash, however small. In fact, however, the timing of transactions is usually far from indifferent, certain schedules of receipts and payments being preferred to others, though overall consumption may be the same. From this perspective, it is the main function of money to permit a more attractive timing of transactions than could be maintained without it. The determination of the demand for cash balances and of payment schedules thus become a joint optimization problem. This is the subject of the remainder of this chapter. It will be shown that *in the absence of other assets* the demand for cash balances can be explained in terms of individual utility maximization without introducing either uncertainty or transaction costs into the analysis.

If the individual is free to vary the time pattern of his consumption, we have to know his preferences for one pattern relative to another. We may suppose that his tastes, as seen at the beginning of the year, are expressed by a utility function,

$$U = U(x_1^1 \cdots x_t^i \cdots x_h^q) = U(x), \tag{2.2.1}$$

where $x_t^i \geqq 0$ is consumption of good i on day t. The utility function relates to one "year" consisting of h "days." With respect to commodities consumed on different days, tastes may exhibit any sort of variation; Christmas trees at Easter may be very imperfect substitutes for the same trees in December. The utility function also leaves room for any sort of intertemporal complementarity and substitutability. This is important because these intertemporal variations and interrelations in tastes are presumably one of the important reasons why an individual may wish to realize a transactions schedule that shows gaps between receipts and payments. For example, forty-eight weeks with excess receipts and four weeks with excess payments (three for vacations and one for Christmas shopping) may be preferable to fifty-two weeks with balanced budgets. The utility function is assumed to be twice differentiable and to have declining marginal rates of substitution and positive marginal utilities. It should be noted that cash balances do not appear as an argument in the utility function. Whatever utility money may have must be of an indirect nature, derived from the more desirable consumption patterns it makes possible.

The individual is endowed with certain resources $\bar{x} = \bar{x}_1^1 \cdots \bar{x}_t^i \cdots \bar{x}_h^q$. This endowment vector can be transformed into certain consumption vectors through exchange; there is no production. Of course, if on day t the value of the consumption bundle exceeds the value of the endowment bundle, the cash balance will be drawn down by the amount of the difference. Adopting the convention that consumption and exchange take place at the end of each day, the individual thus confronts a series of budget constraints

$$\sum_{i=1}^{q} p_t^i (x_t^i - \bar{x}_t^i) = m_t - m_{t+1}, \qquad (t = 1 \cdots h) \qquad (2.2.2)$$

one for each day of the year. This multiplicity of budget constraints is characteristic for the theory of transactions balances, producing a sharp contrast to the Walrasian theory of individual optimization. I suspect it was this feature which held up analytical progress in this area for such a long time, diverting attention to secondary aspects like speculation and risk.

Exchange is subject to the solvency constraints $m_t \geq 0$. Together with the budget constraints they imply that, for every day of the year, initial cash balances plus cumulative receipts up to that day must at least cover cumulative expenditures. For the time being we also make the arbitrary assumption that both the initial and the terminal cash balance are given to the individual from the outside. We thus write $m_1 = \bar{m}_1$ and $m_{h+1} = \bar{m}_{h+1}$. The individual is assumed to maximize his utility subject to these constraints. This is a nonlinear programming problem with a quasi-concave objective function and linear constraints. Once it is solved, consumption, exchange, and the demand for cash balances are known for each day of the year. For cash balances, in particular, we can write demand functions $L_t = L_t (\bar{x}, p, \bar{m}_1, \bar{m}_{h+1})$ for $t = 1 \cdots h$. In terms of the previous graph, the cumulative receipts and expenditure curves and cash balances are determined simultaneously.

For such a problem, as Arrow and Enthoven (1961) have shown, the Kuhn-Tucker conditions are necessary and sufficient for an optimum. We can gain insight into the economic properties of the problem by specifying the Kuhn-Tucker conditions on consumption flows and money stocks. The Lagrange equation can be written

$$L = U (x_1^1 \cdots x_t^i \cdots x_h^q) - \sum_{t=1}^{h} \lambda_t [\sum_{i=1}^{q} p_t^i (x_t^i - \bar{x}_t^i) + m_{t+1} - m_t]. \qquad (2.2.3)$$

By taking the partial derivative with respect to x_t^i we obtain the Kuhn-Tucker conditions on consumption:

$$\left(\frac{\partial U}{\partial x_t^i} - \lambda_t \, p_t^i\right) x_t^i = 0, \qquad \frac{\frac{\partial U}{\partial x_t^i}}{p_t^i} \leq \lambda_t, \qquad x_t^i \geq 0. \qquad (2.2.4)$$

The multiplier λ_t can be interpreted as the marginal utility of a dollar's worth of resources or income on day t. It is, equivalently, the marginal purchasing power of money, measured in terms of utility, and may thus be called the marginal *flow* utility of money. For positive consumption, we obtain the familiar condition that the marginal utility of goods per dollar of expenditure is made equal to the marginal utility of income. For zero consumption, the weighted marginal utility may remain below the marginal utility of income.[6]

The Kuhn-Tucker conditions on money stocks inject a new element into the marginal calculus. By taking the partial derivative of (2.2.3) with respect to m_t, we obtain

$$(\lambda_t - \lambda_{t-1})\, m_t = 0, \qquad \lambda_t - \lambda_{t-1} \leqq 0, \, m_t \geqq 0. \qquad (t = 2 \ldots h).$$

$$(2.2.5)$$

$\lambda_t - \lambda_{t-1}$ measures the marginal utility of money stocks. The marginal *stock* utility of money thus turns out to be the difference (or rate of change) of the marginal flow utility of money from one day to the next.[7] It can be visualized as the benefit from spending a dollar today, minus the sacrifice involved in not spending it yesterday. It is the gain in utility from postponing a dollar's worth of expenditure from one day to the next by holding cash overnight. Whenever cash balances are actually held, their marginal utility will be equalized to their marginal cost, which, in the present model, is zero. In this simple case, the marginal utility of money will never be positive, in the optimal plan, because whenever it is positive it will be advantageous to postpone some consumption up to the point where the marginal utility of money has vanished. On the other hand, it is well possible that the marginal utility of money, in the optimal plan, is negative on some days; no cash will then be held, of course. It would indeed be desirable in such a case to shift some further consumption from tomorrow to today, but since cash balances are already exhausted, this is not feasible. The negative marginal utility of money, $\lambda_{t-1} - \lambda_t$, could be described as the marginal utility of an interest-free overnight loan; it expresses the economic burden imposed by the solvency requirement. In this way the marginal utility of cash balances is rigorously related to the marginal utility of goods.[8]

6. On the interpretation of the Lagrange multipliers as marginal values in such a problem, see Balinski and Baumol (1968), where the necessary qualifications are also given.

7. That the marginal stock value of cash balances is the difference between their marginal flow values for different points of time was clearly stated by Pantaleoni (1898, p. 235). See also Patinkin (1960, p. 91).

8. Friedman (1969a, pp. 14, 18) attributed the utility of money to (1) the non-pecuniary consumption services as a reserve for emergencies and (2) the productive service in reducing transaction costs. It is interesting to note that neither of these sources of utility appear in the present model: Money does not serve as an investment asset and there are no transaction costs, and the source of its utility is the more attractive timing of consumption it permits, a factor not considered by Friedman. It will be shown in chapter 3 that an increase in real cash balances may easily be associated with an increase, and not a saving, in the amount of resources used up in transactions.

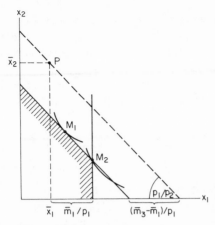

Figure **2.2.1**
Initial and Terminal Balances Given

By shortening the "year" to just two "days" and considering only one good, this argument can be represented graphically (see fig. 2.2.1). Day-1 goods and day-2 goods are measured, respectively, along the horizontal and vertical axis. The individual wishes to transfer his endowment, represented by P, into the consumption bundle with the highest utility. Day-1 goods can be transformed into day-2 goods by selling them at the end of day 1, holding the money during day 2, and buying goods on the evening of day 2. The reverse transformation takes place in an analogous way. This results in the broken budget line through P, whose slope reflects the price ratio p_1/p_2. However, the solvency requirement will generally not permit the individual to move freely along the budget line. The initial cash balance $\bar{m}_1$ limits market purchases of x_1 to a maximum of $\bar{m}_1/p_1$. Furthermore, since the terminal balance $\bar{m}_{h+1} = \bar{m}_3$ is also given, the individual knows that over the two-day period the value of his consumption bundle must differ from the value of his resources by a fixed amount $\bar{m}_3 - \bar{m}_1$. His effective budget constraint for the two-day period, drawn as a solid line, may therefore lie either inside or outside the broken line. The way the graph is drawn, cash balances have to be accumulated and feasible consumption thus falls short of resources. The amount of cash accumulation, measured in terms of x_1, appears as the horizontal distance between the two budget lines, $(\bar{m}_3 - \bar{m}_1)/p_1$. The individual thus finds himself constrained to the shaded polygon.

If the utility function is such that the highest indifference curve is reached at a point of tangency like M_1, then some cash will be held over from day 1 to day 2, and the marginal utility of cash balances during day 2 is zero. However, if the optimum is at the corner M_2, there will (generally) be no tangency, and an overnight loan on day 1, to be repaid on day 2, would increase utility. This graph thus shows in the simplest possible way how the solvency requirement can reflect utility from the commodities on money.

2.3. Initial and terminal balances optimized: Infinite stationary motion

The assumption that initial and terminal balances are imposed on the individual from the outside has often been made in modern monetary theory. Its usual purpose is to assure that individuals do not use up all cash balances on the last day.[9] From every other point of view it is obviously unsatisfactory. With $\bar{m}_{h+1} \neq \bar{m}_1$ it does not even produce a steady state. With $\bar{m}_{h+1} = \bar{m}_1$ it still is not a true equilibrium because the individual, if left free, would generally have preferred different cash balances. Fortunately, the assumption of given initial and terminal balances is not necessary to prevent individuals from always using up their cash.

To get around this assumption, I introduce the concept of infinite stationary motion.[10] By this I mean fluctuations that repeat themselves in identical cycles to infinity. Inasmuch as infinite stationary motion is able to reconcile the nonstationary endowments and tastes that make money useful with the notion of economic equilibrium, the concept may be regarded as the key to an equilibrium theory of money. It makes it possible to develop an indirect-utility theory of money that is an exact monetary extension of neoclassical theory.

This general idea now has to be made precise. Let time be divided into $1 \ldots T \ldots H$ years, with each year consisting of $1 \ldots t \ldots h$ days. The model is dynamic in the sense that things are subject to change from day to day within each year; this provides the general basis for the demand for stocks, at present consisting only of cash balances. The model is stationary in the sense that nothing is allowed to change from year to year; this makes it possible to construct a counterpart to the stationary equilibrium of neoclassical theory. In particular, endowments are the same for a given calendar day of each year, tastes remain the same from year to year, and the individual will be constrained to choose a plan with identical consumption patterns for the same calendar day of different years. This constraint can be formalized by requiring

$$x^i_{(T-1)h+t} = x^i_t,$$

$$m_{(T-1)h+t} = m_t. \qquad (T = 1 \cdots H)$$

9. For an economy with finite horizon, the literature seems to suggest three ways to insure that positive terminal balances are held by some individuals, namely, (1) by imposing it as a constraint (Sontheimer, 1972; Starr, 1971), (2) by imposing taxes payable in money (Lerner, 1947; Starr, 1971), (3) by requiring that money be "covered" by commodities (Kurz, 1974).

10. This was suggested by Kurz (1974, p. 451).

H is infinite and foresight is perfect. We can thus visualize all decisions as being made at the beginning of time. The individual is assumed to maximize utility over the infinite horizon, but since he is constrained to stationary consumption patterns, this is equivalent to the maximization of annual utility. As a consequence, the one-year utility function (2.2.1) is all we have to keep in mind.

This change in perspective means that the previous assumptions $m_1 = \bar{m}_1$ and $m_{h+1} = \bar{m}_{h+1}$ can be replaced by the requirement $m_1 = m_{h+1}$. Both initial and terminal balances are now endogenously determined by the optimization process, subject only to the requirement that they be equal. They thus drop out of the demand functions for money, which are thereby simplified to

$$L_t = L_t (\bar{x}, p).$$

The Kuhn-Tucker conditions (2.2.5) for cash balances on days $2 \ldots h$ are not affected by this change in the model. In addition, however, we now have a condition

$$(\lambda_1 - \lambda_h) \, m_1 = 0, \qquad \lambda_1 - \lambda_h \leqq 0, \qquad m_1 \geqq 0. \tag{2.3.1}$$

Together with $\lambda_t - \lambda_{t-1} \leqq 0$ $(t = 2 \ldots h)$ this implies $\lambda_t = \lambda_{t-1}$ for all t. The marginal utility of money is now equalized to the marginal cost throughout, which is still zero. Solvency does not impose a burden on the individual at any time: The optimal consumption pattern can be determined *as if* solvency did not matter or *as if* everything could be paid for on the last day of the year. In the absence of time preference (and transaction costs), the optimal path of infinite stationary motion is one of satiation with cash balances.

In the two-day graph the transition to infinite stationary motion means two things (see fig. 2.3.1). First, the effective budget constraint now goes

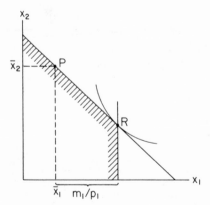

Figure **2.3.1**
Satiation Balances

through P; sales for the year equal purchases, the value of consumption equals the value of the endowment. Second, the initial (and terminal) balance m_1 is now subject to optimization. The individual will thus make his plan in such a way that he can reach the optimum R. This is the same optimum he could have reached for given P if there had been no solvency constraint in the first place. Money behaves as if it did not matter. If initial balances were higher than what is necessary to attain R, they would just be redundant.

2.4. Time preference

I now introduce a psychological cost of wealth holding in the form of time preference at a constant rate θ per day. The utility function (2.2.1) can then be interpreted as expressing the utility as seen at the beginning of day 1. Any discounting due to time preference is *implicit* in it. The same is, of course, true for the marginal utilities $\partial U/\partial x_t^i$. With unchanged tastes, the marginal utilities relating to consumption on July 4 will rise as the individual moves progressively closer to that date.

I now wish to make time preference *explicit*. For the demand functions for money this means simply writing

$$L_t = L_t (\bar{x}, p, \theta).$$

To determine the significance of this change we have to perform the analogous transformation on the marginal conditions. It thus becomes necessary to distinguish between the discounted marginal utilities $\partial U/\partial x_t^i$ and undiscounted marginal utilities, defined as

$$\partial V/\partial x_t^i = (1 + \theta)^t \, \partial U/\partial x_t^i.$$

Similarly, I define an undiscounted marginal utility of income $\mu_t = (1 + \theta)^t \lambda_t$. While the discounted marginal values for a given day will increase as time goes by and that day comes nearer, their undiscounted counterparts remain constant, each change in $\partial U/\partial x_t^i$ or λ_t being exactly matched by an opposite change in $(1 + \theta)^t$.

In the two-day case, the relationship between the discounted and undiscounted concepts can be graphically visualized as follows. Graph the discounted-utility function (2.2.1) as a family of indifference curves with day-1 goods on the horizontal axis and day-2 goods on the vertical axis (as in figs. 2.2.1 and 2.3.1). The slopes of these indifference curves then represent the marginal rates of substitution between goods consumed on different days. Now select a point on the indifference map and twist the tangent at this point counterclockwise to make it flatter in the proportion $(1 + \theta)$. Do the same with the tangent at every other point. The family of twisted tangents can then be integrated to represent the indifference curves of an

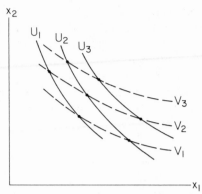

Figure **2.4.1**
Discounted and Undiscounted Utility

undiscounted utility function $V(\ )$ (fig. 2.4.1), where $V(\ )$ represents tastes "purged" from time preference and the partial derivatives $\partial V/\partial x_t^i$ are the undiscounted marginal utilities. For more than two days, as is well known, it may be impossible to integrate the twisted tangents to give $V(\ )$, but since the marginal utilities are all we need for this analysis, this does not have to bother us.

We now express the Kuhn-Tucker conditions in terms of undiscounted marginal utilities. For the marginal conditions on consumption flows this makes no difference, both sides being multiplied by the same discount factor:

$$\frac{\dfrac{\partial V}{\partial x_t^i}}{p_t^i} \leqq \mu_t. \tag{2.4.1}$$

For the cash balance conditions (2.2.5) and (2.3.1), however, the transformation makes a difference. The sign constraints now read

$$\frac{1}{(1+\theta)^t}\mu_t - \frac{1}{(1+\theta)^{t-1}}\mu_{t-1} \leqq 0, \qquad m_t \geqq 0,$$

which can be rearranged to[11]

$$(1+\theta)\frac{\mu_t - \mu_{t-1}}{\mu_t} \leqq \theta, \qquad m_t \geqq 0. \tag{2.4.2}$$

The marginal cost of money on the right-hand side is θ. On the left-hand side we again find the marginal utility of cash balances, now expressed as a percentage. The condition says that whenever cash balances are positive,

---

11. For marginal conditions of similar form, but for a direct-utility approach, see Patinkin (1965, p. 91, eq. 6).

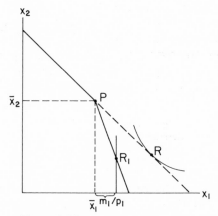

Figure **2.4.2**
Time Preference

their undiscounted marginal utility is equal to the rate of time preference. The cash balance must be zero at least once during the year. If it were positive throughout, the left-hand part of (2.4.2) would hold as an equality throughout. This, in turn, implies that μ_t would be increasing throughout the year, which would be inconsistent with stationary motion. This justifies the assumption made in section 2.1. With $\theta = 0$, the marginal stock utility of money will, of course, be zero.[12] This is the same result as in the preceding section: In the absence of time preference, people will satiate themselves with cash balances.

Again the argument can be illustrated in the two-day graph. The indifference curves are assumed to describe the utility function (2.2.1) with implicit discounting. Because of time preference, the slope of the indifference curve going through a given point is somewhat steeper than it would be in the absence of time preference. If we want to increase x_2 at the expense of x_1, the budget line will be the same as before, moving upward from P with slope p_1/p_2. However, if we consider an increase in x_1 at the expense of x_2, we have to keep in mind that x_1 is now consumption on the first day of the *following year:* The individual reduces his consumption on day 2 in order to accumulate cash balances that can be spent on day 1 of the next year or on day 3 overall. This could be expressed by using another set of indifference curves with x_1 increased in the proportion $(1+\theta)^2$ for any given x_2. It is graphically more convenient, however, to use unchanged indifference curves and instead redraw the segment of the budget line below P to make it steeper in the proportion $(1+\theta)^2$. In other words, in order to make the commodities on day 1 of the following year comparable to the

12. It can never be negative in this case, because this would be inconsistent with the requirement that the second year be the same as the first.

commodities on day 1 of the current year, we have to discount them for 2 days. We thus obtain the kinked budget frontier of figure 2.4.2. The optimum with time preference will be at a point like R_1. It is clear that, in view of time preference, R is out of reach. The individual will no longer behave as if cash balances played no role. Specifically, he will have a lower utility than he would have obtained in the absence of a solvency constraint. Time preference sees to it that individuals will not satiate themselves with cash balances, and whenever cash is held its marginal utility will be positive.

2.5. Interest on cash balances

It was so far assumed that cash balances do not bear interest. We now introduce interest on cash balances, assumed to be compounded daily at the rate ρ. To the extent money consists of coins and banknotes, the administrative difficulties of such a scheme may well be prohibitive. For deposit money it presents no difficulties. In the absence of commercial banks we may imagine that all cash balances are kept in the form of deposits with some branch office of the central bank or with some postal clearing system. In principle, ρ could then be given any positive or negative value.

The payment of interest on bank balances adds a term to the budget constraint, since interest payments are added to the spendable resources:

$$\sum_{i=1}^{q} p_t^i \left(x_t^i - \bar{x}_t^i \right) = (1 + \rho)\, m_t - m_{t+1}. \tag{2.5.1}$$

The Kuhn-Tucker conditions on cash balances thus become

$$\left[(1 + \rho)\, \lambda_t - \lambda_{t-1} \right] m_t = 0, \tag{2.5.2}$$

and the associated sign constraints can be arranged to read

$$(1 + \theta)\, \frac{\mu_t - \mu_{t-1}}{\mu_t} \leqq \theta - \rho, \qquad m_t \geqq 0. \tag{2.5.3}$$

This is a neat expression, because it shows interest as an exact offset to time preference. The expression also shows that interest rates have an influence on the demand for cash balances even in the absence of speculation, uncertainty, and transaction costs, and even in a world in which money is the only asset. The demand functions for money thus become

$$L_t = L_t\, (\bar{x}, p, \theta, \rho).$$

Assuming $\theta > \rho$, what is the comparative-static effect of a change in ρ on the demand for money? Can we be sure that an increase in the yield of cash balances will raise the quantity demanded? In terms of a multi-day model the question is difficult to answer. In general, the stock of money will increase on some days but fall on others. As a consequence, we cannot

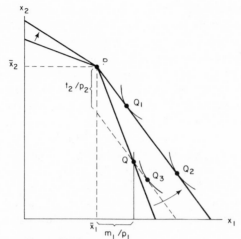

Figure **2.5.1**
Interest on Cash Balances

expect unambiguous statements about the direction of the change in cash balances. A more precise answer can, however, be given in terms of the two-day variant of the model, for it contains only one nonzero cash balance.[13] The argument is best conducted in graphic terms (see fig. 2.5.1). The initial equilibrium is at Q. An increase in ρ from zero to some value $0 < \rho < \theta$ means that the faces of the budget frontier swivel outward around P, thus counteracting the effect of time preference. If the new optimum is further to the right at a point like Q_2, cash balances will indeed increase. If, however, the new optimum is to the left of Q at point like Q_1, cash balances will fall. It seems that, in general, we cannot be sure that the demand for cash balances will rise as their yield goes up. It is clear that this is due to the familiar phenomenon of an income effect of uncertain sign counteracting a substitution effect. If we want to be sure that the demand for cash balances reacts positively to ρ, we have to compensate for the income effect by a lump-sum tax. If the tax is levied on day 2, the required amount, in real terms, is t_2/p_2, resulting in the broken budget line through Q. We can then be sure that in the new equilibrium Q_3 both cash balances and utility will be higher than in Q. With these qualifications we are permitted to say that the demand for cash balances is positively related to their interest rate.[14]

If the rate of interest on cash balances is equal to the state of time preference, the individual will satiate himself with cash balances and thus reach R in figures 2.3.1 and 2.4.2. He will again behave *as if* he had no

13. It will be remembered that cash balances fall to zero at least once during the year.
14. See Samuelson (1947, p. 121).

time preference and thus *as if* money did not matter. Any amount of cash balances beyond the minimum required for satiation would then be indifferent to him. It is conceivable, of course, that for a given individual the rate of interest on cash balances is higher than the rate of time preference. In this case there is no optimal cash balance; whatever the level of cash holdings, a higher amount would always be more profitable. In formal terms, the right-hand side of (2.5.3) would be negative. This implies that the left-hand side is also negative for all t, which means that the undiscounted marginal utilities of resources must be forever diminishing. However, this is incompatible with stationary motion; the marginal utility of resources at the beginning of a given year must be the same as at the beginning of the preceding year. It follows that there is no optimal stationary plan.[15] Of course, this is just a particular instance of the familiar proposition that with a low enough rate of time preference and high enough capital returns there is no upper limit to desired wealth.

2.6. Inflation

The model developed in the preceding sections will now be used to analyze the effect of inflation on the demand for cash balances. The discussion will be restricted to the case of inflation progressing at a constant rate with perfectly adjusted expectations. A rising price level means that the individual, in order to keep his real cash balance at a constant level from year to year, has to give up a certain fraction of his income just to acquire additional nominal balances. Inflation thus imposes a cost on the individual comparable to a negative yield or a tax on cash balances. This argument, made familiar by Friedman (1953), will now be made more rigorous.

To simplify the notation, all commodities are lumped together into one composite good. Its price p_t then measures the price level. p_t is still subject to change from day to day, but it is assumed to be the same for given days of successive years, reflecting the notion of stationary motion. On this stationary price pattern we now impose a constant inflationary trend of π percent per day. Actual prices on the t-th day will thus be $p_t(1 + \pi)^t$. The optimizing problem can thus be written as max $U = U(x_1 \ldots x_h)$, subject to

$$p_t (1 + \pi)^t (x_t - \bar{x}_t) = (1 + \rho) m_t - m_{t+1}, \qquad (t = 1 \cdots h) \qquad (2.6.1)$$

with $x_t \geqq 0$ and $m_t \geqq 0$. Stationarity requires that the nominal cash balance on a given calendar day be the same as the nominal cash balance on

15. Friedman (1969a, p. 17) argued that for $\rho > \theta$ the marginal utility of money would become negative. Cash balances would be held at an inefficiently high level, where they really become a discommodity. The present analysis shows that the problem with this case is not the inefficiency of equilibrium, but its absence.

the same day of the preceding year *adjusted for inflation*, or

$$m_{t+h} = (1 + \pi)^h \, m_t.$$

The way the problem is written, it is not obvious that inflation is indeed equivalent to a negative yield on cash balances. However, a simple transformation will bring this out. Dividing the budget constraints by $(1 + \pi)^t$, they can be rewritten as

$$p_t \, (x_t - \bar{x}_t) = (1 + \rho) \, (1 + \pi)^{-t} \, m_t - (1 + \pi)^{-t} \, m_{t+1}.$$

Defining "deflated cash balances" held at t as nominal balances deflated by cumulative inflation at the beginning of the day,[16] that is,

$$m_t^r = (1 + \pi)^{-(t-1)} \, m_t,$$

the budget constraints can be expressed in terms of deflated balances

$$p_t \, (x_t - \bar{x}_t) = \frac{1 + \rho}{1 + \pi} \, m_t^r - m_{t+1}^r, \qquad (2.6.2)$$

with the stationarity condition $m_{t+h}^r = m_t^r$. In this way, the original problem in terms of actual prices and nominal balances is converted into one in terms of deflated prices and deflated balances. In this modified problem inflation appears as an exact counterpart to the interest rate on cash balances. What matters are not $1 + \rho$ and $1 + \pi$ separately, but only their ratio, and the demand function for money can thus be extended to

$$L_t = L_t \, [x, p, \theta, (1 + \rho)/(1 + \pi)].$$

Inflation is indeed a negative yield on cash balances.

This proposition can be looked at from a different perspective. For a given day t, the loss in income resulting from inflation can be measured by the reduction in consumption necessary to maintain the same level of deflated cash balances. For simplicity we assume $\rho = 0$. In the absence of inflation, the budget constraint (2.6.2) would be

$$p_t \, (\overset{\circ}{x}_t - \bar{x}_t) = m_t^r - m_{t+1}^r,$$

where $\overset{\circ}{x}_t$ denotes consumption for $\pi = 0$. Subtracting (2.6.2) from this expression, we obtain

$$p_t \, (\overset{\circ}{x}_t - x_t) = \left(1 - \frac{1}{1 + \pi}\right) m_t^r = \frac{\pi}{1 + \pi} \, m_t^r$$

or, in current prices,

$$p_t \, (1 + \pi)^t \, (\overset{\circ}{x}_t - x_t) = \pi (1 + \pi)^{t-1} \, m_t^r = \pi m_t. \qquad (2.6.3)$$

In order to acquire continually the additional cash necessary to keep de-

---

16. These are not "real balances" because they are not expressed in terms of commodity units, p_t not appearing in the deflator.

flated balances at an unchanged level in the face of inflation, the individual would thus have to reduce consumption expenditures by a percentage of his cash balances. This percentage is equal to the rate of inflation.[17] Inflation is indeed a proportionate tax on cash balances.

It should be noted that this argument is based on the assumptions (1) that the individual obtains no benefits from the resources "taxed away" by inflation and (2) that the pattern of p_t is not affected by inflation. For an individual experiment in which we confront a household or firm with given changes in market data, these are legitimate assumptions. We have to be careful, however, not to draw unwarranted conclusions about the social benefits or costs of inflation. A change in π would presumably also result in changes in p_t. As a consequence, nothing definite can be said about the benefits or losses to specific individuals. While many may lose, some may gain. The results of the individual experiment, therefore, do not necessarily carry over to the market experiment (on the latter, see section 5.2).

By forming the Lagrange equation for the inflation problem, taking its partial derivatives and expressing these in terms of undiscounted marginal values, the Kuhn-Tucker conditions for cash balances can be written as

$$(1 + \theta) \frac{\mu_t - \mu_{t-1}}{\mu_t} \leqq (1 + \theta) - \frac{1 + \rho}{1 + \pi}. \tag{2.6.4}$$

In the absence of time preference and interest on cash balances, this reduces to

$$(1 + \pi) \frac{\mu_t - \mu_{t-1}}{\mu_t} \leqq \pi.$$

Inflation thus appears as a marginal cost on cash balances of exactly the same form as time preference in section 2.4. If there is interest on cash balances (but still no time preference), the condition reads

$$(1 + \pi) \frac{\mu_t - \mu_{t-1}}{\mu_t} \leqq \pi - \rho.$$

This makes it clear that the payment of interest on cash balances equal to the rate of inflation would prevent individuals from reducing their cash holdings below the satiation level. In the complete condition with time preference, cash satiation would, of course, require that interest on cash balances compensate for both time preference and inflation according to

$$(1 + \rho) = (1 + \theta)(1 + \pi).$$

The effect of gradually rising inflation on the demand for money is

___

17. Alternatively, (2.6.3) can be interpreted as the value of the additional endowment, which would just compensate the individual for inflation at given levels of real balances.

exactly analogous to the effect of a gradually falling interest rate ρ. In particular, we cannot be absolutely certain that the demand for real cash balances will fall, as the normal-signed substitution effect is counteracted by an ambiguous income effect (see sec. 2.5). However, a negative slope of the demand curve for real balances as a function of inflation can be assured by postulating a compensation scheme whereby the losses in real income are made up by lump-sum benefits. The downward-sloping demand curve for cash balances familiar from the inflation literature (see fig. 1.1.1) must thus be interpreted as a compensated ("Marshallian") demand curve.

As can be seen from (2.6.4), whenever cash balances are held an increase in π is reflected in an increase in $\mu_t - \mu_{t-1}$. This means that the marginal utility of tomorrow's consumption goes up relative to the marginal utility of today's consumption. Consumption on more distant dates becomes more scarce, while nearby consumption is made more abundant. Inflation thus leads to a forward shift in consumption which would have lowered utility at stable prices. This forward shift is the result of the individual's efforts to reduce the burden of inflation by cutting down on his cash balances. Subject to the aforementioned qualification about income effects, these efforts will be reflected in an actual reduction in cash balances.[18]

By making the artificial assumption that cash balances are constrained to move in a regular sawtooth pattern, and expressing the disutility of higher synchronization between constant receipts and intermittent payments in the form of higher transaction costs for more frequent payments, this general argument can be illustrated in simple algebraic terms.[19] Suppose an employer produces and sells his annual output Y at a constant daily rate. Since every payday imposes a fixed administrative cost of c_f, he pays wages to his workers only n times a year at regular intervals of length $1/n$. The inflationary tax on cash balances is π and the rate of time preference is θ. What is the optimal pay (or income) period $1/n^*$? Cash requirements on each payday are Y/n. The average cash balance of the employer, therefore, is $L = Y/2n$, on which the cost is $(\pi + \theta)\,Y/2n$. Total transaction costs are $c_f n$. This results in a total cost of

$$C = \frac{Y}{2n}\,(\pi + \theta) + c_f n.$$

Taking the derivative with respect to n, setting it equal to zero, and solving for the optimal income period, we obtain

$$\frac{1}{n^*} = \sqrt{\frac{2c_f}{Y(\pi + \theta)}}.$$

18. The pathbreaking empirical study of this effect is, of course, Cagan's investigation of the demand for money in seven hyperinflations (Cagan, 1956). For an alternative, and highly original, approach see Allais (1972).
19. This illustration is adapted from Barro (1970).

This implies an optimal average cash balance of

$$L = \frac{Y}{2n^*} = \sqrt{\frac{c_f Y}{2(\pi + \theta)}},$$

which corresponds to the familiar Baumol/Tobin formula (see [3.2.2] on page 50). The income period thus gets shorter and shorter with accelerating inflation. For $\theta = 0$ its length is inversely related to the square root of the rate of inflation. The same is true for the demand for money.[20] This is a simple algebraic illustration of the general proposition that a higher rate of inflation results in a more perfect synchronization of receipts and payments, motivated by the effort to reduce the inflationary tax on cash balances.

The first three sections of this chapter developed a new approach to the theory of the demand for money. Its main characteristics can be summarized as follows:

1. Whatever utility money has is indirect, "reflected" from the utility of commodities.

2. The marginal utility of money can be precisely related to the marginal utility of income.

3. The concept of infinite stationary motion permits the determination of an equilibrium that is independent of arbitrary constraints on initial and terminal balances.

4. The theory of individual optimization in a monetary economy appears as a straightforward generalization of the neoclassical approach. In the second half of the chapter, the basic model was extended to include time preference, interest on cash balances, and inflation. The conclusions about their effects on the demand for money were in close agreement with the propositions familiar from monetary theory. However, these propositions have never before been derived rigorously from an indirect-utility model. For the first time it has been possible to derive what so far had to be intuitively postulated.

---

20. If asset and transaction costs for the workers are the same as for the employers, n^* also minimizes total costs of employers and workers, while the average total cash balance would, of course, be $2L$. The (minor) difference in Barro's result (eq. 21) is due to the fact that he disregards transaction costs for workers.

Three

MONEY AND BONDS WITH
GIVEN WEALTH

Introduction

In the preceding chapter money was assumed to be the only store of value. In the present chapter the focus shifts to the choice between money and interest-bearing assets. On the other hand, the flows of receipts and payments for goods and services are now assumed to be predetermined. The joint optimization of commodity flows and asset composition will be the subject of chapter 4.

All bonds appearing in this chapter, like the cash balances, have the character of transactions assets. By this I mean that they are held exclusively to bridge temporary gaps between purchases and sales of commodities, and not for long-term investment purposes. In a formal model of infinite stationary motion (see sec. 2.3) this can be made precise by saying that the transactions assets go to zero at least once every "year." Investment assets, held throughout the year, continue to be disregarded. The assumption of given receipts and payments for goods and services implies that the time profile of aggregate transactions assets is also known. The question is how these will be divided between cash balances and interest-bearing securities.

The large number of households with low and middle incomes will hardly ever keep their transactions funds long enough to warrant a temporary investment in interest-bearing assets. For them, the analysis of this chapter is irrelevant. However, in the case of current transactions occurring at long intervals (like tax payments), and for high-income households and business firms, the temporary investment of transactions funds may play an important role. For example, large corporations may find it profitable to invest excess cash balances in the money market for just a few days. Interest rates on alternative assets may thus be expected to have some influence on the demand for cash balances. Indeed, many econometric studies have found significant negative elasticities of the demand for money with respect to the yield on alternative assets. The analysis of the present chapter, while probably less important overall than the preceding discussion, thus adds a significant element to the total picture.

The discussion will be limited to the choice between money, assumed to be noninterest-bearing, and one alternative asset, namely bonds. Bonds are assumed to have the form of consols, paying a fixed coupon, with a given yield of i. The main question can thus be described as follows. Suppose the individual, by solving the problem of the previous chapter, has determined the daily cash balance which would be optimal in the absence of bonds. Having done this, he is given access to the bond market and confronted with the question of what part of this cash balance he prefers to invest in bonds. It must be recognized that such dichotomized decision-making is not, in general, optimal. Usually the individual can increase his utility by reconsidering his daily excess purchases and sales, and thus his daily asset holdings, in the light of the newly opened opportunity to hold interest-bearing assets. At the present stage this interdependence is disregarded.

Why don't households and firms invest *all* transactions funds in interest-bearing assets? Why do they keep *any* such assets in the form of cash? It appears that the answer to these questions must be sought in the presence of transaction costs on the transfer of bonds. Transaction costs thus begin to play a crucial role in this chapter. By transaction costs I mean any sort of cost that depends only on the purchase and/or sale of the bonds and not on the length of time for which they are held. For the purposes of this chapter they can best be visualized as a broker's fee, but the concept will be given an extended interpretation in chapter 4.

While the significance of transaction costs for the demand for money has always been recognized, Baumol (1952) and Tobin (1956) were the first to analyze it in an explicit inventory model. Baumol's analysis, in particular, was highly successful in offering a simple, convincing and suggestive solution to a problem that seemed before to be quite intractable. For a quarter of a century, the Baumol/Tobin model was regarded as *the* theory of the transactions demand for cash. Since it explains only the division of transactions funds between money and bonds and not their aggregate amount, it is, in fact, nothing of the sort. But the division of transactions assets between money and bonds is precisely the topic of this chapter, and for this limited problem Baumol and Tobin have indeed provided the basic elements of the solution.

Baumol and Tobin restricted their analysis to the highly artificial case of a regular sawtooth profile of transactions assets. It is a commentary on the methods of economic science that there seem to be no published efforts to generalize their analysis to irregular asset patterns and to make sure that the conclusions continue to hold in less special cases. The following discussion will break with this tradition and begin with the general problem, introducing the sawtooth pattern as a special case.

Transaction costs may, in reality, be rather complicated functions of the quantity bought or sold, including fixed and variable components. In the first section of this chapter they will be assumed to be proportional to the amount invested, fixed transaction costs will be considered in the second section, and the third section will introduce uncertainty about interest rates and thus precautionary motives for holding cash balances.

3.1. Proportional transaction costs

Suppose that buying or selling a bond costs c_v for a dollar's worth of consols. This means that there are no scale economies in transactions; the smallest lots can be traded at the same per-dollar cost as the largest. The analysis can be based on the model presented in section 2.3. It will be remembered that the optimization process determined the amount of transactions assets for every day of the year along a path of infinite stationary motion. These assets, in the earlier model held in the form of money, now have to be allocated between cash balances and bonds. It was pointed out in chapter 2 that transactions assets are zero at least once in the course of the year. Without loss of generality we can choose a day with zero assets as the beginning of the year.

Suppose the time profile of transactions assets has the shape of $A(t)$ in figure 3.1.1.[1] The question is what part of A should be held in the form of bonds. Reflection shows that optimal cash holdings have a profile of the type illustrated by the shaded areas, while the remainder of the assets will be held in the form of bonds. There are certain periods like $t_0 - t_1$, $t_2 - t_3$, and so forth, when newly accruing assets are fully converted into bonds, while a decline in assets is fully reflected in sales of bonds. There are other

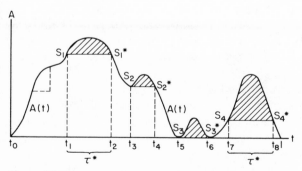

Figure **3.1.1**
Proportional Transaction Costs, Irregular Asset Curve

1. Note that $A(t)$ corresponds to the height of the shaded area in figure 2.1.1.

periods like $t_1 - t_2$, $t_3 - t_4$, and so forth, when the accumulation or de-cumulation of assets is reflected in cash balances only, the bond portfolio remaining unchanged. In the absence of fixed transaction costs it is never profitable to accumulate cash to convert it into bonds at a later moment (as illustrated by the broken part of the curve), for if it is profitable to buy bonds later, it is even more profitable to buy them at once. On the other hand, it is never profitable to sell bonds in order to hold cash for some time, because if the cash is not spent for some time anyhow, it is always more profitable to keep the bonds.

There are thus certain switching points $S_1 \ldots S_n$ where the individual ceases to adjust his bond portfolio and begins to hold accumulating funds in cash, while at the reverse switching points $S_1^* \ldots S_n^*$ cash balances are exhausted and further deficits are financed out of bonds. Determining the optimal portfolio amounts to determining the optimal switching points. Given $A(t)$, the position of the optimal switching points only depends on c_v and i. Holding a marginal dollar in the form of bonds is profitable if the cost of a "return trip" into the bond market is at least covered by the inter-est earned during the holding period. Define the holding period τ as the length of time between the moment A reaches a certain level from below and the moment it again reaches the same level on its way down. The con-dition for further bond accumulation can then be expressed by the condi-tion $2c_v \leqq i\tau$. If the inequality is reversed, further surpluses are held in cash. The switching point, if it is not at a trough of the asset curve, is char-acterized by the condition $2c_v = i\tau$ (see, for example, S_1, S_4). This means that the marginal cost of the round trip into the bond market is just equal to the marginal revenue. Those values of τ at which this occurs may be called the marginal holding period, denoted τ^*. It is clear that the average proportion of assets held in the form of cash balances is highly dependent on the shape of the asset curve; it is easy to construct extreme cases in which either all or nothing will be held in cash.

Now consider the comparative effects of changes in the data. I begin with *real income*. If all commodity flows, and thus receipts and expendi-tures, increase in the same proportion at constant prices, $A(t)$ moves up proportionally, while τ for any given moment remains unchanged. With unchanged c and i, the marginal holding period τ^*, and thus the optimal switching points, remain unchanged, too. The only thing we have to change in figure 3.1.1 is the scale of A. As a consequence, all cash balances and bond holdings will increase in the same proportion as assets. It follows that the demand for cash balances is proportional to real income, provided all commodity flows change in the same proportion.

Suppose, next, that real purchases and sales remain unchanged while all *prices*, including the coupon on consols, change in the same proportion. With given c_v and i the consequences are exactly the same as for a change in real income: The demand for cash balances increases in the same pro-

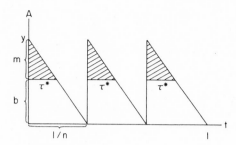

Figure **3.1.2**
Proportional Transaction Costs, Triangular Asset Curve

portion as money income, whether the change in the latter is due to real income or to prices.[2]

If *transaction costs* per dollar worth of bonds go up, the round trip into the bond market becomes more expensive. At a constant rate of interest, the marginal holding period rises. As a consequence, the bond portfolio falls while cash balances increase. There is thus a direct relationship between transaction costs and cash balances. If, on the other hand, the *rate of interest* goes up while the transaction costs are unchanged, τ^* will fall, resulting in higher bond holdings and reduced cash balances. We thus find that cash balances are inversely related to the bond yield.

More specific statements can be made if the asset curve is assumed to have some particular shape. As the simplest possible case we select the sawtooth pattern of figure 3.1.2, where annual income Y is received in n equal installments y at regular intervals of length $1/n$. This is the Baumol/ Tobin case. With proportional transaction costs, each time y is received b will at once be invested in bonds, while m is retained in cash. Once m is used up, further expenditures will be financed by continuous sales of bonds until the next installment of income is received. It is clear that $\tau^*/(1/n) = m/y$, which can be solved to give

$$\tau^* = m/yn = m/Y.$$

We are interested in the optimal size of the average cash holding

$$L = (1/2)m\tau^*n = (1/2)(m^2/Y)n. \tag{3.1.1}$$

Cash balances are optimal if they maximize net revenue P, defined as the excess of interest revenue over transaction costs. Interest revenue per year is

$$R = (1/2) i [(y/n) - m\tau^*]n = (1/2) i [y - (m^2/y)],$$

while transaction costs are

$$C = 2c_v (y - m)n.$$

---

2. Note that the price of a consol will go up with the coupon. With given c_v *per dollar of bonds*, transaction costs for one consol will thus keep pace with commodity prices.

Net revenue can thus be written

$$P = (1/2)\, iy - (1/2)\, i\, (m^2/y) - 2c_v\, (y - m)n. \qquad (3.1.2)$$

For m to be optimal, the partial derivative of P with respect to m must be zero,

$$\frac{\partial P}{\partial m} = -\, i\, (m/y) + 2c_v n = 0,$$

which can be solved for optimal m,

$$m^* = 2\, \frac{c_v}{i}\, ny = 2\, \frac{c_v}{i}\, Y. \qquad (3.1.3)$$

This indicates that the amount to be withheld from the bond market in each income period is independent of the length of these periods; the same absolute amount would be withheld if the total annual income were received, say, in one installment.

Substituting m^* into (3.1.1), the optimal cash balance is seen to be

$$L^* = 2\left(\frac{c_v}{i}\right)^2 Yn. \qquad (3.1.4)$$

It thus turns out that in the case of variable transaction costs with a regular sawtooth pattern of financial assets the demand for money (1) is proportionate to income, both real and nominal, (2) increases with the square of transaction costs, (3) has an interest elasticity of -2, and (4) is higher in proportion as income periods are shorter. Comparing these results with those for the general case of irregular asset curves, we note that the proportionate effect of money income is independent of special assumptions about the shape of the asset curve. However, the elasticities of the demand for money with respect to transaction costs and the rate of interest have not been demonstrated to be applicable for irregular asset curves. The same qualification is necessary with respect to the length of income periods, which cannot even be defined without quite restrictive assumptions about the shape of the asset curve.

The validity of (3.1.4) is subject to the additional constraint that bond purchases b cannot be negative. This means that m cannot exceed y. As a consequence, (3.1.2) only holds if $2c_v\,(Y/i) \leqq y$ or $2c_v \leqq i/n$. If this condition is not satisfied, the return trip into the bond market fails to pay even for the first dollar, and no bonds will ever be held. In this case, $m^* = y$ and thus $L^* = (1/2)\,(Y/n)$; the average cash holdings will amount to half the income received per pay period. For a large number of households this will be the normal state of affairs. Their income periods are too short to warrant any investment in the bond market, the rate of interest and the transaction cost rate have no influence on their demand for money, and the latter only depends on annual income and the length of the pay periods.

3.2. Fixed transaction costs

While variable transaction costs may be an important determinant of the demand for money, the resulting pattern of cash balances has some unrealistic features. Casual observation suggests that people sometimes do accumulate cash to buy bonds at a later time. They also sometimes sell bonds, not to finance immediate purchases, but in order to replenish their cash balances. It seems quite implausible that over some part of the year individuals would finance any excess demand for commodities, however small, by simultaneous bond sales. This shows that a part of the picture is still missing. It is supplied by fixed transaction costs. After all, it must be the fixed cost of bond transactions, in terms of time and trouble and usually also of brokerage fees, which prevents us from adjusting our security portfolio whenever we pay for a telephone call.

To analyze the effect of fixed transaction costs on the demand for money, I assume that these costs are at a rate of c_f dollars per transaction, no matter what its size, while variable transaction costs are now disregarded. The analysis can again begin with the general case of an irregular asset curve (see fig. 3.2.1). Suppose the individual, confronted with $A(t)$, is told that there must be exactly two bond transactions, a purchase and a sale. Since this fixes aggregate transaction costs, profits will be maximized if the interest revenue is maximized. At a given rate of interest, the individual will thus time his two transactions in such a way that his average bond holdings over the year are maximized, which is equivalent to maximizing the area of the solid rectangle. The same problem is then solved for 3, 4, ... k ... transactions, resulting in portfolio profiles of the type illustrated by broken and dotted polygons. Every time the planning has to be done from scratch; it will not generally be optimal just to add another transaction while the others take place at the points of time determined before.

The resulting revenues, R, are plotted as a function of the number of transactions, k, in figure 3.2.2. Strictly speaking, this function is defined

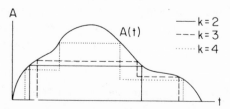

Figure **3.2.1**
Fixed Transaction Costs, Irregular Asset Curve

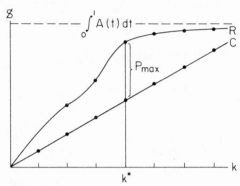

Figure **3.2.2**
Optimizing the Number of Transactions

for integer numbers of transactions only, but this aspect, though considered by Tobin and potentially important, will here be disregarded. The function is usually increasing and in any case nondecreasing; by making more transactions, we never lose revenue. It would be nice if the marginal revenue from additional transactions, expressed by the slope of the R-curve, were nonincreasing, amounting to a law of diminishing marginal returns. Unfortunately, in a strict sense there is no such law; it is conceivable that marginal revenue is sometimes increasing as illustrated in the graph. However, as k goes to infinity, R approaches a finite limit set by total assets, $\int_0^1 A(t)dt$. However marginal revenue may behave for small k, it eventually approaches zero.

The revenue curve has to be confronted with the transaction cost curve C. With given c_f, the aggregate transaction costs are proportionate to k. The C-curve, therefore, is a straight line through the origin. The number of transactions is optimal at the point k^*, where profit P, defined as the excess of revenue over cost, is a maximum. Disregarding discontinuities, optimality requires that the marginal revenue of transactions equal the transaction cost rate. If the R-curve is nowhere above the C-curve for $k \geqq$ 2, no bonds are bought and all assets are held in the form of cash.

The comparative-static effects of changes in data can also be discussed in terms of figure 3.2.2. If the *transaction cost rate* increases, the cost curve becomes steeper while the revenue curve remains unchanged. This tends to reduce k^* and thus the average bond portfolio, while average cash holdings are increased. The higher transaction costs, the higher the demand for money.

If the *rate of interest* rises, it is the revenue curve that becomes steeper in proportion, while the cost curve remains unchanged. As a consequence, k^* tends to increase and the demand for cash balances declines. It follows that the demand for money is inversely related to the bond yield.

The effect of an increase in *real income* is more difficult to determine. Nothing definite can be said, of course, if the asset curve is twisted in some irregular way. The question must thus be again restricted to the special case of a proportionate upward shift in the asset curve. The total effect can be divided into two components. I first consider the effect of a changing real income at given k. From figure 3.2.1 it is evident that for given k the optimal timing of transactions remains the same. For given k, the demand for money and the demand for bonds thus increase in the same proportion as real income. If k^* actually remained the same, the demand for money would thus be proportionate to income. But k^* does not, in fact, remain the same. For each k, returns are now higher. The revenue curve thus turns proportionately upward, just as it did with an increase in interest rates, while the cost curve remains unchanged. As a consequence, the optimal number of transactions k^* increases. We thus find that for each k the demand for money increases in proportion to income, while at the same time k^* rises. It follows that the demand for money rises less than in proportion to real income. This means that fixed transaction costs result in economies of scale in cash holdings. As real income increases, less cash is demanded per dollar of income.

The same is not true if the shift in the asset curve is due to an increase in the *price level*. In this case, the brokerage fee c_f must be assumed to rise in step with commodity prices. The cost curve thus turns upward in the same proportion as the revenue curve, leaving k^* unchanged. It follows that the demand for nominal cash balances increases in the same proportion as prices, and the cash/income ratio remains unchanged. Inflation does not provide economies of scale in cash holding.

In the Baumol/Tobin case of a sawtooth asset curve, the preceding results can again be sharpened (see fig. 3.2.3). Transaction costs, fixed in amount, have to be paid for each purchase or sale of bonds, indicated by a vertical step in the shaded cash holdings. The bond portfolio is represented by the nonshaded part of the area under the asset curve. Again I shall neglect the fact that the number of transactions per income period must be integer, but I shall take into account the fact that it must be at least two. It is evident that bond purchases, if any, will be made at the

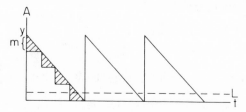

Figure **3.2.3**
Fixed Transaction Costs, Triangular Asset Curve

beginning of each income period, followed by regularly spaced sales in the same amounts as the initial cash balance m.[3] All we have to do, therefore, is to determine m^*, the optimal amount of cash withheld or withdrawn from the bond market in each transaction. The average cash balance will then be $L^* = m^*/2$.

Revenue from the bond portfolio is equal to what it would be in the absence of cash holdings minus the interest lost on cash balances. For the full year of n income periods, using the same symbols as before,

$$R = (1/2)\, yi - (1/2)\, mi = (1/2)\, i\, (y - m).$$

Transaction costs, on the other hand, are

$$C = c_f n\, (y/m) = c_f\, (Y/m).$$

For net revenue we thus obtain

$$P = R - C = (1/2)\, i\, (y - m) - c_f\, (Y/m) = (1/2)\, i\, (y - 2L)$$
$$- c_f(Y/2L), \tag{3.2.1}$$

where $m = 2L$. Taking the partial derivative with respect to L and setting it equal to zero, the necessary condition for optimal cash holdings is seen to be

$$L^* = \sqrt{\frac{c_f Y}{2i}}. \tag{3.2.2}$$

It follows that the demand for money (1) has an income elasticity of 0.5, thus increasing with the square root of real income, (2) increases with the square root of the transaction cost rate, (3) has an interest elasticity of -0.5, (4) is independent of the length of the income periods, and (5) is proportionate to the price level as reflected in an equiproportionate increase in Y and c_f.

While it is gratifying to have a model with such precise empirical implications, the relevance of these implications for the aggregate demand for money is, for several reasons, quite limited. First, (3.2.2) only holds if some transactions assets are held in the form of bonds. No bonds will be held if one return trip into the bond market costs as much as, or more than, the interest it yields, which means, in symbols, if

$$2c_f \geq \frac{1}{4}\, y\, \frac{i}{n}.$$

In this case the demand for money is simply proportionate to income, in-

---

3. For a given number of sales, the shaded area, representing the loss of interest, will be minimized. But the area of each shaded triangle depends on the square of its base. Minimization of the sum of these triangles thus requires equal bases.

versely proportionate to the annual number of income periods, and insensitive to interest rates and transaction costs. For most households and many small firms this is the normal case—which helps to explain why econometric estimates of the income elasticity of the demand for money have usually been closer to 1.0 than to 0.5, while estimates of the interest elasticity have often been lower (absolutely) than 0.5.[4]

Second, transaction costs will normally have both variable and fixed components. This means that the elasticities of the demand for money with respect to the various independent variables will be somewhere in between those for the pure cases.[5] In particular, the real income elasticity of the demand for cash balances could thus be expected to lie between 0.5 and 1.0, while the interest elasticity should range between -0.5 and -2.0. As the volume of transactions increases, the fixed component is increasingly dominated by the variable element, and the income elasticity of the demand for money approaches unity as income goes to infinity. To illustrate by an extreme example, fixed transaction costs are hardly a valid reason to suppose that the demand of central banks for international reserves, as sometimes has been argued, grows at a lower long-term rate than world trade.

Third, one has to remember that the square-root property, strictly speaking, has so far been demonstrated only for the sawtooth case. It is remarkable how many economists are quite willing to accept it as a general proposition without apparently feeling the need to check whether it actually holds in less special cases. Fourth, it is not clear to what extent the square root formula can be applied to the private sector of the economy as a whole as distinct from individual units. Certainly, if the private sector grows by adding more units of the same size, no scale economies can be expected. Finally, it should be noted that the whole issue has nothing to do with the validity of the quantity theory of money. What matters for the quantity theory is a rise in money income because of a price change, and in this case the demand for money increases in proportion for any shape of the asset curve and for any combination of fixed and variable transaction costs.

Regardless of the significance of the square-root property, fixed transaction costs are an important element in the world we live in, particularly in its micro aspects. Unfortunately, economic science finds it very difficult, in general, to cope with fixed costs and is in danger of bogging down whenever they raise their head. This is probably the main reason why the Baumol/Tobin model, despite persistent efforts,[6] turned out to be so resistant to further progress from the sawtooth case to more general cases, from two assets to many, and from individual optimization to general equi-

---

4. For a detailed analysis of this point see Barro (1976).
5. For the income elasticity see Brunner and Meltzer (1967a, p. 426).
6. Due mainly to Barro (1970, 1972, 1976), Santomero (1974), Barro and Santomero (1972, 1976) and Feige and Parkin (1971).

librium. At the present time, the price of such progress seems to be the neglect of fixed transaction costs. From a macroeconomic point of view, the sacrifice seems to be small.

3.3. Uncertainty about interest rates

In the Keynesian theory of liquidity preference, precautionary motives play an important role. Cash balances are assumed to be held, in part, in view of the uncertainty of future market conditions. The uncertainty may, in principle, relate to any of the factors that determine the demand for money, including interest rates, commodity prices, transaction costs, incomes, endowments, wealth, and the dates of incoming or outgoing payments. It may also relate to the individual's own utility function, as in the case of sudden needs arising from illness or accidents. The present discussion will, however, be limited to uncertainty about the bond yield.[7]

Important elements of a theory of liquidity preference with uncertain interest rates were provided by Tobin's classic contributions (1958, 1965). The following analysis will be based on his approach. However, Tobin was not considering transactions assets, arising from current sales and expenditures, but long-term investment portfolios. The demand for cash balances was attributed to the risk that bondholding might involve a capital loss in excess of interest income. As a consequence, Tobin's analysis is open to the well-known objection that usually there exist some interest-bearing assets that are virtually immune to capital losses, so that no cash balances will ever be held. It follows that Tobin's portfolio model, taken literally, has little to say about the demand for cash balances. Its main field of application is in the explanation of diversified noncash portfolios.

This objection loses its force in the context of a theory of transactions balances, exemplified by the Baumol/Tobin transaction cost model. In such a model, cash balances will be held even if interest-bearing assets are immune to capital loss. A valid theory of the demand for money under uncertainty can thus be constructed by grafting Tobin's portfolio approach onto a model of transactions balances. Such a theory is presented in this section.

To keep the analysis simple, the individual is still assumed to make a once-and-for-all decision about the timing and size of future security transactions. However, the model used in the preceding sections will be extended in two respects. On one hand, the price of consols is now assumed to be subject to random fluctuations, resulting in a distribution of i with mean

---

7. Uncertainty about receipts and payments was considered for one period by Whalen (1966), for several successive periods (but with quite similar cubic-root results) by Miller and Orr (1966, 1968) and Orr (1970), and in the context of a Baumol/Tobin model by Tsiang (1969).

$E(i)$ and standard deviation σ_i. On the other hand, the individual, instead of just maximizing expected returns, is assumed to maximize a utility function depending on both the mean and standard deviation of net revenue. An individual with upward-sloping indifference curves will be called a "risk averter"; the analysis will concentrate on the case in which the marginal risk premium, as measured by the slope of the indifference curves, rises with increasing risk. An individual with falling indifference curves will be called a "risk lover," and the analysis will concentrate on the case of a diminishing marginal rate of substitution between expected yield and risk.

What is the effect of introducing uncertainty into the models used in the preceding sections? Will cash balances unambiguously increase or may they conceivably decline? We may first try to conjecture an intuitive answer. Suppose interest rates are known with certainty. At the point where cash balances are optimal the marginal net revenue from bonds, after deducting transaction costs, must be zero. This means that a "small" increase in cash balances at the expense of bonds would not reduce net revenue. But with uncertain interest the same increase in cash balances would clearly reduce risk. It follows that a risk averter, weighing net return against risk, will always find it advantageous to hold a larger cash balance and a smaller bond portfolio than in a riskless situation. In other words, risk will unambiguously raise the demand for cash balances, and the opposite would be true for risk lovers. The following, more formal analysis will show that this conjecture is indeed correct.

3.3.1. PROPORTIONATE TRANSACTION COSTS. I begin with the case of proportionate transaction costs, discussed in the first section of this chapter. The analysis will be restricted to the special case of a regular sawtooth pattern of assets (see fig. 3.1.2). Average assets can be defined as $A = y/2 = L + B$, where L and B are, respectively, average cash balances and average bond holdings. The corresponding asset proportions are denoted

$$\lambda = \frac{L}{A}, \qquad \beta = \frac{B}{A}. \qquad (\lambda + \beta = 1)$$

Dividing (3.1.2) by A, and making obvious substitutions, the net revenue per dollar of assets can be written

$$\pi = \frac{P}{A} = \beta i - 4c_v n (1 - \sqrt{1 - \beta}). \tag{3.3.1}$$

If i is subject to uncertainty, the expected return is

$$E(\pi) = \beta E(i) - 4c_v n (1 - \sqrt{1 - \beta}), \tag{3.3.2}$$

while the risk attaching to a portfolio with bond component β is measured by

$$\sigma_\pi = \beta \sigma_i, \tag{3.3.3}$$

where σ_i is the standard deviation of i.

For a given σ_i, the portfolio risk σ_π is seen to be a linear function of β, just as in Tobin's model. In figure 3.3.1, constructed in analogy to Tobin's familiar graph, it is represented by $\sigma_\pi(\beta)$. Substituting from (3.3.3) into (3.3.2), the expected return can, in turn, be expressed as a function of σ_π,

$$E(\pi) = \frac{E(i)}{\sigma_i} \sigma_\pi - 4c_v n + 4c_v n \sqrt{1 - \frac{\sigma_\pi}{\sigma_i}}. \tag{3.3.4}$$

This is the equation of the opportunity locus, giving all those combinations of expected return and risk which can be obtained from given assets by varying their composition between bonds and cash. Unlike Tobin's opportunity locus, it is clearly not a straight line. Its first component is represented by a straight line through the origin, whose slope, for given σ_i, reflects the expected rate of interest. The second term can be expressed by a parallel downward shift of this line. The last, and most interesting, term can be represented by a curve that begins at $4c_v n$ for $\sigma_\pi = 0$, declines more and more rapidly as σ_π grows, and reaches zero (with a vertical slope) at $\sigma_\pi = \sigma_i$. The sum of these components is a curve like $E(\pi)$ in figure 3.3.1, with a maximum somewhere between zero and σ_i. The marginal expected return, which is constant in Tobin's model, is thus seen to decline as the bond portfolio is increased. Beyond $E(\pi)_{max}$ it actually becomes negative, finally approaching a value of minus infinity. It should be noted that the level of A has no influence on $E(\pi)$; this reflects the fact, noted in section 3.1, that with proportional transaction costs the demands for money and bonds are proportionate to income and thus to total assets.

The opportunity locus can now be confronted with the indifference curves, describing the individual preferences with respect to expected return and risk. For a risk averter, those curves will rise to the right with an increasing slope. As the graph is drawn, the utility-maximizing individual will choose a bond portfolio β^* and cash balances λ^*. In the absence of uncertainty, the individual would choose the point where $E(\pi)$ reaches its maximum.[8] The same would obviously be true for a risk-neutral individual (with horizontal indifference curves) in the presence of risk. It follows that a risk averter will always locate to the left of $E(\pi)_{max}$, which means that he will always hold a higher proportion of his assets in cash than in a risk-free situation. For a risk lover, on the other hand, since he has downward-sloping indifference curves, uncertainty results in lower cash balances. But

---

8. Taking the derivative of (3.3.4) with respect to σ_π, setting it equal to zero, and solving for L, one obtains (3.1.4), which is the optimal cash balance in the absence of risk.

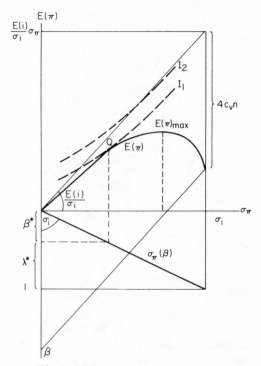

Figure **3.3.1**
Uncertainty with Proportional Transaction Costs

not even an ardent risk lover will ever hold an all-bond portfolio, provided he is not willing to give up a finite amount of expected return for an infinitely small increase in risk. This corresponds well to casual observation about transactions assets: Nobody can manage completely without cash. By grafting Tobin's mean/variance approach onto a transaction cost model, we thus obtain clear-cut propositions about the effect of risk on the demand for money.

This does not mean that any increase in risk, as expressed by an increase in σ_i, will necessarily result in an increase in demand for money. As Tobin pointed out, the effect of a change in σ_i on the demand for money is ambiguous. This is illustrated in figure 3.3.2. The opportunity locus E_1 is derived from E_0 by doubling σ_i, thus doubling σ_π for any level of β, and also doubling σ_π for any given level of $E(\pi)$. In the original situation the optimal bond portfolio is β_0^*. If, with increased risk, the optimal bond portfolio is β_1^*, cash balances $\lambda^* = 1 - \beta^*$ will be increased. If, however, the bond portfolio is increased to β_2^*, cash balances will be reduced.

This ambiguity, as is well known, is due to an income effect of uncertain strength and direction interfering with the substitution effect. For any given β, an increase in σ_i makes the opportunity locus flatter than it was

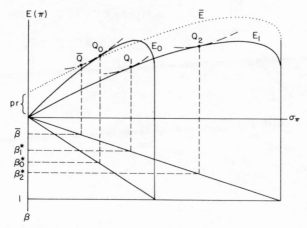

Figure **3.3.2**
The Effect of Risk on the Demand for Money

before. This means that there is a substitution effect that, taken by itself, would result in a reduction in bond holdings and thus an increase in the demand for cash. This substitution effect can be isolated by an experiment in which the individual is paid a premium pr on all assets, both money and bonds, such as to keep him on the same indifference curve. In figure 3.3.2 this results in the dotted opportunity locus $\bar{E}$, which is parallel to E_1 and tangent to the same indifference curve as E_0. The optimum $\bar{Q}$ corresponds to a value of β that is far below β_0^*. The income effect can be isolated by comparing the new optimum excluding premium, be it Q_1 or Q_2, with the new optimum including premium, $\bar{Q}$. As the graph is drawn, the income effect, taken in isolation, works in favor of a higher bond portfolio and thus produces a fall in cash balances. However, other indifference curves may produce other results.

The preceding argument implies that different risk levels may result in the same cash balance. If, starting from $\sigma_i = 0$, risk is newly introduced, a risk averter is certain to increase his cash balance. There may be points, however, at which a further increase in risk results in a decline in the demand for money, reducing it to the same level it has had at a lower risk level. There is thus the possibility of a "reswitching" of cash balances with respect to uncertainty.

By a similar, though not identical,[9] argument it can be shown that in the presence of uncertainty the sign of the interest elasticity of the demand for cash balances becomes ambiguous. Again the ambiguity can be removed by compensating the individual for the loss in utility resulting from a lower bond yield by a premium on both money and bonds.

---

9. The difference is due to the fact that $E(i)$ appears only in the first term of 3.3.4, while σ_i also appears in the last term.

From a policy point of view it is important to note that, with respect to the demand for money and bonds, an increase in the level of the bond yield is roughly similar to a reduction in its uncertainty. This means that a policy of interest stabilization appears as closely, though not perfectly, similar to a policy of easy money: While a policy of easy money lowers interest rates through the relative supply of assets, namely by increasing the money supply and reducing the bond supply, a policy of interest stabilization lowers interest rates through the relative demand for assets, namely by reducing the demand for money and increasing the demand for bonds. By the same token, a policy permitting more fluctuations in interest rates is a close, though not perfect, substitute for a policy of tighter money.

3.3.2. FIXED TRANSACTION COSTS. Qualitatively similar results can be derived for the case of fixed transaction costs (see section 3.2). Dividing (3.2.1) by A and remembering that $y = 2A$, $m = 2L$, $Y = ny$ and $\lambda = L/A = (1 - \beta)$, net revenue per dollar of assets can be written

$$\pi = \frac{P}{A} = \left(1 - \frac{L}{A}\right) i - \frac{c_f n}{L} = \beta i - \frac{c_f n}{A(1 - \beta)}. \tag{3.3.5}$$

With uncertain i, the expected rate of return is

$$E(\pi) = \beta E(i) - \frac{c_f n}{A(1 - \beta)}, \tag{3.3.6}$$

while the standard deviation of the rate of return is

$$\sigma_\pi = \beta \sigma_i. \tag{3.3.7}$$

For given σ_i, the portfolio risk is again a linear function of β as illustrated in the lower part of figure 3.3.3. $E(\pi)$ is the difference of two terms. The first term is simply a linear function of β and thus of σ_π. The second term starts out with a value of $-nc_f/A$ for $\beta = \sigma_\pi = 0$ and declines with increasing slope toward minus infinity as β approaches 1 (which means that σ_π approaches σ_i). The result is a curve like $E(\pi)$ in the upper part of figure 3.3.3. It must be kept in mind, however, that with fixed transaction costs β cannot assume values between zero and one-half. This means that the opportunity locus is not defined for $0 < \beta < 1/2$. For $\beta = 0$, of course, we have $E(\pi) = 0$.

Again we find that the cash balance of a risk averter will always be higher than it would be in the absence of uncertainty, while the cash balance of a risk lover will always be lower, though positive. We also find the same ambiguities as before with respect to the effect of changes in the level and the uncertainty of interest rates on the relative demand for money and bonds.

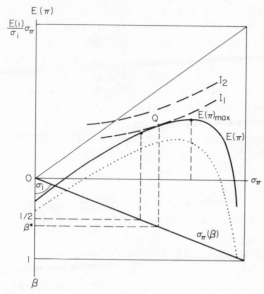

Figure **3.3.3**
Uncertainty with Fixed Transaction Costs

A new element is injected by the presence of A in 3.3.6. It means that with fixed transaction costs a change in the level of income, and thus of assets, produces a shift in the opportunity locus. In particular, a fall in A produces a downward shift in the opportunity locus as indicated by the dotted curve. It can easily be ascertained that this results in a leftward shift in $E(\pi)_{max}$.[10] With lower income and thus lower assets, the expected yield is maximized at a lower proportion of bonds and a higher proportion of cash balances. This simply is a restatement of the proposition that fixed transaction costs result in scale economies in cash balances. However, in the presence of uncertainty, $E(\pi)_{max}$ is not what we are interested in. What is relevant is rather the shift in the optimum Q. It is clear that, depending on the shape of the indifference curves, the optimum on the dotted opportunity locus can be either to the left or to the right of Q. By coincidence, it may just be on the same vertical line as Q. This means that in the presence of uncertainty about interest rates, we cannot be sure about the scale effects of a change in income. It is quite likely that there are still some economies of scale, but it is also possible that the demand for cash, even with fixed transaction costs, is now proportionate to income, and it is conceivable that there are actually diseconomies of scale. As a consequence, the eco-

10. Take the derivative of 3.3.6 with respect to β, set it equal to zero, and solve for $\lambda = 1 - \beta$. The result is simply the familiar square-root formula 3.2.2, divided through by A.

nomic significance of the square-root property in the Baumol/Tobin model is further reduced.

In summary, it has been found that, for risk averters, uncertainty about interest rates increases the demand for money beyond what it would have been under complete certainty. However, in contrast to Tobin's mean/variance model, some money will always be held, no matter how small the uncertainty. In many cases, both an increase in the level of interest rates and a reduction in their uncertainty will reduce the demand for money, but in view of an ambiguous income effect the opposite reaction cannot be excluded. The presence of uncertainty also makes the scale effects arising from fixed transaction costs more unreliable. These propositions were derived from a model with a regular sawtooth pattern of transactions assets. In view of what has been said in the first two sections of this chapter, it seems likely, however, that they would still be valid with irregular asset patterns.

Four

MONEY, OTHER ASSETS, AND
COMMODITY FLOWS

Introduction

Chapter 2 showed how commodity flows and the level of transactions assets are jointly determined by individual optimization, but it allowed for no assets except cash balances. Chapter 3, on the other hand, showed how an individual allocates his transactions assets between money and bonds, but it did not allow for the optimization of commodity flows and thus of the total asset stock. In the present chapter these two points of view will be combined, allowing for the joint optimization of commodity flows and of the size and composition of assets. At the same time, the range of assets will be enlarged to include commodity stocks and debt.

We thus arrive at what may be called "Walras' Problem" (Walras, 1900). In developing the monetary aspects of his general equilibrium system, Walras assumed that all production, consumption, and exchange flows are dated. Stocks are then introduced to bridge any gaps between inflows and outflows, thus providing utility (see sec. 1.3). Inventories are held at such levels that their marginal stock utility, capitalized at the rate of interest, equals their marginal flow utility in consumption. A certain part of the inventories is held in the form of cash balances, subject to the same marginal conditions as commodities. Walras thus provided the outline of a theory that explains the demand for cash balances as a special case of the demand for inventories. He failed, however, to explain why exactly stocks have utility and why it may be efficient to hold some stocks in the form of money. These are the problems we have to solve.

The present chapter (based on Niehans, 1975) shows that these problems can be solved by extending the neoclassical theory to assets, both nonfinancial and financial, which, in turn, requires a multiperiod framework and the introduction of transaction costs. Once the individual optimization model is properly specified, the exact marginal calculus for cash balances and other assets can be shown to flow from it as automatically as the marginal conditions for commodities flow from the neoclassical theory. The theory of value and the theory of money are truly integrated.

4.1. The model in outline

The model to be used is an extension of the time preference model of chapter 2, sections 4 and 5. In order to focus attention on the relationship between commodities (as a group) and financial assets, all consumables will again be lumped together into one composite commodity. There are now three assets, money, bonds, and commodity stocks. The individual can also go into debt by selling and repurchasing his own bonds in the market. Debt thus appears as a negative stock of bonds.

The net yield of each asset consists of its market return, the capital gain or loss, and time preference. The market return on commodity stocks is negative, consisting of a storage cost expressed as a physical shrinkage. Bonds have a uniform and constant coupon r, fixed by the government and payable in money; their market return i fluctuates inversely to their price p^b according to $i = r/p^b$. There may also be a positive market return on cash balances, fixed by the government. Capital gains and losses are created by changes in commodity and bond prices. The analysis thus incorporates the speculative motive for asset-holding familiar from Keynesian models (Tobin, 1958) and stressed by Marschak (1950).

It should be noted that the present analysis, while incorporating speculative motives, is not subject to the same limitations as the Keynesian approach. This is true in two respects. First, while the Keynesian analysis, as pointed out by Leontief (1948) and others, can only be used for disequilibrium situations, the present analysis is valid in full equilibrium. Second, the Keynesian speculative motive, like Tobin's risk preference theory (see above, sec 3.3), is relevant for cash balances only in the case where there are no interest-bearing assets that are protected against capital losses. In reality, however, such assets usually exist. It follows that the Keynesian analysis is really irrelevant for the demand for currency and demand deposits.[1] This difficulty is due to the conceptual separation, in the Keynesian approach, of transactions and speculative motives for holding cash balances. Speculative motives were treated as if they had nothing to do with current transactions, relating not to temporary transactions assets but to long-term wealth. The present model, since speculative motives are inte-

---

1. In fact, this seems to have been Keynes' own view. In the *General Theory* (p. 195) he pointed out that the speculative motive for holding money, like the precautionary motive, applies chiefly to those deposits which in the *Treatise* he had classified as savings deposits. But in the *Treatise* savings deposits are said to correspond roughly to what in the United States is called time deposits (p. 36), though the dividing line is acknowledged to be blurred.

grated into the theory of transactions balances, is immune to this criticism. Speculative motives thus remain potentially relevant for cash balances even though there may be interest-bearing assets that are protected against capital losses.[2]

Despite the possible differences in the yields of different assets, portfolios may be diversified due to transaction costs. An individual will prefer commodity stocks to money balances for short periods, because the saving in storage costs is not worth the transaction costs on the exchange of commodities. For sufficiently short periods, he will also prefer noninterest-bearing cash balances to bonds, because the positive return on bonds is outweighed by the transaction costs on bonds. In a pure exchange economy, all assets have the character of transactions assets, used to "bridge the gaps" between the given time-profile of endowments and the preferred time-profile of consumption. Debt is an alternative way to achieve the same purpose; it is profitable whenever the resulting savings in asset-holding costs at least pay for the additional interest and transaction costs.[3]

For the money/bond model of the preceding chapter, it was convenient and reasonably realistic to interpret the transaction costs as brokerage fees, payable in money. This approach implies that the actual resource inputs are all made by the specialized brokers. Since for purchases and sales of goods and services this looks implausible, I shall adopt a different interpretation under which transaction costs represent an individual's own resource inputs. On the other hand, I shall assume that there are no brokerage fees, so that there is no spread between bid and ask prices.

For the purposes of this analysis, transaction costs may be defined as costs that arise not from the production of goods (including transportation, packaging, lot breaking, etc.) but from the transfer of ownership from one economic agent to another. They are a catchall term for a rather heterogeneous assortment of inputs. The parties have to communicate; information is exchanged; the goods must be inspected, weighed, and measured; contracts are drawn up; title is transferred; and records have to be kept. To a considerable degree these transaction costs have their ultimate basis in uncertainty, and most of the costs listed above are really search and infor-

2. One would expect that speculative motives of the Keynesian type find a particularly pure expression in the stock transactions of mutual funds (net of transactions arising from sales and redemptions of shares). If these motives are indeed significant for the demand for money, such stock transactions should be inversely reflected in the cash holdings of mutual funds. In a detailed statistical analysis of the balance sheets of thirty-three investment companies, Ronald J. Talley (1975) found no significant association between stocks and cash balances, but a strong negative association between stocks and interest-bearing nonmonetary assets. This provides strong evidence for the view that the Keynesian speculative motive, while important for the choice between nonmonetary assets, is irrelevant for cash holdings.

3. In the absence of time preference and storage costs, nobody would go into debt, since asset-holding would be costless. This is the basic reason why the Baumol/Tobin approach cannot explain the supply of debt.

mation costs.[4] The trouble is that, while it is easy to discourse on search and information costs, it is difficult to incorporate them into a general equilibrium framework.[5] The present treatment thus follows the research strategy of trying to make as much progress as possible without an explicit theory of information. As a consequence, transaction costs will be treated as if they were necessary even in a world of full certainty. This can be rationalized by assuming that the exchange system is initially full of uncertainty, that everybody is so averse to risk that he insists on complete certainty, and that the transaction costs are exactly those inputs which are necessary to transform the initial uncertainty into full certainty. While uncertainty, search, and information are certainly important in the world as we know it, the following chapters show that it is possible to construct a coherent model of different exchange systems, both nonmonetary and monetary, without them. Even if transaction costs had nothing to do with uncertainty, we would still find about the same general types of exchange arrangements we find in the real world.

It will be assumed that transaction costs consist of commodity inputs, that they are proportional to the quantity transferred, and that they are the same for purchases and sales. There is little doubt that scale economies do, in fact, play an important role in exchange, just as in other aspects of economic life. In part, they are economies of transactions scale, the transfer of two pounds of sugar imposing less than twice the transaction costs of one pound. If this were not so, there would be no reason why wages and rents, for example, should not be paid by the second instead of by the day, week or month. In addition, there may be economies of market scale inasmuch as transaction costs for a widely traded commodity may be lower than those for one that is rarely traded. Scale economies, however, are difficult to incorporate in a general equilibrium model. Whenever the objective was to build a general equilibrium model, most economists thus felt compelled, and also justified, to abstract from these troublesome factors. I shall follow the same procedure. There were indeed economists who felt that scale economies are not only an important but an essential aspect of monetary exchange (see, for example, Hahn, 1971). This and the following chapters seem to indicate that this is an overly pessimistic view, and that the basic aspects of monetary exchange can be understood even in terms of an exchange technology with proportionate transaction costs.

Before specifying the model in detail, it may be useful to give a non-

---

4. From a more fundamental point of view, the very fact that the economy uses exchange is due to uncertainty. Exchange is a way to make sure that nobody can escape his budget constraint(s). If one could be perfectly certain that everybody always stays within his budget constraint, everybody could be allowed to obtain goods without a specific quid pro quo.

5. For suggestive elements of a monetary theory of information costs, see Brunner/Meltzer (1971).

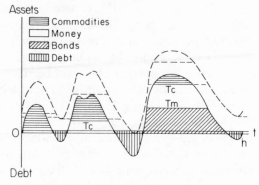

Figure **4.1.1**
Asset Diversification

rigorous description of the type of asset diversification it explains. This description will be based on figure 4.1.1. The graph depicts the annual cycle of an individual's optimal portfolio, disregarding daily price changes, interest on cash balances, and taxes. All of its elements are jointly determined; none are exogenously given.

Endowments accrue to the individual in the form of commodities. Unless the time-profile of endowments, by coincidence, matches the time-profile of preferences, the individual will want to divorce the pattern of consumption from the pattern of endowments by holding assets. Total assets as a function of time are described by the solid curve. The stationarity postulate implies that this curve begins and ends the year at the same level. We assume for convenience that it begins the year at zero. Total assets may, of course, be negative, indicating debt. The layers revealed in a vertical cross-section through the asset profile indicate what portions of total assets are held in the form of commodities, money, bonds, or debt, respectively, at a given moment. A horizontal section shows how long the marginal unit of an asset is held.

Commodity stocks will be held, if the holding period is so short that the transaction cost for a return trip into cash balances would be higher than the storage cost. This determines a critical holding period for commodities, T_c. In the absence of transaction costs on goods, no commodity stocks would ever be held. Cash balances are held, if the holding period, though exceeding T_c, is still so short that the transaction costs for a return trip into the bond market would be higher than the market return on the bonds. This determines a critical holding period for money, T_m. In the absence of transaction costs on bonds, no cash balances will be held, nor will cash balances be held if $T_m < T_c$.

An individual goes into debt in order to shift his asset curve downward. People borrow to reduce the need for accumulating wealth. If debt had been prohibited, the asset curve might have looked as indicated by the broken line. In view of time preference and, for commodities, storage costs, this would have entailed higher holding costs. Debt thus permits a lowering of asset holding costs. On the other hand, it costs interest, both interest foregone on the interest-earning assets (if any) that would otherwise have been held, and interest paid on the debt. In addition, borrowing will often involve additional transaction costs. Debt is incurred up to the point where the marginal benefit from lower asset holding ceases to outweigh the marginal interest and transaction costs.[6] This marginal consideration can be visualized in figure 4.1.1 by moving the vertical scale upward by $1, thus cutting off a narrow strip over the length of the asset profile. This has the following consequences: (1) It saves time preference over the length of the year, reflecting the cost of accumulating a dollar of assets; (2) it saves storage costs during the time inventories are held; (3) it costs interest (paid or foregone) during the period of debt or bond holding; and (4) it adds costly transaction chains commodities/money/bonds and money/bonds where indicated by a heavy line (note that switching from bonds to debt adds no transaction costs). This intuitive explanation of asset diversification will be made precise and more general by the formal model.

4.2. The optimization problem

Let an individual's endowment be described by the vector $(\bar{x}_1, \cdots \bar{x}_t, \cdots \bar{x}_h)$. The task is to transform this into the consumption vector $(x_1, \cdots x_t, \cdots x_h)$ which maximizes

$$U = U(x_1, \cdots x_t, \cdots x_h), \tag{4.2.1}$$

subject to linear constraints. There are three sets of constraints, relating, respectively, to commodities, bonds, and money. In each set there is one constraint for each of h days ($t = 1 \ldots h$). The following notation will be used:

g (superscript) goods (in physical units)
m (superscript) money (in nominal terms)
b (superscript) bonds (in pieces of bonds)
y quantity sold
z quantity bought
s quantity held in stock
p price (in terms of money)

6. It never pays, in a pure exchange model, to go into debt in order to finance the simultaneous holding of assets. Compared to commodities and money, bonds are a low-cost asset. It never pays to reduce a low-cost asset by holding a negative amount of it just for the privilege of holding more higher-cost assets. It also never pays to incur transaction costs for the simultaneous holding of bonds and debt.

c transaction costs (units of goods per unit exchanged)
γ storage costs on goods (percent)
r coupon on bonds (in monetary units per bond)
ρ interest on cash balances (percent)
t tax or transfer (lump-sum, in monetary units) $(t \gtrless 0)$
θ rate of time preference

It will be assumed that $\theta \geqq \rho \geqq 0$ and $\theta + \gamma \geqq 0$. A further restriction will be added, and the significance of these restrictions will be discussed, at the end of section 4.4.

The *commodity constraint* for day t states that the increase in stocks from t to $t+1$ is equal to the sum of the excess of the endowment over consumption and net purchases after deducting what is wasted in storage and used up in transactions of goods and bonds,

$$s_{t+1}^g - s_t^g = (\bar{x}_t - x_t) + (z_t^g - y_t^g) - \gamma s_t^g - c^g (z_t^g + y_t^g)$$
$$- c^b (z_t^b + y_t^b). \tag{4.2.2}$$

Optimization will see to it that either purchases or sales (or both) are zero for both goods and bonds. With transaction costs it is wasteful to buy and sell simultaneously in the same market. The *bond constraints* say simply that the change in the portfolio equals the excess of purchases over sales,

$$s_{t+1}^b - s_t^b = z_t^b - y_t^b. \tag{4.2.3}$$

The *money constraints* state that cash balances are augmented by net sales of commodities and bonds, by the receipt of coupon payments on bonds, and by interest payments on cash balances, after deducting tax payments,[7]

$$s_{t+1}^m - s_t^m = p_t^g (y_t^g - z_t^g) + p_t^b (y_t^b - z_t^b) + rs_t^b + \rho s_t^m - t_t. \tag{4.2.4}$$

To these constraints we have to add the requirement that the stocks of commodities and money and the flows of commodities and bonds be non-negative:

$$a \geqq 0 \qquad a = x, y^g, z^g, y^b, z^b, s^g, s^m.$$

There is no sign constraint for bond stocks, since the individual is free to go into debt.[8] We also have to formalize the stationarity requirement, according to which an individual's choice is restricted to plans resulting in the same cycle of consumption, exchange, and stocks year by year:

$$q_{nh+t} = q_t \text{ for } q = x, y^g, z^g, y^b, z^b, s^g, s^m, s^b$$
$$n = 0 \cdots (H - 1).$$

What an individual is asked to determine is his optimal stationary plan.

7. Note that taxes may vary over time; they may, for example, be zero for every day but one.
8. A corresponding sign constraint for bonds would express the assumption that all bonds are issued by the government.

This is again a nonlinear programming problem with a quasi-concave objective function and linear constraints. Its solution determines the consumption of goods, the purchases and sales of goods and bonds, and the stock of goods, money, bonds, and debt for every day under given conditions, where these conditions are defined by the pattern of endowments, the history of market prices for goods and bonds, transaction and storage cost rates, taxes, the coupon on bonds, and the rate of interest on cash balances. Denoting variables in the optimal plan by an asterisk, we can thus write the demand functions

consumption: $\quad \overset{*}{x}_t = \overset{*}{x}(\bar{x}, p^g, p^b, t, r, \rho, \gamma, c^g, c^b),$ (4.2.5)

commodity stocks: $\overset{*g}{s}_t = \overset{*g}{s}_t(\bar{x}, p^g, p^b, t, r, \rho, \gamma, c^g, c^b),$ (4.2.6)

bonds (debt): $\quad \overset{*b}{s}_t = \overset{*b}{s}_t(\bar{x}, p^g, p^b, t, r, \rho, \gamma, c^g, c^b),$ (4.2.7)

money: $\quad \overset{*m}{s}_t = \overset{*m}{s}_t(\bar{x}, p^g, p^b, t, r, \rho, \gamma, c^g, c^b),$ (4.2.8)

where $\bar{x}$, p^g, p^b, and t are vectors over time. Similar functions can be written for the market demand and the market supply of commodities ($\overset{*g}{z}_t$, $\overset{*g}{y}_t$) and bonds ($\overset{*b}{z}_t$, $\overset{*b}{y}_t$). We can also write the utility under the optimal plan as a function of the given conditions

$$\overset{*}{U} = \overset{*}{U}(\bar{x}, p^g, p^b, t, r, \rho, \gamma, c^g, c^b).$$ (4.2.9)

The fundamental difference between (4.2.1) and (4.2.9) should be kept in mind. While (4.2.1) expresses utility as a function of consumption, (4.2.9) expresses the maximum attainable utility as a function of the endowments and market conditions appearing in the constraints.

It is worth noting that the stocks of assets, $\overset{*g}{s}_t$, $\overset{*b}{s}_t$ and $\overset{*m}{s}_t$, do not appear as arguments in the demand functions. This is because these variables do not express constraints, given to the individual from outside, but endogenous variables subject to optimization. In the present model there are no "real balance effects" or "wealth effects." This is as it should be in view of the demonstration by Archibald and Lipsey, mentioned in chapter 1, that real balance effects play no role in the determination of equilibrium situations. They only come in if we wish to explain the dynamics of the system in disequilibrium, when the individual may be unable or unwilling to keep his asset stocks at the levels indicated by (4.2.6)–(4.2.8). Such a disequilibrium dynamics is beyond the scope of this chapter, but real balance effects will play an important role in the macrodynamic analysis of chapter 11.

It can easily be ascertained that consumption demand (4.2.5), the demand for commodity stocks (4.2.6), and the demand for bonds (4.2.7) are homogeneous of degree zero in commodity prices, bond prices, taxes, and the coupon on bonds. The same is true for the market demand and supply for commodities and bonds. The demand for money (4.2.8), however, is homogeneous of degree one in p^g, p^b, t and r.[9] Consider the three sets of constraints with p_t^g, p_t^b, t_t, r and s_t^m all multiplied by λ. Constraints (4.2.2) and (4.2.3) are not affected at all. In (4.2.4) all terms are inflated in the same proportion λ. It is clear, therefore, that the optimal solution does not depend on λ except for the proportional adjustment in s_t^m. The present model thus permits us to demonstrate the linear homogeneity of the demand function for money that neoclassical models, in one way or another, had to assume.[10]

4.3. A graphical two-day illustration

Some intuitive insight into the optimization problem of section 4.2 (though not into portfolio diversification) can be gained from a graphical representation (fig. 4.3.1) by again shortening the "year" to two "days."[11] The individual wishes to transform his endowment, represented by P, into the consumption plan with highest utility, given transaction costs, storage costs, and market conditions. Day-1 goods can be transformed into day-2 goods (1) by holding goods from day 1 to day 2; (2) by selling goods on day 1, holding money during day 2, and buying goods on day 2; (3) by selling goods to buy bonds on day 1, holding bonds during day 2, and selling bonds to buy goods on day 2; (4) by borrowing to buy goods on day 2, holding a debt during day 1 of the following year, and selling goods to repay the debt on day 1 of that year.

For each sequence, the relevant constraints tell us how much x_2 can be increased by giving up a certain quantity of x_1. We thus obtain the linear segments of the commodity, money, bond, and debt frontiers sloping upward from P. Their slopes are calculated by solving for $-dx_2/dx_1$ from the relevant constraints, omitting those items that do not appear in the par-

9. One could try out the alternative assumption that the coupon is fixed. It is tempting to argue that in this case the demand for both cash balances and bonds are linear homogeneous in p^g and t at constant p^b. This would not be correct, however, since an increase in the number of bonds imposes higher transaction costs, which are a real variable. In a transaction cost model, neutrality requires that the denomination of the bonds, as measured by the coupon, increase with commodity and bond prices; this leaves the number of bonds, and thus transaction costs, unchanged while the dollar value of bond holdings goes up with with the bond price.

10. The expression "in one way or another" takes account of the fact that in those versions of the neoclassical approach which put money into the utility function, linear homogeneity of the demand for money with respect to prices is derived from the assumption of zero homogeneity of the utility function in money and prices.

11. A similar representation can already be found in an original paper by Bernholz (1967).

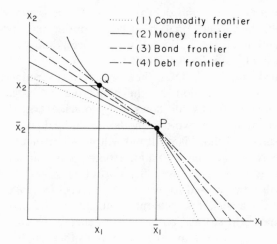

Figure **4.3.1**
The Transformation Frontier

ticular trading sequence:

$$\text{commodities:} \quad -\left(\frac{dx_2}{dx_1}\right) = 1 - \gamma \qquad (4.3.1)$$

$$\text{money:} \quad -\left(\frac{dx_2}{dx_1}\right) = (1 + \rho)\frac{1 - c^g}{1 + c^g} \cdot \frac{p_1^g}{p_2^g} \qquad (4.3.2)$$

$$\text{bonds:} \quad -\left(\frac{dx_2}{dx_1}\right) = \frac{(1 - c^g)(p_2^b + r)/p_2^g - c^b}{(1 + c^g)p_1^b/p_1^g + c^b} \qquad (4.3.3)$$

$$\text{debt:} \quad -\left(\frac{dx_2}{dx_1}\right) = \frac{(1 - c^g)p_2^b/p_2^g - c^b}{(1 + c^g)(p_1^b + r)/p_1^g + c^b}(1 + \theta)^2 \qquad (4.3.4)$$

In sequence (4), the entries relating to day 1 of the following year have to be discounted for two days to make them comparable with the entries for day 1 of the current year in sequences (4.3.1)–(4.3.3). A comparison of the debt slope (4.3.4) with the bond slope (4.3.3) confirms nicely that the advantage of debt, if any, is due to the time-preference effect, working through θ, dominating the interest effect, working through r (transaction costs being the same in both cases).

Another set of frontier segments can be obtained for the reverse shift of consumption from day 2 to day 1 (of the following year), resulting in the rays sloping downward from P. Due to transaction costs, market returns, and time preference, each of the four frontiers has a convex kink at P. The overall transformation frontier consists of the outermost segments of the commodity, money, bond, and debt frontiers. As the graph is drawn, it is efficient either to be in debt or to hold bonds during the first day. With different transaction costs, market returns, prices, and time preference, other sequences could have been efficient.

Once we know the transformation frontier, the optimum is determined by confronting it with the utility function. In the graph the individual chooses Q, hereby determining all stocks and flows. If Q coincides with P, no assets are held. It is clear that, in a two-day model, an individual will never hold assets on both days and that his portfolio will never be diversified. With more days in the cycle, the transformation frontier will generally contain more complex sequences involving diversified portfolios.

The two-day model will now be used to discuss the effects of changes in the data on the demand for assets. The general argument can be illustrated by the effect of a change in storage costs on the demand for *commodity stocks*. The extension to changes in other data and other assets is then straightforward. From (4.3.1) it is clear that a reduction in γ, and thus an increase in the yield of commodity stocks, will make the upper part of the commodity frontier steeper, letting it rotate around P. The lower part becomes, of course, flatter. As long as γ is still high enough to make it inefficient to hold commodities, this has no effect on anything. There is thus a threshold value at which changes in γ begin to have an influence. This is also the point at which, in a two-day model, the holding of other assets becomes inefficient. If some other stock has so far been held, the demand for it will now jump to zero, while the demand for commodity stocks, heretofore zero, will take its place.[12] If γ is further reduced, the effect on the demand for commodity stocks depends on the combination of a substitution and an income effect in the familiar way (see sec. 2.5). In figure 4.3.2, the new equilibrium can be either to the left of Q, as illustrated by Q_1, or to the right, as illustrated by Q_2.[13] In general, therefore, the result is ambiguous. The ambiguity is removed, however, if the income effect is neutralized by a compensatory lump-sum tax keeping real income at the level corresponding to Q, because Q_3 is certain to be left of Q. The compensated or "Marshallian" demand curve for commodity stocks in terms of the holding costs γ thus has an unambiguously negative slope. It can also be stated, at the moment without proof, that, if storage costs are replaced by gradually increasing positive yields ($\gamma < 0$), there is a critical point at which the demand for stocks becomes infinite (see sec. 4.4).[14]

The same argument can be applied to the demand for *cash balances*.

12. If the optimum happens to be at P, the demand for commodity stocks may be zero for a range of γ, even though commodity stocks are the efficient form of asset holding.

13. This figure corresponds to figure 2.5.1, with money stocks replaced by commodity stocks and day-1 stocks replaced by day-2 stocks.

14. This is the point at which the commodity frontier ceases to be convex.

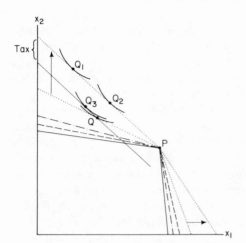

Figure **4.3.2**
The Effect of a Change in Storage Costs

(4.3.2) shows that the money frontier is steeper the higher ρ, the lower c^g, and the higher p_1^q/p_2^q. With the same qualification about threshold values as before, we thus conclude that the demand for cash balances is positively related to (1) a compensated increase in the rate of interest on cash balances, (2) a compensated fall in the transaction costs on commodities, and (3) a compensated fall in commodity prices during the period cash is held. Again, there are data combinations at which the demand for money would become insatiable.

From (4.3.3) it can be seen that the demand for *bonds* during day 2 is negatively related to (1) the transaction costs on bonds and commodities, (2) the (buying) price of bonds on day 1, and (3) the (buying) price of commodities on day 2; and that it is positively related to (1) the coupon, (2) the (selling) price for bonds on day 2, and (3) the (selling) price for commodities on day 1, again provided income effects are properly neutralized. For going into debt during the first day, the effects of changes in the data are the same as for holding bonds during the second day, except that the coupon appears on the other side of the ledger. Both for bonds and for debt there are, of course, critical parameter values at which the demand would become infinite. In general, the demand for assets is thus seen to be related negatively to their costs and positively to their returns. Costs and returns influence the demand for assets in two ways, (1) by pushing different assets into, and out of, the transformation frontier and (2) by influencing the demand for the efficient assets. However, the "normal" sign of the second effect can only be relied upon if the changes in the data are compensated for income effects. In this respect, the present model reveals a close analogy between the demand for transactions assets and the demand for consumption goods.

Finally, the two-day case helps in understanding the effect of changes in "real income" on the demand for assets. An increase in "real income" can be visualized as a movement by the endowment point P in a north-easterly direction. If $\bar{x}_1$ and $\bar{x}_2$ increase in the same proportion *and* if the utility function is homothetic, the demand for assets (as measured by the horizontal or vertical distance between P and Q) will increase in the same proportion as the endowments (see fig. 4.3.3[a]). In this case it can indeed be said that the demand for assets, including money, is proportional to "real income." If either the utility function is not homothetic (see fig. 4.3.3[b]) or the increase in endowments is not equiproportionate (see fig. 4.3.3[c]), this is not true. In this case we cannot even be sure that the demand for assets moves in the same direction as endowments. At the end of the preceding section it was pointed out that the proportionality of the demand for money with respect to prices (including the coupon and lump-sum taxes) can be derived from utility maximization. The reaction of the demand for money to changes in "real income" has no such theoretical basis; at best it is an empirical observation.

4.4. The marginal conditions

It was pointed out in chapter 1 (sec. 1.3) that neoclassical economics was unable to integrate money and other financial assets into the marginal analysis except in a purely formal sense. It was claimed in the introduction to the present chapter that the transaction cost approach provides such an integration. This claim will now be substantiated by deriving the marginal conditions implicit in the optimizing model of section 4.2. As in the theory of value and production, the marginal calculus provides important economic insights by exhibiting the links between the subjective valuations of the individual and the objective market data.

The Kuhn-Tucker conditions on consumption, exchange flows, and stocks are obtained from (4.2.1)–(4.2.4) by taking the partial deriva-

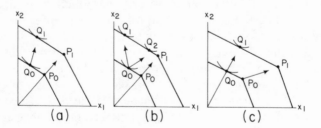

Figure **4.3.3**
The Effect of a Change in Real Income

tives of the Lagrange equation

$$L = U(x_1 \cdots x_h) - \sum_{t=1}^{h} \lambda_t^g \left[(s_{t+1}^g - s_t^g) - (\bar{x}_t - x_t) - (z_t^g - y_t^g) \right.$$
$$+ \gamma s_t^g + c^g (z_t^g + y_t^g) + c^b (z_t^b + y_t^b) \right]$$
$$- \sum_{t=1}^{h} \lambda_t^b \left[(s_{t+1}^b - s_t^b) - (z_t^b - y_t^b) \right]$$
$$- \sum_{t=1}^{h} \lambda_t^m \left[(s_{t+1}^m - s_t^m) - p_t^g (y_t^g - z_t^g) \right.$$
$$- p_t^g (y_t^g - z_t^g) - rs_t^b - \rho s_t^m + t_t \right]. \tag{4.4.1}$$

The multipliers λ_t^g, λ_t^b and λ_t^m can be interpreted as discounted marginal (flow) values of goods, bonds, and money. As explained in sec. 2.4 these can be transformed into undiscounted marginal values $\mu_t^i = (1 + \theta)^t \lambda_t^i$ to make the role of time preference explicit. The marginal values are subjective magnitudes, measured in terms of utility.

The marginal conditions for consumption are obtained by taking the partial derivative of L with respect to x_t. They can be written

$$\left(\frac{\partial U}{\partial x_t} - \lambda_t^g \right) x_t = 0, \qquad \frac{\partial U}{\partial x_t} \leqq \lambda_t^g = \left(\frac{1}{1 + \theta} \right)^t \mu_t^g, \qquad x_t \geqq 0. \tag{4.4.2}$$

This condition is equivalent to (2.2.4), considering that the marginal value of a dollar's worth of goods multiplied by the price of goods equals the marginal value of a unit of goods. If, on a given day, there is any consumption, the direct marginal utility of commodities is equal to their marginal value. Whenever the direct marginal utility is lower than the marginal value, no goods are consumed. In this case goods are valued not because of their direct utility, but because of what they bring in exchange or through storage; their value, like the value of money and bonds, is then of an indirect nature.

For exchange flows the economic interpretation of the Kuhn-Tucker conditions is also straightforward. The conditions state that exchange takes place up to the point where the marginal rate of substitution between goods (or bonds) and money is equal to their price *after transaction costs*. It is because of this wedge between market prices and marginal values, due to transaction costs, that assets may be diversified. For the same reason we have to distinguish between sales and purchases. The marginal conditions for the exchange of commodities and bonds against money are given in turn.

For commodity sales the marginal condition is

$$[(1 + c^g) \lambda_t^g - p_t^g \lambda_t^m] y_t^g = 0, \qquad \frac{\lambda_t^g}{\lambda_t^m} = \frac{\mu_t^g}{\mu_t^m} \geqq \frac{p_t^g}{1 + c^g}, \qquad y_t^g \geqq 0, \tag{4.4.3}$$

while for commodity purchases it reads

$$[(1 - c^g)\lambda_t^g - p_t^g \lambda_t^m]z_t^g = 0, \quad \frac{\lambda_t^g}{\lambda_t^m} = \frac{\mu_t^g}{\mu_t^m} \leqq \frac{p_t^g}{1 - c^g}, \quad z_t^g \geqq 0. \quad (4.4.4)$$

Whenever there is positive supply or demand, the corresponding sign becomes an equality. In the absence of transaction costs, we obtain the familiar condition that, whenever exchange takes place, the marginal rate of substitution between goods and money is equal to the market price. With transaction costs, the marginal rate of substitution will be higher (for sales) or lower (for purchases) than the market price. If the price *after transaction costs* is lower than the marginal rate of substitution, no sales take place. If the price after transaction costs is higher than the marginal rate of substitution, no commodities are bought. There can never be supply and demand at the same time. If strict inequalities hold for both purchases and sales, no exchange will take place on that day.

λ_t^m and μ_t^m represent the *marginal flow values of money*, discounted and undiscounted. They are flow values in the sense that they express the gain in utility resulting from a free gift of a dollar, to be used up as the individual sees fit. Satiation with cash balances, in the sense in which this term is used in the optimal money supply literature, cannot mean that λ_t^m is zero. For the individual, confronted with given market prices, λ_t^m would go to zero only if λ_t^g went to zero, that is, as we approach perfect bliss. As long as there are unsatisfied desires, a free gift of money is always welcome. For society as a whole, with market prices variable, λ_t^m can be pushed toward zero by a progressive increase in the nominal money supply, which drives commodity prices to infinity at given λ_t^g. Neither of these two meanings of satiation is relevant for the optimality problem, which has to do with real balances in a world of continued scarcity of resources. The relevant concept will emerge presently.

The corresponding condition for bond sales is

$$(\lambda_t^b + c^b\lambda_t^g - p_t^b\lambda_t^m)y_t^b = 0, \quad \frac{\lambda_t^b}{\lambda_t^m} - \frac{\mu_t^b}{\mu_t^m} \geqq p_t^b - c^b\frac{\mu_t^g}{\mu_t^m}$$

$$= p_t^b - c^b\frac{\lambda_t^g}{\lambda_t^m}, \quad y_t^b \geqq 0, \quad (4.4.5)$$

while for bond purchases it is

$$(\lambda_t^b - c^b\lambda_t^g - p_t^b\lambda_t^m)z_t^b = 0, \quad \frac{\lambda_t^b}{\lambda_t^m} = \frac{\mu_t^b}{\mu_t^m} \leqq p_t^b + c^b\frac{\mu_t^g}{\mu_t^m}$$

$$= p_t^b + c^b\frac{\lambda_t^g}{\lambda_t^m}, \quad z_t^b \geqq 0. \quad (4.4.6)$$

The interpretation of these conditions is similar to that of the commodity conditions. The only difference is that transaction costs on bonds are valued at the marginal value not on bonds, but again of commodities. This is, of course, because all transaction costs are assumed to consist of commodity inputs. If, in the given period, goods are actually sold or bought, we can substitute for μ_t^g/μ_t^m from either (4.4.3) or (4.4.4) to express μ_t^b/μ_t^m in terms of market prices and transaction costs. The higher the transaction costs, the more likely it is that strict inequalities will appear for both sales and purchases; no bond transactions can then take place. This is the "locking in" effect of transaction costs.

The most interesting marginal conditions are those on stocks. They relate the marginal stock value of an asset to its opportunity cost. The marginal stock value represents the gain in utility an individual derives from *holding* a unit of an asset for one day. It is measured simply by the overnight (percentage) increase in the marginal flow value of that asset or, more simply, its daily valuation gain. In this way, marginal stock values are precisely related to marginal flow values. It is one of the virtues of the approach presented here that the dimensional confusion about the marginal value of money and other assets can be cleared up. The opportunity cost of an asset, on the other hand, is simply its yield, reflecting storage costs, market return, and time preference, but not including capital gains or losses due to price changes. Again the marginal conditions can be expressed in discounted or undiscounted form. It is here where the difference becomes important, because the role of time preference as a component of asset-holding costs, which is implicit in the discounted formulation, becomes explicit in undiscounted terms.

The Kuhn-Tucker condition for commodity stocks is found to be

$$[(1 - \gamma)\lambda_t^g - \lambda_{t-1}^g]s_t^g = 0, \quad \frac{\lambda_t^g - \lambda_{t-1}^g}{\lambda_t^g} \leq \gamma, \quad s_t^g \geq 0. \tag{4.4.7}$$

In terms of undiscounted marginal values the first equality/inequality can be rewritten

$$\frac{\mu_t^g - \mu_{t-1}^g}{\mu_t^g} \leq \frac{1}{1 + \theta}(\theta + \gamma). \tag{4.4.7a}$$

Condition (4.4.7a) says that the daily valuation gain on commodity stocks, expressed as a percentage, cannot exceed the opportunity cost of commodity stocks, $\theta + \gamma$, properly discounted to the same moment. Whenever the marginal stock value of inventories is higher than their holding cost, it is profitable to increase them, which means that equilibrium is yet to be attained. Conversely, if the marginal stock value is lower than the holding cost, there is an incentive to reduce the stock. However, once the stock has reached zero, no further reduction is possible and the inequality persists even in equilibrium. Walras had to pull the "service d'approvisionnement" of inventories out of thin air. The present analysis, by explicitly relating the marginal stock value of goods to their marginal flow value, makes such constructs unnecessary. The "service d'approvisionnement" of inventories, precisely defined by (4.4.7), is automatically determined by the optimizing calculus.

The marginal stock value for bonds

$$(\lambda_t^b - \lambda_{t-1}^b + r\lambda_t^m) s_t^b = 0, \qquad \frac{\lambda_t^b - \lambda_{t-1}^b}{\lambda_t^b} = - r \frac{\lambda_t^m}{\lambda_t^b} \qquad (4.4.8)$$

$$s_t^b \gtrless 0$$

$$\frac{\mu_t^b - \mu_{t-1}^b}{\mu_t^b} = \frac{1}{1 + \theta} \left(\theta - r \frac{\mu_t^m}{\mu_t^b} \right) \qquad (4.4.8a)$$

has the same form as that for commodities, expressing the daily increase in the subjective value of the bond. On the right-hand side, representing opportunity cost, we are not surprised to find the coupon in the place of the storage cost rate, of course with opposite sign. r is weighted with μ_t^m/μ_t^b, because the coupon is paid in terms of money. It should be noted that the opportunity cost of bonds is not, as in the case of commodities and money, fixed exogenously, but is related to the endogenous variables of the model through μ_t^m/μ_t^b.

The marginal condition for bonds appears as an equality, because the individual can always make the marginal stock value equal to the opportunity cost either by holding bonds or by going into debt, thus making s_t^b positive or negative. If the bond stock is negative, the right-hand side can be interpreted as the net marginal benefit of debt; debt permits a reduction in assets and thus in time preference costs, represented by θ, but this benefit is reduced by the interest costs. If we modify the model by excluding private debt, thus leaving only government bonds, the equality is replaced by $\leqq$; once the stock is reduced to zero, nothing further can be done to raise the marginal stock value to the level of the opportunity cost.

The marginal condition on cash balances, finally, is

$$[(1 + \rho) \lambda_t^m - \lambda_{t-1}^m] s_t^m = 0, \qquad \frac{\lambda_t^m - \lambda_{t-1}^m}{\lambda_t^m} \leqq - \rho \qquad (4.4.9)$$

$$s_t^m \geqq 0$$

$$\frac{\mu_t^m - \mu_{t-1}^m}{\mu_t^m} \leqq \frac{1}{1 + \theta} (\theta - \rho) \qquad (4.4.9a)$$

In terms of undiscounted marginal values it turns out to be identical to

2.5.3. The left-hand side of the first equality/inequality, as explained in section 2.2, can be interpreted as the marginal stock value of cash balances, measuring the net benefit from holding a dollar overnight. In addition to the marginal flow value of money, measured by its purchasing power, we thus obtain another value of money, measured in the form of an interest rate. This provides a precise answer to the old question whether "the" value of money is the inverse of the price level or the rate of interest: Both are, in principle, valid measures, but one relates to flows while the other relates to stocks, just as there is a price of land and a rent on land. It should be noted, however, that the relevant interest rate is *not* the interest on bonds or other nonmonetary assets, but the difference between time preference and the interest on money.

While the marginal flow value of money, as pointed out above, does not go to zero for a single individual short of perfect bliss, the marginal stock value may well go to zero, indicating that larger *stocks* of money promise no further benefit. This is the satiation concept that is relevant to the problem of an optimal money supply. The opportunity cost of cash balances is simply the difference between the rate of time preference and the rate of interest on money, if any. Whenever money is held, its marginal stock value is equalized to its opportunity cost. If $\rho = \theta$, satiation with cash balances is consistent with positive cash holdings. In fact, satiation balances will then be held at all times.[15]

Friedman regarded it as "natural" to assume that the marginal utility of money is diminishing (1969a, p. 18). The present model permits one to replace intuition by demonstration. Consider the two-day case for cash balances on day 2. Since commodities are sold on day 1, (4.4.3) holds as equality for that day,

$$\frac{\lambda_1^g}{\lambda_1^m} = \frac{p_1^g}{1 + c^g}.$$

Since commodities are bought on day 2, (4.4.4) holds as equality for day 2,

$$\frac{\lambda_2^g}{\lambda_2^m} = \frac{p_2^g}{1 - c^g}.$$

Solving for λ_1^m and λ_2^m and substituting into the expression for the marginal utility of money, the latter can be shown to be

$$\frac{\lambda_2^m - \lambda_1^m}{\lambda_2^m} = 1 - \frac{p_2^g}{p_1^g} \cdot \frac{1 + c^g}{1 - c^g} \cdot \frac{\lambda_1^g}{\lambda_2^g}.$$

---

15. If $\rho = \theta$, then $\mu_t{}^m - \mu_{t-1}{}^m \leqq 0$ for all t. But stationarity requires that at the end of the year the marginal flow value be at the same level as at the beginning. Thus the marginal stock value must be zero for all t.

λ_1^g/λ_2^g is the marginal rate of commodity substitution. For given prices and transaction costs, there is thus a simple linear relationship between the marginal utility of money and the marginal rate of commodity substitution. This is plausible, since the utility of money derives, basically, from permitting a more advantageous substitution between commodities at different points of time. If s_2^m is increased, x_2 is increased at the expense of x_1. If this is done with utility compensation, we know from the convexity of the indifference curves that λ_1^g/λ_2^g is rising. It follows that the marginal utility of cash balances declines. Friedman's conjecture turns out to be correct for a utility-compensated increase in the money stock.

There are also conditions for the marginal rate of substitution between assets. By relating the discounted marginal stock values for goods and money, we derive

$$\frac{\dfrac{\lambda_t^g - \lambda_{t-1}^g}{\lambda^g}}{\dfrac{\lambda_t^m - \lambda_{t-1}^m}{\lambda_t^m}} = \frac{-\gamma}{\rho}. \qquad (s_t^g > 0, \qquad s_t^m > 0) \qquad\qquad (4.4.10)$$

This means that the ratio between the discounted marginal stock values for goods and money, *if both are held*, is equal to the ratio between the two rates of return. A similar relationship, but in absolute terms, holds for bonds and money,[16]

$$\frac{\lambda_t^b - \lambda_{t-1}^b}{\lambda_t^m - \lambda_{t-1}^m} = \frac{r}{\rho}. \qquad (s_t^m > 0) \qquad\qquad (4.4.11)$$

These conditions are the stock counterpart to the proposition, familiar from neoclassical flow models, that the marginal rate of substitution for any two goods is equal, in equilibrium, to the ratio of their prices. They are the exact marginal conditions for portfolio diversification.

If there is a storage cost on commodities ($\gamma > 0$), the opportunity cost of cash balances is lower than that of commodity stocks (provided $\rho \geqq 0$). Nevertheless, an individual may prefer to hold commodities, because a shift into money would involve transaction costs; for short holding periods these may weigh more heavily than the saving in holding costs.[17] On the other hand, the market will see to it that the opportunity cost of bonds is lower than that of cash balances for most of the time. If it did not, nobody would be willing to hold bonds, and there would be a point at which it would become profitable to borrow money just to hold it idle.

16. This is a counterpart to the condition given in Patinkin (1965, p. 93, eq. 9).
17. For just two days, the relevant comparison is between slopes (4.3.1.) and (4.3.2).

Again, however, transaction costs may prevent a further shift into the lower-cost asset.[18]

Neoclassical models, by introducing the money stock as an argument into the utility function, usually yield a marginal condition of the type $(\partial U/\partial M)/i = \lambda$, where $\partial U/\partial M$ represents the marginal stock utility of money (in absolute terms, not in percent), λ is the marginal utility of income, and i is the rate of interest as a measure of the opportunity cost of cash balances (see sec. 1.3). This is in close analogy to (4.4.9a). We simply rewrite (4.4.9a) as

$$\frac{\mu_t^m - \mu_{t-1}^m}{\theta - \rho} \lesseqgtr \frac{1}{1 + \theta} \mu_t^m. \tag{4.4.12}$$

$(\mu_t^m - \mu_{t-1}^m)$ is seen to correspond to $\partial U/\partial M$, and $(\theta - \rho)$ expresses the opportunity cost of cash balances, while μ_t^m is the marginal *flow* utility of money, analogous to the marginal utility of income. Where the neoclassical models have to *postulate* a marginal stock utility of money, the present model, by a straightforward generalization, is able to derive it.[19]

It is important to note that the marginal stock conditions can only be met if the asset yields satisfy certain constraints. If they don't, there will be no upper limit to profitable asset accumulation and thus no optimal portfolio. For commodities, the relevant constraint simply says that the marginal cost, appearing on the right-hand side of (4.4.7a), must be non-negative. For $\theta \geq 0$ and $\gamma \geq 0$ this constraint is always satisfied, but it could be violated if storage costs were replaced by positive physical growth rates. It is easy to see that there is no equilibrium with $\theta + \gamma < 0$: According to (4.4.7a), $\mu_t^g - \mu_{t-1}^g$ would then be negative for all t, which is inconsistent with stationarity.

The corresponding constraint for money is $\theta - \rho \geq 0$, which can be written $\rho/\theta \leq 1$. But ρ/θ is simply the present value of a dollar held forever. The condition thus says that the present value of a dollar, if held forever, must not exceed a dollar. The relevant marginal stock condition (4.4.9a) makes clear that there can be no stationary equilibrium if this constraint is violated. This shows that the problem with excessively high interest rates on cash balances (or rates of deflation) is not, as Friedman has argued (1969a, p. 20), a wastefully high level of cash holdings, but the insatiability of the demand for cash.

In order to exclude infinite accumulation of bonds, the price of a bond, including transaction costs, must be no lower than its present value,

18. The exact conditions for this to happen in the two-day case are obtained by comparing slopes (4.3.2) and (4.3.3).

19. A similar expression for the marginal utility of money is derived by Grandmont and Younes by replacing the postulate of a direct utility of money with the postulate of a Cambridge-type demand function for money (1973, p. 154).

if held forever. This can be written

$$p_t^b + c^b \frac{\mu_t^g}{\mu_t^m} \geq \frac{r}{\theta},$$
(4.4.13)

setting a lower limit for p_t^b. There is also an upper limit, necessary to prevent an infinite accumulation of debt. It states that the proceeds from selling a bond, net of transaction costs, must be no higher than the present value of the debt maintained forever;

$$p_t^b - c^b \frac{\mu_t^g}{\mu_t^m} \leq \frac{r}{\theta}.$$
(4.4.14)

For bonds it would not be true to say that a negative marginal cost, as appearing on the right-hand side of (4.4.8a), is incompatible with stationarity. Since this marginal cost can fluctuate from day to day, it may possibly be negative on some (but not all) days, if this is compensated by positive values for other days. In general, these constraints mean that, for each asset, some part of the marginal utility must originate in current transactions; it must never pay to hold an asset without buying and selling it at least once a year. These constraints thus reflect the fact that the present analysis is restricted to transactions assets.

This concludes the microeconomic analysis of the demand for money. Like the neoclassical theory of value and production, it was restricted to the bare essentials of the problem. The present chapter concentrated on the case with one commodity and two financial assets in a noninflationary exchange economy with proportionate transaction costs. Additional elements were considered in the preceding two chapters, though for otherwise more restrictive models. Among these elements are the multicommodity case, inflation, fixed transaction costs, and uncertainty about the bond yield. It is obvious that this leaves out many factors that may be relevant for the demand for cash balances in concrete cases. I hope that at this price, which is considerable, I succeeded in laying bare the basic determinants of the demand for money, analogous to the forces that determine the demand for goods and factors in the neoclassical theory. In the following chapters the perspective will be extended from individual optimization to the general equilibrium of an economy.

Five

GENERAL EQUILIBRIUM OF A MONETARY ECONOMY, INFLATION, AND THE OPTIMAL RETURN ON MONEY

Introduction

The three preceding chapters concerned themselves with an individual's demand and supply of money and other things under given market conditions. Once we know the optimal plan for each individual at given prices, these prices can, in turn, be determined by the interplay of individual demands and supplies. The present chapter deals with such a general equilibrium system of a monetary economy. In principle, the model could specify a multiperson multicommodity equilibrium in full detail. However, from the point of view of monetary theory, this would largely be an exercise in notation. A first step toward macroeconomics was already made in chapter 4 by consolidating commodities. Another step will be made in the present chapter by aggregating over individuals. The following analysis thus provides an important link between the microeconomic theory of the preceding chapters and the monetary macroeconomics of later chapters, particularly chapters 10 and 11. The multiperiod character of the analysis, however, is still retained.

The topic of section 5.1 is the statics and comparative statics of a monetary economy in which the government keeps the supply of money and bonds constant over time. The model is used to derive the correct valuation of money in the national income and wealth accounts and to determine the effects of a change in the money supply and in the rate of interest on cash balances. In section 5.2 the model is extended to allow for the continuous expansion of the money supply, resulting in balanced inflation. Section 5.3 analyzes the welfare effects of varying the rate of return on cash balances, either by changing the explicit interest rate or by varying the rate of inflation; this introduces the topic that is usually discussed under the heading of the "optimal money supply."

5.1. General equilibrium with a stationary money supply

I begin with the assumption that the quantities of money and bonds supplied by the government are stationary. As a consequence, prices are also stationary from year to year (though not from day to day). The first step is to derive aggregate demand functions for bonds and cash balances. Equations (4.2.7) and (4.2.8) describe the individual demand for bonds and cash balances as a function of market conditions, including prices. There is a pair of such functions for each of n individuals. Aggregate demand functions are obtained by summing (4.2.7) and (4.2.8) over individuals. Individuals will be identified by left-hand subscripts, and symbols in parentheses will be used to denote the array of a variable over all individuals and days, such as

$$(\bar{x}) = {}_1\bar{x} \cdots {}_n\bar{x} = {}_1\bar{x}_1 \cdots {}_i\bar{x}_t \cdots {}_n\bar{x}_h,$$

and similarly for (t), (γ), (c^g) and (c^b). The aggregate demand functions can thus be written

$$D_t = \sum_{i=1}^{n} {}_i\overset{*b}{S}_t = D_t\left[(\bar{x}), p^g, p^b, (t), r, \rho, (\gamma), (c^g), (c^b)\right], \qquad (5.1.1)$$

$$L_t = \sum_{i=1}^{n} {}_i\overset{*m}{S}_t = L_t\left[(\bar{x}), p^g, p^b, (t), r, \rho, (\gamma), (c^g), (c^b)\right]. \qquad (5.1.2)$$

It will be remembered from 4.2 that p^g and p^b are t-vectors. It will also be remembered that ${}_i\overset{*m}{S}_t \geq 0$, while, in view of debt, ${}_i\overset{*b}{S}_t \gtrless 0$. The aggregate demand functions share the homogeneity properties of the corresponding individual functions (see sec. 4.2). This means that the demand for money moves in proportion to an equiproportionate shift in all prices, taxes, and the coupon, while the demand for consols is not affected by such a shift.

Friedman confessed several years ago that he saw no way to give a meaningful answer to the question about the demand for cash balances at an abstract level (1969a, p. 3 f.). What is summarized in (5.1.2), with the individual demand functions derived in chapter 4 as its infrastructure, constitutes such an answer. It should be noted that exogenous "payments habits" play no essential role in the demand function for money. Whatever payments habits individuals wish to adopt depend on the arguments on the right-hand side of the demand function, and whatever payments habits eventually emerge depend on the general equilibrium described in the following paragraphs.

The aggregate supply of money and bonds is fixed by the government, subject to the government budget constraint

$$T = \rho M + rB. \qquad (M > 0; B \gtrless 0) \tag{5.1.3}$$

It states that, for each day, tax collections must just cover the government interest payments on cash balances and consols. Expenditures on goods and services are disregarded at this stage; they will be introduced in chapter 10. For the purposes of this section, M, B, ρ and r are assumed to be constant over time, and the same must thus be true for T. As a consequence, these variables carry no time subscripts. Cash balances are positive, but the government supply of bonds may be positive, zero, or even negative, with the government holding private bonds in the last case. The individual tax burdens, imposed as lump-sum taxes, must be such that they add to T for each day,

$$\sum_{i=1}^{n} {}_i t_t = T. \tag{5.1.4}$$

In pure logic, ${}_i t_t$ can be chosen freely for all individuals but one, but the size of individual endowments and equity considerations will usually impose upper limits. We may suppose that taxes are chosen freely for individuals $1 \cdots n - 1$, while (5.1.4) is then used to determine ${}_n t_t$.

General equilibrium requires that, for each day, the demand for money equals the money supply,

$$L_t [\,] = M, \tag{5.1.5}$$

and the same must be true for bonds,

$$D_t [\,] = B. \tag{5.1.6}$$

The four equations (5.1.3)–(5.1.6) are just enough to determine p^g, p^b, T and ${}_n t$. This is the multiperiod general equilibrium system we need for the purpose of this chapter. If desired, (4.2.5) and (4.2.6) can be used to determine consumption and commodity stocks.

It should be noted that there are no separate equilibrium conditions for market demands and supplies of commodities and bonds. If there is equilibrium for bond stocks and money stocks, equilibrium in the commodity and bond markets can be derived from the individual budget constraints as follows. Add the bond constraints (4.2.3) over individuals. The left-hand side of the resulting aggregate is zero, the aggregate quantity of bonds, B, remaining constant. This implies that the aggregate excess demand in the bond market, appearing on the right-hand side, is also zero. Now aggregate the money constraints (4.2.4) over individuals. Again the left-hand side is zero in view of (5.1.5). We already know that aggregate excess demand in the bond market is zero. We also know from (5.1.3) and (5.1.4) that the aggregate of $r {}_i s_t^b + \rho {}_i s_t^m - {}_i t_t$ is zero. It follows that aggregate excess demand for commodities is zero. This is the counterpart, for the present model, of Walras' Law.

In general, equilibrium prices for commodities and bonds will fluctuate throughout the year, producing (fully expected) capital gains and losses for holders of commodity stocks and bonds. For each individual there will be a pattern of receipts and expenditures, as pictured in figure 2.1.1. Each individual will also have a determinate pattern of assets, as illustrated in figure 4.1.1. A given quantity of money will circulate through the economy, and while the stocks of commodities and the gross amounts of claims and debts will fluctuate day by day, net bond holdings of the private sector will also be fixed by the government.

There has been a lively debate, provoked by Pesek and Saving (1967), about the correct treatment of the services of money in national income and wealth accounts. The present model implies straightforward answers to these questions to the extent they relate to fiat money (about bank deposits, see chapter 9). The income of an individual on day t can be written as

$$Y_t = \mu_t^g \bar{x}_t + \left(\frac{1}{1+\theta}\right) \left[(\theta + \gamma) \mu_t^g s_t^g + \left(\theta - r \frac{\mu_t^m}{\mu_t^b}\right) \mu_t^b s_t^b \right.$$

$$\left. + (\theta - \rho) \mu_t^m s_t^m\right]. \tag{5.1.7}$$

The first term is the value of the current endowment, while the second term represents property income. The income from commodity stocks is computed by multiplying the value of stocks, $\mu_t^g s_t^g$, by the marginal yield on commodity stocks, $(\theta + \gamma)/(1 + \theta)$, as determined from (4.4.7a). An analogous computation can be made for the income from bonds and cash balances.

It should be noted that these property incomes, being based on *marginal* values, do not measure the *total* contribution of the several assets to an individual's welfare. Consider cash balances. The total service of money reaches a maximum at the point where, in view of $\rho = \theta$, the individual is satiated with cash. However, at this point the marginal service yield is zero. As a consequence, a computation of total income, correctly based on marginal values, would assign cash balances a weight of zero in this case. This conclusion carries over to the aggregate income of all individuals. The services of money properly appear as an item of national income as long as the economy is not satiated with cash; at the point of satiation cash balances vanish from the accounts.

For national wealth, perhaps surprisingly, the conclusion is somewhat different. Individual wealth is simply

$$W_t = \mu_t^g s_t^g + \mu_t^b s_t^b + \mu_t^m s_t^m, \tag{5.1.8}$$

which, using (4.4.7a) $-$ (4.4.9a), can be written

$$W_t = (1 + \theta) \left[\frac{\mu_t^g - \mu_{t-1}^g}{\theta + \gamma} s_t^g + \frac{\mu_t^b - \mu_{t-1}^b}{\theta - r \frac{\mu_t^m}{\mu_t^b}} s_t^b + \frac{\mu_t^m - \mu_{t-1}^m}{\theta - \rho} s_t^m \right].$$

The remarkable point is that cash balances, since μ_t^m in (5.1.8) has no tendency to vanish, appear as an item of wealth even under conditions of satiation. It is true that, with satiation, the marginal service yield $\mu_t^m - \mu_{t-1}^m$ vanishes. At the same time, however, the capitalization factor $\theta - \rho$ approaches zero. As a consequence, the capital value obtained by capitalizing the marginal service yield with the appropriate capitalization factor can still remain positive. Even though fiat money, under conditions of satiation, does not appear in the income account, it still appears in the wealth account. This confirms one of the main propositions of Pesek and Saving, but on the basis of a reasoning that is both very different and, I hope, less confusing to others than theirs.

Once the general-equilibrium system is specified, to determine the effect of a change in the data on the endogenous variables is, in principle, a familiar exercise in comparative statics. In the context of this study, it would be of particular interest to know the effect of two types of changes, namely (1) an equiproportionate change in M, r and all (t), and (2) an increase in ρ, compensated by increases in (t). It can easily be ascertained that an equiproportionate increase in M, r and (t) is neutral in the sense that it results in an equiproportionate change in all commodity prices, bond prices, and money stocks, while the real variables remain unchanged. It can be checked that the constraints (4.2.2)–(4.2.4) and the marginal conditions (4.4.2)–(4.4.9) are not affected by such a change, the marginal flow value of money moving in inverse proportion to its quantity. It needs no saying that this conclusion relates to a once-and-for-all change in the data, not to continuing inflation or deflation. The decidedly nonneutral effects of the latter will be the subject of the following section.

The effects of a compensated change in the rate of interest on cash balances are more difficult to determine; in fact, hardly any general statements can be made. There are two reasons for this. First, the model contains as many prices and interest rates as there are days in the year. Each of them will usually move in a different proportion, and some may rise while others fall. As a consequence, it is hardly possible to generalize about *the* price level and *the* rate of interest. This is a familiar source of ambiguity, present in all multimarket systems. The second source of ambiguity is more specific. To identify it we may imagine that commodity and bond prices are arbitrarily held constant for every day except t. There is also some government equalization fund covering any differences between demand and supply for cash balances and bonds for every day except

$t + 1$. We are thus left with one commodity price, p_t^g, and one bond price, p_t^b (or one interest rate $i_t = r/p_t^b$) to maintain equilibrium for money and bonds during day $t + 1$. The question is how p_t^g and p_t^b (or i_t) will shift in consequence of a change in ρ. The answer can be provided by an argument similar to the familiar IS/LM analysis.

Consider the aggregate demand function for money (5.1.2). Compensation means that the interest payments are financed by lump-sum taxes, which tax away just those additional interest revenues individuals would have earned on the money they held before the increase in ρ. It has been shown (see sec. 4.3) that a compensated increase in ρ, at constant prices of commodities and bonds, will unambiguously increase the demand for money. But the supply of money is unchanged. At unchanged $(\bar{x})$, (γ), (c^g) and (c^b), excess demand will thus have to be choked off by appropriate changes in p_t^g and p_t^b. If p_t^g goes up *ceteris paribus*, since this raises the opportunity costs of consumption of day t and of inventory holdings during day $t + 1$, the private sector will wish to increase its cash L_{t+1}. If p_t^b rises (or i_t falls) *ceteris paribus*, people will find it profitable to switch from bonds to cash. We thus obtain the partial derivatives

$$\partial L_{t+1}/\partial p_t^g \geqq 0, \qquad \partial L_{t+1}/\partial p_t^b \geqq 0, \qquad \text{or} \qquad \partial L_{t+1}/\partial i_t \leqq 0.$$

The locus of all combinations of p_t^g and i_t that keep L_{t+1} constant must thus be an upward-sloping curve like L in figure 5.1.1(a). An increase in ρ makes this curve move to the left.

Now consider the demand function for bonds (5.1.1). For the same reasons as in the case of cash balances, an increase in p_t^g will stimulate the demand for bonds held during day $t + 1$. On the other hand, if p_t^b rises (or i_t falls) *ceteris paribus*, bond portfolios D_{t+1} will be reduced. This results in the partial derivatives

$$\partial D_{t+1}/\partial p_t^g \geqq 0 \qquad \partial D_{t+1}/\partial p_t^b \leqq 0 \qquad \text{or} \qquad \partial D_{t+1}/\partial i_t \geqq 0.$$

A curve connecting all those commodity prices and interest rates which keep D_{t+1} constant will thus be a downward-sloping line like D in figure 5.1.1(a). An increase in ρ, *ceteris paribus*, will lower the demand for bonds. As a consequence, the D-curve will move to the right.

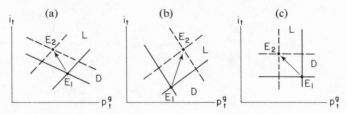

Figure **5.1.1**
Macroeconomic Effects on the Interest on Cash Balances

Simultaneous equilibrium for money and bonds is attained where the two curves intersect. As ρ is increased, this point shifts from E_1 to E_2. As figure 5.1.1(a) is drawn, this results in an increase in the rate of interest and a fall in the commodity price. This is a plausible result. An increase in the return of cash balances, so the familiar argument runs, leads to an increase in the demand for real balances, which, at unchanged nominal balances, can only be satisfied by a fall in commodity prices. At the same time, asset holders find it profitable to shift from bonds to cash balances, thus driving down the bond price and raising the interest rate. With respect to the rate of interest, this argument seems to be quite conclusive. The trouble is that with respect to prices it may be invalid. This is illustrated in figure 5.1.1(b), where the commodity price actually rises. In this case, the increase in the bond rate is strong enough to keep the demand for cash balances at the required level even in the face of an increase in the commodity price. It may be suspected that the familiar argument, consciously or unconsciously, is often based on the assumption that the demand for money is sensitive to the commodity price, but insensitive to the bond yield, while the reverse is true for the demand for bonds. In this special case, illustrated in figure 5.1.1(c), we can indeed be sure that the argument is valid. In general, however, we cannot be certain that an increase in the return on cash balances will lower commodity prices.

In thus experimenting with changes in ρ, we have to observe an important constraint. It was noted at the end of the previous chapter that individual equilibrium requires $\rho \leq \theta$. If this is violated, there can obviously be no general equilibrium either. The demand for money at any set of finite prices would be infinite, and the price level would thus go to zero. If individuals have different rates of time preference, this condition must be satisfied for every one of them. This means that the interest rate on cash balances cannot be higher than the lowest rate of time preference. At the exact point where $\rho = \theta$, the demand for money at given prices would be indeterminate, provided it did not go below the satiation level. As a consequence, the price level would also be indeterminate, provided it did not exceed a certain limit.

There is no corresponding limitation on the bond yield. The level of the coupon, r, is economically irrelevant, and the market will automatically see to it that (4.4.13) and (4.4.14) are satisfied for all individuals at all times. Suppose the bond price is set artificially below the lower limit for just one individual. Bond demand will become infinite, while the supply of bonds is finite. It follows that the assumed bond price cannot be an equilibrium price; it will be bid up until the limiting condition is satisfied for all individuals. The reverse is true if the bond is artificially set above the upper limit for at least one individual: There will be an infinite supply of bonds but a finite demand, and the resulting excess supply will drive the price down.

There is, of course, no general rule that money must always have a positive value in the economy of the present model. It is logically possible to conceive of a case in which each individual's endowments and tastes are synchronized in such a way that no assets and thus no cash balances are ever held. If assets are held, individuals may still be identical; as a consequence, there would be no incentive for exchange and thus no demand for a medium of exchange. Finally, even if individuals are sufficiently different, transaction costs on bonds and storage costs on goods may be so low, and transaction costs on goods so high, that no assets would ever be held in the form of money. Without transaction costs on bonds, bonds would circulate in the place of money. On the other hand, by selecting appropriate values for transaction and storage costs we can always produce asset diversification.[1] Whether a monetary economy is viable depends not on one simple condition, but on the interplay of all the factors determining equilibrium.

5.2. General equilibrium with balanced inflation

Paying interest or levying taxes on cash balances is one way of providing money with a positive or negative return. The other way is through deflation and inflation. The economic equivalence of a positive interest rate on cash balances and deflation was already noted in Section 2.6. However, the discussion in chapter 2 was limited to the individual optimizing problem, regarding market conditions as given and abstracting from noncash assets. We now return to the same problem from the point of view of general equilibrium in an economy that also provides nonmonetary assets. Whereas in section 5.1 the supply of money and bonds to the private sector was assumed to be stationary, it will now be assumed that it expands or contracts at a constant rate, thus imposing an inflationary or deflationary trend on the economy. It will be shown that the effects of such a trend on the real variables are exactly analogous to the effects of the rate of interest on cash balances.

The analysis will be limited to inflationary processes that are balanced in the sense that all real variables are in stationary motion. There will be no discussion of transitory phenomena due to the shift from one rate of inflation to another. This does not mean, of course, that the real variables remain constant from day to day; as before, daily fluctuations are an essential feature of the model. Nor does the stationarity of real variables mean that they are independent of the rate of inflation; in fact, the effect of inflation on the path of the real variables will be one of the main points of the analysis. The limitation to balanced inflation means that there are

---

1. Numerical examples for a basically similar but less general model were given in Niehans (1970). See also section 6.3.

two types of effects that can (and must) be clearly distinguished. First, inflation adds an exponential trend to prices and monetary variables. Second, inflation results in different stationary-motion paths of the real variables, including the path of prices after correction for the inflationary trend. The interesting problem is the relationship between these types of effects.

As the model is constructed—and it will hardly be called unrealistic in this respect—the only possible source of long-run inflation is the government. In particular, the government budget constraint now has to be written with time subscripts,

$$\rho M_t + r_t B_t = T_t + (M_{t+1} - M_t) + p_t^b (B_{t+1} - B_t). \tag{5.2.1}$$

This says that the government finances its interest payments not only by taxes but also by printing new money and issuing additional bonds. In fact, T_t may well be negative, indicating net government transfers to the private sector.

For balanced expansion, every term of the government budget constraint must expand at the same rate ϵ. This is achieved by assuming

$$M_t = (1 + \epsilon)^{t-1} M, \tag{5.2.2}$$

$$r_t = (1 + \epsilon)^t r, \tag{5.2.3}$$

$$B_t = B, \tag{5.2.4}$$

$$T_t = (1 + \epsilon)^t T, \tag{5.2.5}$$

where M, r, B and T refer to initial values. Some explanations are in order. (5.2.2) implies that $M_{t+1} - M_t = \epsilon M_t$. The difference in the exponent between (5.2.2) and (5.2.3) or (5.2.5) is related to the fact that M_t is a stock held during day t, while r and T are flows taking place at the end of day t. The difference in the exponents means that the initial value for r or T is taken to be the one at the *beginning* of day 1, which means it carries subscript $t = 0$, while the initial value for M is the stock supplied *during* day 1, carrying subscript $t = 1$. This is necessary to make the accounting consistent with the definition of deflated variables introduced in chapter 2 (see 2.6.2).

(5.2.4) states that the number of outstanding bonds is constant over time and thus $(B_{t+1} - B_t) = 0$. This expresses the notion that the number of bonds is, in fact, a real variable. The necessary expansion in the value of the government debt is provided by the continuous adjustment in the coupon stipulated in (5.2.3). The same purpose could be achieved by an expansion in the number of bonds with an unchanged coupon, the new bonds being given away to the owners of existing bonds in proportion to their holdings. There are two reasons for preferring the first assumption. First, in the present transaction cost model, where transaction costs depend on the number of bonds, a continuous increase in the number of bonds would necessitate a continuous increase in transactions inputs and thus destroy the balanced character of inflation. Second, in a world with private debt it seems easier to visualize a contractual adjustment of the coupon than a continuous distribution of free bonds. The main point is that balanced inflation requires an escalator clause for coupons or something equivalent to it.

The increase in T, finally, has to be visualized as an equiproportionate increase in all individual lump-sum taxes and/or transfer payments, fully expected by the individuals concerned. It is important to keep in mind that an expansion of the money supply is not enough to produce balanced inflation.

Substituting from (5.2.2)–(5.2.5) into (5.2.1) and dividing through by $(1 + \epsilon)^t$, the budget constraint can be written in terms of deflated (or initial) variables,

$$\frac{\rho - \pi}{1 + \pi} M + rB = \left(\frac{1 + \rho}{1 + \pi} - 1\right) M + rB = T. \qquad (5.2.6)$$

With balanced monetary expansion, if (5.2.6) is satisfied for the initial variables, it will be satisfied for all t.

We now turn to the optimizing problems of individuals as specified in chapter 4. The commodity constraint (4.2.2) and the bond constraint (4.2.3) are not affected by monetary expansion. The money constraint (4.2.4), however, has to be modified, allowing for the price trend and for the adjustment in the coupon and in taxes. It thus reads

$$s^m_{t+1} - s^m_t = p^g_t (1 + \pi)^t (y^g_t - z^g_t) + p^b_t (1 + \pi)^t (y^b_t - z^b_t)$$
$$+ (1 + \epsilon)^t rs^b_t + \rho s^m_t - (1 + \epsilon)^t t_t. \qquad (5.2.7)$$

It is clear that the rate of balanced inflation equals the rate of monetary expansion. Letting $\epsilon = \pi$, deflating by $(1 + \pi)^t$, and rearranging, we have

$$\frac{1}{(1 + \pi)^t} s^m_{t+1} - \frac{1 + \rho}{(1 + \pi)^t} s^m_t = p^g_t (y^g_t - z^g_t) + p^b_t (y^b_t - z^b_t)$$
$$+ rs^b_t - t_t.$$

Using the definition of deflated cash balances introduced in chapter 2,

$$s^r_t = \frac{1}{(1 + \pi)^{t-1}} s^m_t,$$

this can be expressed as

$$s^r_{t+1} - \frac{1 + \rho}{1 + \pi} s^r_t = p^g_t (y^g_t - z^g_t) + p^b_t (y^b_t - z^b_t)$$
$$+ rs^b_t - t_t. \qquad (t = 1 \cdots h) \qquad (5.2.8)$$

This is a money constraint in deflated terms which, except for the presence of π, has the same form as the monetary constraint for the noninflationary economy (4.2.4). More specifically, π appears as the exact counterpart to ρ. What matters is not ρ and π taken separately, but just the ratio $(1 + \rho)/(1 + \pi)$.

The utility function (4.2.1) and the constraints (4.2.2), (4.2.3), and (5.2.8) together constitute the individual optimization problem in terms of deflated variables. This problem is independent of the progress of inflation as expressed by $(1 + \pi)^t$. However, other things equal, the optimal solution is certainly not independent of the rate of inflation, since π appears in the money constraint.

The demand functions for money and bonds that result from the optimizing calculus can now be written

$$\overset{*b}{s_t} = \overset{*b}{s_t} \left(\bar{x}, p^g, p^b, t, r, \frac{1 + \rho}{1 + \pi}, \gamma, c^g, c^b \right), \tag{5.2.9}$$

$$\overset{*r}{s_t} = \overset{*r}{s_t} \left(\bar{x}, p^g, p^b, t, r, \frac{1 + \rho}{1 + \pi}, \gamma, c^g, c^b \right). \qquad (t = 1 \cdots h) \tag{5.2.10}$$

Adding over individuals, the corresponding aggregate functions are

$$D_t = D_t \left[(\bar{x}), p^g, p^b, (t), r, \frac{1 + \rho}{1 + \pi}, (\gamma), (c^g), (c^b) \right] \tag{5.2.11}$$

$$L_t^r = L_t^r \left[(\bar{x}), p^g, p^b, (t), r, \frac{1 + \rho}{1 + \pi}, (\gamma), (c^g), (c^b) \right].$$

$$(t = 1 \cdots h) \tag{5.2.12}$$

Together with the equilibrium conditions $D_t = B$, $L_t^r = M$, the budget constraint (5.2.6), and the tax constraint (5.1.4), this constitutes the general equilibrium model for balanced inflation. It turns out that the analogy between ρ and π carries over to the general equilibrium problem. The real effects of deflation and inflation are indeed identical to the effects of paying interest or levying a tax on cash balances. The difference between the two is just the exponential price trend.

This means, essentially, that the ambiguity found in the effects of changes in ρ carries over to changes in π. First, the multiplicity of commodity prices and bond yields makes it quite likely that some will fall while others rise. Second, while an increase in the rate of inflation is quite likely to produce, in addition to the exponential trend, a once-over rise in commodity prices, the opposite effect cannot be ruled out on logical grounds. It is indeed conceivable that the reduction in the demand for real balances resulting from a rise in π at given bond yields is more than neutralized by the increase in the demand for real balances resulting from the accompanying change in bond yields.[2] There is no such ambiguity about the reduction of bond yields. Since, if we abstract from the aggregation problem, we can be certain that the bond yield rises with increasing ρ, we can also be certain that it declines with increasing π. At the first moment this may look implausible, as we are used to expecting an upward adjustment of interest rates to inflation. It should be remembered, however, that with a fully escalated coupon the yield on consols is a real rate, and it is well known that real rates decline with accelerating inflation (Mundell, 1963). Indeed, if inflation reduces the real yield on cash balances, portfolio adjustments can be expected to produce some reduction also in the real yield on bonds.

The foregoing analysis concentrated on the case where all of the additional revenue from monetary expansion is used to pay lump-sum transfers. Monetary contraction, on the other hand, would be financed by additional lump-sum taxes. Alternatively, the new money could have been used to pay interest on cash balances, while a reduction in the money supply could be achieved by a negative interest rate on cash balances as proposed by reformers like Silvio Gesell. If inflation or deflation are produced in this way, they have no effects on the real variables; the price trend is all that remains. Inflation would indeed be neutral.[3] This is clearly brought out by the model, where the quotient $(1 + \rho)/(1 + \pi)$ is all that matters. What determines the real effects of inflation or deflation is not the total of government payments to the private sector, but the way in which they are allocated.

If, in the case of inflation, the additional money is paid in the form of transfers, the government may still determine the amounts of these transfers in such a way that every individual would be enabled, at the prices and interest rates ruling after the outbreak of inflation, to carry out the plans that were optimal in the absence of inflation. It was shown in 2.6 that for each individual the necessary amount is πs_t^m, so that the proceeds from monetary expansion, πM_t, just provide the required funds. In this way, the government would exactly compensate each individual for the inflationary tax on cash balances. It will be shown in the following sections that such a compensation scheme plays an important role in most arguments about the "optimal rate of inflation" or the "optimal rate of interest on cash balances." It is crucial, however, that such compensation, no matter on what basis the policy-makers may have determined it, be made in the form of lump-sum transfers.

2. Friedman (1969a, p. 12) seems to have overlooked the fact that his argument, originally derived for an economy without bonds, does not necessarily apply in the presence of bonds.

3. For a mathematical elaboration of this point see Grandmont and Younes (1973, pp. 161 ff.).

5.3. The "optimal return on money"

It has long been recognized that a monetary exchange economy with costless token money is exposed to an important externality problem.[4] Society as a whole, acting collectively, could raise real cash balances to any level, however high, by simply deciding to trade at a lower level of prices. As long as we abstract from transitory costs of changing prices, real cash balances would be a free good. The individual, however, acts under the impression that every permanent increase in his cash balance requires a temporary sacrifice in consumption. As a consequence, the level of real cash balances resulting from the interaction of numerous individuals is lower than the optimum from the point of view of society. This is essentially an externality problem, because the benefits a cash-accumulating individual produces for society by bidding down some prices are only fractionally captured by himself and largely spread over the rest of the economy. This is what has been called the "nonoptimality of money under laissez faire" (Samuelson, 1968, p. 106; 1969, pp. 303–8). The standard remedy to such a welfare loss is a subsidy to counteract the externality. This is the problem of the "optimal return on money," often—but somewhat misleadingly—called the problem of the "optimal money supply." In particular, Friedman (1969a) has proposed that the government provide for a return on cash balances equal to the rate of time preference. This proposition may fairly be called the "Chicago Rule" (H. G. Johnson, 1963, p. 113; 1967, p. 170; G. S. Tolley, 1957, p. 477).

So far, the general-equilibrium analysis of the Chicago Rule has been fragmentary.[5] The model presented in section 5.1 will now be used to shed light on its implications. It will be assumed that the return on cash balances is provided by explicit interest payments, financed by lump-sum taxes. It has been shown in section 5.2 that this is equivalent to balanced deflation achieved by continually destroying the money withdrawn from circulation by appropriate lump-sum taxes. It will be assumed that the rate of time preference is the same for all individuals.

Consider first a single individual confronted with given patterns of commodity and bond prices in the 2-day case (see fig. 5.3.1). We assume that he is actually holding cash balances during day 2. In the absence of interest on cash balances his optimum may be at Q, and his cash balance can

4. Friedman seems to have been the first to recognize this clearly (1959, pp. 71 ff.). Samuelson hit upon the same idea a few years later (1963). Friedman also added the qualification that the argument would not apply to commodity money.
5. See Hahn's critique (1971a). Grandmont and Younes (1973) take up the problem, but they make the demand for money simply a function of purchases and sales. They also do not consider credit.

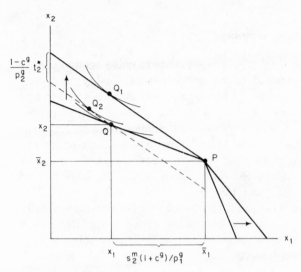

Figure **5.3.1**
Compensated Interest Payment on Cash Balances

be measured by the day-1 commodities he sells to hold cash, $\bar{x}_1 - x_1$.[6] If
the government now pays interest on cash balances equal to $\rho = \theta$, the
money frontier turns outward around P (see sec. 4.3).[7] The new optimum
Q_1 will clearly be on a higher indifference curve than Q. This is the benefit
from the interest payments.

On the other hand, the individual will have to pay an additional lump-
sum tax. In order to provide for an exact compensation, this tax will have
to be equal to the interest payments on the cash balances held at Q, that is,
$t_2^* = \rho s_2^m$. In the graph it is measured by t_2^* $(1 - c^g)/p_2^g$, the amount of x_2
which could have been brought with the tax payment. Why isn't it equal
to the interest payments on the cash balances in the new equilibrium Q_1?
This is because, for the economy as a whole, the nominal money stock does
not change, the desired increases in real cash balances being achieved
by price declines. For the representative individual, the tax thus has to
cover the interest payments on the cash balance held before the increase in
ρ. This additional tax is the burden of the Chicago Rule for the individual.

The point is that the benefit is clearly higher than the cost. The new

6. From constraints (4.2.2) and (4.2.4) we derive

$$s_2^m = \frac{p_1^g}{1 + c^g}(\bar{x}_1 - x_1) = \frac{1}{1 + \rho}\frac{p_2^g}{1 - c^g}(x_2 - \bar{x}_2).$$

7. This does not mean that the shifting of resources over time is no longer costly.
If the store of value consists of commodities there are storage costs, if it consists of
money there are transaction costs on the exchange of commodities for money. The
transaction frontier in figure 5.3.1 does not become a straight line.

equilibrium Q_2 is not only associated with higher cash balances (see sec. 4.3), but is also on a higher indifference curve than Q. A compensated increase in ρ thus turns out to be analogous to the elimination of an excise tax on cash balances, financed by a lump-sum tax. By the well-known argument, this makes the consumer better off. This is the central argument for the Chicago Rule. It is worth noting that this basic welfare gain has nothing to do with economizing on transaction costs, as was argued by Friedman (1969, p. 14). In the present case (though not necessarily in other cases), the amount of resources devoted to transactions actually increases with cash balances. The reason is easy to find. The gain in utility is due to a shift from day-1 consumption to day-2 consumption through the holding of cash balances. It thus involves a higher volume of market exchange and, therefore, of transaction costs. While money has a lot to do with transaction costs, it is simply not true, in general, that it has utility because it frees resources previously tied up in the exchange process.

The above argument does not prove, however, that observance of the Chicago Rule makes the economy unambiguously better off. The economy is unambiguously better off if nobody loses while some people gain.[8] The above argument shows that this would be so, provided prices remained unchanged. However, when we move from the individual to the economy, prices cannot remain unchanged. In fact, if some prices did not decline, there could be no increase in real balances. What is more important, relative prices will also change. The conditions for a neutral change in the price level were given in the preceding section. A compensated increase in ρ does not satisfy these conditions; it will thus affect relative commodity prices for different days of the year as well as the interest rate on bonds.[9] Nothing general can be said about the way relative prices will change. Most likely some individuals will make additional gains while others will lose. It would be an unlikely coincidence if some did not lose more from these price changes than they would have gained at unchanged prices. By the criterion of Pareto-superiority, therefore, the Chicago Rule cannot be shown to produce an improvement in welfare.

In principle, it would be possible to modify the array of lump-sum taxes (possibly changing some into subsidies) in such a way that, without a further change in aggregate T, all losers from the Chicago Rule are at least compensated by the winners. However, as long as we do not possess a workable compensation schedule and have, in fact, no idea where we should look for the gains and losses, this is doubtful consolation.

8. What matters is whether a state with $\rho = \theta$ is Pareto-superior to a state with the same data but $\rho < \theta$. It should be noted that the concept of Pareto optimality is not relevant in this context. Even if it could be proved that a state with $\rho = \theta$ is Pareto-optimal while a state with $\rho < \theta$ is not, this does not prove that the first state is Pareto-superior to the second.

9. In a multicommodity model there would also be changes in relative prices for different commodities.

The Chicago Rule also involves another problem. It was pointed out at the end of the preceding section that with $\rho = \theta$ people are willing to hold any amount of cash balances, provided they hold at least the satiation balances. As a consequence, the price level can be arbitrarily low as long as it does not go below a certain level. The economy would thus be in a liquidity trap, a general-equilibrium counterpart to the Keynesian liquidity trap.[10] Any further increase in ρ, however small, would make it impossible for the economy to achieve an equilibrium. The stock demand for money would become insatiable, and no price level above zero could endure.[11] The Chicago Rule would thus place the economy on a knife-edge between scarcity of money and a pathological addiction to higher and higher cash balances. This is surely an uncomfortable place to be in.

The final question concerns the implications of the Chicago Rule for the demand for bonds and the supply of private debt. With cash balances having the highest yield compatible with equilibrium, it seems intuitively plausible that there can be no incentive ever to exchange money for bonds. One would also suspect that there is no motive ever to go into debt. After all, why should anybody borrow if he is satiated with cash at all times? This conjectures can indeed be shown to be correct.

Consider first the two-day case. By comparing the slopes of the frontiers for money (4.3.2) and bonds (4.3.3) for $\theta = \rho$, and substituting for the bond price (after transaction costs) from (4.4.13) and (4.4.14), it can be shown that the bond frontier cannot lie outside the money frontier. To hold cash is always at least as good as holding bonds. By making a similar comparison for money and debt, it can also be shown that the debt frontier cannot lie outside the money frontier. In order to shift consumption over time, it is at least as good to accumulate the excess supply in cash as to cover the excess demand by borrowing. In the case most favorable to bonds (or debt), an individual would be just indifferent between holding cash and holding bonds (or going into debt).

This argument can be generalized to n days. According to (4.4.13), the buyer of a bond pays (after transaction costs) *at least* r/θ. After n days he can sell the bond, according to (4.4.14), for *at most* r/θ (after transaction costs). While he may make a capital loss, he cannot make a capital gain. In the best possible case, the stream of his costs and revenues will thus be $-r/\theta, r, r, \cdots, r + r/\theta$. If he "invests" his funds in cash, the corresponding stream is $-r/\theta, (r/\theta)\rho, \cdots, (r/\theta)\rho + r/\theta$. In view of $\theta = \rho$, this is identical

10. It is interesting to note that, in this model, to make ρ equal to θ is the only way to catch the economy in such a liquidity trap. In particular, an increase in the nominal money supply combined with a reduction in government bonds, no matter how far it depresses the bond yield, could never have this result. It thus seems Keynes may have looked in the wrong direction for his trap.

11. This is similar to the indeterminacy and nonexistence of equilibrium found by Grandmont and Younes (1973).

to the best possible bond stream. In an economy satiated with cash balances, it never pays to trade bonds. If bonds are exogenously supplied by the government, they must, of course, be held. They will be held indifferently by those who happen to have them, the market pushing the rate of interest on bonds to the level of ρ. The distribution of the bonds is as indeterminate as the amount of real balances, and they are perfect substitutes for money as stores of value. For all economic purposes, they could as well be abolished.

For debt the generalization is equally straightforward. Consider a marginal reduction in the amount of debt, accompanied by an equal increase in the level of cash holdings during the rest of the year.[12] This saves transaction costs on the selling and buying of bonds. At the same time, there is an increase in time preference costs over the whole year. However, this is just matched by the higher interest income over the year, consisting partly of interest earned on the additional cash balances, and partly of interest saved on the debt. As long as there is any debt, a marginal shift from debt to cash holding is always advantageous. Under the Chicago Rule there is no room for private debt. Figuratively speaking, the "Lebensraum" of the credit market is the margin between the rate of time preference and the rate of interest on money. If this margin is compressed to zero, private credit will be squeezed out of existence.

This discussion may be concluded by a comment on its main limitation. The preceding analysis was based on a one-commodity model. There was no production, individuals just consuming, storing, and exchanging their endowments. Even exchange was very limited in scope, since it did not include the exchange of today's commodities against tomorrow's commodities. This raises the question to what extent the results with respect to the demand for money and the yield on cash balances may have been due to the one-commodity assumption. A full answer to this question can obviously not be given here, since it would require a formal extension of the model to production and exchange in a multicommodity model. The following comments will thus have to be interpreted as conjectures about what a full analysis is likely to reveal.

First, the exclusion of multicommodity exchange, taken by itself, is likely to result in an overstatement of commodity stocks. In a one-commodity model, the holding of commodity stocks does not require any transactions; some part of the endowment is just put away for future use. Holding inventories, rather than money or bonds, thus saves transaction costs. In a multicommodity world this is often not true, because the commodities an individual finds in his endowment are generally not those he

---

12. In figure 4.1.1 this corresponds to a marginal downward shift in the vertical scale.

wishes to consume. As a consequence, transaction costs for moving from commodity A to money and from money to commodity B are the same whether stocks are held in the form of commodity A, money, or commodity B. It follows that in a multicommodity world some people would probably prefer to hold money who, in the present model, would have held commodity stocks.

Second, the exclusion of production, by itself, is likely to result in an understatement of commodity inventories. In production, commodity stocks assume the important function of capital goods. This means that their storage cost (or depreciation) rate γ acquires a counterpart in the marginal product of capital, denoted by ϕ. The opportunity cost of commodity stocks, appearing on the right-hand side of (4.4.7a), thus becomes $\theta + \gamma - \phi$. If ϕ were a constant, higher commodity stocks would thus be held. We know, however, that equilibrium requires a nonnegative opportunity cost of commodity stocks. This means that the marginal product of capital cannot be higher than the sum of time preference and the storage cost rate. In fact, of course, ϕ will usually not be a constant. We rather have to assume that the marginal product of capital is high for small capital stocks and declines as the stock increases. The equilibrium condition $\theta + \gamma - \phi > 0$ may thus require a certain minimum amount of capital goods to bring ϕ down to the required level. This implies that commodity stocks cease to be just a transactions asset and may be held as a permanent investment asset.

While an extension of the model to production and multicommodity exchange would have important implications for commodity stocks, I believe that it would leave the monetary aspects of the analysis essentially unchanged. It is true that the overstatement of the demand for commodity stocks due to the one-commodity assumption is likely to be associated with some understatement of the demand for money stocks. But this is about all. In particular, it would still be true that money is only held as a transactions asset and never as a permanent investment asset. What was said about the implications of the Chicago Rule for the demand for money and debt would also continue to be true. The conjecture that an extension of the model to multicommodity exchange and production would not shed new light on the role of money and credit in a fully monetized economy was exactly the reason why the simple one-commodity model was used in the first place. Under what conditions monetary exchange may be preferred to barter will be discussed in a multicommodity framework in the following chapter.

$\mathcal{Six}$

BARTER AND MONETARY EXCHANGE

Introduction

In the preceding chapters it was *assumed* that the economy is fully monetized and that the choice of the medium of exchange has somehow been made. The use of something called money as the quid pro quo in every transaction was treated as a constraint, imposed on individuals from the outside. The question that now has to be faced is under what circumstances, and why, an economy may be monetized. Closely related to it is the further question about the possible advantage of monetary exchange compared to barter and about the reason for using certain commodities as media of exchange. In a sense, these problems are more fundamental than those discussed in the preceding chapters; before analyzing the equilibrium of a monetary economy, we may want to know why the economy uses money in the first place. From the point of view of exposition, however, it seemed more convenient to invert the sequence and to raise the more complex, though more basic, problems only after the discussion of the simpler problems has provided the necessary tools.

To answer these questions we need a general equilibrium theory of exchange in which barter and monetary exchange appear as special cases. Classical and neoclassical theory left exchange arrangements indeterminate. All inputs are devoted to production and consumption; exchange requires no inputs. As a consequence, a given allocation of resources to production and consumption is consistent with an infinite variety of exchange arrangements, none of which is preferable to any other. Exchange is simply not an economic activity. Lacking an economic theory of exchange, neoclassical theory was forced to treat money metaphorically as a potential consumer or producer good, which, in fact, it is not (see chapter 1). The key to an explicit, nonmetaphorical treatment of money is a reversal of this perspective: All commodities must be treated as potential media of exchange, which, in fact, they are. At the same time, every potential exchange has to be treated as a resource-using economic activity. The choice between monetary and nonmonetary exchange arrangements thus becomes a straightforward question of optimal resource allocation. It will turn out that the transaction cost approach developed in the preceding chapters contains all the elements necessary to explain this choice.[1]

The discussion will proceed from the elementary to the complex in three stages. The first section concentrates on the flow aspects of the problem, abstracting from stock holding. It will also be assumed that the final demands for commodities are already known; the exchange arrangements are all that remain to be determined. The second section, while still restricted to flow aspects, will treat final demand, relative prices, and exchange arrangements as jointly determined. In the third section, finally, the analysis will be extended to stocks. The discussion will again be restricted to an exchange economy without production and without financial intermediation.

6.1. Money flows in a dichotomized economy

I shall begin by making two simplifying assumptions, to be dropped in the following sections. First, I shall abstract from any intertemporal, dynamic aspects of the problem. This makes it impossible, of course, to explain the holding of stocks, including money stocks. The analysis will thus be limited to flows in a stationary world. Any money appearing in such an analysis must be commodity money, which, besides serving as a medium of exchange, is also a consumption good.

The second simplification concerns the separation of the theory of money and exchange from the theory of value and allocation. I shall, in fact, assume that some Walrasian auctioneer has already established equilibrium between supply and demand for each commodity, thus determining everybody's *net* sales, the consumption of every commodity and also their exchange ratios. The theory of value and allocation is supposed to have done its job. This leaves the question about everybody's *gross* purchases and sales, together with the question who trades with whom. This is the field of the theory of money and exchange.

In a sense, this dichotomization is in the spirit of neoclassical monetary theory. However, as was pointed out in chapter 1, neoclassical economists were never able to analyze the notion that money can increase the efficiency of the economic system without affecting relative prices. We shall now formalize this idea by postulating an artificial division of consumable resources into two parts. On one side are the resources that are capable of being traded in the market. On the other side are resources that, besides for consumption, can only be used as transactions inputs. We could

1. References to recent contributions on transaction costs were given at the end of chapter 1.

visualize these transactions resources as a particular type of labor that, if not used up in transactions, is used in the form of leisure. Corresponding to the two kinds of resources there are two systems of prices, namely the commodity prices in the ordinary sense of the word and the prices (or shadow prices) of transactions. In this way, the exchange arrangements, including the choice of a medium of exchange, can be analyzed after commodity prices and allocation are already known. It should be noted, however, that this dichotomized system, while being in the neoclassical spirit, does not reduce the monetary part to the function of determining some absolute price level. Both parts of the system have to do with the allocation of resources, though of different parts of them.

The main point of the argument may first be illustrated by what may be called "Wicksell's Problem" (1934, p. 63 f.; 1935, p. 15 f.). Suppose Norway plans to export a certain quantity of fish to Sweden, Sweden plans to ship an equivalent quantity of timber to Denmark, while Denmark closes the triangle by selling wheat of the same value to Norway (see fig. 6.1.1). The components of this shipping program may be called the "ultimate flows." Suppose further that every change in ownership involves the actual shipping of the goods; there are no IOUs and the like. Since there must be a quid pro quo in every transaction, it is clear that the shipping program cannot be confined to the ultimate flows. One of the shipments cannot move directly from the ultimate source to the ultimate destination but must be transshipped by way of the third country, thus becoming for this country a medium of exchange. If there are no shipping costs, it does not matter which commodity is used for this purpose. This is the frictionless world in which there is no difference between various exchange arrangements. In the presence of shipping costs, however, efficiency clearly requires that the commodity with the lowest shipping costs be used as the medium of exchange. This basic idea will now be generalized and formalized, with transaction costs replacing shipping costs.

Consider an economy with n individuals, each endowed with certain quantities of Q resources $\bar{x}_i^q (q = 1 \cdots Q; \ i = 1 \cdots n)$ and given tastes, represented by a utility function. Suppose we permit a Walrasian auctioneer

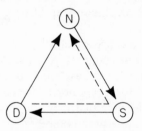

Figure **6.1.1**
"Wicksell's Problem"

to establish an equilibrium in the system. This equilibrium determines net purchases $(z_i^q - y_i^q)$ for every individual and every commodity, constituting the network of ultimate flows. It also establishes the exchange ratio for every pair of commodities. Since the apple price of nuts times the nut price of pears must be equal to the apple price of pears, the matrix of these exchange ratios can be condensed to a vector of q prices p^q in terms of an arbitrarily chosen numéraire (with the price of the numéraire equal to 1). This network will equate aggregate demand and aggregate supply for each commodity,

$$\sum_i^n (z_i^q - y_i^q) = 0, \qquad q = 1 \cdots Q, \tag{6.1.1}$$

and satisfy the budget constraint for every individual,

$$\sum_q^Q p^q(z_i^q - y_i^q) = 0, \qquad i = 1 \cdots (n - 1). \tag{6.1.2}$$

There are $n - 1$ independent budget constraints, the nth being implied in the others together with (6.1.1). For each commodity and trader, net purchases are equal to the excess of consumption over the endowment, or

$$x_i^q - \bar{x}_i^q = y_i^q - z_i^q, \qquad i = 1 \cdots n, \tag{6.1.3}$$

$$q = 1 \cdots Q.$$

In a Walrasian auction hall the exchanges specified by the equilibrium system are carried out by costless trading with an anonymous market. In fact, however, each exchange in a market economy is carried out between specific individuals. The Walrasian equilibrium does not determine who trades with whom. It does not determine gross purchases z_i^q and gross sales y_i^q of a given individual for a given commodity. This is the empty space we now have to fill in. Without further analysis we know only one thing: There must be a quid pro quo in every bilateral exchange. B will refuse to supply C with free apples in the hope that A will, in turn, let him have free nuts. To be sure, the quid pro quo may be an IOU or perhaps just an oral promise, but there must be something. This is the technique by which an exchange economy enforces the budget constraint for every individual.

For given ultimate flows, bilateral balance can generally be achieved in many different ways. From these, an efficient economy will select the one that minimizes aggregate transaction costs. We shall assume that transactions inputs take the form of some particular form of labor, not included in the endowment and not tradeable. We also assume that they are proportional to the quantity exchanged and specific to the commodity, to the pair of traders and to the direction of flow. Each trader has transaction costs both on what he sells and on what he buys. The objective function can thus be written

$$Min \ T = \sum_i^n \sum_j^n \sum_q^Q c_{ji}^q y_{ij}^q + \sum_i^n \sum_j^n \sum_q^Q c_{ij}^q z_{ij}^q,$$

where c_{ij}^q is the transaction cost on commodity q sold by i to j, while z_{ij}^q and y_{ij}^q are, respectively, the purchases and sales of trader i in his dealings with j.

The solution is subject to two sets of constraints. First, for each individual the difference between the total quantity of commodity q bought from all individuals and the total quantity of q sold to all individuals must be equal to his net purchase of q:

$$\sum_j^n z_{ij}^q - \sum_j^n y_{ij}^q = z_i^q - y_i^q, \qquad i = 1 \cdots n,$$

$$q = 1 \cdots Q. \tag{6.1.4}$$

There are nQ such resource constraints. Second, bilateral balance requires that the value of the flows between any two individuals be equal in both directions,

$$\sum_q^Q p^q z_{ij}^q = \sum_q^Q p^q y_{ij}^q. \tag{6.1.5}$$

The number of these constraints is $(1/2)n(n-1) - 1$, bilateral balance for the last pair of traders following from (6.1.1) and (6.1.4).

This is a linear programming problem with the constraints written as equalities. Its optimal solution determines all z_{ij}^q and thus all y_{ij}^q and, therefore, also the gross purchases z_i^q and sales y_i^q for every individual and commodity. This means that we know all flows in the system. As a consequence, we also know whether certain commodities will be used as a medium of exchange, whether one commodity will be used as a common medium of exchange and, if so, which commodity will be elevated to this role.

For a given Walrasian system, the configuration of exchange flows and thus the monetary or nonmonetary character of exchange arrangements depends *only* on the transaction cost rates. Whenever the transaction cost rate for a given commodity is lowered between any two individuals, this increases the chance that the commodity will be used as a medium of exchange. For small numbers of commodities and traders it is possible to compute the effects of different transaction cost rates by solving the above optimization problem (Niehans, 1969a). In the present context it is enough to illustrate some possible outcomes graphically (fig. 6.1.2). Suppose there are four traders. Every commodity is supposed to originate from only one trader. This means that the Walrasian system of the ultimate flows can be graphed as in figure 6.1.2(a), in which every arrow is supposed to represent a flow of the same value, expressed in the numéraire. Except be-

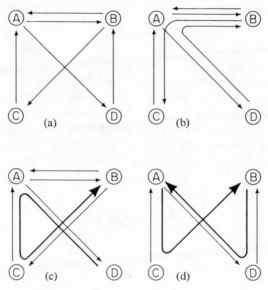

Figure **6.1.2**
Exchange Arrangements

tween *A* and *B*, the bilateral flows are not balanced. Some indirect exchange thus becomes necessary. Its nature will depend on transaction costs.

Suppose that individual *A* has a particular ability as a trader in the
sense that whenever he appears as a party in an exchange the transaction
costs are considerably lower than in exchanges between other parties.
In this case, *A* will emerge as a middleman or "center of exchange" as
illustrated in figure 6.1.2(b). At the same time, none of the commodities
can be said to be a *common* medium of exchange; only *A* uses goods as
media of exchange, while *B*, *C*, and *D* buy nothing for resale. The center
of exchange can thus be substituted for a medium of exchange. One of the
most interesting modern examples is probably the emergence of financial
centers for borrowing and lending of various national currencies as a
substitute for an international currency. The prominence of London in the
Eurocurrency market is not due to the role of sterling as an international
money, but largely to the comparative advantage of London banks with
respect to transaction costs on foreign funds.

Suppose, on the other hand, that transaction costs are made particularly low, not for a certain trader but for a certain commodity, no
matter who is trading it. In this case, this commodity will sooner or later
emerge as the common medium of exchange in the sense that no other
media of exchange are used. This is illustrated in figure 6.1.2(c), where *D*'s
goods are used as the common medium of exchange. It should be noted
that direct barter, such as between *A* and *B*, may still persist. If the hungry

tailor happens to meet the shivering baker, they have no reason to use money.

It is not necessarily true, however, that the same medium of exchange is used in all transactions. We can also visualize dual or, more generally, multiple monetary systems in which different monies each have their particular uses. Thus in figure 6.1.2(d) the commodity A ultimately supplied to B is used to effect trade with C, while the commodity B ultimately supplied to A is used in trade with D. In fact, in most economies we find a multitude of monies, reaching from small coins to large checks, each with its own comparative advantages and thus its specific range of uses.

In this way the choice between barter and monetary exchange can be visualized, *for a predetermined Walrasian system*, as the result of transaction cost minimization. However, this model has several unsatisfactory features. First, transaction cost minimization is attributed to a conscious minimizing calculus, to some kind of central planning.[2] Second, the assumption of a dichotomy between general endowments and transactions endowments is highly artificial. In fact, consumption and exchange flows are determined simultaneously. Both of these objections will be met by the integrated model presented in the following section.

6.2. Money flows in an integrated economy

I now drop the convenient, but highly unsatisfactory, assumption that the economic system is dichotomized into a real part, determining consumption flows and prices, and a monetary part, determining exchange arrangements. Consumption and exchange will thus be jointly determined; monetary and value theory will be fully integrated. As a consequence, it is no longer possible to determine the exchange network by solving a centralized optimization problem. Instead, each individual has to solve its own optimization problem for given market conditions, and the interplay of supply and demand then determines market conditions. In this respect, the present multicommodity model is closely related to the one-commodity model of chapter 5. However, the analysis will still be confined to a timeless world and thus abstract from stocks and token money.

In contrast to the preceding section, I now assume that a given individual is trading not with other individuals but with certain markets or "trading posts." This involves a sacrifice of economic content. In particular, it will no longer be possible to explain who trades with whom, but only what is traded against what. This implies, among other things, that it will not be possible to explain the emergence of middlemen or brokers, earning

2. Duality theory shows that the optimum can also be found by adding certain premiums to the commodity prices, depending on the different nodes of the network, and letting the traders individually maximize their profits (see Niehans, 1969a). It turns out that the optimal exchange arrangement is the only one in which every trader breaks even, just as in perfect competition.

a living from the difference between bid and ask prices. On the other hand, a market approach simplifies notation and makes it possible to focus more clearly on the elements that are most important from the point of view of monetary theory. For a reader who is interested in an individual-exchange approach it should be easy to provide the necessary extension for himself.[3]

We assume that there is a separate trading post for each pair of goods. At one post, apples are traded against nuts, at another post apples are traded against pears. For Q goods there are thus $(Q/2)(Q - 1)$ markets. When the system is in equilibrium, some of these markets will generally turn out to be inactive. The central problem of the present chapter is precisely the determination of the set of active markets. In a fully monetized economy, the $Q - 1$ nonmonetary commodities would be exchanged against money only; the remaining $(1/2)(Q - 1)(Q - 2)$ trading posts would be deserted. Unfortunately, there is no way of predicting which the inactive markets will be without actually determining the complete equilibrium.

For given endowments and tastes, the resulting exchange arrangement will again depend on transaction costs. These costs are assumed to consist of labor (with index Q) and to be proportional to the quantity transferred. They are also assumed to be specific to the trader and the commodity, but now independent of the quid pro quo and the direction of the flow.

It would be possible to generalize this specification in various respects. In some directions, added generality would be quite cheap, but also unrewarding. In particular, it would be a matter of notation to allow for the possibility that transaction costs consist of the inputs of numerous goods and services in fixed proportions and that they do also depend on the quid pro quo and the direction of the exchange. In other respects, added generality would be somewhat more interesting, but also more difficult to achieve. It would be possible, for example, to specify a transactions technology with variable inputs, provided it exhibits no scale economies. In this case, the constraints of the individual optimization problems would no longer be linear. However, the only really worthwhile generalization, namely the introduction of scale economies, is very difficult to achieve,[4] and we are thus forced to leave it to future research.[5]

3. The key to this extension is the realization that for the same pair of commodities there are, in principle, different exchange ratios depending on the pair of traders and also depending on the direction of the flows.

4. In terms of the present model, scale economies in the transactions technology would result in nonconvex exchange opportunities. The emerging competitive equilibrium, if it exists, would most likely not be efficient. Fixed transaction costs are perhaps the most fundamental level at which it may be argued that "money does not manage itself."

5. For a contribution about economies of transactions scale, see Heller (1972). Ostroy's model (1973) can be viewed as an effort to capture certain economies of market scale.

I begin with individual optimization under given market conditions.[6] A given individual is endowed with resources $\bar{x}_1, \cdots \bar{x}_q, \cdots \bar{x}_Q$. By trading in the market he maximizes the utility function (with the characteristics specified in earlier chapters)

$$U = U(x_1, \cdots x_q, \cdots x_Q), \tag{6.2.1}$$

subject to the resource constraints. For every good except Q the resource constraint states that the excess of consumption over the endowment equals net purchases,

$$x_q - \bar{x}_q = \sum_k^Q (z_{qk} - y_{qk}), \qquad q = 1 \cdots (Q - 1) \tag{6.2.2}$$

where z_{qk} and y_{qk} denote, respectively, the quantities of good q bought and sold against good k. Purchases and sales at a given trading post are related through the exchange ratio or price

$$p_{qk} = \frac{z_{kq}}{y_{qk}} = \frac{y_{kq}}{z_{qk}} = 1/p_{kq}. \tag{6.2.3}$$

Substituting for z_{qk} the resource constraints can be rewritten

$$x_q - \bar{x}_q = \sum_k^Q (p_{kq} y_{kq} - y_{qk}). \qquad q = 1 \cdots (Q - 1) \tag{6.2.4}$$

The resource constraint for Q includes, in addition, the term reflecting transaction costs. It can be written

$$x_Q - \bar{x}_Q = \sum_k^Q (p_{kQ} y_{kQ} - y_{Qk}) - \sum_q^Q \sum_k^Q (c_q + c_k p_{qk}) y_{qk}. \tag{6.2.5}$$

In addition, all flows must be nonnegative, $x_q \geqq 0$, $y_{qk} \geqq 0$.

This is, again, a nonlinear programming problem with a quasiconcave objective function and linear constraints. Its solution determines consumption, market demand, and market supply each as a function of endowments, market price, and transaction cost rates. It is important to note that these functions do not have a homogeneity property corresponding to the neoclassical proposition that an equiproportionate change in all prices leaves demand unchanged. Also contrary to the neoclassical model an individual may well be both a buyer and a seller of the same good, though at different trading posts. On the other hand, many trading posts may not be frequented by him at all.

---

6. For a quite similar treatment of this problem, see Karni (1972).

By forming the Lagrange equation

$$L = U(x_1 \cdots x_q \cdots x_Q) - \sum_q^Q \lambda_q [x_q - \sum_k^Q (p_{kq} y_{kq} - y_{qk}) - \bar{x}_q]$$

$$- \lambda_Q [\sum_q^Q \sum_k^Q (c_q + c_k p_{qk}) y_{qk}] \qquad (6.2.6)$$

and taking the partial derivatives we can derive the Kuhn-Tucker conditions. Not surprisingly, they are very similar to those obtained in chapter 4. For consumption, in particular, they are

$$\left(\frac{\partial U}{\partial x_q} - \lambda_q\right) x_q = 0, \qquad \frac{\partial U}{\partial x_q} \leqq \lambda_q, \qquad x_q \geqq 0. \qquad (6.2.7)$$

The interpretation is similar to that of (4.4.2): If a good is consumed at all, its direct marginal utility is equal to its marginal value, but a good may have a marginal value, arising from its services as a medium of exchange, even if it has no direct utility in consumption.

The other set of Kuhn-Tucker conditions relates to market supply

$$[\lambda_k p_{qk} - \lambda_q - \lambda_Q(c_q + c_k p_{qk})] y_{qk} = 0, \qquad p_{qk} \leqq \frac{\lambda_q + \lambda_Q c_q}{\lambda_k - \lambda_Q c_k}, \qquad (6.2.8)$$

$$y_{qk} \geqq 0.$$

The expression in square brackets can be interpreted as the marginal benefit of a sale of q against k. If the first condition on the right-hand side holds as an inequality, commodity q will not be sold at the trading post where it can be exchanged against k. If the corresponding inequality holds also for the sale of k against q, the individual will not visit the respective trading post at all. The conditions for commodity purchases do not have to be specified separately, since they are implied in the conditions for the sales. It should be noted that, in view of transaction costs, there is no reason why the price system should be consistent in the sense that $p_{qk} p_{kh} = p_{qh}$.

I now assume that we know the consumption, supply, and demand functions for each of n individuals as derived from the above optimization problem. The prices on the $(Q/2)(Q - 1)$ markets, on the other hand, become endogenous variables. These prices have to satisfy the requirement that aggregate supply equals aggregate demand for each good. Denoting individuals by left-hand subscripts, we thus obtain the set of $Q(Q - 1)$ equilibrium conditions

$$\sum_i^n {}_i z_{qk}^k = \sum_i^n {}_i y_{qk}^k. \qquad (6.2.9)$$

However, by the definition of prices, if this condition is satisfied for one of the two goods traded at a given trading post, it is automatically satisfied for the other. Therefore, only half of the above equilibrium conditions are independent. This is the counterpart to the neoclassical proposition that equilibrium in $Q - 1$ markets implies equilibrium in the Qth market. The number of independent equilibrium conditions thus matches the number of markets.

Once equilibrium prices are known, consumption, market demand, and market supply for all individuals are determined simultaneously. The result is a general equilibrium of barter. It should be noted that this system has, in general, none of the familiar homogeneity properties found in neoclassical models. In particular, the system cannot be dichotomized into a "real" and a "monetary" part. It will be shown below how the neoclassical properties can be made to result from special assumptions.

It is important to realize that for some markets the equilibrium trade volume may be zero. For two traders and two goods (and thus one market), this aspect can be illustrated graphically. The optimization problem of trader 1 is represented in figure 6.2.1. Note that E is the no-trade point, defined by the given endowments. Trade can take place along the straight line through E whose slope measures the market price of good 1 in terms of good 2. However, in view of transaction costs, the commodity bundle resulting from trade is not fully available for consumption. The consumption frontier is AEB. If transaction costs are paid out of good 2, they are measured by the vertical distance between the consumption frontier and

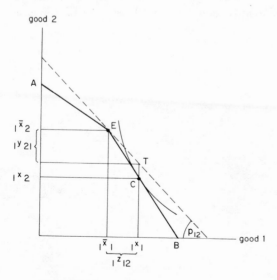

Figure **6.2.1**
Individual Optimization

the trade line. The trader will maximize utility by choosing consumption pattern C. This results in market demand and supply represented by the difference between T and E.

With a change in market price, both the trade line and the consumption frontier will swivel around E. If the initial consumption equilibrium was somewhere along the flat segments AE and EB, this will lead to a change in market demand and/or supply. However, if the equilibrium was initially at the no-trade point E, it is clear that it may stay there for some range of prices. A similar graph can be drawn for the second trader.

The results for market demand and supply are summarized by the offer curves for traders 1 and 2 in figure 6.2.2, where the origin represents the no-trade point. The kink in each consumption frontier, due to transaction costs, is reflected in a kink of the respective offer curve at the origin. The intersection of these curves then determines the direction of trade, if any, the market price, and the quantities exchanged. It may happen, however, that market equilibrium is at the no-trade point, as illustrated in figure 6.2.3. In this case we can generally determine a range of prices only, any price within this (shaded) range making the desired exchange zero for both traders.

This two-person, one-market example shows that the no-trade solution is more likely, *ceteris paribus*, the higher the transaction cost rate. In a multimarket system, various sets of markets can be made inactive by choosing appropriate configurations of transaction cost rates. In one case, all markets may be active, implying that every good is traded against every other good. In another case, all markets are deserted except those where one particular good is traded against other goods; this would be the case

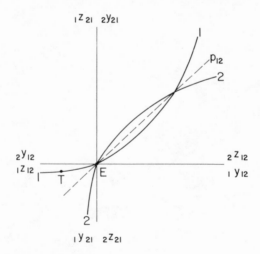

Figure **6.2.2**
Reciprocal Offer Curves

of a fully monetized economy. From the point of view of explaining the emergence of different exchange arrangements, it is thus one of the principal functions of the model to determine which trading posts are active under a given set of conditions.

Different exchange arrangements, some monetary, others non-monetary, can be made to emerge by simply varying the pattern of transaction costs. Suppose, with given tastes and endowments, we start out by assigning arbitrary positive values to transaction cost rates in a random fashion. The result is likely to be a complex network of exchange with some trading posts active while others are idle, including cases of both direct barter and indirect exchange. In the latter cases, goods are bought for resale, thus serving as media of exchange. The same individual may use several such media, each in a different range of applications, and different individuals will often use different sets of exchange media. There is no general reason to expect that any one good will universally or even widely be used as a medium of exchange and thus deserve the name of money. From this general case I shall now derive special (and in some sense limiting) cases by varying transaction costs in some particular way.[7]

I first assume that wherever there is originally an indirect exchange the transaction cost rate on the respective medium of exchange is progressively increased. It is clear that there is always a rate high enough to make it preferable to eliminate that medium of exchange, replacing indirect barter by direct barter.[8] In the course of this process we will sooner or later arrive at an exchange system with direct barter only. It is regarded as commonplace that such a system is wasteful. This is not generally true, however, because *with the given exchange technology*, embodied in a particular set of transaction cost rates, it may well be the most efficient trading pattern available.

In a second experiment we assume that transaction cost rates are increased wherever there is any exchange, be it direct or indirect. In general, this will tend to lower the volume of market exchange. In part this is so

---

7. Proofs for the propositions in the remainder of this section are given in Niehans (1971).

8. The square bracket in equation (6.2.8) is the marginal gain from the direct sale of one unit of q for k. The marginal gain from the corresponding indirect exchange with g as medium of exchange is

$$p_{qg}\lambda_g - \lambda_q - \lambda_Q(c_q + c_g p_{qg}) + p_{qg}[\lambda_k p_{gk} - \lambda_g - \lambda_Q(c_g + c_k p_{gk})].$$

Deducting the first expression from the second, we obtain the extra gain from using the indirect route

$$(p_{qg}p_{gk} - p_{qk})(\lambda_k - c_k\lambda_Q) - 2c_g p_{qg}\lambda_Q.$$

The first term represents the value of the gains in k from using the more favorable indirect prices, net of additional transfer costs, while the second term measures the value of the additional transaction costs on the medium of exchange. There is clearly some c_g high enough to make this negative.

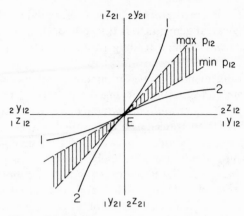

Figure **6.2.3**
Equilibrium Without Trade

because the rise in transaction costs, similar to a tax on exchange, will make it relatively more profitable to consume one's own endowment. A possible result is complete self-sufficiency of individuals. It is logically conceivable, though perhaps unlikely, that even small transaction costs will shut off all trade if tastes and endowments are sufficiently similar. But even if tastes and endowments are such that individuals must trade to satisfy any of their needs, increasing transaction costs can reduce the volume of trade to any level we care to specify, however low. Suppose no work is directly consumed, thus maximizing the amount available for transactions. The exchange programs that can be maintained with this amount at the given transaction cost rates specify a "trade possibility frontier." By increasing transaction cost rates, this frontier can be made to shrink, until finally the smallest trace of market exchange would use up all of society's work. By increasing transaction costs we can thus bring society as close to individual self-sufficiency as we want.

Going to the other extreme, we may reduce all transaction costs to zero. In this case, the model reduces to a neoclassical general equilibrium system. Equations (6.2.7) and (6.2.8) show that, for all nonzero flows, prices will now equal the marginal rates of substitution. The price system will become consistent in the sense that the direct exchange rate for any two commodities equals the quotient of their prices in terms of a third good. As a consequence, the resource constraints can be expressed in terms of any one of the goods, arbitrarily chosen as numéraire, and added over all goods. The result is the familiar budget constraint. The price we pay for these simplifications is that exchange flows at the various trading posts become indeterminate; it is now irrelevant to what extent apples are traded against nuts, oranges, or gold dust. From the point of view of monetary theory, the neoclassical system has often been criticized for being essentially a barter theory. In the light of these considerations this criticism does not seem valid. Its basic shortcoming is rather that the choice between barter and monetary exchange, and, in the case of monetary exchange, the choice of the medium (or media) of exchange, are matters of economic indifference. As a consequence, a neoclassical system is unable to give an explicit analysis of monetization and monetary services.

Finally, starting again from the randomly assigned transaction cost rates, we reduce these rates to zero for one commodity, denoted m, leaving all others unchanged. Perhaps surprisingly, the availability of just one good with zero transaction costs is enough to guarantee consistency of the equilibrium price system in the sense defined above. Once consistency is assured, further conclusions can be drawn. First, if a good with zero transaction costs is available, it is inefficient to use any other good as medium of exchange. The commodity m will thus be elevated to the status of the general medium of exchange, called "money." With consistent prices, we only have to compare transaction costs in the various markets, and these, by assumption, are always lower for m. All nonmonetary goods will thus flow directly from the initial resource owner to the final consumer. Second, there will never be an advantage in using direct barter instead of monetary exchange; the nonmonetary trading posts may just as well be closed down. Third, all commodity flows can again be arranged as if the individual were under no constraint to balance his accounts in each market separately; an aggregate budget constraint is all that matters. We are thus close to a neoclassical model, but with a determinate monetary exchange network.

It should be noted that even in the last case money is still commodity money, being currently supplied and consumed. As a consequence, the money of this section, even if it can be transferred without cost, is not neutral and the quantity theory of money (in the sense of proportionate effects of the money supply on prices) does not apply. If all quantities of the money commodity in people's endowments were exactly doubled, commodity prices, expressed in this commodity money, would not necessarily double. This reflects the old insight, familiar to classical and neoclassical economists, that the quantity theory and the neutrality postulate do not apply to, say, a gold standard world.

6.3. Money stocks and money flows in an integrated economy

The preceding analysis was restricted to flows. It had no room for assets and thus for money stocks. Since it could accommodate only goods having direct utility for *somebody* in the economy (though not necessarily for everybody), it also had no room for token money. This limitation will now be lifted by giving the model a time dimension.

The elements of the solution can again be visualized in terms of a simple example. Suppose A produces good X and consumes Y, while B produces Y and consumes X, all in equivalent amounts. In a timeless world, exchange would pose no problems. But now suppose that, for some reason, A produces and consumes during even weeks, while B's activities take place during odd weeks. Exchange takes place at the end of each week. Without inventories, trade at each weekend would be unbalanced, as indicated in figure 6.3.1(a). In a market economy, this cannot be; there must be a quid pro quo in every transaction. Balance can be provided in various ways. Thus exchange could be concentrated on even weekends, as in figure 6.3.1(b), Y being stored one week by the producer and another week by the consumer. Alternatively, exchange could take place on odd weekends with X being held in stock. Still another possibility is the introduction of a third commodity that is neither consumed nor produced, perhaps consisting of worthless slips of paper called "drafts" or "bank notes," as described in figure 6.3.1(c). In this case, both X and Y can be transferred without storage, but instead A and B have to store bank notes, and there are also additional transfers of bank notes. The optimal arrangement will depend on a comparison of transaction and storage costs in the three (and possibly other) cases. The new element consists in the appearance of storage costs (or yields) as one of the determinants of the optimal exchange arrangement. Depending on the set of transaction and storage costs (yields), this optimal exchange arrangement may involve the use of token money. Again, linear programming makes it possible to generalize this dichotomized model to

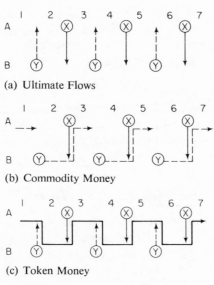

(a) Ultimate Flows

(b) Commodity Money

(c) Token Money

Figure **6.3.1**
Exchange Arrangements over Time

many traders and many goods, including money and other financial assets (Niehans, 1970). I shall not do this here but proceed directly to a fully integrated stock/flow model.

I again use a stationary-motion model for a year of h days closely similar to the model used in chapters 4 and 5. The present variant will be more general in the sense that full monetization is not assumed but rather derived as an important special case along with barter and other exchange arrangements. The present model also is a multicommodity model. On the other hand, it is more special in the sense that it abstracts from time preference, credit, and interest. Whoever finds it interesting to incorporate these features should find it easy to do so, following the example of chapters 4 and 5.

For Q commodities and h days the individual is assumed to maximize the utility function

$$U = U(x_1^1, \cdots x_q^t, \cdots x_Q^h), \tag{6.3.1}$$

given an endowment $(\bar{x}_1^1, \cdots \bar{x}_q^t, \cdots \bar{x}_Q^h)$. In addition to consumption flows, x_q^t, purchases, z_{qk}^t, and sales, y_{qk}^t, the optimization process now has to determine stocks, s_q^t. The daily holding cost per unit of good q will be denoted γ_q, assumed to be invariant over time. Storage costs are again interpreted as a physical shrinkage. As in the preceding section, transaction costs are assumed to arise in the form of inputs of commodity Q. For every good except Q, the resource constraints can be written

$$x_q^t - \bar{x}_q^t = \sum_k^Q (p_{kq}^t y_{kq}^t - y_{qk}^t) - (s_q^{t+1} - s_q^t) - \gamma_q s_q^t. \tag{6.3.2}$$

$$q = 1 \cdots (Q - 1)$$

$$t = 1 \cdots h$$

The h resource constraints for commodity Q include additional terms reflecting transaction costs:

$$x_Q^t - \bar{x}_Q^t = \sum_k^Q (p_{kQ}^t y_{kQ}^t - y_{Qk}^t) - \sum_q^Q \sum_k^Q (c_q + c_k p_{qk}^t) y_{qk}^t$$
$$- (s_Q^{t+1} - s_Q^t) - \gamma_Q s_Q^t. \tag{6.3.3}$$

Since this is supposed to be a stationary-motion economy, terminal stocks are required to be equal to initial stocks, $s_q^h = s_q^0$, but neither of them is exogenously given. Of course, all stocks and flows must be non-negative: $x_q^t \geqq 0$, $y_{qk}^t \geqq 0$, $s_q^t \geqq 0$.

It can be left to the reader to write out the Lagrange expression. The Kuhn-Tucker conditions on consumption and sales are identical, respectively, to (6.2.7) and (6.2.8), except that the variables now carry a time superscript. The new element is the conditions for stocks. These can be derived as

$$[(1 - \gamma_q)\lambda_q^t - \lambda_q^{t-1}]s_q^t = 0, \qquad \frac{\lambda_q^t - \lambda_q^{t-1}}{\lambda_q^t} \leqq \gamma_q, \qquad s_q^t \geqq 0. \qquad (6.3.4)$$

Not surprisingly, this is identical to the condition for commodity stocks derived in chapter 4 (4.4.7), except that we now have one such condition for each of many goods, all of which are potential media of exchange.

Once each individual has decided on his stocks and flows for given market conditions by solving the above optimization problem, market equilibrium is established in the way described in the preceding section by the interplay of individuals in the market. Again the resulting market equilibrium will determine which goods, if any, are used as media of exchange. The only additional element is the observation that this depends not only on transaction costs, but also on holding costs (or yields). Even a commodity with very low transaction costs will not be used as money if its holding costs are high enough, and vice versa. In general, there is no way of identifying the best medium of exchange by just looking at the characteristics of the various commodities as expressed in transaction and holding cost rates. Whether a given commodity will be used as a medium of exchange in a given transaction depends, among other things, on commodity prices. Prices, however, are only known once the whole market equilibrium is determined. As a consequence, only the resulting equilibrium can tell to what extent a given commodity will be used as money. In special cases, however, more specific statements can be made. This is illustrated by the following discussion.

Suppose we start again by assigning positive random values to transaction and storage cost rates, resulting in a pattern of exchange flows and stocks without any particular monetary characteristics. In contrast to the timeless case, certain goods may now be exchanged and held in stock even though they fail to appear in anybody's utility function. Their utility is of a purely indirect nature, being derived from their efficiency as media of exchange. Since they are not consumed, the current (flow) endowments are all used up by storage costs. By assigning low enough values to the respective transaction and storage costs, it is always possible to make one of these goods, again designated m, the general medium of exchange. This will then be token money.[9] The current endowments with token money cover the phenomenon of "seigniorage" for a stationary economy. If there is some attrition of the money stock, those who are able to supply the flow of replacement money obtain a steady stream of other goods and services from those who wear out the money but do not have the power to replace it.

---

9. If the endowment flows of a token money are positive, there must still be some storage costs to make the model stationary over the year. In this case prices will be such that the resulting demand for money stocks is just high enough to make attrition equal to the new supply.

We now assume that money, in addition to being token money, has zero transaction costs. Inspection of the programming problem shows that the system then becomes homogeneous of degree zero in the given monetary resources $\bar{x}_m^t$ for all t, and in money prices p_{km}^t for all t and k.[10] We thus end up with neutral money and the quantity theory. While for each money user at given prices such a money has a positive marginal (flow) value, measured by λ_m^t, a general increase of all monetary endowments in the same proportion will leave everybody's utility unaffected, all λ_m^t moving inversely to money prices. The absence of direct utility and transaction costs for money thus appears as the crucial assumption for neutrality. If desired, the system can now be dichotomized in the neoclassical way.[11]

Finally, let us suppose there is a token money for which there are no current endowment flows, which means that $\bar{x}_m^t = 0$. Correspondingly holding costs must be zero ($\gamma_m = 0$); otherwise the terminal stock could not equal the initial stock. The economy can now be thought to be equipped with an arbitrary stock of such a "perfect money,"

$$\overline{M} = \sum_i^n {}_is_m^t. \qquad (t = 1 \cdots h)$$

This fixes the equilibrium values of absolute money prices and individual cash balances at every moment of time. Since the marginal stock value of money measured by $(\lambda_m^t - \lambda_m^{t-1})/\lambda_m^t$ is now zero (see equation [6.3.4]), the economy is satiated with cash balances. This is the highly special limiting case envisaged in the neoclassical approach to monetary equilibrium but now made determinate by transaction costs on nonmonetary goods.

In this chapter the neoclassical multicommodity system was extended to include transaction and storage costs, providing a general equilibrium theory of exchange. Within this framework, various exchange systems, ranging from no exchange to multilateral barter and further on to various forms of monetization, could be constructed by suitable assumptions about transaction and storage costs. Within its confines, the transaction cost approach is thus seen to be able to deal effectively with three basic problems of monetary theory, inasmuch as it (1) provides full integration of monetary and value theory, (2) gives an explicit analysis of the services of money, and (3) includes the neutral money of the neoclassical theory as a limiting case.

10. In the resource constraint for m, with zero consumption, a doubling of $\bar{x}_m^t$ will be reflected in a doubling of stocks of the money prices of other goods p_{km}^t and also of the money flows y_{mk}^t, while the commodities exchanged for money y_{km}^t are unchanged. In all other resource constraints, the money flows are doubled while the price of money in terms of goods is cut in half, leaving their product unchanged. With unchanged commodity flows and zero transaction costs on money, transaction costs in the constraint for q are not affected either.
11. It should be noted that this is quite different from the dichotomy postulated in section 6.1. For one thing, the latter did not involve neutrality of money.

Seven
MONEY AS A MEDIUM OF ACCOUNT

Introduction

The choice or construction of a "standard of value" was one of the leading themes of classical economics; Ricardo debated it with his friends, and himself, to the end of his days. In this chapter I shall return to this topic, though from a different direction. Ricardo was concerned with a problem of analytical technique, namely with the best way to compare economic aggregates if relative prices are subject to change. I shall be concerned with a problem of economic life, namely with the best way for economic agents to measure prices and incomes. In the preceding chapters money was considered as a medium of exchange, that is, in view of its ability to be exchanged for other goods. I shall now take up the other basic function of money, namely to serve as a medium of account. By a medium of account or "numéraire" I shall mean a good in terms of which prices are quoted and accounts are kept. It is the good that appears in the numerator of the prices of all other goods, while its own unit price is 1 by definition.[1]

In most cases, and for good reasons to be discussed presently, the same good serves both as medium of exchange and as medium of account. It is logically conceivable, however, that the two functions are performed by different goods, and such cases have actually occurred. For example, bank notes may serve as medium of exchange while accounts are kept in terms of ounces of gold. It is even possible that the medium of account, at first sight, appears to be no good at all, being purely abstract in nature. Thus certain prices in England were traditionally quoted in guineas, even though guineas had long vanished from the scene as economic goods, except perhaps as collectors items whose prices, characteristically, have no rela-

---

1. Money is here called a medium and not, as customary, a unit of account because, clearly, money itself is not a unit, but the good whose unit is used as the unit of account. For an illuminating sample of economists' notions—often profound-sounding but confused—about the concept of a unit of account see the references in Eagly (1964).

tionship to their services as medium of account. In such cases it is necessary, however, to fix the price of at least one economic good in terms of the abstract unit of account. Thus it was specified that 1 pound sterling equals 20/21 guineas. In this way what seems to be an abstract unit is, in fact, firmly tied to the universe of economic goods. For truly abstract media of account there is no room in the economic system. We thus have no reason to give them any thought.

In the economic writings about media of account there are two distinct strands. On one hand there is a tradition to consider the numéraire as a concept without operational significance.[2] On the other hand, most older treatises on money were careful to explain how the use of a unit of account simplifies the price system and thus increases economic efficiency.[3] There is also a long history of references to the economic advantages of a unit of account that is reasonably stable in value, and it is said to be one of the evils of inflation that money ceases to be an efficient medium of account.[4] It seems clear that these contradictory propositions consider the medium of account in the context of different, though often not explicitly specified, models. An effort to disentangle the various strands of the arguments will be made on the following pages. The discussion will be concerned with the question whether the choice and use of a medium of account can be explained as the result of economic considerations.

The key concept will be what may be called "accounting costs." These will turn out to play a role for the medium of account similar to the role transaction costs were shown to play for the medium of exchange. Just like transaction costs, accounting costs are meant to reflect various things. Basically, they express the fact that it takes time and trouble to compare prices. From a fundamentalist point of view they are largely costs of search and information, thus resulting from uncertainty. A full analysis of accounting costs may thus require a theory of decision-making under uncertainty. As in the case of transaction costs, some progress can fortunately be made by assuming that each individual aims at a predetermined, and possibly zero, level of uncertainty. The accounting costs are then defined as the resources that have to be spent to reach this level, and they can be treated like any other input in a world of perfect certainty. While this is a drastic simplification of the complex problems of accounting costs, it still permits a meaningful analysis of essential points. This analysis, however, will be less detailed and rigorous than in the preceding chapter in the case of transaction costs. It will also be more tentative and exploratory, being a first systematic attack on a problem largely ignored by modern economic theory.

2. It has recently been reaffirmed by Patinkin (1965, p. 16).
3. J. St. Mill (1857, 2:3 ff.) and Jevons (1875, p. 5) are representative examples.
4. See Jevons (1875, pp. 38 ff.), Marshall (1923, p. 15 f.), and Wicksell (1935, p. 7).

In section 7.1 the use of a medium of account is considered from the point of view of simplifying the price system. In section 7.2 it will be argued that the choice of the medium of account may be relevant for the amount of variability in prices. Section 7.3 is about the problem of measuring income in a capitalist economy and the dilemma created by inflation, even if it is fully expected, in such an economy: Either there is a misallocation of resources resulting from money illusion, or there is an accounting cost for using deflators, or there is the cost of using an inefficient medium of exchange. Section 7.4 deals with the corresponding problem for unexpected (or, better, uncertainly expected) inflation, which raises the question of escalator clauses.

7.1. The accounting costs of a complex price system

The subject of this section is the classical argument that the use of a general medium of account increases the efficiency of the economy by permitting a simplification of the price system. This argument can be made more precise in terms of the one-period flow version of the multilateral barter model used in chapter 6 (see sec. 6.2). There is a trading post for every pair of commodities. For q commodities there are, in general, $(q/2)(q-1)$ prices, counting $p_{hk} = 1/p_{kh}$ as one price. For the present purpose I shall remain close to the classical model by abstracting from transaction costs. If accounting costs are absent as well, the exchange arrangements in such a system were shown in chapter 6 to be indeterminate. There is an infinite number of indifferent ways to assign the equilibrium set of exchange flows to the various trading posts. A direct exchange of apples against oranges can always be replaced by an indirect exchange of apples against nuts and nuts against oranges. We may thus assume that the assignment of transactions to trading posts, within the constraints of the equilibrium solution, is random. Very likely, most trading posts will be active, though perhaps with small trading volumes.

In equilibrium, the prices quoted at the various trading posts will be consistent in the sense that the price of apples in terms of nuts times the price of nuts in terms of oranges equals the price of apples in terms of oranges, that is,

$$p_{gh}p_{hk} = p_{gh}/p_{kh} = p_{gk}.$$

If the price system were not consistent, everybody could increase his utility ad infinitum by arbitrage, which is not compatible with equilibrium. It should be noted that consistency of the price system results from the fact that individuals are constantly alert to arbitrage opportunities, monitoring carefully any deviation from the consistency rule.

Into this system I now introduce accounting costs. For the present purpose these may be regarded as depending simply on the number of market prices an individual has to watch. If accounting costs are a penny for each price, an economy of 1,000 commodities, each traded at 999 trading posts, would impose on each household an accounting cost of slightly less than $5,000. Even seemingly trivial accounting costs can thus add up to substantial amounts. However, $(1/2)(q - 1)(q - 2)$ markets are, in fact, redundant. Without economic loss, the whole exchange program can be carried out at just $q - 1$ trading posts by exchanging each of $q - 1$ commodities against the qth commodity serving as the medium of account. In the above-given numerical illustration the aggregate accounting costs can thereby be reduced to about $10.

It should be noted that the advantages of a common medium of account can only be realized if the medium of account is also elevated to the role of the common medium of exchange. Clearly, as long as all $(1/2)q(q - 1)$ potential trading posts are active, it does not help to provide each individual with a price list giving all prices just in terms of apples; he would still have to take the time and trouble to compute the prices at all other trading posts from this basic set. The saving of accounting costs only materializes if the other markets are closed down. While in chapter 6 the monetization of the economy was explained as the result of particular sets of transaction costs, it is here explained as the result of accounting costs.

However, the simplification of the price system only explains why some common medium of account is used. It does not explain which commodity is so used. On the basis of the present argument, every commodity is as suitable as any other. In order to obtain a determinate choice of the medium of account, the concept of accounting costs has to be provided with additional dimensions.

The preceding argument did not include transaction costs. In the presence of transaction costs, as was shown in chapter 6, the price system will no longer be consistent. This reflects the fact that the concentration of all exchange activity in $q - 1$ markets may involve an economic loss. As long as multilateral barter is efficient from the point of view of transaction costs, the use of a common medium of exchange (in order to have a common medium of account) involves a cost. It is conceivable that this loss is more than offset by the saving in accounting costs, but an analysis of this problem would require a model with both transaction and accounting costs. In any case, once we have to consider transaction costs, it is no longer generally true that the use of a medium of account lowers costs by simplifying the price system. However, whenever transaction costs are such that the economy is fully monetized even in the absence of accounting costs, it is evident that efficiency requires the common medium of exchange to be used also as the medium of account. In the timeless economy considered in this section, every other arrangement would involve unnecessary accounting costs and thus be inefficient. It will be seen below that in an economy with a time dimension it may well be efficient to divorce the medium of account from the medium of exchange.

7.2. The accounting costs of price variability

7.2.1. FLUCTUATIONS IN RELATIVE PRICES. I shall now extend the concept of accounting costs by assuming that these costs depend not only on the number of relevant prices but also on their variability. The accounting cost of a highly variable price would thus be higher than the cost of a stationary price. It is easily seen that the variability of absolute prices does indeed depend on the choice of the medium of account. As a consequence, this choice can be imagined to be determined by the economic calculus. The nature of this calculus will now be explained in more detail.

I begin with fluctuations in relative prices in the absence of inflation. Consider a stationary-motion general equilibrium system without transaction costs. The accounting cost argument of the preceding section showed that it is efficient to trade all other commodities against a common medium of exchange in such a case. The question is which commodity should be chosen for this purpose. The price variability criterion can be made intuitively clear by a simple example. Suppose endowments consist only of wheat and strawberries. For both goods the endowments are highly seasonal, but storage costs for wheat are low, while for strawberries they are very high. As a consequence, the terms of trade between the two commodities show a marked seasonal fluctuation, strawberries being relatively cheap in summer while wheat is cheap in winter. It is not clear, in detail, how price variability has to be measured to make sure that accounting costs are monotonically related to it. It may be reasonably assumed, however, that the squared variations in individual commodity prices will somehow have to be weighted with the shares of these commodities in total income. With respect to these shares I assume that the annual income from strawberries is much smaller than the annual income from wheat.[5]

If, under these conditions, strawberries are chosen as the numéraire, their absolute price will be constant while the wheat price will vary. Since the weight of strawberries is low while the weight of wheat is high, most any reasonable measure of price variability will show a relatively high value. If, on the other hand, wheat is chosen as the numéraire, the price with the high weight will be constant, while the variable price carries a low weight. As a consequence, overall price variability will be low. To the

---

5. In general, since relative prices are changing, the income shares, too, will depend on the choice of the numéraire, but the above assumption is taken to mean that wheat income clearly dominates for any numéraire.

extent accounting costs depend on price variability, wheat would thus be a more efficient numéraire than strawberries.

It would be easy, but at the present point also unrewarding, to translate this argument into algebra and to extend it to any number of goods. The important point is that for given fluctuations in relative prices the overall variability of money prices depends on the choice of the medium of account. To the extent accounting costs depend on price variability, the minimization of accounting costs thus provides a criterion for the choice of the medium of account.

Again it is difficult to name characteristics that are likely to make a commodity a promising candidate for the monetary role without looking at the price system as a whole. In particular, it is not generally true that the appropriate medium of account is simply the commodity with the highest share in the value of the endowment as the wheat/strawberry example seems to suggest. In fact, the optimal medium of account, from the present point of view, might well be a commodity that, in itself, accounts for only a small share of aggregate income, provided its relative prices in terms of other commodities are sufficiently stable. It may thus turn out that something like gold, for example, is a better medium of exchange than wheat or petroleum.

So far there has been no mention of token money. Token money has the property that the supply, for every day of the year, can be controlled by the state, in the present model within the stationary-motion constraint whereby the money supply must be the same for a given calendar day of successive years. Couldn't token money be made to provide a better medium of account than any commodity money? It is easily seen that this indeed is the case. Suppose we have selected, according to the above accounting cost calculus, the best medium of account from among the various commodities. If this optimal commodity money is now replaced by a token money, it is easy, in principle, to control the token money supply in such a way that the aggregate variability of prices in terms of token money is no larger than the variability of prices in terms of the optimal commodity money. All the government has to do is to supply the token money at such a rate that the price of the optimal money commodity is constant over time. In fact, it will usually be possible to do somewhat better by producing appropriate fluctuations in the token money price of the optimal money commodity. A token money thus has the potential of being as good or better as a medium of account than any commodity money.

On the other hand it is easy to supply token money in such a way that it is inferior to the best commodity money or, for that matter, to any commodity money. All the government has to do is to make the fluctuations in the money supply large enough. This is a conclusion that will also emerge in other contexts: An ideal token money is superior to any commodity money, but token money also introduces the risk of doing worse than a reasonably well-selected commodity money.

7.2.2. BALANCED INFLATION. While the preceding argument applies to a stationary-motion pattern of the money supply, the same type of reasoning can be used in the case of an inflating token currency. Suppose there are still no bonds, and both endowments and tastes follow a stationary-motion pattern. The supply of token money, however, is assumed to increase at a constant daily rate π through the payment of interest on cash balances at the same rate $\rho = \pi$. It was shown in section 2.6 that in the absence of accounting costs all real variables of such a system, including relative prices and real cash balances, are the same as under a stationary money supply. The only effect of monetary expansion is a steady rate of fully expected inflation. The economy is in neutral inflation.

Now consider accounting costs, assumed to depend on the variability of prices. With a constant inflationary trend superimposed on the steady-motion pattern of prices, the individual can choose between two alternatives. Either he extends his optimization problem to an infinite number of years with prices different from one year to the next, or else he follows the procedure described in section 2.6 and reduces the problem to one for a sequence of identical years by deflating all prices by the corresponding rate of inflation. In both cases there are accounting costs. In the first case these result from the necessity to solve an infinite-horizon optimization problem instead of a one-year problem. In the second case the accounting costs arise from the necessity to deflate money prices. In either case the costs could have been avoided by maintaining a noninflationary pattern of the money supply. In view of accounting costs, even expected inflation at a constant rate, fully compensated by the rate of interest on cash balances, turns out to be nonneutral. This means that in an inflationary environment every individual, no matter how well he is adjusted to it, has a more complicated life, spending more resources on solving his economic problems, than under a stationary price pattern. This burden is more fundamental than the distortions in allocation and distribution arising from unexpected inflation, inasmuch as it is not transitory but permanent. It is also more fundamental than the reduction in real cash balances, inasmuch as it cannot be avoided by paying interest on cash balances. It may be argued that it is the most fundamental, if not necessarily the largest, economic burden of inflation.

7.3. Misallocation of resources under expected inflation

7.3.1. RELATIVE PRICES GIVEN: THE PROBLEM OF CAPITALIST INCOME AC-COUNTING. In the two preceding sections the medium of account was considered in its primary function as the "common denominator" (which means, mathematically, the common numerator) of market prices. In modern capitalist economies this becomes the basis of a secondary function, namely to serve as the medium in which income is measured. Because of this function, inflation may result in a misallocation of resources over time due to money illusion. This aspect will now have to be discussed.

Income is essentially a collection of different goods, evaluated in terms of a common medium of account. The use of the income concept is not inherent in any exchange economy. In fact, it is specific to the system we call capitalism. It is customary (and convenient) to distinguish two types of private agents, namely households and firms. A household is defined by the fact that it reckons directly in terms of subjective utility. In an economy consisting only of households the economic calculus does not require the concept of income. Factor endowments and technology of each household determine its production possibilities. These, together with market prices, determine the consumption opportunities. Optimal consumption is determined by confronting these with the utility function. There is no need to measure income.

This is changed with the appearance of firms. The existence of firms gives rise to a two-stage decision-making process. In the first stage, the firm maximizes the income from the resources obtained from its owners in the light of its technology and the expected market conditions. This income is distributed among the owners according to contractual provisions. In the second stage the owner-households maximize utility subject to the income received from the firm together with whatever other endowments they may have. In this case income plays a crucial part in the economic calculus as the link between the two stages.

It is easy to imagine an economy without firms, consisting of the households of peasants (possibly up to the scale of large manors), craftsmen, merchants, and laborers. This is indeed the picture of the precapitalist economy. Except for the presence of producers, this was also the type of economy described by the exchange models of the preceding chapters. In such a system, balanced inflation does not give rise to any particular distortion in the allocation of resources over time, though it may increase accounting costs as pointed out in the preceding section.

The modern industrial economies, however, to the extent they are market economies, are characterized by the dominance of firms over households in production, enabling individuals with different utility functions to pool their resources for a common venture. It is evident that the separation of firms from households, originating probably from the joint ventures in Mediterranean trade, was one of the fundamental economic advances of the last thousand years. It is also clear that this system depends on the possibility of keeping income accounts (or, what amounts to the same thing, capital accounts) in terms of some medium of account. In fact, it was precisely this observation which caused Marx to call such an economic system "capitalism." If it becomes impossible or inefficient, possibly because of inflation, to express income in terms of a medium of account, the capitalist technique of organizing an economy will have to be abandoned and replaced by another system. This is why the performance of money as a unit of account is of far-reaching significance for the evolution of the economic system.

This argument will now be made more precise. Consider a monetized economy with a constant, fully expected rate of neutral inflation in the familiar sense that the expansion of the money supply is matched by the payment of interest on cash balances, while the coupon on bonds and tax/transfer rates are adjusted to inflation, thus leaving relative prices unchanged (see section 5.2). If this is a capitalist economy with firms and households, the allocation of resources over time has two aspects.

On one hand, the firms have to decide about their investment plans. In a profit-oriented system they will do this by maximizing the present value of future quasi-rents, each properly discounted. This implies that they are also maximizing the income accruing to the owner-households in the sense of a permanent constant stream. This aspect of resource allocation is not affected by neutral inflation. It is true that the money value of future quasi-rents, each valued at concurrent prices, will be inflated. At the same time, however, the rate of inflation raises the nominal rates of interest, thus increasing the discount factor for each year in the same proportion as the quasi-rent. As a consequence, the plan that maximizes the present value of the firm in the absence of inflation will still maximize it with inflation.[6]

The other aspect of allocation over time has to do with the choice of households between present and future consumption. It is here where neutral inflation introduces potential distortions. The firms, by stating their profits, present owner-households with a set of possible consumption paths over time. If the investment problem has been correctly solved, each of these consumption paths is efficient in the sense that consumption cannot be increased in any period without a reduction in at least one other period. With money as a unit of account, these consumption possibilities will be stated in money terms. In making their choices among these consumption paths, households may be assumed to be guided by an intertemporal utility function in terms of present and future consumption bundles. These bundles are defined in terms of physical quantities of commodities (with relative prices constant, consumption in each period can be measured in terms of any one commodity, say, wheat). The distortion problem arises because the consumption possibilities, presented by the firms to the households, are stated in money terms, while household preferences are stated in real terms.

6. Hanke, Carver, and Bugg (1975) have recently stressed the point that the results of a cost-benefit analysis are distorted if quasi-rents are evaluated at constant, non-inflating prices while the rate of interest is taken from an inflationary economy.

The problem can be resolved in one of three possible ways (or possibly a combination of them). The household can treat its money income as if it related to real commodities. In this case, it is said to be suffering from "money illusion." Provided consumption in a given period is never an inferior good, money illusion will distort present consumption upward at the expense of future consumption. Resources are used up that would have been necessary to maintain the capital required to provide for the hoped-for future consumption. In future periods the individual will thus be disappointed to find that money income is insufficient to buy the hoped-for consumption bundle; he is left with an inefficient allocation of consumption over time. This phenomenon became well recognized and was widely discussed in the wake of the German inflation after World War I. For the accountant it appears in the form of a firm that determines its profit distributions in such a way that capital, in money terms, just remains intact. Such a firm will later find that its owners have actually dissaved, consuming capital in the guise of profits.[7]

Alternatively, each of the money values of possible consumption can be deflated by the corresponding rate of inflation. In an ideal world, the distortion of resource allocation is hereby avoided. The actual situation, however, will hardly ever be ideal. What is more important, even in the best case the deflation of future money values will cause accounting costs. It is hard to know how large these might be. I suspect they could become very serious. In all his planning for the future, including insurance, pension plans, savings, mortgages, and the like, the consumer would be involved in almost continuous compound-interest computations, either absorbing considerable time, skill, and/or equipment or else resulting in error. In the income accounting of firms it is possible, at least in principle if not always in practice, to avoid the misstatement of income by appropriate accounting techniques. Accountancy has, in fact, produced a large literature on the subject.[8] But again these techniques impose an accounting cost on the economy, well illustrated by the resources that have gone into writing, reading, and debating (and to some extent even applying) that literature. It is also generally agreed that the practical results are quite imperfect; considerable distortions seem to remain.[9]

The third way to resolve the problem consists in abandoning the use of token money as a medium of exchange, thus reverting to a commodity-money system. Token money would be replaced by gold, cigarettes, and the like. This, too, would avoid the intertemporal misallocation of resources and would also avoid the accounting costs of using deflators. However,

7. On the possible implications for business fluctuations, see Haberler (1958, pp. 49 ff.), with references to Schiff and Schmidt.
8. The most elementary step is, of course, to base depreciation on market value instead of initial cost.
9. For a recent discussion see Fabricant (1971).

there would be an economic burden from employing a monetary arrangement that, by assumption, is not efficient in the absence of inflation. Again the burden may be large, as illustrated by the persistence with which even highly inflationary economies seem to cling to the use of token money. The general conclusion is that inflation, even if it is of the (highly artificial) balanced type, involves a capitalist economy in economic losses of one kind or another.

7.3.2. RELATIVE PRICES VARIABLE: THE INDEX-NUMBER PROBLEM. Inflation also raises an index-number problem: Which price or combination of prices needs to be held constant to avoid the inflationary misallocation of resources? Which price or combination of prices should be used to deflate money income if inflation occurs? The preceding discussion has been limited to the case of balanced inflation where relative prices follow a stationary-motion path, independent of the rate of inflation. Under these conditions the index-number problem has a trivial solution: Every individual price and every linear combination of prices can serve equally well. In reality, inflation tends to be accompanied by changes in relative prices, partly because the newly created money is not issued in payment of interest on cash balances with fully adjusted coupons and tax/transfer rates, and partly because there are always parallel changes in endowments, technology and tastes. Under these more realistic conditions the construction of the appropriate deflator is more difficult; the index-number problem becomes nontrivial. This problem will now be briefly considered.

Consider a utility function for q commodities over h periods

$$U = U(x_1^1, \cdots x_i^t, \cdots x_q^h),$$

and an arbitrary consumption bundle $\overset{o}{x}_1^1, \cdots \overset{o}{x}_i^t, \cdots \overset{o}{x}_q^h$. Now select any period T and contemplate variations in $x_1^T, \cdots x_q^T$, leaving consumption unchanged at $\overset{o}{x}_i^t$ for all other periods $t \neq T$. Some of these variations will have the property that they leave U unchanged; the individual is moving along an indifference surface. Other variations will result in higher or lower utilities. The result of this experiment is a partial indifference map for period T, the remainder of the consumption path being fixed.

In order for the consumer to select a given point on this map, he must find himself somewhere on the budget plane that is tangent to the indifference surface at this point. We wish to characterize each of these budget planes by the amount of real income it represents. Real income is obtained by dividing money income by some price index. The problem is that the ranking of real incomes is generally different for different index numbers. Consider figure 7.3.1. If real income is measured in terms of milk by deflating money income by the price of milk (that is, by the vertical intercept of the budget line), then real income is higher in A than in B. If real income is measured in terms of wheat (that is, by the horizontal

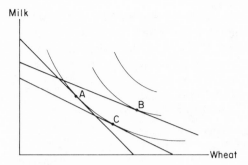

Figure **7.3.1**
Measurement of Real Income

intercept of the budget line), the reverse is true. If some combination of the two prices were used, the result would presumably be somewhere in between. What we seek is a price index number with the property that the resulting real incomes, obtained by deflating money income by this number, are monotonically related to utility. In particular, real income should stay constant for movements along an indifference surface.

It is clear that none of the individual commodities entering into the utility function can be a perfect medium of account or, to use the classical term, standard of value in the sense that its price, if used as a deflator, converts money income into the desired measure of real income. If in figure 7.3.1 the individual moves along the same indifference curve from A to C, neither income in terms of wheat nor income in terms of milk stays constant. Remarkably, however, token money may *conceivably* be a perfect medium of account and money income may possibly be a correct indicator of utility. This is basically because money does not enter into the utility function. While relative commodity prices are determined for every point on the indifference map by the slope of the indifference surface, absolute prices in terms of token money can, in principle, be freely chosen. For a given indifference map, therefore, it is always possible to vary the absolute price level in such a way that money income stays constant as the individual moves along an indifference curve.[10]

A numerical illustration, while trivial, may help at this point. Suppose in figure 7.3.1 the quantities demanded, x_m and x_w, and the relative prices, p_m/p_w, in the indifferent situations A and C are as follows:

	x_m	x_w	p_m/p_w
A	3	3	1
C	1.5	5	2

10. Adjustments may also have to be made in the price levels for other periods. A movement along the indifference curve for period T with the rest of the consumption path unchanged will, in general, change the marginal rates of substitution and thus the required relative prices for the other periods. In order to keep money income for these other periods constant, absolute prices will have to be adjusted.

Suppose further that the money prices in A were $p_m^A = 1$ and $p_w^A = 1$. It follows that in order to keep money expenditure at C, since it is indifferent to A, at the same level (namely 6) it had at A, the new money prices must be $p_m^C = 1.50$ and $p_w^C = 0.75$. Such an absolute price level can be found for every point along an indifference curve. This price level can, in principle, be realized by supplying the appropriate amount of token money at every point of time, which means that token money can be made to be superior to any commodity money as a medium of account. The same point can be expressed by saying that for any arbitrary variation in money prices there is some number that, if used as deflator, converts money income into a true measure of utility.

This proposition is, however, subject to two serious limitations. First, if the individuals in an economy do not have identical utility functions, different individuals will generally require different deflators. No monetary policy will then make money income a correct measure of utility for everybody. Second, even for a single individual the appropriate deflator can generally not be expressed in an index-number formula. In fact, as Samuelson (1947, p. 154 f.) has shown, such an index number can be constructed only for a limited class of utility functions.

A particularly simple example is $U = \sqrt{xy}$. In this case a price index of the form $p = \sqrt{p_x p_y}$ satisfies the requirement. To see this, consider expenditure

$$E = p_x x + p_y y = p\left(\frac{p_x}{p} x + \frac{p_y}{p} y\right) = p\left(\sqrt{\frac{p_x}{p_y}} x + \sqrt{\frac{p_y}{p_x}} y\right). \quad (7.3.1)$$

With utility maximization the marginal rate of substitution is equal to the price ratio, which for the given utility function means $p_x/p_y = y/x$. Substituting into expenditure, we obtain

$$E = p\left(\sqrt{\frac{y}{x}} x + \sqrt{\frac{x}{y}} y\right) = p(2\sqrt{xy}) = p(2U). \quad (7.3.2)$$

It follows that if p is held constant as the individual moves along an indifference curve, expenditure in money terms will also remain constant; constancy of the specified index number makes money a perfect medium of account.[11]

This is, however, a very special case. In general, the price policy that would make token money a perfect medium of account, if it exists, cannot be expressed in an index formula, and in view of the differences between

11. About classes of utility function for which a true index number can be constructed see the references in Samuelson (1947, p. 155) and Geary (1950). For the limiting case of a linear utility function $U = ax + by + c$ the Paasche price index satisfies the requirement. From utility maximization it follows that $a/b = p_x/p_y = \bar{p}_x/\bar{p}_y$ where $\bar{p}_x, \bar{p}_y$ are the given base prices. Hence, for the Paasche index $p = (p_x x + p_y y)/(\bar{p}_x x + \bar{p}_y y) = p_y/\bar{p}_y$, expenditure is $E = p_x x + p_y y = p_y[(a/b)x + y] = (\bar{p}_y/b)(U - c)p$. As long as p is held constant, a move along an indifference curve keeps E constant.

individuals it is unlikely to exist in the first place. No matter what index number is used to deflate money incomes, the resulting real incomes will generally not be correct measures of utility and thus involve the individual in a certain misallocation of resources over time. Furthermore, the more complex the index number formula, the higher the accounting costs will be.

While it is not possible, in general, to specify a perfect deflator, something on prices can nevertheless be said. If *all* money prices move up, it is clear that the performance of money as a medium of account can always be improved by a less inflationary policy; the reverse is true if all money prices fall. This is because changes of all prices in the same direction make it impossible for expenditures to stay constant for movements along an indifference curve, whatever its shape.[12] For money to be a satisfactory, if not perfect, medium of account, it is a necessary condition that there be no general inflation or deflation.

7.4. The costs of uncertain inflation: Escalator clauses

In the preceding section, expectations about future inflation were assumed to be perfectly certain and correct. In reality they are likely to be quite uncertain. Some implications of this uncertainty for the use of money as a medium of account will now be considered.

There are perhaps some reasons to believe that the uncertainty about the rate of inflation (as measured by, say, the standard deviation of the distribution of future rates) is positively related to the rate itself (as measured by, say, the mean of this distribution): If the mean is 100 percent per year, rates of 10 percent above or below the mean will probably be regarded as more likely than if the mean is around 10 percent. To the extent this is true, the following considerations will be more relevant for rapid inflation than for slow inflation.

One way of coping with the uncertainty of future prices is through futures markets. If somebody contracts for retirement benefits scheduled to be paid thirty years hence, he could, ideally, assure himself of their purchasing power by simultaneously buying his retirement market basket in the futures markets for meat, eggs, instant coffee, shoes, and housing. As a practical matter, futures markets of this sort do not exist, the actual futures markets being restricted to relatively few standardized commodities and rather short maturities. The only futures market that covers all maturities from a few hours to many decades is the market for money debts.[13] As a consequence, an individual dealing in the debt market has little

---

12. Any change in relative prices along an indifference curve causes income to rise in terms of at least one commodity. If the money price of that commodity has risen, income in terms of money must have risen, too.

13. The traditional monetary literature used to express this by saying that money serves as the standard for deferred payments.

opportunity to hedge his monetary commitment in the commodity futures markets.[14]

The typical substitute for more extensive commodity futures markets are escalator clauses, linking interest payments and repayment of principal (if any) to some price index.[15] Escalated money debts are similar to commodity futures contracts inasmuch as they stipulate a claim to future commodities. They differ from a commodity futures contract inasmuch as (1) the claim is not expressed in terms of an individual commodity, but in terms of a composite commodity defined by the weights of an index number; and (2) settlement is made in terms not of commodities but of money, which means that the transaction costs are different. Escalator clauses are like deflators in reverse: While the latter reduce the inflated market prices to a constant-purchasing-power basis, the former adjust the constant-purchasing-power prices to an inflating market.

Escalator clauses have three main fields of application. The primary field, as noted, is in debt contracts, both for private and government debt. A secondary application is in administered forward prices, fixed for several months or years at a time. Wage agreements are the most important and, at the present time, perhaps the only really important example. The price of petroleum set by the cartel of oil-producing countries may become another illustration. Such administered forward prices are fundamentally different from debt contracts inasmuch as they only specify the price while the quantity is left open. They are not an agreement to buy or sell anything, but fix just the price at which future transactions, if any, will take place. Still another application is in schedules for taxes and transfer payments. In this case the escalator clause is essentially a particular technique for the legislator to express its will, which, alternatively, could have been expressed by taking legislative action each year in the light of current inflation.

There has been some discussion about a fourth application, namely to government fiat money.[16] However, there seems to be general agreement that the monetary base, consisting of currency and central bank deposits should not be subject to escalation. One reason is the obvious technical difficulty in providing the equivalent of escalating bank notes and coins through the use of tokens, stamp money, and the like. The main reason is

14. In the precapitalist economy, debts like tithes, rents, and annuities were often expressed in terms of commodities. Such arrangements became obsolete with the advent of reasonably stable currencies, but they are being revived in proportion as the monetary system deteriorates. It may be conjectured that the fragmentary nature of commodity futures markets is largely due to the same factors that make money the preferred medium of exchange, namely the high transaction costs for commodities coming into existence many years from now. Another major factor may be the uncertainty about future technology, endowments, and tastes. It is indeed difficult to imagine a contract for an automobile to be delivered twenty years from now.

15. For a survey, see Finch (1956).

16. See Baumol (1966).

that an economy with an escalated monetary base would not be viable. Imagine some arbitrary disturbance in the price level above the equilibrium level. The government would be obliged to supply the owners of cash balances with a corresponding amount of additional money, thus ratifying the higher price level. There would thus be no force pulling prices back to their old level; the price level would become indeterminate. This does not mean, however, that the owners of cash balances cannot be protected against the inflationary tax. It only means that this protection cannot take the form of an escalator clause. In its place the government could follow the rule of using any additional money for the payment of interest on cash balances. Of course, there would still be the technical difficulty of paying interest on coins and bank notes, but the price level would now be determinate.

The economic effects of escalation can be summarized under six headings, namely (1) the elimination of distribution effects, (2) the reduction of risk, (3) the reduction of the output effects of changes in monetary policy, (4) the reduction of the inflationary tax, (5) the neutralization of an automatic stabilizer in the government budget, and (6) accounting costs. These effects will now be discussed in turn.

7.4.1. THE ELIMINATION OF DISTRIBUTION EFFECTS. In the absence of escalation, every acceleration of inflation involves a gain to debtors, but a loss to creditors. If the acceleration is fully expected, these gains and losses are reflected in the initial terms of the debt, particularly in a higher interest rate. As a consequence, they do not require any special attention, no matter how large. However, if the acceleration is unexpected, these gains and losses distort the distribution of income compared to what it would have been under perfect foresight. Escalator clauses eliminate, or at least reduce, this distortion. Of course, for every dollar's worth of goods someone has lost through inflation, there must be a dollar's worth of goods someone else has gained. The reduction of the distribution effects, therefore, is not an obvious gain for society as a whole. However, it may be argued, plausibly if not rigorously, that the hardships from losses count more heavily than the blessings from gains. A high variability of the income distribution with its unsettling effects on the structure of society may be regarded as an evil in itself. It seems to be on the basis of such arguments that escalation of debts has been advocated by illustrious economists like Stanley Jevons, Alfred Marshall, Irving Fisher, and Keynes.[17]

17. If the losses and the gains from unexpected inflation had the tendency to be concentrated in different classes of society, escalation could also be advocated on the basis of the argument that the gainers are somehow less deserving (because, say, they are richer, less industrious, etc.) than the losers. Remarkably, however, decades of research have revealed no major and persistent differences in the incidence of gains and losses among social classes. Almost everything seems to depend on the circumstances of individual cases and the nature of specific inflationary episodes. See Nordhaus (1973) and Niehans (1962).

7.4.2. THE REDUCTION OF RISK. There is a more rigorous way to derive a social benefit from escalation.[18] The availability of escalated bonds adds to the menu of debt instruments a new type of assets with low risk in real terms. Both the creditor and the debtor thus have additional options for their portfolio choice. Such new options cannot make them worse off and in most cases will make them better off. To make this more specific, suppose individuals have identical expectations about future rates of inflation, π, expressed by some distribution $F(\pi)$ with mean $\bar{\pi}$. Suppose a one-year escalated bond has the same mean yield, consisting of the basic interest and the expected value of the escalator adjustment, as a conventional bond. In this case, both the borrowers and the lenders, provided they are free from money illusion, will prefer the escalated bond, since it promises the same mean yield with lower variance in terms of goods. As a consequence, conventional bonds will disappear. Borrowers would issue them only if their mean yield were lower, and lenders would buy them only if their mean yield were higher, than the mean yield of escalated bonds. Both parties gain from the switch to escalated bonds. Under these circumstances the problem is not the existence of escalated bonds, but rather the existence of conventional bonds. Some countervailing forces will be noted presently.

The effect of escalation on the nominal rate of interest including the expected value of the escalator allowance is uncertain. Since escalation shifts both the supply curve and the demand curve for bonds to the right, there is no presumption that the bond yield with escalation will be either higher or lower than without escalation. The result will depend on differences in risk preference and price expectations between borrowers and lenders.[19] The effects of escalation on total saving will, for well-known reasons, also be uncertain, but a larger part of assets will be held in the form of interest-bearing debt and a smaller part will be held in the form of commodity inventories, capital goods, and equity. It is also likely that escalation will increase the average maturity of debts, increasing the willingness to enter into long-term commitments.[20]

The risk-reducing effects of escalation are subject to two important qualifications. First, escalated debt contracts are more difficult to state

18. See Sarnat (1973). A detailed theoretical analysis of index bonds is provided by Fischer (1975).

19. If the bond supply curve is not affected by escalation, the increased demand by lenders will, of course, lower the nominal rate of interest, including the escalator adjustment. Similarly, a monopolistic borrower may be able to lower his borrowing costs by offering escalated bonds. Keynes emphasized the potential savings for the government from this source.

20. Characteristically, the gradual extension of the Eurodollar market into long-term credits has been accompanied by the development of "roll-over" arrangements whereby the interest rate is adjusted to the current London interbank rate, usually every six months. While this is not strictly an escalation on the basis of the rate of inflation, it is economically closely related.

unambiguously than ordinary obligations. As a consequence, they are more likely to result in litigation, and the outcome of litigation, if any, is more uncertain. This is particularly important in view of the frequent changes in official index numbers. In addition, legislators and courts have an impressive record of declaring escalator clauses illegal or unenforceable from time to time, whenever this seems economically or politically expedient. It is quite likely that for moderate degrees of uncertainty about future inflation, this legal risk of escalated contracts dominates the risk-reducing effect described above.

The second qualification has to do with the selection of an appropriate escalator. The argument about the risk-reducing effect of escalation implies that there is indeed a price index that, if used as escalator, would make debt free from inflation risk in real terms for everybody. In fact, as was pointed out in the preceding section, such an index is unlikely to exist. Different people are likely to require different index numbers, and the same individual is likely to require a different index number in different situations. Some may actually prefer the price of a single commodity— say, cotton, wheat, or coal—to an index number. The logic of the risk-reduction argument thus tends to lead to a multiplicity of index numbers, each with its own range of applications. If the availability of one escalator clause, by increasing the range of options, increases welfare, then a choice of index numbers would seem to increase it even more. On the other hand, however, the parties would now have to haggle about index numbers in about the same way they haggle about other aspects of a contract, thus paying higher transaction costs. At the same time, as a consequence of more and more complex and more varied escalator clauses, the legal risks would rise further.

7.4.3. THE REDUCTION OF THE OUTPUT EFFECTS OF CHANGES IN MONE-TARY POLICY. Inasmuch as unexpected inflation affects distribution through debt contracts, its effects are a matter of equity and risk. I see no clear-cut effect on aggregate output, employment, and the price level. Correspondingly, the elimination of such effects through escalated debt contracts cannot be expected to have significant repercussions on such aggregates. This may be different for administered forward prices. In particular, the temporary rigidity of money wages due to collective bargaining contracts, by adding to the stickiness of wages from other causes, may have important macroeconomic effects. The nature of these effects is familiar from the Keynesian system with its short-term rigidity of wages. The main effect is that monetary expansion has a stronger stimulating effect on output and employment (see chaps. 10, 11). Escalation of wage rates, on the other hand, would reduce the rigidity of money wages and thus weaken the effect of monetary expansion on real output. Conversely, escalation would reduce the initial decline in output and employment resulting from a restrictive monetary policy. In other words, escalation of wages would make the short-term Phillips curve steeper and thus more similar to the long-run curve.[21]

Friedman makes this one of his main arguments for escalator clauses (1974; Shanahan, 1974). It is doubtful that this is warranted. First, it is not clear that collective bargaining contracts are really a major reason for the temporary employment effects of monetary expansion and contraction. Strong output effects of such monetary policies were observed in periods and countries in which there were probably not many contracts fixing wages for extended periods. By implication, it is not clear that escalation of wages would make a significant difference for the behavior of output and employment. Recent episodes suggest that in economies with virtually universal escalation of wages the employment effects of monetary contraction were not visibly smaller than in, say, the United States, where only a fraction of wages are covered by escalators.

Second, even if escalation indeed made the short-run Phillips curve steeper, it is not clear that this would be a blessing. It would certainly be desirable in periods of contraction; it is hardly an accident that the recent enthusiasm for escalation in the United States came in a period of anti-inflationary efforts. But escalation cannot be turned off and on every few years. In order to reduce the legal risk to tolerable proportions it has to be treated as a permanent change in the structure of the economy. This means that, once introduced, it will also be with us during episodes when monetary policy is used to stimulate output and employment. During such episodes, most economists would typically prefer a flatter Phillips curve; in fact, economists have devoted a large (and probably inordinately large) amount of energy to the very question how the short-run Phillips curve could be made flatter. Friedman argues that the greater difficulty of stimulating employment by monetary expansion would help the government to resist the temptation to use such policies. However, one may well argue, as Fellner did (Shanahan, 1974), that it would rather induce the government to use larger doses of monetary expansion (and thus to produce more long-run inflation) in order to achieve the temporary stimulation of employment which it believes the voters demand.

7.4.4. THE REDUCTION OF THE INFLATIONARY TAX. By escalating bonds, government wages and tax/transfer schedules, the government would lose an important part of the real revenue from inflation, thus reducing the

21. This argument does not automatically apply to commodity prices. If in an inflationary period some prices are temporarily made more rigid by past contracts, the situation is analogous to a price ceiling, creating excess demand in the respective markets. As is well known, the effect of price ceilings on aggregate output and employment is ambiguous. It follows that the effect of escalator clauses, being equivalent to the elimination of such ceilings, is also ambiguous.

inflationary tax on the private sector. (By also using all new money to pay interest on cash balances, the government would lose, in fact, all of its inflationary revenue.) Friedman has argued that this would reduce the incentive for the government to initiate inflationary policies (Shanahan, 1974). Again it is hardly less plausible to argue with Fellner that the decline in the real tax yield from a given rate of inflation would exert strong pressure to increase the rate of inflation to obtain about the same real tax yield. As so many assertions about government behavior, not grounded in coherent theory, both arguments will probably continue to be used, though by different people, without much supporting evidence on either side.

7.4.5. THE NEUTRALIZATION OF AUTOMATIC STABILIZERS. Under a progressive income tax system, tax brackets and exemptions are usually stated in dollar amounts. It is similar with transfer payments like social security benefits. For tax purposes, capital valuation gains resulting from inflation are usually treated as profits.[22] In an inflationary economy, tax revenues in real terms thus rise even without an increase in real incomes, while real transfer payments fall. Taxes net of transfers as a proportion of income rise. In some of the European tax literature, this effect has been discussed under the quiet expressive heading of "cold progression." By inserting appropriate escalator clauses into the pertinent provisions of tax/transfer legislation, the cold progression could, in principle, be eliminated.

Considerations of short-run equity seem to argue in favor of such escalation. On the other hand, the cold progression is one of the effective automatic stabilizers in the fiscal system. If fiscal legislation were fully escalated, this stabilizer would be neutralized. I believe this is a significant disadvantage of escalation. In periods of monetary expansion, every mechanism that helps to shift the financing of government expenditure from inflation to explicit taxation should be welcome. The same argument applies, *mutatis mutandis*, in contraction. It is true that, even without formal escalation, legislatures are always free to adjust the tax/transfer rates whenever this finds a majority, but I think the responsibility for lowering tax rates in a period of inflation and for increasing rates in a period of deflation should be clearly on the shoulders of the elected representatives, undiluted by automatic escalator clauses.

7.4.6. ACCOUNTING COSTS. Escalator clauses in debt contracts, like the use of deflators, involve accounting costs. In a sense, the nature of these accounting costs is the opposite of that of deflators: With escalation, there are no accounting costs at the moment the contract is made, but there are costs for figuring out the appropriate adjustment each time a payment on

22. The classical study of this subject is Viner (1923).

interest or principal is due. In monitoring his solvency, an economic agent will constantly have to apply prospective inflation rates to his claims and liabilities of different maturities. This will be especially onerous if escalation is only partial, including, say, long-term debt but excluding short-term debt and cash balances. For financial intermediaries, both bank and nonbank, these costs will be particularly heavy. Both firms and households, in order to avoid distortions in their resource allocation, will have to make sure that their economic calculus is either uniformly in terms of current (inflating) prices or uniformly in terms of constant (noninflating) prices. In the first case escalated items will have to be "blown up" by applying the expected rate of inflation. In the second case nonescalated items will have to be deflated.

In summary, it seems that the risk-reducing effects would make escalation virtually irresistible for debt contracts under high and long-lasting uncertainty about future inflation. This is the basic microeconomic justification of escalator clauses. It is closely associated with the distortion-reducing effects on the distribution of income. However, for the low degrees of uncertainty typically associated with low and moderate rates of inflation, the associated accounting costs and the additional legal risks tend to make escalation unattractive. An evaluation of the benefits and costs can be left to the parties concerned. Legislation should give the private parties the option of using escalator clauses; the degree of their adoption can be left to the competitive mechanism. The macroeconomic aspects, related to the Phillips curve, the inflationary tax, and the working of automatic stabilizers, are much less clear and probably of minor importance overall. Escalators, like deflators, make it easier for individuals to live with inflation, but they cannot be expected to facilitate the task, or improve the performance, of monetary policy to a significant extent. While these conclusions will probably be objected to by both the protagonists and the opponents of escalation, there is general agreement that escalator clauses can never be more than second-best expedients: Whatever they can achieve can be achieved better and cheaper by avoiding inflation.

In this chapter, money was considered as a medium of account. It was found that money may conceivably be superior as a medium of account to any single commodity. It not only saves the costs of keeping accounts in terms of something other than the medium of exchange, but it may also minimize the misallocation of resources resulting from changes in relative prices. This requires, however, that the absolute level of money prices remain stable at least in the vague sense that general movements of all prices in the same direction are avoided. If the violations of this condition become sufficiently large and persistent, a correct intertemporal allocation of resources requires deflation of money values. Escalator clauses will be used in debt contracts, wage agreements, tax schedules, social security benefits, and the like. What is perhaps more important, profit calculations of firms will have to be corrected for inflation. All this imposes accounting costs on the economy.

Inflation thus confronts a capitalist economy with a three-way dilemma (if there can be such a thing): (1) Either money is used both as medium of exchange and medium of account without deflation and escalation, but at the price of a less efficient allocation of resources; or (2) money is used as medium of exchange, but another good is used as medium of account (which is equivalent to keeping accounts in terms of "deflated" money values), the burden appearing in the form of added accounting costs; or (3) another good is used both as medium of exchange and medium of account, amounting to the "repudiation" of money, but at the expense of higher transaction costs for a less efficient means of payment. The main point is that the stability of prices is significant for economic welfare even if the transitional problems, which usually dominate the public discussion about inflation to the near-exclusion of long-run problems, are disregarded. If the government does not provide a money that is a tolerable medium of account, private trade, if left to itself, could have an incentive to create one.[23] As soon as accounting costs are duly considered, it turns out to be advantageous for a modern economy to have a medium of exchange that is also an efficient medium of account, which in turn, as the monetary tradition correctly emphasized, requires a reasonable degree of stability of the money price level.

23. This is likely to be the underlying reason for the tenacious survival of a commodity component, represented by gold, in modern monetary systems, surprising as it may seem if the economic role of the medium of account is disregarded.

Eight

COMMODITY MONEY

Introduction

By and large, the first part of this study was about the demand for money. While chapter 5 provided a general-equilibrium analysis of a monetary economy, attention was still concentrated on the demand side, the supply side being pushed into the background by the assumption that all money was fiat money created by the state in a fixed quantity. In the second part the perspective will be reversed, the main topic now being the supply of money, while the demand side is treated in a summary fashion. The present chapter is about the supply of commodity money and thus, in particular, the gold standard. Chapter 9 introduces commercial banks and other financial intermediaries. The following two chapters return to fiat money for a macroeconomic analysis, both static and dynamic, of alternative money policies. Chapter 12, finally, considers the modifications introduced by the activities of the central bank.

Commodity money is defined by the fact that it is convertible into a certain commodity (or certain commodities) at a fixed rate. Commodity money does not exist today. It is also not ideal in the sense that it is relatively easy to imagine noncommodity systems that are intellectually more satisfying than commodity money. In fact, a noncommodity system, since it gives monetary policy more freedom, can, if it is ideally managed, always do at least as well as any commodity money system and probably better. Commodity money has therefore been denounced as a "barbaric relic" from less enlightened stages of human society.[1] Yet, from a practical point of view, commodity money is the only type of money that, at the present time, can be said to have passed the test of history in market economies. Except for short interludes of war, revolution, and financial crisis, Western economies have been on commodity money systems from the dawn of their history almost up to the present time. More precisely, it is only since

---

1. Keynes (1923, p. 172; see also 1930, chap. 35). It is remarkable to what extent the contemporary discussion about gold still echoes Keynes' diatribes.

1973 that the absence of any link to the commodity world is claimed to be a normal feature of the monetary system. It will take several more decades before we can tell whether the Western world has finally embarked, as so often proclaimed, on a new era of noncommodity money or whether the present period will turn out to be just another interlude. An understanding of commodity money, therefore, is important because it played an essential role in shaping the world we live in, because it is still one of the main issues in current policy debates, and because it may conceivably play a role again in the future.

The analysis of commodity money has made hardly any progress in the last fifty years. Actually, more knowledge was forgotten than was newly acquired. Economists seemed to feel that the books contained whatever there was to know in this field and tended to be bored whenever the subject was mentioned.[2] I think this complacency was not quite justified. In particular, some of the most fundamental and seemingly intractable problems of recent monetary policy were analytically similar to the "classical" questions of the nineteenth century, and some of the leading economists around the turn of the century might have been better equipped to cope with these problems than many present-day experts, raised on models in which currency is printed costlessly and handed out for nothing. In what follows I shall concentrate on those aspects of commodity money which are particularly important for the understanding of recent developments and may have potential significance for the future.

There are different types of commodity standards. In the simplest case, money is convertible into a single commodity. The most important example is the gold standard. If, under a gold standard, the value of monetary gold is equal to the money supply, it may be called a pure gold standard. If the monetary gold covers only a fraction of the money supply, I shall use the term fractional gold standard. However, there may be more than one monetary commodity. The historical paradigm of such multicommodity standards is bimetallism, but it will be shown that the postwar gold/dollar standard shares some of its basic features. These types of commodity standards will be discussed in successive subsections.

8.1. The pure gold standard

8.1.1. THE GOLD SPECIE STANDARD: FUNDAMENTAL RULES. A pure gold standard may be either a gold specie standard or a gold bullion standard. Under the gold specie standard gold coins actually circulate as currency. Under the gold bullion standard the currency consists of bank notes or other token money, convertible into gold ingots with a 100 percent gold

---

2. Noneconomists were bored even more, as we know from Cecily in Oscar Wilde's *The Importance of Being Earnest* (act 2).

reserve. The following discussion will be based for the most part on the gold specie standard. but from a macroeconomic point of view the difference between the two is insignificant.

The analysis will be limited to the most basic features of the gold standard. The latter never existed in the stark simplicity in which it is presented here, and a large part of the gold-standard literature was precisely concerned with the techniques, often sophisticated and complex, that were used to mediate between those basic principles and the real world. For a classic survey of gold-standard theory the reader is referred to Viner (1937), while analytical interpretations of the historical and empirical evidence are given by Brown (1940) and Bloomfield (1959, 1963).

Under a gold specie standard the supply of money is based on two fundamental rules. The first rule consists of a technical definition of the various pieces of currency, specifying the material from which they are made, their weight, and their value in terms of the unit of account. For a U.S. "eagle," for example, the rule says that it shall contain 232.20 grains of pure gold, nine-tenths fine, and shall be worth $10. The second rule says that everybody can either obtain from the mint as much currency as he likes, provided he pays for the required raw material and the manufacturing cost, or have his coins melted down. This is the principle of free coinage.

Both the definition of coins and the actual coinage could be left, in principle, to competitive, profit-seeking enterprise. In this case, currencies issued by different mints would circulate side by side at variable exchange rates, each having certain comparative advantages on the basis of transaction and holding costs. Monetary history provides many examples of this sort of competition.[3] Under modern conditions, however, the application of both rules will be typically left to a government monopoly. The rules then imply that the government freely buys and sells gold metal for gold currency at fixed prices, with the buying and the selling price differing by the costs of coinage and melting.

8.1.2. THE ALLOCATION OF RESOURCES AND THE VALUE OF MONEY. For a closed economy under a pure gold standard, the allocation of resources between gold mining and other industries holds the center of the stage. The money supply is governed by real factors. The basic relationships can be summarized in the following model. Let all money consist of uniform gold coins with the coining of metal and the melting of coins assumed to be costless. The economy is endowed with given resources, $\bar{R}$. These can be used to produce two goods, namely consumer goods (or commodities), C, and gold, G, according to a production possibility frontier

$$\bar{R} = R(C, G). \tag{8.1.1}$$

3. For a recent attempt to provide an analysis of a competitive money supply process, see Klein (1974).

Increases in the production of consumer goods can be achieved at the expense of gold mining by a shift of resources between the two industries. The owners of resources earn an aggregate income that, measured in gold, is

$$Y = (p_C/p_G)C + G, \qquad (8.1.2)$$

where p_C and p_G are, respectively, the money prices of commodities and gold. Profit maximization by competitive producers will see to it that the price of consumer goods in terms of gold is equal to their marginal opportunity cost as expressed by the marginal rate of transformation,

$$\pi = p_C/p_G = R_C/R_G. \qquad (8.1.3)$$

A rise in the commodity price or a fall in the gold price thus induces a shift of resources from gold mining into consumer goods. In equilibrium, resources in each industry will be paid their marginal value product

$$w = p_G/R_G = p_C/R_C.$$

If resources are thought to be represented by labor, this means that the wage rate, measured in gold, equals the amount of gold mined by the marginal worker. The marginal worker can just make himself paid by keeping the gold he dug out of the ground.

The flow demand for consumer goods and the stock demand for monetary gold (or the demand for real cash balances in terms of gold) are assumed to depend on income, the relative price of consumer goods and the cost of holding money, δ:

$$C = C(Y, \pi, \delta), \qquad (8.1.4)$$

$$M/p_G = L(Y, \pi, \delta). \qquad (8.1.5)$$

Both C and L will normally increase with income. C will certainly fall with increasing π, while L will fall with increasing δ. It may also be assumed that a rise in π, since it makes newly mined gold relatively cheaper, raises L, while an increase in δ, since it makes the consumer worse off, lowers C. It should be noted, however, that there is, strictly speaking, no homogeneity postulate with respect to the demand for money. Since π is a relative price, there is no reason why, for given Y and δ, M/p_G should be proportionate to π; if commodity prices change, the velocity of circulation of money will, in general, change also.

These macroeconomic functions are in the spirit of the demand functions derived at the macroeconomic level from explicit utility maximization in chapters 4 and 5. The present model goes beyond those in the first part by including production; endowments are thus replaced by income. On the other hand, gold coins are the only asset, and there is neither time preference nor credit. Transactions costs, assumed to be given, are suppressed, and there are no taxes.

The flow demand for newly mined gold is

$$G = \delta(M/p_G) + G_{nm}. \tag{8.1.6}$$

The first term represents replacement demand with a proportion δ of monetary circulation disappearing each year by abrasion, destruction, or loss. δ is thus a storage cost rate analogous to the physical shrinkage rates used in earlier chapters. The second term represents the nonmonetary consumption demand for gold. By virtue of the household budget constraint, the implied demand function for nonmonetary gold can be derived, if desired, by subtracting from income the demand for consumer goods and new money,

$$G_{nm} = Y - \pi C(\quad) - \delta L(\quad).$$

The cost of holding money can be given an alternative interpretation by regarding the model as relating to balanced growth. Stocks and flows can then be made independent of time by expressing them in intensive form per unit of resources. With small letters standing for the intensive counterpart of the same variable in the previous model, the modified model reads

$$1 = R(c, g) \tag{8.1.1a}$$

$$y = \pi c + g \tag{8.1.2a}$$

$$c = C(y,\pi,\omega) \tag{8.1.4a}$$

$$m/p_G = L(y,\pi,\omega) \tag{8.1.5a}$$

$$g = \frac{\Delta M}{p_G \cdot \bar{R}} + g_{nm} = \frac{\Delta M}{M} \cdot \frac{M}{p_G \cdot \bar{R}} + g_{nm} = \omega(m/p_G) + g_{nm}, \tag{8.1.6a}$$

where ω is the growth rate of the economy. ωm is the amount of new currency per unit of resources that is needed to keep the money stock growing in step with the rest of the economy. The resulting growth model is formally identical to the original model, with growth taking the place of the storage cost rate. The more rapid economic growth, the higher the burden of a commodity currency. The following discussion will make use of both the stationary and the growth interpretations of the model.

The six equations determine Y, C, G, G_{nm}, M, and π for given δ (or y, c, g, g_{nm}, m, and π for given ω). This means that the government, in principle, can fix either the money price of gold or the money price of commodities, but not both. Under a gold standard, where the price of gold is fixed, the authorities are forced to accept the corresponding commodity price level. To a large extent, the breakdown of the postwar gold exchange standard, though it was more complex than a pure gold specie standard, can be attributed to the simple fact that the authorities permitted prices to develop in a way that was inconsistent with the fixed price of gold. This is, then, the main virtue of the gold standard: By fixing the purchasing power of money in terms of gold, the government implicitly fixes the purchasing power of money in terms of commodities, thus giving a guarantee against persistent inflation and deflation. Of course, this is strictly valid only if all the functions in the model remain constant. In reality, however, these functions are subject to change, and as a consequence, a fixed price of gold may result in a variable price of commodities. This is the main vice of the gold standard. More about this will be said presently.

The model has a more specific property: Equations (8.1.1) to (8.1.4) are enough to determine Y, C, G, and π without reference to equations (8.1.5) and (8.1.6). The interplay of the relevant elements is depicted in figure 8.1.1. The production possibility curve appears on the right-hand side. Income at point Q is measured by the G-intercept of the tangent at Q, and the slope of this tangent expresses the relative commodity price. The left-hand panel describes the demand for consumer goods as a function of income, with a separate demand curve for each price ratio. In equilibrium the price ratio must be such that the supply of consumer goods as determined on the right is equal to demand as determined on the left.

The observation that equations (8.1.1) to (8.1.4) suffice to determine π means that, once the government has fixed p_G, the consumer goods price p_C and thus the value of money depend only on cost conditions and the demand for consumer goods. In particular, they are independent of the demand for money, which only serves to determine the division of G between monetary and nonmonetary gold. This is the valid core of the cost of production theory of the value of money in a gold standard world.[4]

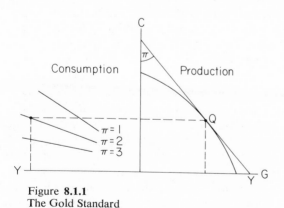

Figure **8.1.1**
The Gold Standard

4. The classic analysis was provided by Nassau Senior (1829). In the special case of a linear production possibility curve, even the demand for commodities becomes immaterial for the commodity price level; the opportunity cost of commodities (or gold) is all we have to know.

8.1.3. COMPARATIVE STATICS. The effects of given changes in data can be worked out by the usual techniques of comparative statics. The results may be briefly summarized as follows. A change in the price of gold will obviously result in nothing but a corresponding adjustment in commodity prices, all real aspects of the system remaining unchanged. An increase in the demand for money has different effects, depending on what other shift in demand it has as its counterpart. While the primary change is in the stock demand for money, this inevitably affects the flow demand for monetary gold through δ or ω. By virtue of the budget constraint, this must be associated with a corresponding decline in the demand for either nonmonetary gold or consumer goods (or a combination of both). If the matching decline is in the demand for nonmonetary gold there is no further change in the system. In the more interesting case where the matching decline is in the demand for consumer goods, there will be a fall in consumer prices. This will make gold production more profitable, thus drawing resources from the consumer goods industry into gold mining. In the face of an increase in liquidity preference, gold mining thus acts as an automatic stabilizer for employment. Even the demand for money is thus translated into a demand for current output.

However, these effects may take a long time to work themselves out. Since the annual flow of new gold typically is only a fraction of the stock of monetary gold, even a moderate increase in the stock demand for money may require many years of temporary above-equilibrium production of gold to be satisfied. In the meantime, commodity prices will be depressed even below the new equilibrium level, thus increasing the purchasing power of existing cash balances. If, instead of gold, the monetary system were based on a commodity with a much larger share in annual output, potential adjustment problems of this type would probably be less severe.

An increase in the growth rate of the economy (or the replacement rate of the money stock) means that a larger flow of new gold will be needed to maintain the money stock at the equilibrium level. This, in turn, requires a higher price of gold relative to commodities. An acceleration of growth thus tends to produce a tight liquidity situation with pressure to deflate commodity prices. An increase in resources and technological progress have the common effect that they shift the transformation curve outward. The main question is how this affects the marginal rates of transformation. If there are new gold discoveries or rapid advances in gold-mining technology, the transformation curve will become flatter as it moves out, as indicated in figure 8.1.2(a). The consequence will be rising commodity prices as experienced toward the end of the nineteenth century. If, on the other hand, there is stagnation in gold discoveries and/or if technical progress in gold mining lags behind other industries, the curve will become steeper as it moves out. In this case, illustrated in figure 8.1.2(b), the gold price will have to be adjusted upward or else commodity prices will have

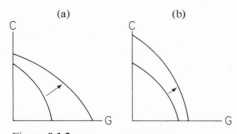

Figure **8.1.2**
Two Cases of Technological Progress

to fall. In an extreme but not implausible case it is even possible that the transformation curve, in view of the gradual exhaustion of gold mines, moves inward. It is these shifts in technology which expose a gold standard system to the risk of long-term fluctuations in commodity prices.

Such shifts, like those arising from an increase in the stock demand for money, take time. However, since we are now considering changes in flow relationships, the small size of new gold production relative to the stock of monetary gold helps to make the adjustment easier. Even the opening of rich new gold fields will take a long time to fill the equilibrium demand for additional currency stimulated by the decline in π, and over short periods of time the increase in commodity prices will be small. Short-run changes in supply conditions, each time reversed after a few years, may leave hardly any trace in commodity prices. From this point of view, the small output/stock ratio thus helps to make gold a good money commodity.[5]

It is not always realized that in such a gold standard world the quantity theory of money, while perhaps valid as a broad tendency, does not strictly apply.[6] While gold discoveries will certainly tend to push prices up, it would be a coincidence if the money supply and commodity prices moved up in proportion. The above model shows how in a gold standard system the commodity price level, together with real income, is determined without reference to the demand for money. (8.1.5) then determines the money supply consistent with these price and income levels. Since (1) equation (8.1.5) cannot be assumed to be linear-homogeneous in π, and (2) Y also changes, money and prices will generally vary in different proportions. Once the government has fixed the price of gold, there is no reason why

5. The gold standard may be compared to a large lake with a small flow-through. If there are disturbances in the flows, there will be a small and very gradual adjustment in the level of the lake, but a given change in the level of the lake will take large and prolonged adjustments in the flows.

6. Foremost among those who didn't realize it was J. Stuart Mill, with his attempt to "reconcile" the cost of production theory and the quantity theory of the value of money (1857, bk. III, chap. 9, sec. 3). His error was that he overlooked the fact that under a gold standard the demand for money cannot be expected to be proportional to commodity prices.

resources, technology, tastes, and growth rates should always move in such a way that the resulting commodity price level or output in current prices is just proportionate to the resulting money supply. Quite generally, the quantity theory of money implies a denial of an economic theory of the money supply with respect to those types of money for which the quantity theory is said to hold.

8.1.4. EXTENSIONS AND SUMMARY. The analysis so far was for a gold specie standard where gold coins actually circulate. One of the components of the real cost of money in such a system is coinage and the physical attrition of coins. This cost can be reduced by replacing the gold specie standard by a gold bullion standard where the monetary gold is kept in the reserves of the central bank. The central bank buys any amount of gold offered and sells any amount demanded at a fixed price, paying in paper money. In this way, the replacement cost of gold coins is replaced by the replacement cost of bank notes (which may be higher or lower), and the gold need not be coined but can be held in ingots. This modification of the gold standard does not require a change in the analysis; the previous model remains applicable except that the storage costs of the central bank have to be covered by the margin between the buying and selling price for gold. In particular, the money supply is still rigidly tied to monetary gold. All that takes place is a possible change in δ. In a stationary economy, δ may go practically to zero; bullion does not wear out, it may be cheap to store, and the production costs of bank notes may be low. In this case, the flow demand for monetary gold and the marginal cost of money approach zero, and the economy will virtually satiate itself with money. While gold coins ceased to circulate as money with the Great Depression, Switzerland was on a virtually undiluted gold bullion standard throughout the 1950s and 1960s, except that a small amount of reserves was held not in bullion but in convertible foreign exchange.

I finally lift the assumption of a closed economy producing its own gold, thus taking account of the fact that most countries either produce no gold or in any case only a fraction of their needs, the rest being imported from abroad. In this case, as the mercantilists used to say, "Foreign trade is the gold mine of Peru." Fortunately, the model can be easily adapted to this case by a simple reinterpretation of some of its components. First, I assume that all imports consist of gold. While this assumption is not crucial for the analysis, it simplifies the exposition. I further assume that the rest of the world is also on the gold standard. World market prices, including the price of gold in terms of foreign currencies, are given. Transportation costs on gold are negligible. The two industries can then be reinterpreted as producing, respectively, domestic goods, C, and export goods, E. At given foreign commodity and gold prices, $\bar{p}_C$ and $\bar{p}_G$, each unit of exports buys a certain quantity of gold $\bar{\pi} = \bar{p}_C/\bar{p}_G$. It follows that gold inflows will be proportionate to exports, $G = \bar{\pi}E$. From the transformation curve for domestic goods and exports we can thus derive a transformation curve for domestic goods and gold, $\bar{R} = R(C, \bar{\pi}E) = R(C, G)$.

After this reinterpretation of the transformation curve, all the rest of the analysis remains unchanged. A country can still fix the price of gold at some arbitrary level (which is equivalent to fixing the exchange rate at some arbitrary level). The domestic price level and the output of domestic and export goods are then determined endogenously. Instead of allocating resources to gold mines, these resources are now allocated to export industries to produce an export surplus. If domestic prices are maintained at an above-equilibrium level, resources will be diverted from export industries to domestic output. At the same time, the demand for nonmonetary gold will rise. As a consequence, there will be a deficiency of monetary gold inflows, producing a "liquidity crisis." If the international gold standard mechanism works well, this will, in turn, exert deflationary pressure on domestic prices and thus act as a self-correcting mechanism. For a detailed analysis of this mechanism and its possible failures the reader is referred to the literature on international monetary theory. It may again be useful, however, to add a word of caution about the validity of the quantity theory in an international context. While some quantity-theoretic adjustment process between gold flows and domestic prices, loosely interpreted, is, of course, an essential element of the international gold standard mechanism, equilibrium prices cannot be expected to be proportionate to the flows or stocks of monetary gold. Again this is due to the fact that the demand for gold currency cannot be expected to be proportionate to commodity prices.

In conclusion I shall try to summarize the main characteristics of the gold standard. Its basic feature is the close link between the money supply and the resources devoted to gold production. In equilibrium, we can fix either the price of gold or the commodity price level; the other is then determined endogenously by the system. For given tastes, technology, demand for cash balances and growth (and/or replacement) rates, in a world of fully flexible prices, fixing the price of gold is thus a means to stabilize commodity prices. Deviations of prices from their equilibrium level will set in motion a self-correcting adjustment mechanism.

The question may be raised why commodity prices are not stabilized directly by appropriate economic policies, while the gold price is left to itself. The main part of the answer probably is that in the real world, with its numerous heterogeneous commodities, it is technically easy to stabilize the gold price; defining the coins and maintaining free coinage are enough. Direct stabilization of commodity prices, however, is difficult, requiring enlightened macroeconomic policies. Also, what we want to accomplish is not rigid day-to-day stability of some particular price index, but only a rough stability in the long run. But this is exactly what a fixed gold price, under favorable conditions, may be expected to accomplish. Similar considerations apply if prices are not fully flexible, resulting in fluctuations in total output and employment. Again, the gold standard acts as an automatic stabilizer, producing countercyclical output fluctuations in gold mining or export industries.

On the other hand, a gold standard has shortcomings. First, other goods, either singly or in "bundles," may provide more efficient short-run stabilizers for prices and output than gold.[7] Second, the gold standard keeps commodity prices stable in the long run only if other conditions are constant. This may not be so. Shifts in resources and technology may twist the transformation curve, growth and/or replacement rates may change, tastes may shift, and the demand for money may vary. Fixing the price of gold will then result in fluctuating commodity prices. Third, the gold standard is expensive to operate, absorbing resources in gold mining that otherwise could have been used for something else. Fourth, the pure gold standard leaves no room for an active monetary policy to stabilize output and employment; the mint can do nothing but passively supply the money demanded by the private sector.

8.2. The fractional gold standard

The cost of operating a gold standard can be lowered, the consequences of fluctuating supply conditions can be reduced, and some room for an active monetary policy can be gained by replacing the pure gold standard by a fractional gold standard. This was the dominant monetary system in the postwar years up into the late 1960s.

To capture the basic features of the fractional reserve standard, the model of the preceding section has to be modified. The discussion will be based on the growth version of the model with attrition of the gold stock assumed to be zero. As the point of departure I use a gold bullion standard under which the circulating medium consists of costless bank notes, convertible into gold ingots at a fixed price, while the government keeps the monetary gold reserves. The main modification is that under a fractional gold standard the monetary gold stock amounts to only a fraction, ρ, of the money supply. The central bank thus acts in some respects like a commercial bank that keeps only a fraction of its deposits in the form of reserves, relying on the law of large numbers to prevent all depositors from demanding cash at the same time.

In other respects, however, the central bank presumably acts very

7. On this aspect see Friedman (1951).

differently from a commercial bank inasmuch as its reserve ratio is not primarily determined by the profit motive but by considerations of economic policy. To the extent money is not issued to pay for monetary gold, it is issued to pay for government consumption of commodities, c_g. A fractional gold standard thus allows the government to finance government expenditures by newly printed bank notes. As a consequence, private consumption is limited to $c_p = c - c_g$.

With these modifications the model reads as follows. The production sector is unchanged:

$$1 = R(c, g), \tag{8.2.1}$$

$$y = \pi c + g, \tag{8.2.2}$$

$$\pi = R_C / R_G. \tag{8.2.3}$$

Consumption demand includes an additional term for government consumption,

$$c = c_p + c_g = C(y, \pi, \omega) + c_g, \tag{8.2.4}$$

while the demand for money remains

$$m/p_g = L(y, \pi, \omega). \tag{8.2.5}$$

The demand for new monetary gold is now only a fraction of the total addition to the money stock required by economic growth,

$$g = \rho\omega(m/p_g) + g_{nm}. \tag{8.2.6}$$

To this must be added the government budget constraint determining c_g,

$$\pi c_g = \omega(1 - \rho)(m/p_g). \tag{8.2.7}$$

It says that the government can use the annual addition to the money stock to buy goods and services to the extent the money is not needed to acquire additional gold reserves.

As in the original model, the households use a part of their income, amounting to $\omega(m/p_g)$, to accumulate additional cash balances. However, in contrast to the pure gold standard, only a part of this amount is reflected in additional gold stocks. The remainder, namely $\omega(1 - \rho)(m/p_g)$, has its counterpart in government consumption. In this sense, a fractional reserve standard imposes a "growth tax" on the economy. It is similar in nature to the "inflationary tax," but, while the latter has its source in rising prices, the former arises even in balanced growth with constant prices.

By substituting from (8.2.7) and (8.2.5), (8.2.4) can be rewritten

$$c = c(y, \pi, \omega) + \frac{\omega}{\pi}(1 - \rho)L(y, \pi, \omega). \tag{8.2.8}$$

The subsystem (8.2.1), (8.2.2), (8.2.3), and (8.2.8) can be used to determine y, c, g, and π, just as in the original model. In graphical terms, the demand curves for consumer goods in the left-hand panel of figure 8.1.1 are moved upward by the amount of government consumption as expressed by the second term of (8.2.8).

The main implications of operating a fractional gold standard in a closed economy can be set out under five headings. First, the resource costs of the money supply are lowered for a given growth rate of the economy. Second, with a constant reserve ratio, fluctuations in the gold supply have a multiple effect on the money supply. An inflow of gold permits a large temporary expansion of government expenditure, while a gold outflow imposes a severe temporary contraction of expenditures until the new equilibrium is reached. Third, fluctuations in the stock demand for money have only a fractional effect on the demand for monetary gold. The effectiveness of gold mining as an automatic stabilizer is further weakened.

Fourth, by selecting the reserve ratio, the government can influence the price level and resource allocation. As (8.2.8) shows, the lower ρ the higher the total demand for consumption. As a consequence, the level of commodity prices rises and commodity output expands at the expense of gold mining, but the private demand for consumer goods falls while the non-monetary consumption of gold rises. Lowering the gold reserve ratio thus permits an expansion of commodity output, associated with an even larger expansion in government consumption, partly at the expense of private consumption and accompanied by higher commodity prices. To put the argument the other way around, an expansion of government consumption, paid for by new money, results in an expansion of commodity output but by a smaller amount, so that private consumption falls. This has to be paid for in terms of higher commodity prices and a lower reserve ratio. If the money supply is progressively increased, the reserve ratio will sooner or later reach a crisis point at which the confidence in the continued convertibility is impaired. At this point, the demand for conversion will grow rapidly, so that convertibility will have to be suspended; the gold standard collapses. This is, in essence, what happened to the gold standard in the late 1960s. It should be noted that the eventual collapse was in no way inherent in the mechanism of the system; it was the consequence of expanding the money supply at a rate that was incompatible with the system. It is hardly surprising that a system, carefully designed to be incompatible with long-run inflation, has to be abandoned if governments insist on pursuing a policy of long-run inflation.

Fifth, the fractional gold standard creates a range of discretion for an active monetary policy. This flexibility is achieved by permitting the reserve ratio to fluctuate around its trend. The transition of the system to a balanced growth path with a lower reserve ratio takes considerable time. During this period of expansionary policies the ratio between the flow of new monetary gold and the flow of new money may be much lower than in the new equilibrium; the incremental reserve ratio falls below the desired average ratio. For a period, the absolute gold reserve may actually decline. The reverse applies for the transition to a higher reserve ratio through contractionary policies. In the short run, a fractional gold standard thus leaves considerable room for a flexible monetary policy. This flexibility can be used to insulate the economy against fluctuations in gold production, or, in an open economy, in foreign trade. It can also be used to reduce fluctuations in output and employment. If the reactions of the economy to monetary policy are reasonably well known, this discretion will be regarded as a crucial advantage of the fractional gold standard over the pure gold standard. However, if the effects of monetary policy are very imperfectly known and often misjudged, the economy may be better off under the strict rules of the pure gold standard.

In the long run, the range of flexibility is much more limited, being restricted to variations in the balanced growth path as described under heading four. This means that a period of vigorous expansion has to be followed by a period of contraction, imposing a severe long-run constraint on monetary policy. However, this constraint is, in principle, quite desirable. It is known from macroeconomic theory that monetary expansion can stimulate output and employment only in the short run, while the long-run effect will be only on prices. This means that a long-run expansionary trend has no desirable real effect. It may thus be argued that a fractional gold standard permits, by and large, just those shortrun variations in monetary policy which are necessary for an effective stabilization policy, while at the same time prohibiting those long-run inflationary (or deflatonary) trends which result from weak governments or bad economics.

8.3. Multicommodity standards: Bimetallism

Under a multicommodity standard, currency is convertible into several commodities. In one case, money is convertible at a fixed rate into each of several commodities separately. Such systems have played an important historical role in the form of bimetallism. Under the other variant, money is convertible at a fixed price into a bundle composed of specified quantities of different commodities. Thus Marshall (1925, 188f.; 1926, p. 14f., 27f.) proposed "symmetallism," under which bank notes would be convertible into metal plates consisting of fixed quantities of gold and silver. Under the commodity-reserve standards devised by Benjamin Graham (1937, 1944) and Frank Graham (1942), currency would be convertible into bundles of warehouse warrants for specified commodities. The basic virtue of such schemes is that they fix only an average of prices while leaving each individual price free to vary. While this is, in principle, a desirable feature, none of these proposals have so far been realized. The following discussion will therefore be limited to the traditional type of multicommodity standard, with bimetallism as the paradigm.[8]

In nineteenth-century treatises on political economy there are few chapters that, on the surface, look more dreary and dated than those on bimetallism. But many of these books were written by authors who were not much more inspiring on other subjects either, and when men like Walras (1886, 1900), Marshall (1923, 1926), Barone (1919), or Fisher (1911) wrote about bimetallism, things appeared intellectually in a different light. These eminent writers understood the central problem of bimetallism, which is the relationship between commodity prices and the money supply under a dual standard. Today bimetallism has disappeared, but, as will be shown below, its basic problem is the same as that which assumed such serious proportions under the international gold standard during recent years. For these reasons a brief theoretical survey of the working of a bimetallic system is enlightening even from a modern point of view.

Under bimetallism the standard currency consists of two metals, usually gold and silver, both subject to the two basic standard currency rules (see section 8.1.1). Obviously this implies a fixed price ratio between the two metals: If a double eagle of $20 is defined to contain one ounce of gold, while 20 silver dollars contain sixteen ounces of silver, then the ratio between the gold price and the silver price must be 16:1. The basic question is whether it makes good economic sense to fix the relative prices of gold and silver in the face of perpetual fluctuations in supply and demand conditions for each metal. It is evident that this question is very similar to the question whether under a modern gold-exchange standard it makes sense to fix the price of gold in terms of dollars in the face of constant fluctuations in supply and demand conditions for both gold and dollars. It is for the sake of this analogy that bimetallism is discussed here.

Following Marshall's example (1923), the analysis may be introduced by recalling briefly the elementary idea on which both bimetallism and the gold-exchange standard are based. Suppose natural and synthetic rubber are perfect substitutes, pound per pound, in the manufacturing of automobile tires. For other purposes, however, they are imperfect substitutes; perhaps one of them cannot be used at all. The area of perfect substitution will then stabilize the price ratio between natural and synthetic rubber at the level of 1:1, even though there may be shifts in supply and shifts in demand for other purposes as well.[9] However, this stabilizing effect will only hold as long as not all tires are made of the same type of rubber. Also, once the general price level is given, the prices for both

8. An authoritative discussion of commodity-reserve currencies can be found in the classic paper by Friedman (1951). On the history of silver money, see Leavens (1939).
9. If natural and synthetic rubber are imperfect substitutes even for tires, the stabilization of the price ratio will be imperfect, too.

natural and synthetic rubber are determined by supply and demand. If somebody wanted to fix the rubber price without obstructing the free-market mechanism, he would have to provide for the appropriate adjustments in the general price level.

A bimetallic standard for a closed economy is essentially a straightforward application of these principles. There are, however, certain additional points that have to be considered.

1. In the rubber example, the ratio of substitution was assumed to be fixed by technology. For gold and silver money, however, this ratio can be fixed by the monetary authorities. There are no compelling technical reasons why one ounce of gold should provide the same payments services as sixteen ounces of silver rather than fourteen or eighteen ounces. The choice of the appropriate ratio thus becomes a problem of economic policy.

2. In the rubber example there appear only flows, no stocks. For money, however, stocks play an important role. On one hand, we have the flow supply of newly mined metals flowing into the economy every year and the flow demand for nonmonetary purposes. There is also a flow demand for monetary purposes because the economy grows and thus, at constant prices, needs more money, and also perhaps because there is a replacement demand for coins that have been destroyed or lost. On the other hand, there is a stock demand for currency. What moves into the center of the stage is a problem of stock/flow equilibrium.

3. In view of the stock/flow relationship, expectations about the future stability of the system become important.

4. It is no longer the general commodity price level that is given, while the particular commodities adjust. Rather it is the gold and silver prices that are fixed by the government, while the general price level is left to adjust. Keeping these points in mind, the working of bimetallism for a single country can be explained more formally in terms of figure 8.3.1.

It is assumed that the government has fixed both the gold price and the silver price, and thus their ratio. Both gold and silver are measured in units that cost, say, \$35. Gold is thus measured in ounces, while silver is measured in bars of, say, sixteen ounces. Along the N-axis we measure the ratio between commodity prices and the given gold price. The commodity price level relative to the silver price is similarly measured along the W-axis. Considering the way we measure gold and silver, their price ratio is one; this is reflected in the 45°-ray in the NW-quadrant. The scale of the price axes gives the corresponding price level for given p_G and p_S.

The NE-quadrant summarizes information about the gold market. All quantities, both stocks and flows, are thought to be divided by the amount of resources. In this way, we again obtain a picture that is invariant if the economy moves along a balanced growth path. g is gold production, falling with rising commodity prices. g_{nm} is the flow demand for nonmonetary gold; it rises with rising commodity prices. The difference between the two curves

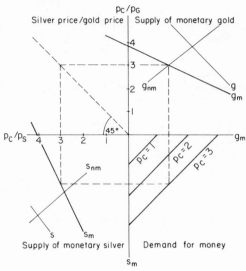

Figure **8.3.1**
Bimetallism

is the excess flow supply g_m available for monetary purposes. If commodity prices are high enough, the excess supply will turn into an excess demand. The SW-quadrant contains the same information for silver, resulting in the supply curve for new monetary silver, s_m.

The SE-quadrant, finally, expresses the aggregate demand for money. At a given commodity price level of, say, $p_C = 3$, the stock demand for money can be satisfied by any number of combinations of gold coins and silver coins. If people feel perfectly indifferent about gold and silver money, these combinations lie along a straight line. This is assumed here for simplicity, though it is not essential for the analysis. If we adhere to a strict quantity theory, albeit not strictly valid for a commodity money system, the desired money stock will increase *pari passu* with the general price level. Otherwise the relationship of successive iso-price lines will be more complicated. If the economy grows, the stock demand for money has its counterpart in a flow demand for new money. In the special case of balanced growth, these flow demand curves are scale replicas of the stock demand curves. They are represented by the parallel lines in the SE-quadrant, showing what combinations of new gold and silver would satisfy the economy's need for new money at different commodity price levels. In reality they may well be curved and unequally spaced.

We now have all the elements to determine the balanced growth path of the system. We may try to start out with an initial price level of 3. The supply curves for monetary gold and silver determine the total supply of new money. In the SE-quadrant we find that this just corresponds to the demand for money at this price level. The initial price level thus turns out to be the equilibrium price level. If supply and demand had not been equal, it would have been necessary to try another price level, making a downward correction if the supply of currency falls short of demand and going upward if there is excess supply of money. There is only one price level that provides equilibrium.

As is well known, such a system may well be able to survive fluctuations in supply and nonmonetary demand for gold and silver. If there is, say, an increase in the supply of monetary gold because new deposits are discovered, more new gold and less silver will flow into monetary circulation. The increment in silver may actually become negative for a time, thus reducing the stock of silver money while gold circulation grows. Profits can be made by having gold coined at the mint, exchanging the gold currency against silver currency, and melting down the silver. These changes in the composition of the monetary circulation were long ago summarized in Gresham's Law, according to which "bad money drives out good money." In the present context it would be more appropriate to say "Cheap money drives out expensive money." Thanks to these variations in monetary circulation, the prices of gold and silver, despite the assumed increase in gold production, can stay at their fixed levels. If, in the course of time, the fluctuations in the supply and the nonmonetary demand of the two metals tend to be of the same order of magnitude, but independent of each other (but not necessarily in other cases), the resulting fluctuations in commodities prices will be smaller than in a monometallic system based on either gold or silver. This mutual buffer-stock action of gold and silver, if it works, is the main virtue of the system.

However, this buffer-stock action operates only if the exchange ratio between gold and silver remains within certain limits. These limits are of two kinds. A wider, absolute limit is set by the fact that each of the two components of the money stock must be nonnegative. If the authorities fix p_S/p_G above the upper limit, gold currency will disappear; if p_S/p_G is set below the lower limit, the same will happen to silver currency. In either case the buffer-stock mechanism will become inoperative. This is more likely to happen the more elastic the two supply curves are. In a small open economy the two curves may be almost horizontal and the two limits, therefore, very close together. In this case, the range of discretion in fixing p_S/p_G may become negligible.

There is also a more narrow, but less well defined pair of limits. It is set by the fact that, long before one of the absolute limits is reached, people begin to speculate on the possible breakdown of the system. This produces adverse shifts in the supply curves for monetary gold and silver, thus precipitating the movement toward the breakdown point. Confidence in the maintenance of the system thus plays a crucial role. As a matter of historical experience, bimetallic standards tended to hit one of these limits sooner or later and thus turned out to be not very durable.

Bimetallism is subject to another qualification, which is even more fundamental. Even within the above-mentioned limits, the system only works if commodity prices are properly adjusted to every shift in supply and demand of money metals. As a consequence, the government still has no freedom in its economic policies, and if these policies result in price developments that are incompatible with monetary equilibrium, there will be an excess or shortage of liquidity in the system. This is the problem whose counterpart in the gold/exchange standard system has become of such far-reaching importance in recent years.

8.4. The gold/exchange standard

8.4.1. THE SYSTEM IN OUTLINE. After bimetallism had yielded to Gresham's Law and the gold standard had finally succumbed to war inflation in the Great Depression, international monetary arrangements evolved into the gold/exchange standard. Institutionalized by the Bretton Woods system, the gold/exchange standard dominated the scene for the first quarter-century of the postwar period, until it became, in turn, the victim of secular inflation.

While the gold standard had directly regulated the national money supplies, the gold/exchange standard related to transactions between central banks. Central banks guaranteed to each other the convertibility of their currencies into gold at fixed prices, which also made their currencies convertible into each other at fixed exchange rates. Legally, central banks had no obligation to buy or sell gold in the private market at fixed prices, and the national monies were inconvertible fiat currencies. Economically, however, the system could only endure if the market prices of gold, expressed in the various currencies, stayed close to the respective parities; if they were allowed to move higher, as Gresham's Law shows and the experiment with a "two tiers" market confirmed, the system would collapse. The functioning of the system thus required central banks collectively to buy and sell gold in the free market at the parity prices much as if the gold standard rules had been legally binding. This means that in the last analysis the centerpiece of the system was still the interplay between commodity price levels and the supply of monetary assets. In the following analysis, therefore, prices will play the same crucial role as in the preceding sections.

In principle the gold/exchange standard rules applied symmetrically to every member currency. There was a technical asymmetry arising from the fact that countries other than the United States had the choice of expressing their parities in terms of gold or of the dollar, but since the relevant dollar was defined as being worth one-thirty-fifth of an ounce of gold, this difference was of little substantive importance. However, there was an important economic asymmetry in the sense that, besides gold, the dollar was by far the dominant reserve asset. The working of the system can thus be best understood if it is assumed that gold and dollars were the only reserve assets, which implies, of course, that the United States held only gold. The following analysis will be based on this simplification.[10]

The gold/exchange standard can be regarded as a combination of some of the features of a fractional-reserve standard with some of the elements of bimetallism. It was a fractional-reserve standard, inasmuch as the U.S. gold reserve covered only a small fraction of the dollars that might be presented for conversion through the intermediary of foreign central banks. On the other hand, it has often been observed, by Aliber (1967) among others, that the mechanism of the gold/exchange standard is in many respects similar to bimetallism. Just as the private sector under bimetallism holds currency in the form of gold and silver coins, so the associated central banks held their reserves in gold and dollars. Just as the government under bimetallism guarantees a fixed exchange rate between silver and gold, so the United States guaranteed a fixed exchange rate between the dollar and gold. Just as under bimetallism fluctuations in the relative demand and supply of gold and silver can be absorbed, within limits, by shifts in the composition of the monetary circulation, so fluctuations in the relative demand and supply of gold and dollars could be absorbed, within limits, by shifts in the composition of international reserves. It will now be shown that the fractional-reserve and dual-reserve feature gave the gold/exchange standard a flexibility and a margin of freedom for national monetary policies that a pure monometallic standard does not have.

8.4.2. A MODEL OF THE GOLD/DOLLAR STANDARD. The argument of the preceding section will now be made precise by a model of the international gold/dollar standard, stripped of all institutional and technical details (like the role of the International Monetary Fund) and reduced to its essential building blocks.[11] For the omitted elements the reader is referred to the vast literature on international monetary economics.[12] The exposition will be limited to the case of two areas and two reserve assets. Full employment is assumed throughout, which means that price variations, to some extent, take the place of short-run fluctuations in employment.

Suppose the trading world is divided into the United States and what, for simplicity, may be called "Europe." In particular, Europe is defined to include South Africa, while U.S. gold production is disregarded. The United States stands ready to convert the dollar holdings of European central banks into gold at a fixed price, while the European central banks

10. The multicurrency reserve case is analyzed in Niehans (1974b).
11. The derivation of the model is explained in more detail in Niehans (1973).
12. On the Bretton Woods system, Horsefield and De Vries (1969) offer the basic material.

maintain fixed dollar rates for their currencies. Capital flows and interest rates are disregarded. The main question is under what conditions such a system is viable in the long run. The model thus concentrates on the path of balanced growth at a constant rate.[13] As a consequence, all stock and flow variables can again be expressed per unit of resources and thus made invariant along the balanced growth path.

In view of short-run disturbances along the long-run growth path, European central banks hold monetary reserves consisting of gold, m_E (measured in dollars at the fixed gold price), and dollars, e, while the United States holds gold to assure the convertibility of dollars.[14] By virtue of the balanced-growth assumption, the annual increments of gold and dollars are a constant fraction of the respective stocks. Disturbances may, of course, result in temporary deviations between stocks and flows. Since the annual increments are small relative to the reserve stocks, such deviations may last for extended periods. The viability of the system requires, however, that in the long run stocks and flows move in step.

The European demand for monetary reserves will probably depend mainly on the expected disturbances in imports and exports, influenced by many factors outside the scope of this model. The relevant point is that this demand is also positively related to the level of European and American commodity prices, p_E and p_A. Alternatively, the demand for reserves can be said to depend on the level of world prices, p, defined as a suitably weighted average of p_A and p_E, and the ratio of American prices and European prices, $q = p_A/p_E$. The demand for both m_E and e is increasing with p. The influence of relative prices on reserve demand, however, is not clear and may well be negligible; in a first approximation it can thus be disregarded. With this simplification, the European demand for reserves can be described by the function

$$p = r(m_E, e), \tag{8.4.1}$$

which specifies those combinations of gold and dollars which satisfy European reserve needs at a given price level. This function is pictured in the SE-quadrant of figure 8.4.1.

If gold and dollars are perfect substitutes, the reserve-indifference curves will be straight lines with slopes of 45 degrees. If the preference for gold rises with the proportion of reserves held in the form of dollars, the curves will be convex to the origin. In the extreme case where the two

13. This requires, among other things, that diminishing returns in gold mining are just matched by new gold discoveries and technical progress. The experience of recent decades gives no indication that, at constant commodity prices and wages, gold mining suffers from some fundamental inability to expand at about the same rate as the rest of the world economy.

14. The present model is thus consistent with the view, prominently expressed by Despres, Kindleberger, and Salant (1966), that the role of the United States was that of the banker of the system.

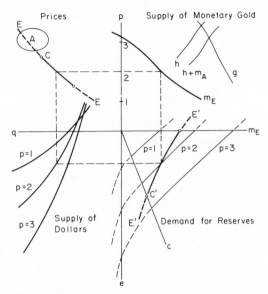

Figure **8.4.1**
The Gold/Dollar Standard

reserve assets are demanded in fixed proportion, the indifference curves would be rectangular. In the graph it is assumed that to the right of the c-line gold and dollars are perfect substitutes. However, if the gold/dollar ratio falls below the critical level represented by the c-line, more and more dollars are required to compensate central banks for one dollar's worth of gold. It will turn out that the flexibility of the gold/exchange standard depends crucially on the size of the area in which the two reserve assets are perfect substitutes.

The U.S. demand for monetary gold, m_A, is, for the moment, treated as an exogenously given policy variable. The consequences of changing U.S. gold reserves will be discussed in the following subsection.

The demand for reserve assets must now be confronted with the supply. The NE-quadrant summarizes information about the supply of monetary gold, also measured in dollars. With given relative prices gold production declines with rising world prices, as expressed by the g-schedule. The nonmonetary demand for gold, h, on the other hand, increases. This means that with rising prices smaller and smaller quantities of gold flow into monetary reserves, and at some point this flow becomes negative (as it actually did during the 1960s). The same is true for the gold flow into European reserves, taken separately, obtained by subtracting the given increment in U.S. reserves from the total flow of monetary gold. The m_E-schedule, being the graph of

$$m_E = g(p) - h(p) - m_A, \tag{8.4.2}$$

is thus a downward-sloping curve which intersects the p-axis at some positive level.

In principle, a new set of the curves in the NE-quadrant would have to be drawn for each price ratio. However, it is not clear a priori in what direction gold production and private gold demand are influenced by an increase in q at a given world price level, the result depending on the geographical distribution and the price elasticities of supply and demand. Without doing undue violence to the substance of the analysis, it may thus be assumed that the effects of q on the American and European side cancel out, leaving p as the only significant variable.

While under bimetallism the second reserve asset is supplied by another mining sector, under the gold/dollar standard it is created by European payment surpluses. Some deficit of the U.S. balance of payments was thus required by the equilibrium of the system. The annual flow of dollars into European reserves is the sum of the European commodity trade balance, depending on absolute and relative prices, and the American gold imports, both monetary and nonmonetary:

$$e = b(p, q) + m_A + h_A(p, q). \tag{8.4.3}$$

This function is graphed in the SW-quadrant of figure 8.4.1. At a given level of world prices, the European trade surplus, taken in isolation, increases with q. Since exports and imports in real terms must be presumed to be independent of the absolute price level, the trade surplus for given q, measured in dollars, may be assumed to be proportional to the world price level. By varying the price level, the trade balance can thus be represented by a bundle of dollar supply curves intersecting the zero-balance axis in the same point. Each of these curves is then shifted upward or downward to allow for the associated gold inflow, $m_A + h_A(p, q)$.

For given m_A this model consists of three equations in the four variables p, q, m_E and e. It can thus be used to determine the equilibrium positions of q for given p. Let us start with an arbitrary p. The m_E-curve shows the corresponding flow of gold into European reserves. Going down vertically to the appropriate reserve-indifference curve, we find the required amount of dollars. The corresponding balance of payments curve then shows what price ratio is necessary to produce this dollar flow at the given price level. This operation can be repeated for other price levels. In this way, we construct the price-equilibrium curve E-E as the locus of all those combinations of p and q which produce equilibrium in the system. The higher the level of world prices, the higher must be the American prices relative to European prices to provide the required reserves. In the absence of such an adjustment in relative prices, the drain of monetary gold will not be compensated by higher exchange reserves, thus producing a reserve shortage.

The fact that normally there will be many equilibrium combinations of p and q is the source of flexibility for the gold/exchange standard system. It means that equilibrium is consistent with different price ratios between the United States and Europe, provided the world price level is adjusted accordingly (or vice versa). Remembering that both p and q are functions of p_E and p_A, this is equivalent to the statement that equilibrium is consistent with different levels of U.S. prices, provided European prices are adjusted accordingly (or vice versa). Now prices in each area are determined by economic policies in the United States and Europe. The existence of an E-line thus implies that one of the two areas is free to choose its economic policies, provided the other is willing to adjust. Alternatively, a combination of policies can be selected by international cooperation. This is the main virtue of the gold/exchange standard.[15]

The price that has to be paid for the flexibility of the gold/dollar standard consists in shifts in the *composition* of reserves, reflecting Gresham's Law. To each equilibrium point in price space there corresponds an equilibrium point in reserve space. The locus of these points is the reserve-equilibrium curve E'-E'. For a proper functioning of the gold/exchange standard it is crucial that central banks are willing to move along this curve. In particular, as the world price level rises (and U.S. relative prices rise along with it) they must be willing to accept an increasing share of their reserves in the form of dollars, while the share of monetary gold declines. The willingness to accept such moves can clearly not be unlimited. These limits will be discussed presently.

8.4.3. THE GOLD/DOLLAR STANDARD UNDER INFLATION. As the crises of the Bretton Woods system followed each other more and more rapidly, it became popular to argue that a gold/dollar standard is inherently unstable.[16] Since the growth in the stock of monetary gold, so the argument ran, falls short of the growth rate of reserve demand, an increasing proportion of reserves consists of dollars. As a consequence, U.S. gold reserves gradually decline, at first only relative to dollars, but ultimately even absolutely. This leads to a gradual erosion of confidence in the convertibility of dollars and ultimately to the collapse of the system. As a summary description of actual events, this may be adequate enough. The preceding section has shown, however, that the collapse was not inherent in the construction of the system; if policy makers choose the "right" prices, there is no intrinsic reason why a gold/dollar system should not be viable indefinitely. What the system cannot survive are commodity prices that are out of line with the fixed prices of gold in terms of the various currencies.

15. It should be noted that the degree of freedom inherent in the gold/dollar standard is entirely different from the apparent "redundancy" of a policy instrument discussed by Mundell and others. The latter arises simply from the neglect of the stock demand for reserves by the economic theorist.
16. For a concise restatement of this argument, see Harry G. Johnson (1967).

The limits this imposes on prices, and thus on economic policies, will now have to be made precise.

In graphical terms, these limits can be expressed by saying that the price-equilibrium line E-E extends only over a limited range of prices. In the first place this is because gold and dollar holdings cannot be negative. If p, and thus q, are raised along the E-E line, gold will be drained from European reserves, being replaced by dollars. For short periods this may not be particularly alarming. In the long run, however, it is not compatible with the working of the system. From the point of view of balanced growth, therefore, the point where $m_E = 0$ provides a ceiling to admissible prices, both absolute and relative. Similarly, the point at which the dollar component becomes zero provides a floor for admissible prices.

In most cases, there will also be more narrow limits of a different nature. Whenever the slope of the reserve-indifference curves is not 45 degrees, central banks will find it advantageous to convert dollars into gold or vice versa. Equilibrium, therefore, requires that dollars and gold be perfect substitutes. The willingness of central bankers to regard gold and dollars as perfect substitutes, however, depends on their confidence in convertibility. For the convertibility of dollars into gold, this confidence in turn depends largely on U.S. gold reserves. For given U.S. reserves there is likely to be some gold/dollar ratio at which central banks become reluctant to accept further dollars for gold at the given gold price. In the graph, this critical ratio is represented by the c-line. Once the system pushes against this line, it will be in crisis, either collapsing in a scramble for gold or freezing in disequilibrium because central banks, out of self-protection, agree to a sort of moratorium for gold conversions.

There may conceivably be another crisis line with a high gold/dollar ratio at which central banks, uncertain whether the United States will continue to supply dollars for gold, refuse to accept gold at the given price. It is difficult to say anything definite about this line, though. While confidence in the dollar has a lot to do with objective reserve conditions, confidence in gold is more a matter of international economic warfare and may have little to do with the quantitative relationships used in this model.

The robustness of the gold/dollar standard thus depends crucially on the size of the area of perfect substitution. As the graph is drawn, the system can range over the solid part of the E- and E'-curves. If, on the other hand, European central banks decide to maintain a fixed ratio between gold and dollars, the area of perfect substitution shrinks to a line, and each of the two equilibrium curves shrinks to a point. The system thus becomes perfectly rigid. This is the basic reason why those well-meant proposals for fixed proportions in international reserves, while apparently intended to save the gold/dollar system, would actually have robbed it of its main advantage.

It should be noted that the range of admissible prices and thus the robustness of the system depend to a large extent on U.S. gold reserves. So far m_A was regarded as given; I shall now consider what happens if it is varied. On one hand, an increase in m_A reduces the flow of gold into European reserves at given prices, while the supply of dollars is increased, all by the same amount. On the other hand, it strengthens confidence in the dollar and thus raises the maximum amount of dollars European central banks are willing to hold. Whenever an increase in U.S. gold reserves by one dollar raises this maximum by more than one dollar, the increased movement of gold to the United States makes the system more flexible and pushes the crisis point further out. From the point of view of the flexibility of the system, the optimum is reached where the increases in U.S. reserves and in maximum European dollar holdings are just equal at the margin. It may be conjectured that by the middle of the 1960s U.S. gold reserves had fallen well below this point, thus making the system increasingly vulnerable to price variations.

In any case, continuing price increases pushed the system gradually toward the upper crisis point and, finally, into the area A, where a drain of monetary gold is associated with the unwillingness to hold the accruing dollars. The question is what could have been done to bring the system into equilibrium again. The United States tended to advocate the revaluation of European currencies and more expansionary policies in Europe. Both, however, would not have had the desired effect. Revaluation would have lowered the price of gold in terms of European currencies even further, thus aggravating the drain of monetary gold. More expansionary policies in Europe, by producing a decline in q and an additional rise in p, would have pushed the system further away from equilibrium in a NE-direction. That these policies were advocated could only reveal the basic lack of understanding of the gold/dollar standard.

In fact, there was only one thing that could have saved the gold/dollar system without a prolonged period of disastrous deflation, namely an increase in gold prices combined with the transition to noninflationary policies. The increase in gold prices would have pushed the supply curve for monetary gold in the NE-quadrant to the right, (1) by raising the physical quantity of gold flowing into European reserves, and (2) by raising the dollar value of a given quantity of gold. As a consequence, the whole price-equilibrium line would have been shifted upward toward higher world price levels, thus making a point in the A-area compatible with equilibrium. The transition to noninflationary policies, on the other hand, would have prevented a recurrence of the experience of the 1960s. As long as world prices continue to rise, no amount of technical ingenuity can make a system with fixed gold prices viable in the long run. The gold/dollar standard thus succumbed not to inherent flaws, but to inflationary policies, particularly of the United States during the 1960s.

Nine

THE SUPPLY OF BANK MONEY

Introduction

In the first eight chapters, money was synonymous with currency. The analysis is now extended to bank money, consisting of bank deposits or bank notes. The topic of this chapter thus becomes the economic theory of banking and the role of financial intermediaries for the money supply. In the first section the economic functions of financial intermediation are described in general terms.[1] The second section considers asset transformation and liquidity creation from the point of view of an individual bank, thus providing elements of a theory of the firm for banks. In the third section the perspective is extended to the banking system as a whole and its interplay with the rest of the economy. The supply of fiat money by the government and the existence of central banks are disregarded throughout, and we may assume that banks operate in a gold standard economy.

9.1. The economic functions of financial intermediation: A preliminary view

Financial intermediaries are economic agents whose balance sheets consist mainly of financial assets and liabilities. In the American terminology they are called banks if their liabilities include demand deposits that, for their holders, can serve as medium of exchange.

The economic functions of financial intermediaries are, in principle, the same as those of other firms. Nonbank firms have two basic functions. Some are producers, using factors of production to transform raw materials into technically and/or locationally different products. Others are dealers, using factors of production to facilitate the exchange of technically and locationally unchanged commodities and thus helping to lower transaction

---

1. For a classic, and much more detailed, description of the economic functions of intermediation, see Gurley and Shaw (1960), particularly pp. 116 ff., 191 ff.

costs. To some extent most firms are, of course, both producers and dealers.

Similarly, financial intermediaries may be brokers, middlemen, or dealers in assets, bringing borrowers and lenders together at lower costs than if the parties had to get together directly. The basis of their existence, from this point of view, is the cost of transactions in the credit market, including the cost of evaluating credit risks. In a competitive system, the difference between the interest such brokers pay to their creditors and the interest they receive from their debtors simply reflects their own marginal transactions costs. As dealers, financial intermediaries do not transform the claims they help to exchange. Their assets and liabilities relate to funds of the same type; in particular, they have the same liquidity or "moneyness." An impressive example of a highly developed intermediary system in which the brokerage function predominates is the Eurodollar market.[2] While the brokerage function may be very important for the efficiency of the monetary system, it has no significant influence on the aggregate liquidity of the nonbank sector. In particular, it cannot create money. "Passing the buck" may well help to redistribute liquidity; it does not create any.

On the other hand, financial intermediaries may perform a qualitative transformation on the funds they handle, comparable to the technical transformation performed by the nonbank producers. In this case, the funds they borrow (such as checking or savings deposits) are qualitatively different from the funds they lend (such as commercial loans or mortgages). This transformation of assets is of crucial importance for the composition of assets and liabilities of the nonbank sector, including, in particular, its liquidity and money supply.

Assets transformation by financial intermediaries increases the liquidity of the rest of the economy if the claims of the nonbank sector against the banks are, in the aggregate, more liquid than its debts to the banks. This may be called "positive asset transformation." In the opposite case of negative asset transformation, the liquidity of the nonbank sector is reduced. If we could suppose that the liquidity of different assets and liabilities can be expressed by a number between zero and one, this argument could be made numerically precise. Each item in the balance sheet would simply be weighted with its liquidity. The difference between the weighted sum of bank liabilities and the weighted sum of bank assets could then be used as a measure of liquidity creation. Since, in fact, there is no objective way to translate liquidity into a number, such an aggregation is difficult to carry out, but the mere notion of it helps to clarify the concept of liquidity creation. It is clear that liquidity for the nonbank sector is not created out

2. This interpretation of the Eurodollar market is elaborated in Niehans and Hewson (1976).

of thin air; it is merely the counterpart of a less liquid balance sheet of the banks.

The creation of money is a special case of liquidity creation, where attention is focused on the most liquid liabilities and assets, namely those that serve as medium of exchange. A bank supplies the rest of the economy (including other banks) with money if its monetary liabilities (like checking deposits) exceed its monetary assets (like currency reserves and demand deposits with other banks). In the reverse case, the bank reduces the money supply in the rest of the economy.

There is no logical or economic reason why financial intermediaries should always increase the money supply. Nonbank intermediaries, for example, while perhaps increasing the liquidity of the rest of the economy, typically reduce its money supply. This is because they hold some monetary assets as reserves, while even their most liquid liabilities (like savings deposits) are not monetary. There is also no logical or economic reason why financial intermediaries should always increase the liquidity of the rest of the economy. One could imagine banks that find it profitable to maintain balance sheets implying a reduction in nonbank liquidity by borrowing (in the aggregate) long to lend (in the aggregate) short—a possibility more fully analyzed in the following section. By and large, however, asset transformation by banks is usually of a sort to add both to the liquidity and to the money supply of the rest of the economy. The remainder of this section will concentrate on this typical case of positive liquidity transformation.

I shall now try to explain the economic significance of positive liquidity transformation in a preliminary way; a fuller analysis will be given in section 9.3. Suppose nonbank firms are the ultimate borrowers and households are the ultimate lenders. There are two debt instruments, called "deposits" and "loans," each of them standardized.[3] Deposits, with interest i_D, are legally defined in such a way that the default risk is relatively low, while their liquidity is relatively high in the sense that the lender finds it cheap to convert them into money at short notice. Loans, with interest i_L, are legally defined in such a way that the default risk is relatively high, while their liquidity is relatively low. It is clear that with equal interest rates lenders would always prefer deposits while borrowers would always prefer loans. Equilibrium thus requires $i_L > i_D$. In order to get the clearest possible picture of asset transformation, it is assumed that both assets can be transferred without transaction costs.

In the absence of intermediation, firms solicit deposits and loans directly from households. The firms' demand for loans depends jointly on both interest rates, negatively on i_L and positively on i_D. The household supply of loans, on the other hand, depends positively on i_L and negatively

3. We thus visualize firms as accepting deposits and households as making commercial loans—if the interest is right.

on i_D. By subtracting household supply from firm demand we obtain the excess demand for loans, L, which depends negatively on i_L and positively on i_D. For certain combinations of i_D and i_L the excess demand for loans is zero. In figure 9.1.1, these combinations are represented by the upward-sloping loan-equilibrium curve L-L. By analogous reasoning we can derive a curve along which the excess demand for deposits is zero, as illustrated by the deposit-equilibrium curve D-D. D-D is drawn flatter than L-L, because each market will be relatively more sensitive to its own rate than to the other market's rate. Since $i_L > i_D$, both curves lie wholly below the 45-degree line. Equilibrium will be attained at E, where both markets are in equilibrium. The corresponding interest margin $i_L - i_D$ reflects both the marginal cost to firms of switching from loan financing to deposit financing and the marginal cost to households of shifting from deposits to loans. These costs may consist of both resources and risk.

Suppose now that some individuals, discovering that they can transform loans into deposits at a marginal cost lower than $i_L - i_D$, begin to act as bankers. On one hand, this adds to the supply of loans, lowering i_L. On the other hand, it increases the demand for deposits, pushing up i_D. In figure 9.1.1 both curves shift upward and to the left as indicated by the broken lines, and the new equilibrium is at E'. Marginal costs, as measured by the interest margin, are lowered for both firms and households. The firms are now able to reduce risk by financing a larger share of their credit needs by loans, while the households reduce their risk by holding a larger share of their assets in the form of deposits. Conceivably, firms may switch completely to loan financing and/or households may decide to hold only deposits. If both of these occur, all credit flows through the banking system.

It has often been argued that the emergence of intermediation is accompanied by an expansion of saving and investment and an overall

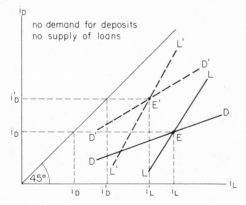

Figure **9.1.1**
The Market for Deposits and Loans

decline in interest rates. While this argument, on the surface, is plausible enough, it is not necessarily valid and requires more analysis. In particular, the level of interest rates is not unambiguously lower at E' than at E, since one interest rate is higher while the other is lower. In any case, such aggregate effects are not what matters in the present context. The important point is that the available funds, if the credit market works well, are channeled from households to firms with lower costs and thus more efficiently. That there is a gain from the entry of banks shows up in the fact that the first dollar's worth of asset transformation can be performed by the banks at a cost that is lower than the marginal cost to firms and households as reflected in the interest margin $i_L - i_D$. Banks will then enter up to the point where marginal costs are again equalized at $i_L' - i_D'$, creating consumer and producer surpluses in the process.[4]

This discussion left open the question why exactly the banks can transform loans into deposits at a lower marginal cost than firms and households. It also leaves open the question about the determinants of assets transformation by banks. These questions will be the subject of the following section.

9.2. Asset transformation by an individual bank

The supply of bank money is the aggregate result of asset transformation performed by each individual bank. To understand the determinants of the bank money supply we thus need a theory of the banking firm. Three variants of such a theory, selected from the point of view of monetary macroeconomics, will be presented in this section.

9.2.1. FIXED COEFFICIENTS. Under the first, most primitive approach, bank behavior is described by a set of fixed coefficients, comparable to fixed technical coefficients in production theory. Based on Phillips's classical contribution (1920), it dominated the field for about half a century. Since it is well known, the exposition can be brief.

Suppose the simplified balance sheet of a bank looks as follows:

Assets	Liabilities
Reserves (R)	Deposits (D)
Loans (L)	Equity (E)

Each of these items is assumed to be homogeneous. Deposits may be either demand deposits, time deposits or savings deposits. Capital goods like buildings and computers are assumed to be rented and thus do not appear in the balance sheet. By the balance-sheet identity, $R + L = D + E$.

---

4. For a more detailed analysis of this equilibrium condition, see Mangoletsis (1975), where, however, liquidity is treated as continuously variable, and the analysis is restricted to the polar cases in which all financing is either direct or indirect.

There are three fixed coefficients. Per dollar of deposits the bank holds r dollars of reserves to assure the convertibility of deposits; thus r is the reserve ratio. Per dollar of loans the bank maintains e dollars of equity to protect its creditors against unexpectedly large default losses on loans; e may be called the "equity ratio." Out of every dollar lent, s dollars will be held on deposit in the lending bank; s may be called the "redeposit ratio." Suppose now the bank experiences an inflow D^* of deposits that are autonomous in the sense that they are not created by its own lending activity. From the balance-sheet constraint and the three equations

$$R = rD,$$

$$E = eL,$$

$$D = sL + D^*,$$

we can then determine its loans, deposits, reserves, and equity capital, each as a multiple of autonomous deposits:

$$L = \frac{1 - r}{(1 - e) - s(1 - r)} D^* \qquad \text{Credit Multiplier}$$

$$D = \frac{1 - e}{(1 - e) - s(1 - r)} D^* \qquad \text{Deposit Multiplier}$$

$$R = \frac{r(1 - e)}{(1 - e) - s(1 - r)} D^* \qquad \text{Reserve Multiplier}$$

$$E = \frac{e(1 - r)}{(1 - e) - s(1 - r)} D^* \qquad \text{Equity Multiplier}$$

These multipliers can be interpreted either as level multipliers, based on average coefficients, or as marginal multipliers giving the effects of *changes* in D^* on L, D, R, and E, based on marginal coefficients. Stability requires that the common denominator be positive.

Among the four multipliers, the credit multiplier deserves particular attention. For individual banks, assuming realistic reserve, redeposit, and equity ratios, it will usually be less than unity. This means that for a dollar of additional deposits the bank can extend less than a dollar of additional loans. This is particularly true for banks that are small relative to the whole banking system and thus have a low redeposit ratio. It is conceivable, however, that the credit multiplier is more than unity even for a single bank. In this case the additional loans are larger than the additional deposits that caused the expansion. This case may be relevant for banks that, in view of their large size relative to the banking system, have a large redeposit ratio.

The economic significance of the credit multiplier depends on the type of bank in question. For commercial banks, D^* remains part of the depositor's cash balance. Extending loans means supplying additional cash balances to the nonbank sector. L/D^* thus measures the increase in the total money supply per dollar of initial deposits through the operations of the bank in question. For savings banks, D^* consists of savings deposits, which do not serve as a medium of exchange. As a consequence, the increase in the money supply through the operations of the individual bank is measured by $(L - D^*)/D^*$. This will normally be negative, implying that the operations of a savings bank reduce the money supply. At the same time, however, the savings bank increases the supply of savings deposits, which are a close substitute for money and thus tend to reduce the demand for cash balances.

It should be noted that the credit multiplier rises with an increasing equity ratio. For many short-run purposes, the equity ratio may be disregarded. This is the justification for the omission of e in most elementary expositions of banking multipliers. From a long-run point of view, however, the omission of e may lead to errors. If there is a sustained expansion of deposits, the equity base of the bank will have to be adjusted. The additional capital will be used, at least in part, to make additional loans. As a consequence, the expansion becomes stronger than it would be in the absence of equity considerations. Except for the inclusion of equity capital, the above model is stripped down to the most essential elements. It can easily be extended to include various types of deposits, different types of loans, and real capital like buildings and equipment. In each case, another fixed coefficient would, of course, have to be added.

While such fixed-coefficient models are useful to elucidate certain basic quantitative relationships in the money supply process, their value is severely limited by the fact that the economic calculus behind them is not made explicit. In particular, it is not made clear how the coefficients depend on market conditions like interest rates, prices, wages, and the like. These models thus make it difficult to explain the economic role of financial intermediation in a general equilibrium system of optimizing households and firms. More than half a century after Phillips, we should be able to do better. The "new view" of financial intermediation, initiated by Gurley and Shaw (1960) and Tobin (1963), was the response to this criticism. While it seemed perhaps new to a generation of monetary theorists reared on the fixed-coefficient approach, it was, in fact, a renaissance of the old tradition of banking and finance.

Various optimizing approaches to credit transformation have been developed, where the behavior of banks is derived from explicit cost minimization and profit maximization. Their common feature is the crucial role of uncertainty. It is uncertainty that explains the holding of reserves and the need for equity capital. Approaches differ (among other things) in their choice of the elements subject to uncertainty. Two such approaches will be presented here, shedding light on different aspects of the credit transformation process. In one model, uncertainty is concentrated in future interest rates, while deposits have perfectly certain maturities. In the other model, interest rates are perfectly certain, while deposits have uncertain withdrawal dates. In reality, these elements will generally be combined, but from an analytical point of view it is more instructive to treat them in isolation.

9.2.2. UNCERTAIN INTEREST RATES. The first model may be regarded as an idealized picture of the Eurocurrency banking system. One of the "stylized facts" about this system is the definite maturity of most deposits and loans. While this was even more pronounced in the earlier stages of the market, it still remains one of its distinctive features. As a consequence, the uncertainty about the withdrawal of deposits, so important in other banking systems, did not play a dominant role. On the other hand, interest rates in the Eurodollar market are free to fluctuate freely under the pressure of market forces, and their future is, as a consequence, quite uncertain. Under these conditions, credit transformation by banks becomes a problem of the term structure of interest rates under uncertainty.[5]

To formalize this idea, I use a two-period framework.[6] At the beginning of the first period the bank can accept both one-period deposits and two-period deposits. It can also make one-period loans and two-period loans. The need for equity capital is disregarded. The bank's revenues and costs will depend on the current rates of interest for one-period and two-period funds, where the relevant lending rate is the market rate net of the expected value of default losses. Usually the bank will face different borrowing and lending rates, with the margin reflecting transaction costs. This margin is the basic source of the bank's profits. Part of the interest income will go to pay for inputs like labor, computers, communications, and the like. If the bank is in pure competition in the sense that it can borrow and lend any amount at the respective market rates, then a determinate bank size requires marginal costs to be increasing with the scale of operations. In reality, the size of the bank will often be limited by the size of its market for deposits and loans.

For the present purpose it is assumed that the margin between borrowing and lending rates is perfectly certain for both periods, and that the current level of one-period and two-period rates is also certain. The future

5. An effort to solve this problem in terms of portfolio analysis is found in Pyle (1971), but instead of exploiting the term structure of assets and interest rates, Pyle treats deposits highly artificially as assets with a negative yield (compared to currency) and thus held in negative amount.

6. For a mathematical and graphical exposition of the following argument, though for a simplified case, see Niehans and Hewson (1976, appendix).

level of one-period rates ruling at the beginning of the second period, however, is subject to uncertainty. Suppose, first, that the bank maintains a perfectly matched balance sheet in the sense that all one-period loans are financed by one-period deposits, while all two-period loans are financed by two-period deposits. There is, as a consequence, no asset transformation and no liquidity creation. In this case, the bank's portfolio decisions at each moment are not affected by the uncertainty of future interest rates. At each moment, current decisions can be made in the light of known interest rates.

Suppose, however, the bank decides to use funds from one-period deposits to finance two-period loans, thus borrowing short to lend long and creating liquidity for the nonbank sector by positive liquidity transformation. It will then have to refinance these two period loans at the beginning of the second period with new one-period deposits, the cost of which is uncertain. Alternatively, the bank may decide to use two-period deposits to finance one-period loans, thus engaging in negative asset transformation and thereby reducing liquidity for the nonbank sector. In this case, it will have to reinvest the proceeds from the one-period loans at the beginning of the second period, again at uncertain rates. It should be noted that this model does not allow for liquidity risks in either case, as any amount of deposits can always be obtained by the bank at the going market rate. As a consequence, no reserves need to be held against liquidity risks. (It is interesting to note that Eurodollar banks indeed operate with surprisingly low reserves.) However, the uncertainty of future interest rates makes bank profits subject to risk whenever the portfolio deviates from the perfect matching of maturities.

The bank will not run such a risk unless by so doing it can increase the expected value of its profits. Such an expected gain requires that the expected value of the future one-period rate deviate from term-structure parity. If it is cheaper, on the average, to finance a two-period loan by two successive one-period deposits than by one two-period deposit, the bank will obtain a reward for accepting the risk of positive maturity transformation (and a punishment for negative transformation). If it is more lucrative, on the average, to invest a two-period deposit in two successive one-period loans than in one two-period loan, the bank will obtain a reward for accepting the risk of negative liquidity transformation (and a punishment for positive transformation).

Credit transformation by the bank thus becomes dependent on the term structure of current and expected future interest rates. With a term structure close to parity, with considerable uncertainty about the future, and/or with high risk aversion of bankers, balance sheets will tend to be closely matched and asset transformation will be insignificant. This seems roughly to have been the situation in the Eurodollar market, at least in its first decade. In this case the banks are essentially brokers of funds, and the source of their profits is their comparative advantage with respect to transaction costs. If, however, factors outside the banking system put a persistent liquidity premium on short-term funds, and if the uncertainty about future interest rates and/or the risk aversion of the bankers are small, "borrowing short to lend long" and thus liquidity creation will become a dominant feature of the banking system. If the short-term deposits circulate as money, the creation of liquidity appears in the particular form of the creation of bank money. Conversely, if there should be a persistent premium on long-term funds, we would begin to regard "borrowing long to lend short" as a characteristic feature of banks, and their contribution to the liquidity of the nonbank sector would be negative.

This model of the asset transformation by banks, while close to portfolio and term structure theory, is very different in spirit from the usual banking models with their deposit risks, reserve requirements, and multipliers. It shows that money creation by banks does not necessarily result from the discovery by goldsmiths that currency deposited for safekeeping is not all withdrawn at the same time, but may grow out of the discovery by bill brokers that open positions for certain maturities may be worth the risk. Since this model does not require any sort of market imperfection (except uncertainty of interest rates), it is more basic than the traditional approach, which has to assume that banks find it difficult to borrow on short notice. As the debate about liquidity creation in the Eurodollar market has shown, the preoccupation of economists with the traditional model at the virtual exclusion of more basic alternatives may result in a serious misinterpretation of reality.

9.2.3. UNCERTAIN MATURITY OF DEPOSITS. In the preceding model of asset transformation, the maturities of all deposits and loans were known with certainty, while interest rates were uncertain. I now reverse the perspective, assuming that interest rates are certain, while deposits have an uncertain maturity. This reflects an important aspect of reality, particularly in the U.S. banking system, since demand deposits can be withdrawn at any time, while the interest rate on demand deposits is held at zero by law.[7] If banks use such deposits to make loans with definite maturities, they run the risk of running out of reserves. If this imposes a cost, the bank will want to balance the marginal revenue from additional loans against the marginal cost of running out of reserves, thus creating a demand for reserves and putting a limit on asset transformation. The first to develop a stochastic theory of the bank money supply based on the uncertainty of deposit withdrawal was Edgeworth (1888). His idea lay dormant during

7. It should be noted that this legal provision is important here only inasmuch as it eliminates or reduces uncertainty about the future deposit rate, and not because it introduces an imperfection into the market.

the long reign of the fixed-coefficient approach, until it was taken up and further developed by Orr and Mellon (1961).

The maturity of bank loans may be subject to similar uncertainty if the loans have the form of an open credit line or an overdraft facility, where the borrower can decide day by day what amounts, within the stated limit, he wishes to borrow. The consequences for the demand for bank reserves would be very similar to those of uncertain deposit withdrawal, and this aspect will not be further considered here. However, bank loans are also subject to default losses. To the extent these are known from experience, they can be treated like any other cost. To the extent, however, that default losses are uncertain, they will force the bank to maintain a certain amount of equity capital, balancing the cost of capital against the need to protect its creditors against losses from a bank failure. Stochastic elements thus play a crucial role in the determination of both the reserve ratio and the equity ratio. It is essentially the importance of these risk elements that distinguishes the theory of the firm for banks (and other financial intermediaries) from the textbook case of the theory of the firm. The following model is designed to make these considerations analytically explicit.[8]

I again use a simplified balance sheet consisting of demand deposits, loans, reserve, and equity, related by the identity

$$R + L = D + E. \tag{9.2.1}$$

Capital goods are assumed to be rented and thus do not appear as an asset. Each item is supposed to be perfectly homogeneous, all deposits are of equal size θ, and all loans are of equal size λ. Banks strive to arrange their balance sheets in such a way that the expected value of pure profits, in excess of the normal competitive return on equity, is maximized. In doing so, they are subject to a number of constraints.

A *deterministic* constraint, analogous to the production function in the theory of the firm, arises from the fact that bank operations require inputs of capital and labor, depending on the volume of loans and deposits they handle. For given loan and deposit sizes, this "technological production function" can be written implicitly as

$$f(K,N,L,D) = 0, \tag{9.2.2}$$

8. The model is of the same general type as Klein's model (1971). It differs from it in the following respects: (1) monopolistic elements in the loan and deposit market are disregarded; (2) default losses and the resulting demand for equity capital are explicitly considered; (3) the model determines not only the structure of the balance sheet, but also the absolute scale of bank operations; (4) a less arbitrary distribution for deposit withdrawals is used; (5) inputs of labor and capital goods are part of the optimizing model. A similar approach was used by Baltensperger (1972a, 1972b) who actually took as his point of departure an earlier version of the present model. However, Baltensperger was not able to integrate the reserve/deposit calculus, the equity/loan calculus, and the factor input calculus.

with $f_K > 0, f_N > 0, f_L < 0$, and $f_D < 0$. The marginal product of capital in terms of loans is thus represented by

$$dL/dK(\bar{N}, \bar{D}) = -\frac{f_K}{f_L},$$

and other marginal relationships are defined in an analogous manner.

In addition, there are two *stochastic* constraints not commonly used in the theory of the firm. One of them relates to the withdrawal risk on deposits. To formalize it in a simple way we can again use a two-period framework. Loans are due at the end of the second period. Deposits, however, can be withdrawn or added to at the end of the first period. The dollar amount of net withdrawals after one period, W, (which can be positive or negative) is assumed to have a distribution $\phi(W)$ with zero mean, reflecting stationary conditions, and standard deviation σ_W. Whenever $W > R$, the bank experiences a reserve deficit $W - R$. Such deficits have to be financed by borrowing at a "penalty rate" i_P during the second period.[9] Whenever $W < R$, the bank has an excess of liquid funds in the amount of $R - W$ during the second period. It is assumed that the market for emergency financing is imperfect in the sense that such excess funds cannot be lent out at all.[10] The expected dollar value of (positive) reserve deficits is a function of D and R,

$$\rho = E(W - R) = \int_R^\infty (W - R)\phi(W)dW = \rho(D, R). \tag{9.2.3}$$

A rise in D clearly produces an increase in ρ, while an increase in R works the other way. The locus of points with a given expected reserve deficit is thus a rising curve. The further properties of these iso-deficit curves depend on $\phi(W)$. For a triangular distribution it is shown in the appendix to this section that (1) the iso-deficit curves are concave from below, (2) for an equiproportionate increase in deposits and reserves the reserve deficit first rises to a maximum and then declines, and (3) if the reserve deficit increases with an equiproportionate increase in D and R it increases in a lesser proportion. The family of iso-deficit curves thus has the general shape of figure 9.2.1.

ρ is the expected value of the amount the bank will have to finance through emergency borrowing. If there are legal reserve requirements,

9. It should be noted that loans and mean deposits are for two periods, while the reserve deficits only last one period. i_P thus has to be interpreted as half the rate actually observed in the market.

10. A more general treatment could include a "federal funds market" for interbank loans, with transaction costs producing a difference between borrowing and lending rates. In the absence of a market imperfection of this sort, no reserves would be held, and the expected cost of emergency borrowing would just be matched by the expected revenue from lending excess funds. In this sense, the Edgeworth-type models of banking are indeed based on market imperfections.

this is increased by the amount of required reserves; penalty costs are incurred long before reserves are exhausted. As a consequence, banks subject to minimum reserve requirements will usually wish to hold some excess reserves for exactly the same reason reserves are held in the absence of legal requirements.

The other stochastic element is default losses on loans, F. These are assumed to have a distribution $\psi(F)$ with a mean default ratio $\beta > 0$ and standard deviation σ_F. Whenever $F > E$, the bank fails. This is not the place to enter into a discussion of the proper treatment of bankruptcy risks in profit maximization. Such a treatment would certainly require a much fuller analysis of behavior under uncertainty than the present topic warrants. For the present purposes it is sufficient to assume that the bank maximizes profits subject to the constraint that the expected bankruptcy loss does not exceed a prescribed value[11]

$$\bar{\pi} = \int_{E}^{\infty} (F - E)\psi(F)dF = \pi(L,E), \tag{9.2.4}$$

with $\pi_L > 0$ and $\pi_E < 0$. The properties of (9.2.4) are assumed to be exactly analogous to those of (9.2.3). The analysis in the appendix thus applies with D replaced by L and R replaced by E. For a specific $\bar{\pi}$, E is a rising function of L with diminishing slope, as depicted in figure 9.2.2.

The bank maximizes expected pure profit

$$E(P) = (i_L - \beta) L - i_D D - i_p \rho - eE - wN - rK, \tag{9.2.5}$$

subject to the constraints (9.2.1) − (9.2.4), where

i_L loan rate	e normal profit rate
β expected default ratio	w wage rate
i_D deposit rate	r capital goods rental
i_P penalty rate	

All markets are assumed to be competitive so that the bank believes it can borrow, raise, and lend any amounts at the respective market rates.

Forming the Lagrange function and taking its partial derivatives, three marginal conditions are found to be necessary for an optimum. The first condition provides for the optimal combination of factors in banking operations at given levels of loans and deposits. It thus corresponds to the familiar condition for cost minimization and reads

$$\frac{w}{f_N} = \frac{r}{f_K}. \tag{9.2.6}$$

It means that banking technology should be used in such a way that the

---

11. To keep π at zero would evidently require equity as large as loans and would thus preclude the financing of loans from deposits. Most banks would probably be willing to incur a somewhat higher risk of failure for the sake of higher profits.

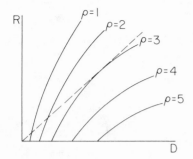

Figure **9.2.1**
The Expected Reserve Deficit

marginal costs of loans in terms of different factors are equalized, and the same is true for deposits.

The second condition relates to the optimization of loans at a given level of deposits and can be written[12]

$$ i_L - \beta = r\left(\frac{-f_L}{f_K}\right) + e\left(\frac{\pi_L}{-\pi_E}\right) + i_P\left[1 - \left(\frac{\pi_L}{-\pi_E}\right)\right](-\rho_R). \qquad (9.2.7) $$

The condition says that the marginal revenues from loans, net of expected default losses, should be equal to their marginal cost. The first cost component is the marginal factor cost of a loan. The second term is the marginal equity cost of loans; it arises because each increment in loans, to keep bankruptcy risk at $\bar{\pi}$, requires additional equity in the amount $-\pi_L/\pi_E$, which has to be paid at rate e. The third term is the marginal penalty cost of loans. At a given level of deposits, any increase in loans that is not financed by new equity has to come out of reserves, thus increasing the withdrawal risk, which is chargeable at the penalty rate i_P.[13]

The third condition provides for the optimization of deposits at a given level of loans. It can be arranged to read

$$ i_P(-\rho_R) = i_D + r\left(\frac{-f_D}{f_K}\right) + i_P\rho_D. \qquad (9.2.8) $$

12. Partial derivatives that are negative are written with a minus sign, so that the expressions in round brackets are all positive.
13. If we abstract from resource costs, equity, and default losses, the loan condition reduces to

$$ i_L/i_P = -\rho_R = \int_R^\infty \phi(W)dW \leq \frac{1}{2}. $$

The equality/inequality holds because the probability of running out of reserves cannot exceed one-half, the value it has for $R = 0$. The implication that, for an interior optimum, the penalty rate would have to be at least twice the loan rate seems to cast a shadow of implausibility over the model. However, in view of β, π_L/π_E and f_L/f_K, an interior optimum is, in fact, compatible with penalty rates well below the loan rate.

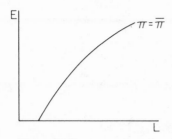

Figure **9.2.2**
The Expected Default Loss

On the left-hand side is the marginal benefit of reserves through the reduction in penalty costs. On the right-hand side appear the components of the marginal cost of deposits, consisting of interest cost, factor cost, and penalty cost.[14] In addition, all four balance-sheet components must, of course, be nonnegative.

While the first-order conditions are necessary for a profit maximum, they are, of course, not sufficient. The second-order conditions require, among other things, that the marginal cost of loans increase with increasing loans and that an increase in deposits produce an excess of marginal cost over marginal benefit. While there is nothing in the model (or in reality) to ensure that these conditions are satisfied,[15] it may be conjectured that they usually are. It would indeed be unusual if a bank, at a given level of deposits, would find it advantageous to expand loans to the point where reserves are zero. It would also be unusual if, at a given level of loans, the bank found it profitable to expand its deposits beyond all limits just to increase reserves. In any case, it will here be assumed that the conjecture is valid. More serious qualifications with respect to a joint increase in both deposits and loans will be discussed presently.

The three marginal conditions imply demand functions for deposits, loans, reserves, equity capital, capital goods, and labor in terms of interest rates and factor prices. If the loan rate i_L goes up, the volume of loans, and

14. Again, no particular relationship between the two interest rates is required for an interior optimum except that no deposits would be demanded if the penalty rate were below the deposit rate. In particular, the deposit rate may conceivably be negative, amounting to a service charge.

15. Whether the marginal factor cost of loans (at given deposits) and the marginal factor cost of deposits (at given loans) rise or fall depends on the degree of complementarity or substitutability of D and L in (9.2.2). It is reasonable to assume that they rise at least after a point. The shifts in the stochastic components of the marginal benefits and costs can be assessed on the basis of the second-order partial derivatives of the expected reserve deficit and the expected default loss derived in the appendix. It turns out that the marginal penalty cost of loans rises, but the marginal equity cost of loans declines with increasing loans, while the marginal penalty cost of deposits, net of the marginal benefit of the additional reserves, is likely to decline with rising deposits. The last two components, reflecting stochastic economies of scale, may cause the second-order conditions to fail, even if the factor costs are well behaved.

thus equity requirements, will rise. The demand for deposits will also rise as it becomes more profitable to transform deposits into loans. The aggregate effect on reserves is uncertain, as the substitution of loans for reserves will tend to reduce them, while the expansion of bank operations will work in the opposite direction. The average reserve ratio, however, will certainly fall, both because the higher loan rate makes it profitable to assume a somewhat higher expected reserve deficit and because the expansion in operations, thanks to the law of large numbers, makes it possible to achieve the same expected reserve deficit with a lower reserve ratio.

If there is an increase in the deposit rate i_D, the aggregate amount of deposits will certainly contract. Loans, and thus equity requirements, will contract also. The demand for reserves will decline, as the reduction in deposits reduces the expected reserve deficit. However, it will decline less than in proportion to deposits, because the law of large numbers now works in reverse, thus raising the reserve ratio for a given reserve deficit, while the reduced margin between the penalty rate and the deposit rate reduces the willingness to accept reserve deficits. As a consequence, the reserve ratio rises.

A rise in the penalty rate will, of course, induce the bank to increase reserves and to shift to a higher reserve ratio. The aggregate effect on deposits is ambiguous, as the increase in the reserve ratio[16] and the lower overall profitability of bank operations work against each other. The volume of loans, however (and thus of equity), will certainly contract, both because it is now marginally more profitable to hold funds than to lend them and because the level of bank operations contracts.

It was so far assumed that banks are characterized by diminishing returns to scale. If they are not, there is no upper limit to the size of the individual bank under pure competition. Scale economies may originate either in the technological production function or from the stochastic elements. The possible scale economies in the technological production function were extensively investigated on the basis of accounting data by Benston (1965, 1970, 1972), Greenbaum (1967), and Longbrake/Haslem (1975). They are of the same nature as in other industries, and there are no specific reasons why factor costs should generally rise or generally fall with the scale of operations. Nobody will be surprised to find many instances of scale economies that, in the real economy, are counteracted by imperfect competition in the market for loans, deposits, and equity.

Of more interest are the stochastic scale effects, for which the basic analysis, both theoretical and empirical, has been provided by Baltensperger (1972a, 1972b). Thanks to the law of large numbers, an equipro-

---

16. Note that, with given L and thus $dR = dD$, an increase in the reserve ratio requires an increase in deposits.

portionate increase in all items of the balance sheet raises the expected reserve deficit in a smaller proportion, and the probability of bankruptcy declines. From the stochastic point of view, larger banks are always better off, *ceteris paribus*, than smaller banks. Unless these stochastic scale economies are overbalanced by diminishing returns in the factor inputs, larger banks will also be better off overall under pure competition. This does not mean that smaller banks cannot, in fact, survive. It does not even mean that they are actually worse off and that there is a tendency toward increasing concentration. It only means that the size of the banking firm, like the size of firms in so many other industries, will be limited not by increasing costs, but by the size of the market under imperfect competition. Given the size of local markets and the costs of transportation, communication, and information, even very small banks may be prosperous.

The stochastic scale economies seem to be different for different types of banks. For demand deposits, characterized by relatively large withdrawal risks, and for commercial loans with their relatively large default risks, scale economies seem to be stronger than for mortgages and time deposits. As a consequence, in the absence of regulatory constraints, banks of different size tend to have a different structure of their balance sheets, small firms tending to concentrate on assets and liabilities with relatively low risk, while the higher-risk markets are dominated by larger banks (or less risk-averse bankers). For the same reason, large banks can afford to hold large-size deposits and loans, while small banks have to keep their risks low by concentrating on smaller deposits and loans.

Appendix to Section 9.2: The expected reserve deficit

Consider a bank that is going to be liquidated after two periods. There is a population of homogeneous deposits of equal initial size θ. Each deposit is characterized by the percentage of θ, x_i, which is withdrawn after the first period. x_i is distributed with mean zero, expressing the assumption of stationary conditions, and standard deviation s. For an amount of deposits D the bank draws from this population a sample of $n = D/\theta$ deposits. Withdrawals after the first period will thus be $W = \Sigma x_i \theta$. If $\phi(W)$ is the distribution of W, the expected value of withdrawals in excess of reserves R is

$$\rho = E(W - R) = \int_R^\infty (W - R)\phi(W)dW = \rho(D,R).$$

This will be called the "expected reserve deficit."

For large n, by virtue of the central limit theorem, $\phi(W)$ is approximately normal, with mean zero and a standard deviation proportionate to the square root of D, namely, $\sigma_w = s\theta\sqrt{n} = s\sqrt{\theta D}$. However, some of the relevant properties of $\rho(R,D)$, particularly the first and second order derivatives with respect to D, are hard to evaluate for a normal distribution. It should also be kept in mind that withdrawals cannot exceed 100 percent of the original deposit (thus $x_i \leqq 1$), while additions have no upper limit. To the extent that $\phi(W)$, in view of the finite character of n, deviates from normality it will thus reach zero at a finite value of W.

For these reasons the analysis will be based on a triangular distribution, valid for positive values of W,

$$\phi(W) = \frac{1}{h}\left(1 - \frac{W}{h}\right),$$

where h stands for the upper limit of W. It will be assumed that the standard deviation is still proportionate to $\sqrt{D}$. As a consequence, h is also proportionate to $\sqrt{D}$ since $h = 2\sqrt{3} \cdot \sigma_w = c\sqrt{D}$. By evaluating the above integral, the expected reserve deficit can be written in terms of h and R,

$$\rho^*(h,R) = (h/6)\left(1 - \frac{R}{h}\right)^3. \qquad 1 - \frac{R}{h} > 0$$

Some characteristics of this function can be found by considering the shape of the "iso-deficit" curves as the locus of points of given ρ^*. Analysis shows that these curves rise to the right, as the expected deficit is positively related to D but negatively to R, and they do so with increasing slope, which implies that an equiproportionate increase in h and R will always result in a higher expected deficit. More specifically, it is evident that the function is linear-homogeneous in h and R.

What we would ultimately like to know, however, are the properties of the expected reserve deficit in terms of D and R,

$$\rho(D,R) = \frac{c}{6} D^{1/2} \left(1 - \frac{1}{c} RD^{-1/2}\right)^3.$$

The derivatives of this function turn out to be

$$\rho_R = -\frac{1}{2}\left(1 - \frac{1}{c} RD^{-1/2}\right)^2 < 0,$$

$$\rho_D = \frac{c}{12} D^{-1/2} \left(1 - \frac{1}{c} RD^{-1/2}\right)^2 \left(1 + \frac{2}{c} RD^{-1/2}\right) > 0,$$

$$\rho_{RR} = \frac{1}{c} D^{-1/2} \left(1 - \frac{1}{c} RD^{-1/2}\right) > 0,$$

$$\rho_{RD} = -\frac{1}{2c} RD^{-3/2} \left(1 - \frac{1}{c} RD^{-1/2}\right) < 0,$$

$$\rho_{DD} = -\frac{c}{24} D^{-3/2} \left[1 - 9\left(\frac{1}{c} RD^{-1/2}\right)^2 + 8\left(\frac{1}{c} RD^{-1/2}\right)^3\right] \lessgtr 0.$$

The ambiguous sign of ρ_{DD} tells us that the bank cannot be sure whether the marginal reserve deficit with respect to deposits will rise or fall as deposits increase. Further analysis shows that ρ_{DD} is zero for $R = h$ and also for a value of R slightly below $R = h/2$. It has a maximum at $R = (3/4)h$ and a minimum at $R = 0$. We conclude that $\rho_{DD} < 0$ for values of reserves below about 40 percent of maximum withdrawals, which must be considered as the normal state of affairs, but $\rho_{DD} > 0$ for very high values of R.

By taking the differential of $\rho(D,R)$ and setting it equal to zero (or, alternatively, by taking the ratio $- \rho_D/\rho_R$) we can determine the slope of the iso-deficit curves,

$$\frac{dR}{dD} = \frac{c}{6} D^{-1/2} \left(1 + \frac{2}{c} R D^{-1/2} \right),$$

which is positive. The curvature of these curves,

$$\frac{d^2 R}{dD^2} = - \frac{c}{36} D^{-3/2} \left(1 + \frac{8}{c} R D^{-1/2} \right),$$

turns out to be negative. In terms of deposits and reserves, the iso-deficit curves thus have the shape of those in figure 9.2.1. This suggests that for an equiproportionate increase in D and R the reserve deficit first rises to a maximum and then declines. This can be confirmed by evaluating $\partial\rho/\partial D$ on the assumption that the reserve ratio is constant at $R/D = r$. The maximum is found to be at $R = h/2 = (c/2) D$.

While $\rho(D,R)$ is clearly not linear-homogeneous in the arguments, it can be ascertained that the expected reserve deficit per dollar of deposits,

$$\frac{\rho}{D} = \frac{c}{6} D^{-1/2} \left(1 - \frac{r}{c} D^{1/2} \right)^3,$$

declines as deposits are increased at a constant reserve ratio $R/D = r$,

$$\frac{\partial}{\partial D} \left(\frac{\rho}{D} \right) = - \frac{1}{12} \left(1 - \frac{r}{c} D^{1/2} \right)^2 \left[c D^{-3/2} \left(1 - \frac{r}{c} D^{1/2} \right) \right.$$

$$\left. + 3r D^{-1} \right] < 0.$$

This is an important aspect of scale economics. Other things equal, a larger bank has lower expected reserve deficits relative to its deposits than a small bank.

9.3. The supply of money by the banking system

The preceding section described asset transformation, and thus implicitly the supply of demand deposits, by an individual bank under given market conditions. Progressing from the equilibrium of the firm to the general equilibrium of the economy, I shall now consider the aggregate level of bank money resulting, jointly with interest rates and prices, from the interplay of producing firms, banks, and households. A preliminary view of this topic was given in section 9.1; it will now be analytically elaborated, using the banking model presented in subsection 9.2.3.

The analysis is restricted to a closed economy. This economy is supposed to be on a gold standard, with gold coins circulating as currency. The only function of government is to fix the price of gold in terms of the unit of account. In particular, there is no government fiat money, no government debt, and no central bank. Entry into banking is free, and there are no regulations with respect to reserve requirements and the like.

This way of restricting the problem is designed to focus attention on the basic problems of the money supply by commercial banks. Specifically, the following questions will be raised:

1. What are the effects of the banking system on resource allocation, the composition of output, the supply of financial assets, and interest rates?

2. Does such a system result in a determinate price level, or does it result in an infinite expansion of the bank money supply?

3. Are bank deposits and commercial bank notes a component of national wealth?

4. Can such a system be expected to work efficiently, if left to itself, or does efficiency require government regulation?

Questions like these have been hotly debated in the last two decades,[17] and the character of this debate is vivid testimony to the imperfect understanding of the economics of the banking system. What seems to be needed is an integration of banking theory with general economic analysis.[18]

9.3.1. A GENERAL EQUILIBRIUM MODEL. Imagine a stationary economy without banks, similar to the economy analyzed in the preceding chapter on commodity money. For the present purpose, it is convenient to introduce the following modifications:

1. Instead of working with one amorphous resource, I now distinguish between labor and capital. This makes it possible to raise the question about the relationship between the interest rates on loans and deposits and the yield on capital goods.

2. I shall assume that in the vicinity of equilibrium the relative price of gold is high enough to exclude any nonmonetary use. While this simplifies the analysis, we have to keep in mind that it is the potential nonmonetary

---

17. The most recent round of this debate was provoked by Pesek and Saving (1967).

18. The following analysis is in the spirit of Stanley Fischer's paper (1972), though the latter uses a Golden Rule growth model and, having a different purpose, is less explicit about the banking aspects of the problem.

demand for gold, appearing at a sufficiently low relative price, that ultimately puts a ceiling on commodity prices.

3. It is assumed that national wealth is exogenously given by past history, though its composition is subject to the economic calculus. This assumption, while arbitrary, serves to exclude the whole problem of the determination of steady-state wealth, which is not specific to monetary theory.

We know that in the absence of banks the market mechanism in such an economy allocates certain shares of labor and capital to the consumer goods industry and gold production and, by so doing, determines the currency supply and the consumer price level. There may well be borrowing and lending in such a system, and some of it may even have the form of loans similar to bank loans or of deposits similar to bank deposits. However, for the nonbank sector in the aggregate the net amount of each type of borrowing (or lending) must be zero.

Into such a system we now introduce commercial banks. These banks accept demand deposits, consisting of gold currency, paying either a positive interest or charging a fee, depending on the state of supply and demand. The deposits can be transferred by check, thus serving as a medium of exchange, and they can be withdrawn at any time. The nonbank sector is thus allowed to hold a positive aggregate amount of demand deposits. These are assumed to be close but still imperfect substitutes for currency, the imperfection arising from the fact that bank deposits are not subject to attrition and that the services a bank provides are different from those of coins. As a consequence, currency and deposits may have different yields.

The banks make loans to the private sector, again denominated in standard currency. However, some standard currency is held by the banks as reserves. The transformation of deposits into loans also requires inputs of labor and capital goods. We thus imagine the economy to be divided into two sectors, with the producers' sector using labor and capital to produce consumer goods and commodity money while the banking sector uses labor and capital, plus some commodity money, to process loans into deposits.

This general idea is now formalized in an analytical model. There are two factors, labor and capital. A part of each is used in the producers' sector, while the remainder is used in the banking sector:

$$\bar{N} = N^P + N^B, \tag{9.3.1}$$

$$K = K^P + K^B. \tag{9.3.2}$$

The aggregate supply of labor is given, while K is determined endogenously. Firms use their factors to produce consumer goods, X, and gold, G, according to the implicit production function

$$Q(N^P, K^P, X, G) = 0. \tag{9.3.3}$$

Cost minimization will see to it that

$$\frac{Q_G}{Q_X} = \frac{p_G}{p_X}, \tag{9.3.4}$$

$$\frac{Q_N}{Q_K} = \frac{w}{r}, \tag{9.3.5}$$

$$-\frac{Q_N}{Q_X} = \frac{w}{p_X}, \tag{9.3.6}$$

where p_G and p_X are, respectively, the prices of gold and commodities, while r and w are again the rental on capital and the wage rate. The ratios of partial derivatives on the left-hand side of each condition can be interpreted, respectively, as the marginal rate of transformation of commodities into gold (with given factors), the marginal rate of factor substitution (with given outputs), and the marginal product of labor in terms of commodities (with given capital and gold). There is assumed to be free entry into the producing sector so that all income becomes imputed to labor and capital.

The households are endowed with given labor $\bar{N}$ and with total real wealth $\bar{W}$. Within this overall wealth constraint they are free to determine the amounts of real capital, K, real currency, M/p_X, and real demand deposits, D/p_X, they wish to hold and the amount they want to borrow from banks, L/p_X:

$$\bar{W} = K + M/p_X + D/p_X - L/p_X. \tag{9.3.7}$$

Since there will generally be borrowing and lending within the nonbank sector, D and L have to be interpreted, respectively, as excess demand and supply.

The households are also subject to an income constraint. It tells them that they can spend on goods and services whatever they earn on their labor, on their capital goods, on their demand deposits, and on risk-bearing (to be explained presently), minus the replacement demand for currency at the depreciation rate δ and the interest on bank loans:

$$p_X X = w\bar{N} + rK + i_D D + i_p p_X \bar{\rho} - \delta M - i_L L. \tag{9.3.8}$$

It was shown in the preceding chapters how, for given market yields, demand (or supply) functions for financial assets can be obtained on the assumption that these assets have no direct utility. It was also pointed out that it does not seem to be possible to use this indirect-utility approach to derive a surrogate utility function in which financial assets appear as arguments having direct utility. It is nevertheless instructive, in the present context, to proceed as if such a direct-utility function

$$U = U(X, M/p_X, D/p_X)$$

were maximized subject to the income and wealth constraints.

This yields the marginal conditions

$$\frac{r}{p_X} = i_L, \tag{9.3.9}$$

$$\frac{U_M}{U_X} = i_L + \delta, \tag{9.3.10}$$

$$\frac{U_D}{U_X} = i_L - i_D. \tag{9.3.11}$$

The first condition says that consumers allocate their wealth in such a way that the rate of return on capital goods is equal to the loan rate. The second and third conditions imply that the marginal stock utility of each financial asset, capitalized on the appropriate yield, is equalized to the marginal flow utility of commodities. For money the appropriate yield, not surprisingly, turns out to be the loan rate plus the holding cost of currency. For demand deposits the corresponding yield is the loan rate minus the deposit rate.

By dividing the second condition by the third, the marginal rate of substitution of money for deposits can be determined as

$$-\frac{dM}{dD} = \frac{U_D/U_X}{U_M/U_X} = \frac{i_L - i_D}{i_L + \delta}.$$

If there is a positive holding cost on currency and a nonnegative yield on deposits, portfolios will be arranged in such a way that the marginal utility of deposits is lower than the marginal utility of currency. If deposits and currency are perfect substitutes in the sense that $U_D = U_M$ for all quantities of D and M, there must be a service charge $-i_D = \delta$ on deposits or else either currency or deposits will disappear.

The banks, finally, are assumed to be similar to the individual bank with uncertain deposit maturities modeled in the preceding section. For the present purposes, the following modifications are introduced:

1. Equity capital and default risk are disregarded.

2. Banks are assumed to maintain the expected reserve deficit, $\bar{p}$, at a fixed level.

3. The expected reserve deficit depends not only on the level of deposits and reserves, but also on the factor inputs. This expresses the idea

that the size of deposits, θ, is variable and that for given D and R the withdrawal risk can be reduced by using more labor and capital to maintain a larger number of smaller accounts.

These modifications mean that the banks maximize expected profit

$$E(P) = i_L L - i_D D - \delta R - wN^B - rK^B - i_p p_X \rho,$$

subject to the balance-sheet constraint

$$L + R = D \qquad (9.3.12)$$

and the risk constraint (in real terms)

$$\bar{\rho} = \frac{1}{p_X} W(D,R,N,K). \qquad W_D > 0 \qquad W_N < 0 \qquad (9.3.13)$$

$$W_R < 0 \qquad W_K < 0$$

On their currency reserves banks have to pay the same holding costs as households. If their reserves, in the aggregate, fall short of withdrawals, they can borrow from households at the penalty rate i_p, which, for simplicity's sake, is assumed to be fixed.[19] With the assumption of a given $\bar{\rho}$, the expected value of the penalty cost can be treated as a fixed income transfer from the banking sector to the household sector, which greatly simplifies the exposition.

The optimizing calculus for the banks yields the marginal conditions

$$\frac{w}{r} = \frac{W_N}{W_K}, \qquad (9.3.14)$$

$$r \frac{W_R}{W_K} = i_L + \delta, \qquad (9.3.15)$$

$$- r \frac{W_D}{W_K} = i_L - i_D. \qquad (9.3.16)$$

Free entry is assumed to see to it that aggregate profits, if maximized for given market conditions, are just zero. The first marginal condition provides for an efficient factor combination in banking operations. Comparing it with the corresponding condition for producers, we find, as expected, that the two marginal rates of factor substitution must be the same. The second condition, by using (9.3.9), can be written

$$\frac{p_X W_R}{W_K} = \frac{i_L + \delta}{i_L}.$$

19. In a more general analysis, i_P would be endogenously determined by the interplay of supply and demand for emergency financing.

Since $i_L + \delta$ is the marginal cost of currency reserves, the condition says that the marginal rate of substitution between reserves and capital is equal to the ratio of their marginal costs. The third condition establishes the corresponding relationship for the marginal capital requirements per dollar of deposits.

Combining these conditions, we derive an expression for the marginal reserve ratio

$$MRR = \frac{dR}{dD}(\bar{N},\bar{K}) = -\frac{W_D}{W_R} = \frac{i_L - i_D}{i_L + \delta}.$$

In words, the optimizing banks of this simplified model make the marginal reserve ratio equal to the ratio between the interest margin and the opportunity cost of reserves.[20] Alternatively, we can say that the marginal benefit of deposits, measured by $i_L - i_D$, is made equal to their marginal cost, measured by the reserves held on the marginal deposit, MRR, times the marginal cost of reserves in foregone interest and holding costs.[21] Competition will thus see to it that the marginal reserve ratio in the banking sector is equalized to the marginal rate of substitution between currency and deposits for households.

This completes the exposition of the model.[22] Its sixteen numbered equations determine endogenously the capital stock (K); the allocation of capital and labor to the two sectors $(K^P, K^B, N^P,$ and $N^B)$; the output of commodities and gold (X,G); the nominal amounts of the four financial assets $(M, D, L,$ and $R)$; the yields on real capital, deposits, and loans $(r, i_D$ and $i_L)$; wages (w); and the price level (p_X). There is no assurance, however, that perfect competition is, in fact, compatible with equilibrium, even if the usual assumptions about utility and production are made. This is due to the scale economies introduced by the stochastic elements in banking. In particular, there is no assurance that the marginal reserve ratio $MRR = -W_D/W_R$ increases with the volume of deposits. Detailed analysis of $(d/dD)(-W_D/W_R)$ shows that there are both positive and negative components, and it is not clear which will dominate. In this respect,

20. This condition was mentioned by Alvin Marty (1968, p. 866).

21. It is interesting to note that factor costs do not enter into the marginal costs of deposits to banks, at least not directly.

22. It may be thought that there should also be a statement to the effect that the annual replacement demand for currency and reserves adds up to gold production,

$$G = \delta(M/p_G + R/p_G).$$

While this statement is indeed true, it is already implied in the remainder of the model, including the zero-profit condition for producers and banks. It can also be verified that wealth is equal to real capital and the real value of the gold stock,

$$W = K + (1/p_x)(M + D - L) = K + (1/\delta)(p_G/p_x) G.$$

banking is similar to other industries with scale economies in production. If the marginal cost of deposits is indeed falling, the size of individual banking firms will be limited by the extent of their individual market, as pointed out in the preceding section. Assuming, for the moment, that a competitive equilibrium exists, we can now use this model to consider the specific questions raised at the beginning of this section.

9.3.2. ALLOCATIVE EFFECTS OF BANKING. There is, first, the question of the allocative effects of banking on the rest of the economy. How does the emergence of bank money affect the price level, the allocation of factors, the composition of output, and the level of interest rates? A perfectly general answer is hard to obtain in a model of this complexity. We have to be satisfied with reasonably convincing propositions, based on plausible assumptions. These assumptions include, in particular, the following:

1. Commodities are no substitute for currency and deposits.

2. A dollar of deposits reduces the nonbank demand for currency by more than it increases the bank demand for reserves.

3. The factor intensities are the same in banking as in production (the justification being just the absence of specific information on possible differences).

4. The production function for commodities is linear-homogeneous.

5. The emergence of banks is brought about by progress in banking technology represented by a proportionate decline in the factor inputs necessary to achieve a specific reserve deficit for given values of D and R. We can visualize this by interpreting N and K in terms of efficiency units and relating these to the physical quantities N^* and K^* by $N = tN^*$ and $K = tK^*$. The emergence of banks would then be caused by an increase in t to the level that allows some banks to reach the break-even point.

Under these conditions, the emergence of bank money first of all reduces the demand for currency. The composition of output thus shifts from gold to commodities. In order to induce firms to carry out this shift, the price of commodities has to rise. At the same time, factors of production will be shifted from commodity production into banking. Total output in the producing sector will thus decline in favor of financial intermediation. The effect on commodity output is uncertain, the favorable shift in the composition of output being opposed by the reduction in total output. Since wealth is constant by assumption, the reduction in the real value of the gold stock means an increase in capital goods, which, at given labor and uniform factor intensities, increases the capital intensity of production and produces a decline in the rental on capital relative to wages. Before the advent of banks, i_D had to be at a level to make the excess demand of the nonbank sector for deposits zero. Similarly, i_L had to be at a level to make the excess supply for loans zero. With the emergence of banks, there will be an excess demand of deposits, reflected in a positive D, which implies a higher level of i_D. At the same time, there will now be an excess supply of loans, implying a lower level of i_L.[23]

9.3.3. THE DETERMINATENESS OF THE PRICE LEVEL. The second question has to do with the price level. As long as bank deposits, being effectively gold certificates, are convertible into gold at a fixed price, the price level is obviously determinate and finite. The determinateness of the price level thus does not depend on the presence of a monetary base of government-created fiat money or on limitations of entry into banking. It also does not depend on the need of banks for reserves or on their factor costs. Even if a bank could maintain convertibility without reserves and could operate costlessly, the price level would still be determinate, provided gold has some nonmonetary use if its relative price is low enough. The deposit rate i_D would, of course, be pushed up to the loan rate i_L, bank deposits would thus become costless, and the nonbank sector would satiate itself with deposit money.

The opposite argument that the price level would be infinite, often heard during recent years,[24] cannot be valid for a banking system of the type described here. It is based on the assumption that banks, acting like legalized forgers, have the privilege to buy goods and service for an irredeemable and costless paper currency in unlimited amounts.[25] It is evident that such a privilege in the hands of profit-seeking and competitive banks would lead to an infinite expansion of the money supply.[26] While this proposition is formally correct, it is uninteresting because (1) it is analytically trivial and (2) it abstracts from just about all essential aspects of real commercial banks, whose deposits are always convertible into some other assets that cannot be created by the banks themselves.

If imaginary banks with the above privilege, through a limitation of competition, limit collectively the quantity of the currency they are going to print, the nonbank sector will determine its value and thus the price level. If the imaginary banks collectively specify the price of the goods (in terms of their paper money) they are willing to pay, the nonbank sector will determine the quantity of money demanded. In these cases, the banks behave collectively exactly as if they were a government, supplying fiat money against goods and services.

It was pointed out above that the emergence of money-creating banks,

23. In a growth model with maximization of steady-state consumption according to the Golden Rule there would be no decline in i_L, as the rate of return to capital would remain equal to the rate of growth. See Fischer (1972).

24. Gurley and Shaw called it the "traditional view," though without much justification. For an example see H. G. Johnson (1968, p. 976).

25. This is clearly the type of model Johnson had in mind. See also Patinkin (1969, p. 1144).

26. As has long been recognized, this would also be true for the banking system as a whole if each bank maintained convertibility of its deposits into the deposits of other banks.

under the present assumptions, results in an increase in the commodity price level. It should be noted that this has nothing to do with the quantity-theory effect of "more money chasing fewer goods." Under a system of convertible bank deposits, just as under the gold standard, the quantity theory of money does not strictly apply and the price level is determined by cost conditions.

9.3.4. BANK DEPOSITS AS COMPONENTS OF NATIONAL WEALTH. The third question is about bank deposits as a component of net wealth of the private sector (including banks). The question came up, like about half of all confused questions in recent monetary theory, in connection with the quest for real balance effects. If bank deposits are indeed a component of private wealth, they could contribute, it seems, to those real balance effects. If not, such effects could only arise from the financial liabilities of the government. According to the traditional view, reflected in national accounting practices, bank deposits are not a component of aggregate private wealth, since the claims of the nonbank sector are offset by the corresponding liability of the banks. This view is also implied in the present model, as total wealth is represented by capital goods and gold. Pesek and Saving (1967) criticized this view on the grounds that the appearance of banks, by the creation of deposits, increases welfare and thus the real wealth of the economy. Gold and other things, which would otherwise be used as media of exchange, are now freed for other purposes. If banks, so they argued, are given the privilege to issue a fixed amount of deposits and can do so without cost, this contribution to welfare would show up in a balance sheet entry for net worth equal to the amount of deposits, and this net worth should be counted as a component of net social wealth.

The ensuing discussion succeeded in clearing up two points. The first point has to do with the relationship between welfare and wealth. From the (undisputed) contribution of deposits to welfare it does not follow that deposits should show up in the wealth account. The components of wealth are stocks of assets, each valued at the margin. It follows that intramarginal contributions to welfare in the form of consumer or producer surpluses are not, and should not be, reflected in the wealth accounts.[27] In particular, at the point of satiation goods contribute a maximum to welfare, but a minimum, namely zero, to wealth. Whether or not bank deposits are a component of national wealth, therefore, depends not on their contribution to total wealth, but on their marginal value, and this marginal value may conceivably be zero even though the total contribution to welfare is large.

---

27. From this proposition arise all those familiar discrepancies between welfare and wealth, exemplified by the water-diamond paradox, which should have ceased to confuse economists a century ago.

The second point concerned the source of the banks' net wealth in the argument of Pesek and Saving. It was made clear that this net worth is not, in fact, due to the supply of bank deposits, but to the monopoly privilege granted to the banks by the state.[28] It is thus analogous to other rents originating from barriers to entry, and except in the special case constructed by Pesek and Saving there is no reason why it should have any particular relationship with the amount of demand deposits.

While these two issues were thus settled, the main issue of the off-setting character of deposit claims and deposit liabilities was not even clearly perceived and remains unresolved. The assumption of Pesek and Saving of banks issuing costless fiat money precludes an economic theory of banking, and subsequent participants in the controversy did not correct this deficiency.[29] The present model permits a resolution of this issue.

The crucial question is whether bank deposits have a negative marginal value for banks that offsets their positive marginal value for the holder. If both banks and their customers regard interest rates as given by the market, as assumed so far in this model, the answer is yes. In this case, both the marginal benefit of deposits to households as measured by U_D/U_M and the marginal cost of deposits to banks as measured by $-W_D/W_R$ are equal to $(i_L - i_D)/(i_L + \delta)$ and thus equal to each other. If the correct marginal value is used in the valuation of deposits on both sides, the two entries will just cancel. It should be noted that this conclusion depends only on banks and nonbanks regarding interest rates as being independent of their own actions. It remains valid even if barriers to entry result in positive profits and thus net worth in the banking industry. What matters is pure competition in the sense of horizontal demand and supply curves as seen by individual agents and not in the sense of free entry.

This argument is illustrated in figure 9.3.1. The amount of deposits is measured on the horizontal axis, while $(i_L - i_D)/(i_L + \delta)$ on the vertical axis represents the "price" of deposits in terms of currency. The solid curve with negative slope is the demand curve for deposits, derived from the condition that the marginal monetary benefit of deposits, that is the amount of currency households are willing to give up for the marginal unit of deposits, is made equal to the price of deposits (see 9.3.10 and 9.3.11). The rising curve is the marginal reserve ratio (see 9.3.15 and 9.3.16), which must be interpreted, for the present purpose, as the banks' marginal cost of deposits in terms of currency. Under pure competition, banks accept deposits up to the point where their marginal cost is equal to the

28. Johnson (1969) and Patinkin (1969).

29. While Patinkin's analysis, based on accounting statements, is admirable for its lucidity, it is flawed by the lack of the proper distinction between average and marginal concepts. This can be most easily seen from the impossibility of applying the argument on pp. 1150–51 to banks with several classes of earning assets and deposits. Joint products continue to be the crux of average cost approaches.

price, and the marginal cost curve thus becomes the supply curve. Market equilibrium will be reached at C, where the marginal value of deposits for households, AC, is equal to their marginal cost to banks, while the area $OACB$ represents both the positive total value of deposits to their owners and their negative value to the banks, each correctly evaluated at the margin.

The situation is different for a banking market in which each bank is a local monopolist confronted with a falling demand function for deposits,

$$D = D\left(\frac{i_L - i_D}{i_L + \delta}\right),$$

whose elasticity with respect to i_D can be defined as

$$\epsilon = -\frac{D'}{D} \cdot \frac{i_D}{i_L + \delta}.$$

In this case the profit-maximizing bank equates its marginal cost of deposits to the marginal revenue

$$\frac{i_L - i_D\left(1 + \dfrac{1}{\epsilon}\right)}{i_L + \delta},$$

while the depositor, being in pure competition, still equates his marginal benefit to $(i_L - i_D)/(i_L + \delta)$. As a consequence, the marginal benefit of the depositor remains higher, in equilibrium, than the marginal cost of the bank, as indicated in figure 9.3.1 by $F - E$. This difference, multiplied by the amount of deposits, represents the net contribution of banks to private wealth. In the graph it is measured by the shaded area. Generally,

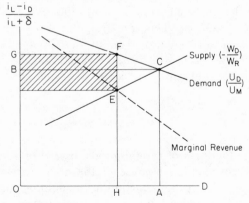

Figure 9.3.1
The Market for Bank Deposits

this will be smaller than the value of deposits, $OHFG$, but in the limiting case of zero marginal costs of deposits to banks the full amount of deposits will appear in the wealth account. It is clear that the contribution of deposits to wealth, properly measured, is positive exactly because imperfect competition has reduced their contribution to welfare. It is also clear that this contribution to wealth has nothing to do with the net worth of banks, for free entry will keep pure profits to zero even if a falling demand curve for deposits opens a wedge between the marginal value of deposits to holders and their marginal cost to banks.

While the question about the contribution of bank deposits to private wealth has thus a fairly straightforward answer, the preoccupation of monetary theorists with real balance effects has lent it an apparent importance that it does not, in fact, have. Discrepancies in marginal values due to imperfect competition are a commonplace occurrence in our economic system. While they are the legitimate concern of welfare economists, they are probably of minor importance for the accountant of national wealth, and they have no specific monetary significance. While the proper accounting for bank deposits is a nice test for the underlying theory of banking, it is hardly a major issue.

9.3.5. THE EFFICIENCY OF BANK MONEY SUPPLY. The fourth question concerns the efficiency of the deposit supply by banks. The question is whether the bank money supply as determined by the interplay of utility-maximizing households and profit-maximizing firms is efficient in the sense of providing the maximum of real bank deposits for given quantities of commodities and real currency.

The answer depends largely on the laws of return in banking. Suppose returns to scale are diminishing, at least after a point. Forgetting all about utility maximization by households, profit maximization by firms, wages, prices, and interest rates, we adopt a planning point of view to determine the maximum D/p_X that can be obtained from a given labor force, for given real wealth and given X and M/p_X. This is a straightforward maximizing problem. Its solution leads to two marginal conditions. First, labor and capital must be combined efficiently, which means that the marginal rate of substitution between labor and capital must be the same in production and banking,

$$Q_N/Q_K = W_N/W_K.$$

Second, wealth must be allocated efficiently to real capital and gold. If an additional unit were held in the form of capital goods instead of gold, the labor saved in commodity production because of the higher capital intensity plus the labor saved because of the reduction in the holding costs on gold must just be matched by the higher labor requirements in banking to keep the expected reserve deficit at the prescribed level despite the lower gold reserve. Mathematically, this is expressed by

$$\frac{Q_K}{Q_N} - \delta \frac{p_X}{p_G} \frac{Q_G}{Q_N} = p_X \frac{W_R}{W_N}.$$

It can easily be verified that both of these efficiency conditions are implied in the marginal conditions for firms, (9.3.4)-(9.3.6), and banks, (9.3.14)-(9.3.16) together with (9.3.9). With diminishing returns, the competitive supply of bank money is efficient.

In equilibrium, the interest rate on deposits can be positive, zero, or negative. The marginal reserve ratio must be between zero and one, and thus

$$0 < \frac{i_L - i_D}{i_L + \delta} < 1.$$

If there is a positive holding cost on currency, efficiency may be compatible with a zero interest on demand deposits or even with a service charge. However, if there is no holding cost on currency or perhaps even a positive yield, efficiency requires a positive interest on demand deposits. If the government imposes a ceiling on i_D at a level below the equilibrium rate, the deposit supply will no longer be efficient, the deposit balances of the nonbank sector being inefficiently low while currency holdings and bank reserves are inefficiently high.

Certain aspects of static efficiency are not included in this model. One of them is the cost of bank services aside from the cost of maintaining an account.[30] In an efficient banking system, banks would charge for these services at marginal cost. If an interest ceiling (possibly at zero) were imposed by the government, the banks would react by providing free services to customers. To the extent that these services would not be otherwise provided by the bank (the distribution of kitchenware being a case in point), this would be inefficient, inasmuch as the banks have no comparative advantage for them. To the extent that the services would be provided by the bank in any case, but at a cost, the depositor would still lose the incentive to economize on payments services. It may be conjectured that in the American banking system both the rate of interest on demand deposits and the charges for services are inefficiently low. It is not clear, however, whether these inefficiencies, if they exist, are large enough to matter.

This was all based on the assumption of diminishing returns. It is likely, though, that there are significant elements of increasing returns in

30. H. G. Johnson has rightly emphasized the difference between the costs of maintaining deposits at a certain level and the costs of the payment services on these deposits (1968, p. 973). This paper is also the principal reference on the following points.

banking. These have different sources. In part they are due to the stochastic scale economies discussed in subsection 9.2.3 and incorporated into the present model. If they dominate, banks will expand up to the point where further expansion is prevented by the rising supply curves for loans and/or the falling demand curves for deposits. Competition becomes imperfect and the resulting equilibrium is likely to be inefficient. However, banking hardly differs in this respect from many other industries. As long as entry is free, I doubt that the resulting distortion would be serious enough to warrant extensive regulation.

A different source of scale economies is the advantage of a centralized payments and clearing system, reducing interbank transfers. At a still different level of analysis there is the advantage of uniform bank notes, issued by the same bank, in the place of notes issued by many different banks, possibly with complicated and fluctuating exchange rates. Such scale economies will often not be realized by a competitive system, and they may be valid reasons for appropriate government intervention.

For government banking policy this poses the familiar dilemma, well illustrated by different banking systems. By maintaining a highly decentralized system, as in the United States, we may hope to preserve many of the static and dynamic advantages of competition, but at the cost of diseconomies of small scale in the payments and credit system. By permitting high concentration, as in the United Kingdom, government policy may give the economy the advantages of large scale, but at the expense of competition. One possible strategy is the separation of functions according to economies of scale. Services with strong scale economies and little significance of competition could be provided by a centralized public utility. In this spirit, the provision of coins and bank notes has long been monopolized by the state. In many countries, a large part of payments by check is also handled by a centralized giro system.[31] On the other hand, services with relatively weak economies of scale would be left to small banks. Savings deposits, small commercial credits, and mortgages seem to be fields in which small banks have proved to be highly resistant. In between there would be functions with considerable scale economies, but at the same time with a high degree of competitive dynamics. The market for large commercial loans, large time deposits and Eurodollar deposits are typical cases. These would be fields for relatively large, possibly oligopolistic commercial banks.[32]

31. In such a system, the payer sends his check to the clearing agency. The agency debits the account of the payer and credits the account of the payee, sending a notification slip to the latter. Only two accounts are affected and only two mailings are necessary. Every account holder can obtain cash immediately anywhere in the system.

32. It is interesting to note that the Swiss banking system, characterized by little regulation and a highly competitive spirit, has gravitated to such a structure, a large part of the payments system being centralized in the hands of the government, while banks of different sizes tend to concentrate on different types of business.

In view of the static nature of the banking model used in this chapter, this discussion of efficiency has been confined to static aspects. The problem has, however, important dynamic aspects, arising from the fact that both deposit withdrawals and default losses may be subject to marked variations in the course of economic fluctuations. It is these variations which produced the recurring "bank panics" of the nineteenth century. The emergence of central banks and of bank regulation as we know it today are probably more a response to these dynamic experiences than to the static aspects discussed in this subsection; the dynamic problems will be taken up in chapter 12.

Ten

MONETARY MACROSTATICS

Introduction

Chapter 1 began with a brief summary of the neoclassical tradition in monetary theory. The preceding nine chapters can be regarded as a progressive elaboration and reinterpretation of this tradition to the extent it relates to economic equilibrium. It was also pointed out, however, that an important part of the neoclassical tradition, reaching back to classical and mercantilist times, relates to the powerful effects of money on output, interest rates, and the price level during temporary stages of economic disequilibrium. These will be the subject of this and the following chapter.

The analysis will be confined to a closed economy in which all money is noncommodity or token currency supplied by the government. In the present chapter it will be based on static models for successive time periods or "runs." In the following chapter the successive phases will be linked together by an explicit dynamic analysis. The banking system is assumed to be consolidated with the rest of the private sector; as a consequence, the money supply is identical to the monetary base. It should be borne in mind that this study is about money and not about macroeconomic theory in general. The treatment of topics like fiscal policy, labor markets, expectations, Phillips curves, or investment behavior, which are not specifically monetary, will thus strive for expository simplicity rather than sophistication and realism.

About the substantive effects of monetary policy on output, interest, and prices—as distinct from concepts and doctrines—there is, at least since classical times, a wide area of agreement. In particular, the following propositions seem to be almost universally accepted:

1. The immediate impact of an increase in the money supply is on the prices of existing assets, like common stocks, bonds, land, or stocks of raw material, reflected in their rates of return.[1]

---

1. Keynes is sometimes credited with a historic reversal of the roles assigned to prices and quantities, in as much as he thought that quantities reacted quickly while

2. In the short run, though with a lag of several months, an increase in the money supply stimulates output and employment.[2]

3. In the long run, whose length is in dispute, the main effect is on the prices of commodity flows and on wage rates, while the output effects recede.[3]

4. In the ultimate steady state, all capital stocks are fully adjusted, and monetary policy affects the real variables mainly through its effect on the capital stock.

These propositions will now be considered in terms of a basic macro model, which, by suitably chosen modifications, is made to reflect the characteristic features of the various stages. The formal analysis is preceded by a brief review of the issues.

10.1. The issues

Despite a wide area of agreement, monetary macroeconomics is also one of those perennial battlegrounds on which, through the centuries, each generation fought its own wars. The debate about "monetarism" is the most recent episode in this continuing controversy.[4] As in many of the earlier episodes—and also in other fields of human history—the issues (and sometimes the contestants) are confused, the battle lines often meet at obtuse angles, alliances shift, and there are no objective criteria of victory and defeat. At the risk of provoking objections from both (or all) sides, I shall try to characterize monetarism, to the extent it is really concerned with matters of monetary theory (and not, say, of fiscal policy, the wisdom of governments, or the Phillips curve) by three propositions:

1. Economic fluctuations are largely due to variations in monetary policy and not to fluctuations in the demand of the private sector. As a consequence, economic stabilization requires a steady course of monetary policy rather than discretionary shifts to counteract the fluctuations in private demand.

2. What matters for the macroeconomic effects is primarily the

---

prices were sluggish, whereas in the Marshallian adjustment mechanism prices react promptly while quantities take their time. I do not believe there was such a reversal. The Marshallian short-run reaction was meant to take place in the price of fish already caught, that is, of existing stocks, while the price of current output was assumed to react slowly. What was not clear (not even to Irving Fisher) is the relationship of asset prices and output prices, though the Cobweb-analysis can be regarded as a treatment of this problem in the Marshallian tradition.

2. This was well known to the mercantilists. For the classical period see Thornton (1802/1939, p. 118).

3. This was recognized, for example, by Thornton (1802/1939, p. 196).

4. The state of this debate in 1974 can best be judged from the collection of essays and comments in Stein (1976).

quantity of money and not the way it is created. While the effect of a given increase in the money supply may be somewhat different depending on whether it is brought about by, say, open-market operations or by additional expenditures, these differences are of secondary importance. This implies, as a corollary, that increases in government expenditures *not* accompanied by a monetary expansion have a relatively small effect.[5]

3. The transmission mechanism from the money stock to output flows includes other links besides the bond yield; a fall in the latter is not a reliable indicator of the macroeconomic effects.

On each of these propositions the debate continues. The first of them, requiring a historical and empirical investigation, is outside the scope of this study. Propositions two and three, however, will be recurring themes of the following analysis. From this point of view, the central problem of the theory of monetary macroeconomics, first formulated this way by Metzler (1951), is the *modus operandi* and the relative macroeconomic effects of an exogenous change in the money supply, depending on the way it is brought about.

The underlying issue, of course, is the precise meaning of the quantity theory of money as the classical conceptual instrument to elucidate the link between the money stock and commodity flows. More specifically, the quantity theory is a macroeconomic proposition about the effect of the money supply on the price level. Friedman, in his "restatement" (1956), tried to reinterpret it as a homogeneity proposition about the demand function for money. However, it seems inefficient terminology to waste a well-accepted term with an interesting macroeconomic meaning on a mere homogeneity postulate. I shall, therefore, use the term "quantity theory" in its classical sense of a theory of the price level in terms of the quantity of money. As a comparative-static, long-run proposition for an economy in which money is the only exogenous asset, its validity is not in dispute. In such an economy, the equilibrium price level is indeed proportional to the quantity of money. It is less clear to what extent and under what circumstances it retains its validity if, besides money, there is also a government debt. It is still less clear what happens along the adjustment path from one equilibrium to another. In these general terms, the present analysis, though it is not conducted in terms of velocities, can be said to be about the quantity theory of money.

These issues will here be considered in terms of a model that is eclectic in the sense that it logically admits a wide range of propositions, reaching from extreme nonmonetarism, according to which money hardly matters, to extreme monetarism, according to which anything but money hardly

---

5. It has never been seriously maintained by leading monetarists that such expenditures would actually be contractive. Efforts to focus the debate on this issue seem to be beside the point (Blinder/Solow [1973] and Stein [1976]).

matters. It is then shown which parameters of the model—and thus, in principle, what observations—decide on the various outcomes.

10.2. The basic model

The model represents an economy in steady growth with an exogenously given population growth rate ω. This makes it possible to reconcile positive investment, saving, and unbalanced budgets with full stock/flow equilibrium.[6] The stock/flow inconsistencies that have plagued this part of economic analysis will thereby be avoided.

The model does not allow for continuing inflation or deflation. The growth rate of money and debt is always equal to the growth rate of population. What is allowed to change is the *level* of money and debt. As a consequence, the model traces the effect of money and debt on the level of prices and not on the rate of inflation. This may seem to exclude what many regard as the central problem of present-day macroeconomics. While this may be true from a policy point of view, it is different from the point of view of economic analysis. Long-term inflation simply does not pose particularly difficult or interesting analytical problems at the macroeconomic level. Its causes are fairly simple and well understood, its macroeconomic consequences are well known, and the main analytical problems are at the microeconomic level. Of more interest is the transition from one rate of monetary expansion to another, but this transition is in many respects quite similar to the transition from one level of the money supply to another, which is the main subject of this chapter.

The basic model, while non-Keynesian, is in the spirit of Tobin's general equilibrium approach (1969; Tobin/Brainard 1963).[7] It consists of three building blocks, namely a production sector, the asset demand functions, and the government budget constraint. By various sets of additional assumptions it will be modified to exhibit the characteristic features of the different time periods.

The production block is neoclassical and conventional. It simply states that output, Q, is a linear-homogeneous function of real capital, K, and employment, E,

$$Q = Q(K,E), \qquad Q_i > 0 \qquad Q_{ii} < 0 \qquad Q_{ij} > 0 \qquad (10.2.1)$$

$$(i,j = K,E)$$

while the real rental on capital, r, and the real wage, w/p, equal the respec-

---

6. An earlier version of this model is found in Niehans (1974a).
7. The present model may also be interpreted as a further development of the type of model used by Tobin and Buiter (1976) along the lines suggested in their concluding comments.

tive marginal product,

$$r = Q_K, \tag{10.2.2}$$

$$w/p = Q_E. \tag{10.2.3}$$

There are three assets, money, bonds, and capital goods. As a consequence there is no need to make a doctrinal decision whether bonds are closer substitutes for money or for capital goods.[8] Capital goods are owned by wealth owners and rented out to producers; they are measured in the same units as output. In equilibrium their price, p_K, is equal to the price of output; r can thus be interpreted as the yield of capital goods. If p_K differs from p and thus $\pi = p_K/p \neq 1$, then the yield of capital goods is r/π and their real value is πK. Government bonds, B, consist of perpetuities paying a fixed coupon of \$1, while private debt is netted out in the consolidated balance sheet of the private sector. While usually positive in practice, B could, in principle, be negative, the government holding private bonds in its portfolio. Money, M, may be thought to consist of currency and central bank deposits. It bears no interest and, since the commercial banking system is consolidated with the private sector, it is identical to the monetary base.[9]

For each asset the supply in real terms must be equal to the demand by wealth owners, which, in turn, depends on disposable income, X, the rate of return on capital, and the bond yield:

$$\pi K = K(X, r/\pi, i), \qquad K_X > 0 \qquad K_r > 0 \qquad K_i < 0 \tag{10.2.4}$$

$$B/ip = D(X, r/\pi, i), \qquad D_X > 0 \qquad D_r < 0 \qquad D_i > 0 \tag{10.2.5}$$

$$M/p = L(X, r/\pi, i). \qquad L_X > 0 \qquad L_r < 0 \qquad L_i < 0 \tag{10.2.6}$$

For the purposes of this static analysis, these functions are assumed to hold at every moment of time; the wealth effects resulting from lagged adjustment will be one of the main topics of the following chapter.

The asset demand functions are related to the microeconomic optimization model of chapter 4 and the general equilibrium analysis of chapter 5 in the following way. The demand for capital goods (10.2.4) takes the place of the demand for commodity stocks (4.2.6). While the microeconomic

---

8. The classical example of treating bonds as if they were capital goods is, of course, Metzler's influential paper (1951). This assumption is, among other things, responsible for his conclusion that the quantity theory of prices is valid for money-financed expenditures.

9. If the government holds no private bonds, Gurley and Shaw (1960) would classify the money stock as "outside money." In the special case where all money was created by buying private bonds, so that $M = -B/i$, they would call it "inside money." The following analysis applies unchanged in either case. The distinction between outside money and inside money is simply irrelevant. It is part of the analytical fallout from the confusion about "real balance effects."

analysis relates to a pure exchange economy in which capital goods appear only in the form of temporary inventories, the present model relates to a production economy with durable capital goods. The demand functions for bonds and cash balances, (10.2.5) and (10.2.6), can be derived, respectively, from (5.1.1) and (5.1.2), which in turn were based on (4.2.7) and (4.2.8). The derivation is described by the following steps: (1) Suppress the time subscripts and transaction cost rates; (2) replace the storage cost rate on inventories by the rate of return on capital goods;[10] (3) put the interest on cash balances equal to zero; (4) replace endowment and taxes by disposable income; (5) assume that the coupon is fixed at \$1; (6) assume that the transaction costs on bonds depend on the *real* value of bond transactions, so that the last term in (4.2.2) is changed into $c^b (z_t^b + y_t^b) (p^b/p^q)$.[11]

The existence of a demand function for bonds is not meant to deny that future tax liabilities may be capitalized. The underlying view is rather that there is such a demand function even with complete capitalization of tax liabilities, because the government still plays a role analogous to that of a financial intermediary. As a consequence, the question of the capitalization of future tax liabilities, while empirically interesting, is not of crucial analytical importance.

Real disposable income is equal to real output plus real government interest minus real taxes,

$$X = Q + (B/p) - T. \tag{10.2.7}$$

Real taxes are assumed to consist of a component that depends on real private income, which implies that tax schedules are indexed, and an autonomous component,

$$T = T\left(Q + \frac{B}{p}\right) + \tau. \tag{10.2.8}$$

It turns out that the comparative-static analysis is made considerably more messy by the change in government interest (net of taxes on this interest), though this item and its consequences are probably minor. To simplify the exposition I shall therefore assume that any increase in government

---

10. Note that r now denotes the rate of return on capital, while in earlier chapters it represented the coupon on bonds.

11. The last modification results in homogeneity of the demand functions for financial assets of the following degrees:

Argument	Money (4.2.8)	Bonds (4.2.7)
commodity prices	+1	+1
bond price, coupon	0	−1

If the bond price and the coupon are doubled, the number of bonds demanded will be cut in half. This makes it possible to write the demand for bonds in the form of 10.2.5, with $i =$ coupon/bond price.

interest is offset by an equal increase in autonomous taxes. As a consequence

$$d\tau = (1 - T') \, d(B/p) \tag{10.2.9}$$

and thus

$$dX = (1 - T') \, dQ. \tag{10.2.10}$$

The price that has to be paid for this simplification is the elimination by assumption of some of the problems that have been debated in recent discussions about fiscal policy.[12] In particular, the paradox of a possibly contractive effect of debt-financed expenditures, noted by Blinder/Solow (1973), does not arise. I think this price is not too high for the simplification it allows. Except for (10.2.9), tax schedules are assumed to be constant throughout this analysis.[13]

There are no wealth effects in the asset demand functions. Suppose $W = K + (B/ip) + (M/p)$ is initially included as an argument in each demand function. If the implicit function theorem holds, these initial functions can be solved simultaneously to give (10.2.4) $-$ (10.2.6). Indeed, Archibald and Lipsey (1958) have taught us that wealth effects do not matter in stock/flow equilibrium. Macroeconomic theory since the discovery of the Haberler/Pigou effect was nevertheless characterized by an almost compulsive effort to treat wealth effects in terms of comparative statics. I believe this is one of the main reasons for its unsatisfactory state. By postulating, for static purposes, that people hold exactly those assets they wish to hold under given conditions, it is possible to achieve a remarkable simplification and symmetry of results. The wealth effects arising from imperfect adjustment of actual asset stocks to desired stocks will be extensively discussed in the dynamic analysis of the following chapter.

There are also no explicit consumption, savings, or investment functions, but they are implied in the asset demand functions. In steady growth, investment is $I = \omega K$. Private saving is simply the change in private wealth, $S = \omega(K + B/ip + M/p)$ with

$$\partial S / \partial X = \omega(K_X + D_X + L_X),$$

$$\partial S / \partial r = \omega(K_r + D_r + L_r),$$

$$\partial S / \partial i = \omega(K_i + D_i + L_i).$$

---

12. An equivalent simplification has been used by Tobin and Buiter in their model I (1976).

13. To make it possible to investigate balanced-budget multipliers and money paid out in the form of transfer payments, (10.2.9) would have to be expanded to include exogenous changes in τ.

Consumption, finally, can be derived as $C = X - S$ with

$$\partial C/\partial X = 1 - \partial S/\partial X,$$

$$\partial C/\partial r = - \partial S/\partial r,$$

$$\partial C/\partial i = - \partial S/\partial i.$$

In the present context it was found most convenient to focus on the three asset functions, since these can be treated in perfect symmetry. For those who regard the emphasis on stocks as the hallmark of monetarism (Brunner/Meltzer, 1976), the present model must thus appear as a monetarist extreme. However, I regard this as a matter not of doctrine but of expositional convenience. It will turn out that this stock model can produce both monetarist and nonmonetarist propositions.

The government is assumed to be consolidated with the central bank. Its budget constraint states that the excess of expenditures for goods, services, and debt service over taxes is financed by increases in the monetary base and/or in debt, all in real terms:

$$G + B/p - T = \Delta M/p + \Delta B/ip = \frac{\Delta M}{M} \cdot \frac{M}{P} + \frac{\Delta B}{B} + \frac{B}{ip}. \qquad (10.2.11)$$

In steady, noninflationary growth both M and B expand at the rate of population growth:

$$G + B/p - T = \omega(M/p + B/ip). \qquad (10.2.12)$$

The *flows* of government expenditures and revenues are thus related to the *stocks* of real balances and the real debt.[14]

The basic model now consists of equations (10.2.1)–(10.2.8) and (10.2.12). In a final step this model is reinterpreted in per capita terms by assuming that all stock and flow variables have been divided by the labor force, N. E, for example, thus measures employment per head of the labor force or the employment rate. With this reinterpretation, the variables become invariant under balanced growth. N is thought to be defined as that level of employment that can be permanently maintained without producing either progressive inflation or progressive deflation. While $E = 1$ will, for simplicity, be called "full employment," it should be borne in mind that it is equivalent to what has recently been called the "normal" or "natural" rate of employment.

---

14. During the transition to another steady-state path with a higher money supply, additional government expenditures can temporarily be financed out of the new money necessary to build up the money stock to its new steady-state level. The same is true for bonds. This tends to produce a strong impact effect common to both monetary expansion and debt expansion. In the static analysis of the present chapter, these accelerator effects are eliminated by the assumption that any changes in the steady-state stocks of money or bonds are accomplished instantaneously, at unchanged G, through transfer payments or a capital levy.

Making use of the assumption (10.2.9), the budget constraint (10.2.12) can be differentiated to read

$$dG - T'dQ = \omega(dM/p + dB/ip) - (\omega/p)(M/p + B/ip)dp$$

$$- (\omega/i)(B/ip)di. \tag{10.2.13}$$

dQ, dp, and di are determined endogenously by the rest of the model. The government budget constraint thus means that the government is free to assign exogenous changes to any two of the remaining three variables, G, M, and B.

This leaves room for three policies, which, for the purpose of this discussion, will be labeled, respectively, "monetary expansion," "debt expansion," and "open-market operations." In the case of monetary expansion, the money supply is increased to pay for additional expenditures so that $dG = (\omega/p)dM$ and $dB = 0$. By a policy of debt expansion additional expenditures are financed by bonds, whence $dG = (\omega/ip)dB$ and $dM = 0$. Under an open-market policy, the central bank increases the money supply by buying bonds at the going market price, so that $dB = -idM$.[15] It is evident that each of these policies can be regarded as the combination of the other two. With these definitions, policies are comparable dollar for dollar. In the discussion about the relative effectiveness of monetary and fiscal policies, based on IS/LM models, this was often not the case, monetary policy being defined as a "once-over" change in the money supply, while fiscal policy would be defined as a "maintained" increase in public expenditures. It is clear that the resulting effects on, say, national income cannot be compared. The present definition of policies avoids this problem.

In terms of this catalogue of policies, the second of the above-mentioned issues in the debate about monetarism can now be made more precise. A monetarist would be inclined to argue that monetary expansion and an open-market purchase have roughly the same effect on output and prices, at least in the longer run, while the effect of debt expansion, being the difference between the two, is relatively small, except perhaps in the short run. Most monetarists would still feel, however, that money-financed expenditures have somewhat stronger effects than open-market operations and that debt-financed expenditures, therefore, are expansionary rather than restrictive.

A nonmonetarist, on the other hand, would tend to argue that money-financed expenditures and open-market purchases have very differ-

---

15. It should be noted that an open-market operation, as here defined, generally implies a change in tax rates and/or government expenditures. If such a change is excluded, the initial open-market purchase, since it reduces government interest, produces a surplus resulting in secondary changes in M and/or B. This is the case which Blinder and Solow have shown to result in the possible paradox of contractionary open-market purchases.

ent effects. While money matters, it also matters a great deal how it is supplied. Typically he would expect that the effects of monetary expansion are markedly stronger than those of open-market operations. This implies that debt expansion also has a considerable effect. The nonmonetarist may agree with the monetarist that this effect is bound to be small if we wait long enough, but he would expect it to be considerable for quite an extended period. The question is, of course, what qualifiers like "roughly," "relatively," "somewhat," "very," "a great deal," "markedly," and "considerable" really mean. As the debate progresses, it is becoming gradually less clear that the remaining differences are about more than just words.

10.3. Instantaneous effects: Asset revaluation

The basic model described on the preceding pages will now be used to determine the effect of different policies on output, employment, interest rates, and prices. The results are different, depending on the adjustment period, as we move from the immediate reaction through the short and the long run to the ultimate steady state.[16] The essential features of each of these time periods are expressed by adding special assumptions to the basic model. These sets of assumptions are designed to provide what could be called "still pictures" of successive stages in the dynamic process of adjustment to monetary change.[17] It will turn out that each of these still pictures can be represented by some appropriate variant of an *IS-LM* diagram.[18]

The present section will concentrate on the instantaneous effects of monetary policy. These are taken to be characterized by the fact that neither employment and money wages nor the real capital stock have time to adjust. An increase in government purchases is reflected simply in a drawing-down of inventories. As a consequence output, disposable income, the rental on capital goods, and commodity prices remain unchanged. In symbolic terms, $dE = dK = dQ = dw = dp = dr = dX = 0$. The whole burden of adjustment is thus on the yields of capital goods and bonds, r/π and i; the impact effect of monetary policy shows up in the valuation

16. These "runs," a device to treat a dynamic problem in terms of comparative statics, are in the Marshallian tradition. For an application to monetary macro-economics, see Keynes (1936, chap. 21). Brunner and Meltzer (1976) have recently used the same device.

17. In reality, of course, the processes here described as successive are going on simultaneously with weights that shift gradually from the short-run to the long-run elements. This will become apparent in the dynamic analysis of the following chapter.

18. Theologians in our profession have claimed that the use of *IS-LM* diagrams is a fundamental doctrinal issue. I regard this as a matter of expository convenience. It should be noted that without simplification (10.2.9) the diagrams would already become too cumbersome to be instructive.

of existing assets. This phase may be thought to be measured in terms of weeks, lasting up to a few months.

The narrowing of the focus to asset revaluation has an additional implication. Cash balances, since their money price is one by definition, have no asset price that could adjust instantaneously to equalize demand and supply.[19] As a consequence, the equilibrium condition for cash balances (10.2.6) becomes inoperative. Excess demand for money is not eliminated instantaneously. At the same time, cash balances must be thought to have a "real balance effect" on the demand for capital goods and bonds. At unchanged asset yields, a certain proportion of any increase in the money supply would translate itself into a demand for additional bonds and/or capital goods. Real balance effects thus appear in their proper short-term role.

With these changes, the model is reduced to equilibrium conditions for capital goods and bonds:

$$\pi K = K(r/\pi, i, M/p), \tag{10.3.1}$$

$$B/ip = D(r/\pi, i, M/p), \tag{10.3.2}$$

where K, r, and p are constants, M and B are policy variables, and i and π are determined by the model.

By taking differentials, the effects of monetary expansion can easily be determined as

$$\frac{d\pi}{dM}(dB = 0) = \frac{1}{\Delta}\frac{1}{p}\left[D_M K_i - K_M\left(D_i + \frac{B}{i^2 p}\right)\right] > 0, \tag{10.3.3}$$

$$\frac{di}{dM}(dB = 0) = \frac{1}{\Delta}\frac{1}{p}\left[D_M\left(K + K_r\frac{r}{\pi^2}\right) - K_M D_r\frac{r}{\pi^2}\right] < 0, \tag{10.3.4}$$

with

$$\Delta = -\left[\left(K + K_r\frac{r}{\pi^2}\right)\left(D_i + \frac{B}{i^2 p}\right) - K_i D_r\frac{r}{\pi^2}\right] < 0.$$

The statement $\Delta < 0$ is based on the consideration that the direct interest effects dominate the cross effects. It can be shown that $\Delta < 0$ is also necessary for stability. It follows that monetary expansion instantaneously raises the market prices of bonds and capital goods, while the yields decline. The strength of these effects depends crucially on the real balance effects K_M and D_M. If people should decide to hold additional balances entirely in the form of cash, monetary expansion would have no further short-run effects.

---

19. The payment of interest on cash balances by the government would make no difference in this respect, since it could still not adjust hour by hour under the pressure of market forces to eliminate excess demand.

In the case of debt expansion, capital goods prices fall (and their yield rises),

$$\frac{d\pi}{dB/i}(dM = 0) = -\frac{K_i}{\Delta p} < 0,$$

(10.3.5)

while the yield of bonds rises (and their price falls),

$$\frac{di}{dB/i}(dM = 0) = -\frac{1}{\Delta}\frac{1}{p}\left[K + K_r\left(\frac{r}{\pi^2}\right)\right] > 0.$$

(10.3.6)

The effects of money-financed and debt-financed expenditures thus go in opposite directions. Not surprisingly, the effects of debt expansion do not depend on the real balance effect.

Since open-market purchases can be regarded as the difference between monetary expansion and debt expansion, with the changes in government expenditures canceling out, their effects must be qualitatively the same as those of monetary expansion but reinforced by the additional effect of debt retirement. We thus obtain a strong rise in both asset prices and a correspondingly strong decline in yields.

These policy effects can be visualized graphically by plotting π on the horizontal axis and i on the vertical axis (see fig. 10.3.1). The KK-curve is the locus of those combinations of i and π which keep the market for capital goods in short-run equilibrium according to (10.3.1); its slope is nonpositive. The BD-curve is the graph of (10.3.2), representing all those combinations of i and π which maintain equilibrium in the bond market; its slope is also nonpositive, but $\Delta < 0$ implies that it is flatter than the KK-curve.

Monetary expansion shifts the two curves in opposite directions. The consequent changes in i and π are expressed by an arrow in panel (a). Debt expansion produces a rightward shift in the BD-curve, while the KK-curve is not affected. The equilibrium thus moves along the KK-curve as indicated in panel (b). Open-market purchases combine the effects of monetary expansion and debt contraction as illustrated in panel (c).

Of course, the effects of monetary policy cannot be "bottled up" in the

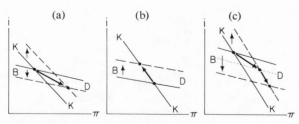

Figure **10.3.1**
Instantaneous Policy Effects

asset market except for a brief period. Gradually, the depletion of inventories, the disparity between the price of existing capital goods and their cost of production, and the excess supply of money will stimulate current output and employment. One of the interesting questions is to what extent the relatively strong impact effects of open-market operations on asset yields foreshadow a relatively strong employment effect. Do cheaper money and higher stock prices *now* presage more output and employment *later?* It will turn out that the answer is likely to be negative.

10.4. Short-run effects: Variable employment

In the short run, the money wage rate and the real capital stock used in production are still fixed, but employment is now variable. This is the phase Keynes and the Keynesians concentrated their attention on, at times almost forgetting its temporary character. With the modifications appropriate for this phase, the basic model thus turns into a summary restatement of Keynesian economics. This phase may be thought to be measured in terms of months, lasting up to several quarters or perhaps a few years.

The price of capital goods is now assumed to be equalized to the price of current output, so that $\pi = 1$. However, there is still no mechanism to equilibrate the capital stock used in production and the capital stock desired by wealth owners. There may be changes in the capital stock per capita, but their effect on the productive capacity of the economy is not accounted for. This corresponds to the Keynesian economy in which investment takes place but is not allowed to affect the productive capacity. As a consequence, the demand function for capital goods just serves to separate investment from consumption and can be disregarded in determining the other variables.

In terms of the basic model, these assumptions mean that output, disposable income, the rental on capital (which now is also the rate of return), and the price level are all hitched to employment,

$$dQ = Q_E \, dE, \tag{10.4.1}$$

$$dX = (1 - T')Q_E \, dE, \tag{10.4.2}$$

$$dr = Q_{KE} \, dE, \tag{10.4.3}$$

$$dp = - p \, \frac{Q_{EE}}{Q_E} \, dE, \tag{10.4.4}$$

while the equilibrium condition for real capital (8.2.4) is suspended.[20]

Differentiating the equilibrium conditions for bonds (10.2.5) and cash

20. Instead of assuming that variable employment of labor is associated with continuous full employment of capital, we could have assumed that the utilization rates

balances (10.2.6) and substituting for dX and dr, the model can be reduced to two equations[21]

$$(D_i + B/i^2p)di + [D_X Q_E (1 - T') + D_r Q_{KE}$$

$$- (B/ip)(Q_{EE}/Q_E)]dE = 1/ip \; dB; \qquad (10.4.5)$$

$$L_i \; di + [L_X Q_E (1 - T') + L_r Q_{KE}$$

$$- (M/p)(Q_{EE}/Q_E)]dE = 1/p \; dM. \qquad (10.4.6)$$

Simplifying notation, this can be rewritten

$$a_{11} \; di + a_{12} \; dE = 1/ip \; dB; \qquad (10.4.7)$$

$$a_{21} \; di + a_{22} \; dE = 1/p \; dM. \qquad (10.4.8)$$

Restrictions on parameters in addition to those embodied in the basic model are provided by stability requirements. We can postulate a dynamic system in which, in the neighborhood of the equilibrium values $i°$ and $E°$, excess supply of bonds produces an increase in i, while excess supply of money results in an expansion of output:

$$di/dt = k_i \left[-a_{11} (i - i°) - a_{12} (E - E°) \right], \qquad (10.4.9)$$

$$dE/dt = k_E \left[-a_{21} (i - i°) - a_{22} (E - E°) \right]. \qquad (10.4.10)$$

Metzler (1945) has shown that for such a system to be stable for any combination of nonnegative adjustment speeds the Hicksian conditions for perfect stability must be satisfied. This implies that the conditions

$$a_{11} > 0$$

$$a_{22} > 0$$

$$\Delta = a_{11}a_{22} - a_{12}a_{21} > 0$$

are necessary for dynamic stability independently of adjustment speeds. With these restrictions in mind, the effects of various monetary policies can be determined as follows.

---

for labor and capital move together. This alternative interpretation of the Keynesian short run means that every newly hired worker can be put to work behind a previously idle machine. With a linear-homogeneous production function, this implies that changes in employment take place at a constant rate of return of capital, a constant real wage rate and thus, with rigid money wages, at a constant price level. It also means that output is proportional to employment. In symbols, $dr = dp = 0$ and $dQ = (Q/E) \; dE$. This, *plus* the assumption that the income-elasticity of the demand for money is one, seems to be what it takes to make output and employment proportionate to the quantity of money. The result is the short-run application of the quantity theory to real output suggested by Keynes (1936, p. 295).

21. Under the alternative interpretation described in the preceding footnote, the coefficients of dE would reduce to $D_x(Q/E)(1 - T')$ and $L_x(Q/E)(1 - T')$.

Monetary expansion results in a short-run expansion of employment

$$\frac{dE}{dM} (dB = 0) = \frac{a_{11}}{\Delta p} > 0, \tag{10.4.11}$$

and thus an increase in output, disposable income, the rate of return on capital, and the price level. In the short run, the improved capacity utilization at given money wages is necessarily accompanied by an increase in commodity prices and thus a fall in real wages. The effect on the bond yield is, in principle, ambiguous,[22] since

$$\frac{di}{dM} (dB = 0) = -\frac{a_{12}}{\Delta p} \gtrless 0. \tag{10.4.12}$$

The ambiguity in the interest effect is due to a substitution effect struggling against an income effect. The expansion in disposable income calls forth an increase in the demand for bonds as reflected in $D_X Q_E (1 - T')$. The increase in commodity prices, on the other hand, reduces the real supply of bonds as expressed in $-(B/ip)(Q_{EE}/Q_E)$. These effects, taken together, tend to produce an excess demand for bonds at a given rate of interest and thus a decline in i. At the same time, however, the increase in the rate of return of capital, resulting from the improved capacity utilization, gives asset holders an incentive to switch from bonds to real capital and thus to drive up i, as reflected in $D_r Q_{KE}$.[23] While a decline in the bond yield, considering the probable orders of magnitude, is more likely than an increase, it is important to note that i does not act as a "link" in the transmission mechanism from money to employment. Even if i, because of $a_{12} = 0$, does not react at all, employment may still be stimulated. In fact, in this short-run model the bond market is something of a side show that gives no clue to the main-ring program. This is what monetarists have always contended against Keynes who wrote that "the primary effect of a change in the quantity of money on the quantity of effective demand is through its influence on the rate of interest" (1936, p. 298).

The employment effect of debt expansion is qualitatively similar to that of monetary expansion,

$$\frac{dE}{dB/i} (dM = 0) = -\frac{a_{21}}{\Delta p} > 0. \tag{10.4.13}$$

---

22. In the alternative interpretation of the short run, the bond yield would unambiguously decline as the square bracket reduces to $D_X(Q/E)(1 - T') > 0$.

23. In the limiting case where the interest-elasticity of the demand for money is infinite and thus $\Delta = \infty$, the effects of monetary expansion on both employment and the price level vanish. This is the "liquidity trap" case that Hicks popularized as his interpretation of Keynesian "depression economics," misleading a generation of textbook writers. On Keynes' real view about the liquidity trap as a relatively uninteresting possibility, see (1936, p. 207).

We approach the monetarist position with weak employment effects if bonds are a close substitute for real capital as reflected in a large value for D_i (and thus for Δ), but a bad substitute for money as reflected in a low absolute value for L_i. If either $D_i = \infty$ or $L_i = 0$, we arrive at the monetarist extreme where "money is all that matters" and debt-financed expenditures are powerless.[24] If, on the other hand, bonds are a good substitute for money, but, in view of a weak substitutability for capital goods, nevertheless have a low sensitivity to their own yield, the short-run employment effects of debt-financed expenditures become more significant.[25] It thus turns out that the interest-elasticities of the demand for bonds and money, as Keynesians like Tobin have so often pointed out, are of decisive importance for the short-run employment effect of debt-financed expenditures.[26]

In any case, however, the output and employment effects of money-financed expenditures are likely to be much stronger than those of debt-financed expenditures. This is due to two factors. First, the direct interest effect on bonds D_i is likely to be higher absolutely than the cross effect L_i; a considerable part of the funds an increase in i attracts to bonds does not come from cash balances, but from real capital and additional savings. Second, an increase in i not only raises the real demand for bonds, but also reduces the real supply through the fall in the bond price, for which there is no counterpart on the side of money. The higher the level of the government debt relative to the monetary base, the weaker are the effects of debt-financed expenditures relative to those of monetary expansion, and the less inaccurate will be the statement that money is practically all that matters.

Once we know the effect of debt expansion on employment, we also know its effect on Q, X, r, and p, since these move with E. It can also be ascertained that the interest rate is certain to rise, as the increased supply

24. Hicks popularized the interest-inelastic demand for money ($L_i = 0$) as the "classical case." This was, of course, an inaccurate interpretation of classical economics. Quantity theorists (correctly) argued that, disregarding bonds, money income reacts proportionally to exogenous changes in the quantity of money in full equilibrium, with fully adjusted prices. The interest-elasticity of the demand for money was irrelevant to this proposition, since in full equilibrium interest rates would be unchanged. The notion that the quantity theory had something to do with the reaction of money income in the short run, before prices were fully adjusted, and thus with real income, seems to be due to Hicks.

25. It may be worth pointing out that in Hicks' "Keynesian case" with $-L_i = \infty$, debt expansion is still effective.

26. It has sometimes been suggested, somewhat loosely, that the effect of debt expansion switches sign at the point where bonds begin to be a closer substitute in portfolios for capital than for money (Tobin/Buiter, [1976], p. 5). (10.4.13) shows that there is no such watershed, the employment effect of debt expansion always being nonnegative and gradually declining as we approach the monetarist extreme.

of bonds drives up their yield,

$$\frac{di}{dB/i}(dM = 0) = \frac{a_{22}}{\Delta p} > 0. \tag{10.4.14}$$

If the employment effects of monetary expansion and debt expansion are qualitatively similar, the short-run effect of open-market purchases, which is their difference, may be less clear. This is indeed the case, as shown by

$$\frac{dE}{dM}(dB = - idM) = \frac{a_{11} + a_{21}}{\Delta p} \gtrless 0. \tag{10.4.15}$$

However, as pointed out above, the direct effect of the interest rate on the bond market, measured by $a_{11} = D_i + B/i^2p$, is almost certain to dominate its cross effect on the demand for money, measured by $a_{21} = L_i$. As a consequence, open-market purchases are almost certain to result in a short-run expansion of employment, accompanied by rising output, disposable income, capital returns, and prices. The significant fact is that even if these effects are "normal" they are smaller than those of money-financed expenditures. In general it matters how money is created, and nonmonetarists are right if they regard money-financed public expenditures as more effective in stimulating employment in the short run than open-market operations. It is only in the limiting case $a_{21} = L_i = 0$ where open-market purchases have the same effect as money-financed expenditures. In this short-run perspective, monetarism thus turns on the interest-sensitivity of the demand for money, which is exactly what has been said (but also denied) so often in the debate. The weaker employment effect of open-market purchases stands in contrast to their stronger impact effect on asset yields noted in the preceding section. This indicates that the impact effect on asset yields cannot be used as a predictor of subsequent employment effects.

The short-run interest effects of open-market operations, like those of monetary expansion, are, in principle, ambiguous:

$$\frac{di}{dM}(dB = - idM) = - \frac{1}{\Delta}\frac{1}{p}(a_{12} + a_{22}) \gtrless 0. \tag{10.4.16}$$

The ambiguity again arises from the substitution term in a_{12}, but in view of the addition of a_{22} this is now extremely unlikely to dominate the sign. As a consequence, a decline in the bond yield can be taken as practically certain.[27] Assuming there is a decline in the bond yield for both policies, it is

27. In Hicks' "Keynesian case," with $a_{21} = L_i = -\infty$ in the denominator, the interest effect vanishes, but the employment effect is still positive. While this case does not tell us much about the real world, it nicely illustrates the fact that expansionary monetary policy, here represented by open-market purchases, can be effective for employment even though it is powerless to lower the bond yield.

stronger, and probably much stronger, for open-market operations than for money-financed expenditures, as the effect of the reduction in bonds is added to the effect of the increase in the money supply. This means that the relative interest effects of monetary policy cannot be used as an indicator of their relative employment and output effects: It is not true that a stronger decline in interest rates, either as an immediate reaction or in the short-run, is associated with a stronger expansion in output and employment. In fact, it is the other way around.

These arguments can be summarized in terms of an *LM-BD* diagram (fig. 10.4.1). Since $a_{21} < 0$ and $a_{22} > 0$, the combinations of interest rates and employment that maintain equilibrium between demand and supply for money lie on an upward-sloping *LM*-curve. Since $a_{11} > 0$ and $a_{12} \gtrless 0$, the *BD*-curve, representing equilibrium between demand and supply for bonds, can slope downward (left-hand panel) or upward (right-hand panel), but in view of the stability condition $\Delta < 0$ it cannot be steeper than the *LM*-curve.[28]

Debt expansion raises both employment and the rate of interest, except in the limiting case of a vertical *LM*-curve where the employment effect vanishes. Monetary expansion certainly stimulates employment, but its effect on i is ambiguous. Open-market purchases, the sum of monetary expansion and debt contraction, have, in pure logic, uncertain effects along both axes, with the more likely cases illustrated in the graphs.[29] The divergent directions of the various arrows illustrate the fact, already noted

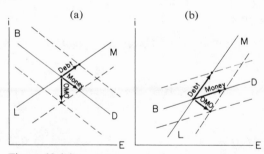

Figure **10.4.1**
Short-Run Policy Effects

28. We may suspect that there is also an implied *IS*-curve. In fact, there is. It can easily be shown from the model that investment equals saving for all those combinations of i and E for which the excess demand for money equals the excess supply for bonds. As always, the *IS*-curve thus goes through the intersection of the *LM*-curve and the *BD*-curve, and it is likely, though not absolutely certain, to have a negative slope.

29. In fact, just as the fiscal arrow follows the LM-curve and the monetary arrow follows the *BD*-curve, so the open-market arrow can be shown to follow the *IS*-curve. The ambiguity in the direction of the open-market arrow thus reflects the ambiguity in the slope of the *IS*-curve.

in another context, that the market yield on bonds is not a reliable indicator of the associated employment effects in the short run.

The Keynesian effects described in this subsection do not, of course, represent a steady state. Sooner or later, changes in employment and commodity prices will set the money wage in motion. The Keynesian short run is shading into the classical long run.

10.5. Long-term effects: Full employment with a fixed capital stock

If we wait long enough, wages are flexible and employment must thus be assumed to be at its equilibrium or "full employment" level. This is the phase of the classical long run. However, changes in the per capita capital stock continue to be disregarded. As a consequence, capital used in production is still not equated to capital demanded by wealth owners. In terms of the basic model this means that the equilibrium condition for capital goods (10.2.4) is still suspended and the factor inputs K and E, and thus Q, X, r, and w/p, are constant. Such a model may be visualized as summarizing the effects of monetary policy over periods from several quarters up to a few years.

The resulting full-employment model is extremely simple. The equilibrium conditions for bonds (10.2.5) and money (10.2.6) reduce, upon differentiation, to

$$(D_i + B/i^2p) \, di + B/ip^2 \, dp = 1/ip \, dB, \tag{10.5.1}$$

$$L_i \, di + M/p^2 \, dp = 1/p \, dM. \tag{10.5.2}$$

Monetary expansion unambiguously raises the price level and lowers the rate of interest, as

$$\frac{dp}{dM} (dB = 0) = \frac{1}{\Delta p} (D_i + B/i^2p) > 0, \tag{10.5.3}$$

$$\frac{di}{dM} (dB = 0) = -\frac{1}{\Delta p} (B/ip^2) < 0, \tag{10.5.4}$$

with

$$\Delta = (D_i + B/i^2p)(M/p^2) - L_i(B/ip^2) > 0.$$

As (10.5.3) shows, the increase in the price level will generally be smaller, percentagewise, than the underlying expansion in the money supply. For the money supply alone, the quantity theory of prices does not hold. This is essentially due to the presence of debt. With $B = 0$ we indeed obtain $dp/p = dM/M$. The same is true even in the presence of debt in the limiting case where the demand for money is insensitive to the rate of interest and thus $L_i = 0$. The quantity theory of prices also holds for an equiproportionate increase in both money and bonds. It can easily be ascertained that for $dB = (B/M)\,dM$ the proportionate change in prices is again equal to the proportionate change in money. In principle, the quantity theory applies not to money in particular, but to the whole array of exogenously determined financial assets.

It may be worth repeating that the quantity theory does not maintain that all changes in the price level are caused by changes in the money supply. In terms of the present model, any number of shifts in the underlying functions may result in price changes. The historical observation, therefore, that movements in the price level do not always parallel the movements in the money supply does not invalidate the quantity theory for at least two reasons, namely, (1) because other exogenous assets like bonds would also have to be considered, and (2) because the quantity of financial assets is only one of the forces determining the price level. The quantity theory does not ask us to adopt a monetarist view of economic history. It does claim, however, that the historical course of prices would have been different if the supplies of financial assets by the government had been different, all in roughly the same proportion. In this sense, which seems to be the correct one, it is neither false nor trivial, but one of the important, if elementary, insights of economic science.

For debt expansion, both long-term multipliers

$$\frac{dp}{dB/i}(dM = 0) = -\frac{L_i}{\Delta p} > 0, \tag{10.5.5}$$

$$\frac{di}{dB/i}(dM = 0) = \frac{M/p^2}{\Delta p} > 0, \tag{10.5.6}$$

are unambiguously positive, but the price effect vanishes if the demand for money is interest-inelastic. The lower the interest-elasticity of the demand for money, the weaker, *ceteris paribus*, will be the long-run price effect of debt-financed expenditures. It is also likely, though not certain, that the price effect of debt-financed expenditures will be weaker than those of money-financed expenditures because, as argued above, the excess demand $D_i + B/i^2p$ produced by an increase in i in the bond market is likely to be stronger than its cross effect L_i in the money market.

The full-employment effects of open-market operations are

$$\frac{dp}{dM}(dB = -idM) = \frac{1}{\Delta p}\left[(D_i + B/i^2p) + L_i\right] \gtrless 0, \tag{10.5.7}$$

$$\frac{di}{dM}(dB = -idM) = -\frac{1}{\Delta p}\left[M/p^2 + B/ip^2\right] < 0. \tag{10.5.8}$$

While the bond yield, as expected, will unambiguously decline, the effect on the price level cannot be signed with absolute certainty. Open-market sales are not an infallible method to lower prices. However, if the above argument about the domination of direct effects over cross effects is accepted, that is, if monetary expansion has stronger price effects than debt expansion, then open-market operations can be relied upon to have the normal effect. This seems to be the likely case.[30]

In the LM/BD diagram for the full-employment case, with p on the horizontal axis, the BD-curve is unambiguously downward sloping, while the LM-curve has positive slope (fig. 10.5.1). This means that the monetary arrow now points unambiguously not only to the right but also downward. The downward movement of the open-market arrow is also unambiguous, but it may still point either to the right or to the left, though the latter is much less likely. The fiscal arrow continues to point unambiguously upward and to the right, though an interest-insensitive demand for money would make it vertical. Just as in the short-term under-employment model the market yield on bonds could not be used as an indicator of the associated employment changes, so in the long-run full-employment model it cannot be used as an indicator of price effects.

10.6. Steady-state effects: Full adjustment of capital stock

The long-run analysis of the preceding section, while classical in spirit, was still characterized by the Keynesian or Wicksellian assumption that investment (beyond the requirements of a growing labor force) is not added to the capital stock used in production. While this simplification is justifi-

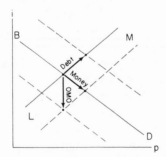

Figure **10.5.1**
Long-Run Policy Effects

30. In the Gurley/Shaw "pure inside-money" case, that is with $M = -B/i$, it can easily be verified that $dp/dM = p/M$ and $di/dM = 0$. If all money is created by buying private bonds, an increase in the level of this operation raises the price level in proportion, of course, while the bond yield remains unchanged. This is because an open-market operation amounts to a proportionate change in both M and B in this case.

able for limited time periods, it ultimately becomes illegitimate. In the very long run it thus has to be replaced by the assumption of full stock/flow equilibrium for real capital goods. What has to be determined are the macroeconomic effects of monetary policy along a balanced-growth path. In terms of the formal model this means that (10.2.4) now becomes operative. The basic model specified in section 10.2 is thus in full force, with the additional proviso that $\pi = 1$.

By taking the total differentials of the asset-equilibrium conditions (10.2.4) $-$ (10.2.6) and substituting for dX from (10.2.10), for dQ from (10.2.1) and for dK from (10.2.2) we obtain the following system of equations:

$$\left[K_X(1 - T') \frac{Q_K}{Q_{KK}} - \frac{1}{Q_{KK}} + K_r \right] dr \qquad + K_i \, di$$

$$= 0, \qquad (10.6.1)$$

$$\left[D_X(1 - T') \frac{Q_K}{Q_{KK}} + D_r \right] \qquad dr + (D_i + B/i^2 p) di$$

$$+ (B/ip^2) dp = (1/ip) dB, \qquad (10.6.2)$$

$$\left[L_X(1 - T') \frac{Q_K}{Q_{KK}} + L_r \right] \qquad dr \qquad + L_i \, di$$

$$+ (M/p^2) \, dp = (1/p) \, dM. \qquad (10.6.3)$$

As the counterpart to this comparative-static system, we can again postulate a dynamic system (see section 10.4)

$$dr/dt = k_r \left[-b_{11} (r - r^\circ) - b_{12} (i - i^\circ) \qquad \qquad \right], \qquad (10.6.4)$$

$$di/dt = k_i \left[-b_{21} (r - r^\circ) - b_{22} (i - i^\circ) - b_{23} (p - p^\circ) \right], \qquad (10.6.5)$$

$$dp/dt = k_p \left[-b_{31} (r - r^\circ) - b_{32} (i - i^\circ) - b_{33} (p - p^\circ)\right], \qquad (10.6.6)$$

where b_{ij} is the corresponding coefficient of the comparative-static system and r°, i°, and p° are the equilibrium values of, respectively, r, i, and p. From the assumption underlying the basic model we know that

$$b_{12} < 0 \qquad b_{22} > 0 \qquad b_{31} < 0 \qquad b_{33} > 0$$
$$b_{21} < 0 \qquad b_{23} > 0 \qquad b_{32} < 0.$$

Again using Hicks' condition for perfect stability, based on Metzler's result, we find that the necessary conditions for stability under any combination of adjustment speeds include the following additional constraints on the parameters:

$$b_{11} > 0, \qquad b_{11}b_{22} - b_{12}b_{21} > 0, \qquad \Delta = \begin{vmatrix} b_{11} & b_{12} & 0 \\ b_{21} & b_{22} & b_{23} \\ b_{31} & b_{32} & b_{33} \end{vmatrix} > 0.$$

It is now easy to determine the comparative-static effects of various policies on the balanced-growth path. I begin again with monetary expansion, characterized by $dM > 0$, $dB = 0$. It clearly leads to a lower return on real capital,

$$\frac{dr}{dM}(dB = 0) = \frac{1}{\Delta p}(b_{12}b_{23}) < 0. \tag{10.6.7}$$

The bond yield also falls,

$$\frac{di}{dM}(dB = 0) = \frac{1}{\Delta p}(b_{11}b_{23}) < 0, \tag{10.6.8}$$

while the price level rises,

$$\frac{dp}{dM}(dB = 0) = \frac{1}{\Delta p}(b_{11}b_{22} - b_{12}b_{21}) > 0. \tag{10.6.9}$$

Normal expectations are thus confirmed.

Since employment is given at the full-employment level, the fall in r means that more real capital per unit of labor is used ($dK/dM > 0$), per capita output rises ($dQ/dM > 0$), and so does the wage rate. These real effects of monetary expansion are essentially due to the fact that, with a positive government debt, an increase in the money supply lowers the bond yield and thus, at unchanged r, induces wealth holders to switch into capital goods. If either there are no bonds ($b_{23} = 0$), or the demand for capital goods is insensitive to the bond yield ($b_{12} = 0$), these real effects disappear. We note that r and i change in the constant proportion b_{12}/b_{11}, and this will turn out to be true for the other types of policies, too. This means that for given b_{11} and b_{12} the market yield of bonds can indeed be used, in this steady-state context (and except for $b_{12} = 0$), as an indicator of the associated real effects. While the monetarist objections against the use of the bond yield as an indicator of real effects are valid in the short run, they lose their force in the steady state.

As is well known, the positive output effect of higher money-financed expenditures along a balanced-growth path does not mean that such expenditures are always desirable. First, the increase in the level of per capita output is generally associated with a change in the proportion of government expenditure in total output, which, in itself, may be desirable or undesirable. Second, an increase in per capita output is not necessarily associated with an increase in per capita consumption, since an increasing proportion of output is absorbed by investment. It can easily be shown that the present model conforms to the Golden Rule, whereby steady-state consumption is maximized if the rate of return on capital is equal to the rate of growth.[31] Third, the present analysis does not take into account the associated changes in real cash balances and their services. In the presence of government debt, a higher level of nominal cash balances, since the price level rises less than in proportion, is associated with a higher level of real balances, which would make the monetary expansion all the more desirable, but only up to the point where the economy is satiated with real cash balances.

In the presence of government debt the price level will generally rise less than in proportion to the increase in the money supply. In two special cases, however, the quantity theory of prices is valid. The more trivial case is again the absence of public debt. The same result emerges even in the presence of public debt if both $K_i = 0$ and $L_i = 0$. The smaller the public debt and the weaker the reaction of the demand for capital and money to the bond yield, the closer we come to the quantity theory. Again it can easily be ascertained that a proportionate increase in both money and bonds produces an equiproportionate increase in the price level.

I now consider debt expansion, characterized by debt-financed government expenditures at a constant money supply. Provided $b_{12} = K_i < 0$, such a policy will certainly raise the rate of return on capital, as

$$\frac{dr}{dB/i}(dM = 0) = -\frac{1}{\Delta p}(b_{12}b_{33}) > 0. \tag{10.6.10}$$

It will also result in a higher bond yield,

$$\frac{di}{dB/i}(dM = 0) = \frac{1}{\Delta p}(b_{11}b_{33}) > 0. \tag{10.6.11}$$

For given K_i, this can again be expressed verbally by saying that the increase in debt raises the bond yield, which, in turn, requires a higher equilibrium yield on real capital. The latter will, of course, be associated with lower capital intensity of production, lower output, and a lower real wage. However, debt expansion has no real effects in the long run if $K_i = 0$.

The effect on the price level,

$$\frac{dp}{dB/i}(dM = 0) = -\frac{1}{\Delta p}(b_{11}b_{32} - b_{12}b_{31}) > 0, \tag{10.6.12}$$

will normally be positive as the supply of financial assets is increased. In fact, in the absence of government-supplied money, that is with $M = 0$,

---

31. Note that total consumption is equal to output minus investment, $C + G = Q - \omega K$. Total consumption is maximized where its derivative with respect to M vanishes:

$$\frac{d(C + G)}{dM} = \frac{dQ}{dM} - \omega\frac{dK}{dM} = \left(\frac{r}{Q_{KK}} - \frac{\omega}{Q_{KK}}\right)\frac{dr}{dM} = 0, \text{ or } r = \omega.$$

the quantity theory would be valid for bonds, since in this case

$$\Delta = -\frac{B}{ip^2}(b_{11}b_{32} - b_{12}b_{31})$$

and thus $dp/dB = p/B$. This illustrates the earlier statement that the quantity theory is not specific to money, but relates to any exogenous financial assets. On the other hand, debt expansion has no long-run effect on the price level if $b_{12} = K_i = 0$ and $b_{32} = L_i = 0$. Once again the cross effects of the bond yield on the demand for capital and money are seen to be important for the monetarist position.

The macroeconomic effects of open-market operations ($dB = -idM$) again differ from those of money-financed expenditures by the corresponding effects of debt expansion. In the limiting case where $K_i = L_i = 0$, this difference vanishes for all variables except the bond yield. The real effects of money become the same whether it is created by expenditures or by open-market purchases. Extreme monetarism triumphs. In general, however, the effects of open-market operations are different from those of monetary expansion; what matters is both the money supply and the way it is brought about.

Specifically, the rate of return on capital,

$$\frac{dr}{dM}(dB = -idM) = \frac{1}{\Delta p} b_{12}(b_{23} + b_{33}) < 0, \tag{10.6.13}$$

will fall even more than under pure monetary policy, and the effects on capital intensity, output, and real wages will be correspondingly stronger. The fall in the bond yield,

$$\frac{di}{dM}(dB = -idM) = -\frac{1}{\Delta p} b_{11}(b_{23} + b_{33}) < 0, \tag{10.6.14}$$

is also stronger. The price effects, however, perhaps no longer surprisingly, are, in principle, ambiguous,

$$\frac{dp}{dM}(dB = -idM) = -\frac{1}{\Delta p}[(b_{11}b_{22} - b_{12}b_{21})$$

$$+ (b_{11}b_{32} - b_{12}b_{31})] \gtrless 0. \tag{10.6.15}$$

While the increase in the money supply, represented by the first term in the square bracket, pulls prices up, the reduction in debt, represented by the second term, is pulling them down. It can plausibly be argued that the monetary effects will normally dominate the debt effects, but without empirical estimates one cannot be sure. While an open-market policy is quite reliable in its qualitative influence on interest rates and real output, it is not reliable, in purely qualitative terms, in its influence on the price level. It will later appear, however, that a perverse price effect is extremely unlikely.

The steady-state model, since it has three interdependent assets, cannot be directly represented in a two-dimensional LM/BD-diagram. However, observing that the capital goods equilibrium is independent of the price level, we can still achieve an indirect representation in a three-quadrant diagram (fig. 10.6.1). In the NW-quadrant we plot those combinations of r and i which keep the excess demand for real capital at zero. As $b_{11} > 0$ and $b_{12} < 0$, its slope is positive. We then assume that the system is always moving along this curve. This permits us to substitute for r in the equilibrium conditions for bonds and money. It can easily be shown that the r-compensated BD-curve in terms of i and p is unambiguously nonpositive, while the r-compensated LM-curve is unambiguously nonnegative, as drawn in the NE-quadrant. In the SW-quadrant we finally plot the output level associated with a given level of r. The NW- and SW-quadrants, taken together, relate a certain output to each level of the market yield on bonds. This is the graphical expression of the fact, noted above, that in the steady state i can indeed be used as an indicator of the real effects of various policies. The NE-quadrant, on the other hand, illustrates the fact that the market yield of bonds, just as for shorter time periods, cannot be used as an indicator of price effects.

Monetary expansion moves the system downward along the BD-curve to higher prices, lower asset yields, and higher output. Debt expansion produces a move along the LM-curve toward higher prices, higher interest rates and lower output. Open-market operations, being the difference

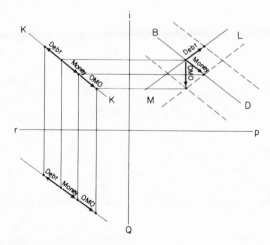

Figure **10.6.1**
Steady-State Policy Effects

between the other two policies, certainly lower interest rates and raise output, but the effect on prices remains uncertain.

The steady-state model finally represents full stock/flow equilibrium. While the shorter-term equilibria all carried the seed of their own destruction, the steady-state equilibrium can, in principle, be maintained forever.

10.7. Comparison of effects

Each of the preceding four sections established the macroeconomic effects of different monetary policies for a particular adjustment period. The results are illustrated in table 10.7.1. It lists the changes in seven variables resulting from monetary expansion, debt expansion, and open-market purchases, depending on the length of the adjustment period. An asterisk indicates that the variable in question is held constant by assump-

TABLE 10.7.1

Effects of Change in Money and/or Debt by 5% of Money Supply

Variable		Instantaneous	Short-Term	Long-Term	Steady-State
			Monetary Expansion		
K	($ per capita)	*	*	*	+37.86
E	(percent)	*	+8.04	*	*
$1/\pi$	(percent)	−4.41	*	*	*
r	(basis points)	0	+53.42	0	−0.74
i	(basis points)	−3.09	−1.05 ?	−6.25	−6.32
Q	($ per capita)	0	+557.86	0	+3.41
p	(percent)	0	+2.62	+4.38	+4.32
			Debt Expansion		
K		*	*	*	−16.22
E		*	+0.49	*	*
$1/\pi$		+6.30	*	*	*
r		0	+3.27	0	+0.32
i		+4.41	+2.99	+2.68	+2.71
Q		0	+34.15	0	−1.46
p		0	+0.16	+0.28	+0.29
			Open-Market Expansion		
K		*	*	*	+54.09
E		*	+7.55(?)	*	*
$1/\pi$		−10.71	*	*	*
r		0	+50.14(?)	0	−1.06
i		−7.50	−4.04(?)	−8.93	−9.03
Q		0	+523.71(?)	0	+4.87
p		0	+2.46 ?	+4.11 ?	+4.03 ?

NOTE: Explanation of signs:

+ increase	* zero by assumption	? sign likely, but not certain
− decrease	0 zero by implication	(?) sign logically ambiguous, but practically certain.

tion, while a zero means that the variable remains unchanged by implication. The differences between the adjustment periods originate from the different assumptions about K, E, and π. Of these, only the relative price of capital goods can react simultaneously. In the short run, it is employment that reacts, while the adjustment of the capital goods price is over and that of the capital stock has not yet begun. In the long run, employment is back at its equilibrium level and all three variables are thus unchanged. In the steady state, finally, capital goods are allowed to adjust.

To obtain a summary of the *qualitative* propositions of sections 10.3–10.6, we concentrate on the signs in the table, disregarding the numbers. Wherever there appears a question mark, the sign is, in principle, ambiguous. Asset yields react instantaneously. Debt expansion consistently raises both r and i as we move through successive stages. Monetary expansion is likely to produce an equally simple picture for the bond yield, though with the opposite sign. However, its effect on the rate of return on capital is more complex, a minus sign succeeding a plus sign as the adjustment process advances. The effect of open-market operations on the rate of return on capital, being the difference of the two other effects, is similarly complex. There is no simple rule that would permit forecasting the changes in employment, prices, and output from the asset yields.

The short term is characterized by an expansion of output and employment, associated with rising prices. In the long run, these real effects recede and the expansion is concentrated in the price level. In the steady state, finally, output increases again, now due to the accumulation of capital, while prices continue at a high level. About the qualitative effects of monetary and debt expansion there is little ambiguity. For open-market purchases, however, about half of the non-zero signs cannot be established with logical necessity, but it was pointed out in the preceding sections that in most cases the sign is nevertheless practically certain; the remaining doubts are mainly concentrated in the price effects.

To obtain *quantitative* comparisons between different stages and different policies, we have to replace the symbols of the model by numbers. While the true numbers are not known, it is instructive to consider the results for a plausible and fairly realistic set of initial conditions and parameters, intended to be roughly representative of the U.S. economy in 1970. This will be called the "reference set."

The initial conditions for stocks and flows in the reference set are listed in table 10.7.2, where the sources are also given. The most significant aspects are the low levels of financial assets relative to real capital goods and the low level of the monetary base relative to government debt. The fraction of government-supplied currency in total wealth is small indeed. The assumption that disposable income and government expenditures add up to total income implies a balanced budget, which, in turn, reflects the assumption that the growth rate is zero. While this is not quite realistic, it

TABLE 10.7.2

The Reference Set: Initial Stocks and Flows

		Aggregate		Per capita
Variable	Symbol	Observed ($ bill.)	Assumed ($ bill.)	(N = 85 mill.) ($)
Capital goods	K	2720[a]	2720	32000
Bonds	B/ip	182.2[b]	178.5	2100
Money	M/p	77.1[c]	76.5	900
National income	Q	798.6[d]	799	9400
Government expenditures	G	97.2	95.6	1125
Disposable income	X		703.4	8275

SOURCES:
[a] Christensen and Jorgensen (1973, p. 358), roughly extrapolated from 1969 to 1970.
[b] Christ (1973), net government debt, privately held, 1970.
[c] Christ (1973), monetary base, 1970.
[d] Federal Reserve Bulletin.

hardly distorts the conclusions about monetary policy. The initial price level is set at 1.00, the initial employment rate is 94%, the initial bond yield is assumed to be 5 percent, while the initial capital yield is 9 percent.[32]

The assumptions about the coefficients of the asset demand functions are given in table 10.7.3. The elasticities can be derived from the partial derivatives by standardizing the latter with the corresponding initial conditions. The assumptions about the interest effects were chosen to satisfy the following requirements:

1. For each rate of return, the positive direct effect should exceed the

TABLE 10.7.3

The Reference Set: Asset Demand Parameters

Asset		Argument of Demand Function		
		Disp. Income (X)	Capital Yield (r)	Bond Yield (i)
		Elasticities		
Capital goods	(K)	1.00	0.40	−0.10
Bonds	(B/ip)	1.00	−1.00	2.50
Money	(M/p)	1.00	−0.30	−0.50
		Partial Derivatives		
Capital goods	(K)	$K_x = 3.867$	$K_r = 142222$	$K_i = -64000$
Bonds	(B/ip)	$D_x = 0.254$	$D_r = -23333$	$D_i = 105000$
Money	(M/p)	$L_x = 0.109$	$L_r = -3000$	$L_i = -9000$

32. The rates of return on different types of tangible assets given by Christensen and Jorgensen (1973, p. 344) vary from 8.7 to 9.3 percent.

sum of the negative cross effects, so that a *ceteris paribus* increase in any rate of return raises total desired wealth.

2. The elasticity of the demand for money with respect to the bond yield should be inside the range of econometric estimates.

3. Since money is a better substitute for bonds than for capital goods, $|L_i| > |L_r|$.

4. Bonds are assumed to be a good substitute for real capital, but their relatively low initial level makes their elasticity with respect to the bond yield (absolutely) much higher than that of capital goods.

5. Both bonds and capital goods react absolutely more strongly to their own yield than to the yield of the other asset.

The production function is assumed to be

$$Q = 408.68\ K^{0.31}E^{0.69},$$

where the exponents are close to the estimates of factor shares for 1969 given by Christensen and Jorgensen (1973, p. 336), while the constant factor follows from the initial conditions for Q, K, and E. The marginal tax rate was set at 0.40.

This reference set will be extensively used in chapter 11 as a benchmark for dynamic simulations of the adjustment path. At the present stage, it is used to give a numerical interpretation to the comparative-static effects of different monetary policies. The strength of these effects is expressed by the numbers in table 10.7.1. All policy actions are supposed to take place at a level of 5 percent of the initial money supply, which means $45 per capita. Attention is drawn, in particular, to the following observations:

1. Except on the bond yield, monetary policy has much stronger effects than debt expansion. One reason is that the U.S. monetary base is only a fraction of net government debt, so that an expansion of money and debt by the same amount implies a much smaller percentage change in debt than in money. The larger government debt relative to the money supply, the more potent are, dollar for dollar, money-financed expenditures relative to debt-financed expenditures. Another reason is the fact that the direct elasticity of the demand for bonds with respect to the bond yield is likely to be higher than the indirect elasticity of cash balances with respect to the bond yield.

2. In view of the preceding observation, the effects of open-market purchases are close to those of monetary expansion. It is my impression that it would be difficult to choose plausible parameters for the U.S. economy in such a way that this implication is reversed. While the parameters were chosen without regard to a particular doctrinal position, they seem to illustrate the monetarist point of view. However, it will be argued in the following chapter that this impression may be misleading.

3. Debt expansion does have a short-run effect on output and employment, but it is relatively weak. Again it may be premature to label this

result monetarist, as long as it is not known exactly how large an effect a nonmonetarist would expect.

4. The differences between the long run and the steady state are very small. With these parameters, the neglect of capital accumulation would not have introduced a serious quantitative error.

5. In the Keynesian short run, the effects of monetary expansion on employment and output are of the same order of magnitude, percentage-wise, as the monetary expansion itself. The application of the quantity theory to the short-term changes in real output (instead of to the long-run change in prices), while not analytically valid, may be a tolerable first approximation.

6. In the long run, the increase in the price level is somewhat smaller than the monetary expansion; this is essentially due to the presence of bonds.

7. The effect of monetary policy on the bond yield, while moderate, persists even in the long run and actually gets larger; this is mainly due to the fact that an increase in the value of existing bonds is necessary to maintain the desired level of real bond holdings in the face of a higher price level.

The changes in variables from the short run to the steady state, by and large, exhibit the features familiar from the tradition of macroeconomic theory. The numerical comparison between the three policies seems to support the monetarist view: The effects of fiscal policy on prices, output and employment are relatively weak, and an increase in the money supply has about the same effect whether it is brought about by government expenditures or by open-market operations. However, this apparent support for the monetarist position is qualified in three important respects. First, while the initial conditions correspond closely to American data, the elasticities of the asset demands had to be chosen arbitrarily. Other sets of elasticities may, conceivably, produce results that are less monetarist. On the basis of many simulations I would conjecture, however, that this is not very likely and that it is difficult to choose plausible demand parameters in such a way that the monetarist position is clearly contradicted. The main reason for this is the large size of debt relative to the monetary base and the fact that a change in the bond yield tends to have a much larger effect on the excess demand for bonds than on the excess demand for money.

The second qualification relates to the disregard of acceleration effects in the government budget constraint. The static model implies that any additional cash balances or bonds required to switch the economy to a higher steady-state level of M or B are instantaneously provided, without any additional expenditures, by temporary transfer payments, so-to-say "overnight." In reality, such adjustments in asset stocks are more likely to be accomplished by temporary increases in expenditures, which may provide additional impact effects. Since these dynamic impact effects are essentially the same for monetary and debt expansion, they tend to militate against the monetarist position. In fact, it is exactly these impact effects of fiscal expansion the non-monetarists have typically relied upon. For this reason, the conclusions from the static analysis are likely to be biased in favor of monetarism.

Thirdly, and perhaps most importantly, it will be shown in the following chapter that the conclusions derived from nonmonetarist econometric models of the U.S. economy are not really very different from those given in table 10.7.1. A nonmonetarist may well feel that the effects of debt expansion derived from the present model, though small compared to the effects of monetary policies, are just those effects he always regarded as significant and potentially important. At the purely analytical level there is possibly more consensus in macroeconomics than is commonly supposed.

The preceding discussion of the "potency" of monetary policy turned on the relative size of asset stocks and the elasticities of asset demand. I conclude with a more fundamental consideration. In the world we live in, the yield on cash balances, at least under noninflationary conditions, is exogenously determined, often at zero, while the bond yield is free to respond to market forces. This was reflected in corresponding assumptions in the present model. We can, however, imagine a world, though perhaps with some difficulty, in which the yield on bonds is exogenously fixed, while the yield on the monetary base is free to respond to supply and demand. It was first pointed out by Tobin (1969, p. 25 f.) that the relative potency of money and bonds would be reversed in this case; debt expansion would normally be more potent than monetary expansion, and open-market purchases would thus be contractive. By rewriting the present model on the assumption that $di = 0$, while money carries an endogenous yield ρ, it can easily be checked that this is indeed correct.[33] The relatively higher potency of monetary policies compared to purely fiscal measures can thus be attributed to the fact that it is the rate of interest on money, and not the bond yield, that is exogenously fixed.

Tobin concluded from his observation that any higher potency of money compared to other financial assets is not due to its role as the medium of exchange, but to the authorities' choice of the yield that should be exogenously fixed. I believe, however, that the crucial difference is indeed the role of money as the medium of exchange. It is this role (and not, say, the failure of the government to pay a coupon yield on the monetary base) which makes it impossible for the market forces to bid up or down the

33. Complete symmetry would also require that there can be capital gains on cash balances replacing those on bonds. As long as the yield on cash balances varies because of a changing coupon yield on a market price fixed at 1, there are no such capital gains. As a consequence, the term B/i^2p appearing in a_{11} has no counterpart for a variable interest rate on money, and the contractive effect of open-market purchases in the latter case is correspondingly weakened.

money price of money (since it is always unity), and thus to adjust its yield. Any endogenous variability of the interest on cash balances would thus have to be achieved by the government adjusting the coupon payments credited to base money balances hour by hour in such a way that the bond yield stays at the exogenously fixed level. This is clearly a highly contrived sort of endogeneity, which would be virtually impossible to achieve in practice. This is consistent with the observation that under a gold standard, in the absence of government intervention, the interest on gold coins is also fixed at zero. To have an exogenously fixed yield must thus be regarded as a typical property of the medium of exchange, at least in a noninflationary system.[34] It is ultimately this property which makes money more potent than bonds.

34. This seems to be what Barro and Grossman (1971), though diverted by some irrelevant complications, seemed to be driving at.

Eleven
MONETARY MACRODYNAMICS

Introduction

The macroeconomic effects of monetary expansion in full stock/flow equilibrium, described in section 10.6, are relatively simple and well understood: The price level rises almost in proportion to the money supply, the increase in money relative to the public debt produces a slight decline in interest rates, and the consequent increase in capital stock results in an increase in output, albeit a minor one. The main subject of debate and controversy is the process of adjustment as the economy gradually progresses from the old steady state to the new. For example, there seems to be general agreement that the differences between the output effects of money-financed expenditures and the output effects of open-market purchases (and thus, by implication, the effects of debt-financed expenditures) are insignificant if we wait long enough. However, about the strength and duration of the shorter-term effects of debt-financed expenditures opinions seem to differ widely.

In the preceding chapter the macroeconomic adjustment process was described in terms of a sequence of static models, designed to idealize the characteristic features of successive stages. In the present chapter, these stages will be described as phases of a continuous dynamic process. Its main feature is the assumption that the adjustment of assets to changing market conditions, so far regarded as instantaneous, takes time. In addition, it will be recognized that wages are neither perfectly rigid nor perfectly flexible, clearing labor markets with some inertia. Some use will also be made of expectations about future inflation. The result is a rather complex dynamic model. In such a model it is difficult, and in many respects impossible, to derive qualitative propositions of the same generality as those obtained from the static model in chapter 10. The analysis will thus be largely based on numerical simulations. However, a strong effort will be made to focus on propositions whose validity transcends a specific set of parameters or even a specific economy.

This chapter was written in collaboration with Paul McNelis.

Section 11.1 introduces asset or wealth effects as the principal dynamic force propelling the system from one equilibrium to another. In section 11.2, these dynamic elements are formally incorporated into the static model of chapter 10. Section 11.3 illustrates the type of adjustment paths generated by this dynamic model in one particular case, called the "reference path." It would clearly be important to know to what extent the shape of this path for a given monetary policy depends on the various behavior assumptions. Answers to such questions are provided in section 11.4 by determining the sensitivity of the reference path to variations in parameters. Section 11.5 returns, now from a dynamic point of view, to the issues of the monetarist debate by comparing the adjustment paths for money-financed expenditures, debt-financed expenditures, and open-market operations. Section 11.6, finally, examines the paths of inflation and unemployment resulting from different time profiles of monetary expansion, tracing out loops in Phillips-curve space. Economic growth will now be disregarded, so that saving, investment, and budget deficits become transitory phenomena.

11.1. Asset effects

During the last three decades, no problem of monetary macro-economics has absorbed more theoretical energy than the effects of wealth on the demand for consumption, investment, and assets.[1] In a fundamental sense this can be said to reflect the overriding concern of macroeconomic theory with problems of economic dynamics. In their critique of Patinkin, Archibald and Lipsey (1958) made it clear—and Patinkin later acknowledged—that the real balance effect is a transitory phenomenon, resulting from a difference between desired and actual cash balances; in stock/flow equilibrium the effect disappears, since assets become endogenous.[2] Preoccupation with wealth effects must thus be understood as an implicit preoccupation with dynamics.

One would thus expect to find that, in the wake of Archibald and

---

1. Originally the problem arose in the form of the Pigou effect. The next stage was initiated by Metzler's pathbreaking analysis of the differences between different monetary policies. Then came Patinkin's challenge of the real balance effect, the distinction between inside and outside money by Gurley and Shaw, and the controversy around Pesek and Saving. In recent years, the monetarist debate seemed to turn increasingly on wealth effects, as illustrated by Blinder and Solow (1973).

2. While the insight of Archibald and Lipsey was important and correct, their analysis was flawed. Since their error, to my knowledge, has never been corrected in print, it may be appropriate to point it out. Archibald and Lipsey drew their long-run budget line for goods and cash balances in figure 2 with a slope of -1. The correct budget line, however, is the vertical line Y-Y'. In the absence of time preference and interest, it is costless for the individual to accumulate any amount of real balances in the long run. A finite demand for money thus requires that there is a satiation point at which the indifference curves turn backwards. Alternatively, a negatively-sloped budget line could be produced by time preference and/or interest.

Lipsey, macroeconomic theory had gradually learned to analyze wealth effects in an explicitly dynamic framework. In fact, this is not quite true. To the present day, wealth effects are typically introduced as static relationships, even in otherwise dynamic models, just as if Archibald and Lipsey had never made their point. This "poor man's dynamics" is clearly deficient: These static wealth effects cannot be expected to remain constant, but vary widely in the course of time. Quite possibly, they may even switch signs. This is, I think, why the static approach to the wealth effect has tended to produce so much confusion in macroeconomic theory; almost anything seems to become possible.

In the present analysis, asset effects will be expressed in dynamic terms. They are supposed to relate, not the level of the demand for a given asset to actual asset holdings, but the change in the demand for an asset to the difference between desired and actual asset holdings. Essentially, the wealth effects thus appear as adjustment speeds. Whenever desired assets are equal to actual assets, they automatically lose their force. The functions describing the change in an asset will be called accumulation functions. There will thus be accumulation functions for cash balances, bonds, and capital goods. The difference between desired and actual stocks will be called excess demand. It should be noted that this is conceptually different from the market excess demand resulting from prices below the market-clearing price; all prices in the present model except wages clear the respective markets at all times. Excess demand refers, rather, to the fact that more rapid adjustment of assets may be more expensive than slow adjustment, so that the individual finds it efficient to spread the adjustment over time. This approach to asset accumulation is familiar from investment and portfolio analysis. It was generalized to a multicommodity stock/flow model by Bushaw and Clower (1957) twenty years ago, and it has been used in many econometric studies of asset demand. Indeed, one might have expected that it had long become the standard approach to wealth effects in macroeconomic theory.

In general, the accumulation of a given asset will depend on the excess demands for all assets. If an individual finds himself with excess demand for cash balances, this may affect not only his cash accumulation, but also his accumulation of bonds and capital goods. If his house burned down, this will not only cause him to replace it and thus to accumulate capital goods, but also to draw down his cash balance and liquidate some of his securities. Defining $L = M/p$ and $D = B/ip$ we can thus express the asset accumulation due to the dynamic wealth effects as

$$dK/dt = \kappa_K(K^* - K) + \kappa_B(D^* - D) + \kappa_M(L^* - L), \qquad (11.1.1)$$

$$d(B/ip)/dt = \beta_K(K^* - K) + \beta_B(D^* - D) + \beta_M(L^* - L), \qquad (11.1.2)$$

$$d(M/p)/dt = \lambda_K(K^* - K) + \lambda_B(D^* - D) + \lambda_M(L^* - L), \qquad (11.1.3)$$

where the starred variables denote desired asset stocks, while the unstarred variables represent the components of wealth inherited from the past. It will turn out that some cross effects are of far-reaching significance for the shape of the adjustment process.

It should be noted that these cross effects are quite different from the "spillovers" of excess demand widely discussed in the 1950s. At that time the question was whether, in the course of a tâtonnement process, market excess demand for one commodity should be assumed to call forth a direct change in the price of another commodity. In the present model, since all prices are market-clearing, this question does not arise. Rather than the behavior of markets, the present spillovers describe the behavior of individuals.

While the direct adjustments may be assumed to be positive, the cross adjustment effects will typically be negative. Excess demand for cash balances will be reflected in a temporary reduction in securities or inventories rather than in an increase, excess demand for capital goods will probably result in a temporary reduction in cash balances and securities, and an effort to increase the security portfolio will probably be associated with temporary reductions in cash balances and capital goods. We thus postulate

$$\kappa_K > 0 \qquad \kappa_B \leqq 0 \qquad \kappa_M \leqq 0$$

$$\beta_K \leqq 0 \qquad \beta_B > 0 \qquad \beta_M \leqq 0$$

$$\lambda_K \leqq 0 \qquad \lambda_B \leqq 0 \qquad \lambda_M > 0.$$

In addition, it is reasonable to assume that excess demand for any asset does not result in a reduction in total wealth. Since wealth accumulation is

$$\frac{dW}{dt} = \frac{dK}{dt} + \frac{dD}{dt} + \frac{dL}{dt} = (\kappa_K + \beta_K + \lambda_K)(K^* - K)$$

$$+ (\kappa_B + \beta_B + \lambda_B)(D^* - D) + (\kappa_M + \beta_M + \lambda_M)(L^* - L), \quad (11.1.4)$$

this means that the direct effects dominate the cross effects:

$$k = \kappa_K + \beta_K + \lambda_K \geqq 0,$$

$$b = \kappa_B + \beta_B + \lambda_B \geqq 0,$$

$$m = \kappa_M + \beta_M + \lambda_M \geqq 0.$$

Further constraints on the adjustment speeds can be derived from stability requirements.

In the absence of capital gains, dW/dt is total saving. For $dp/dt = di/dt = 0$, (11.1.4) can thus be interpreted as the savings function implied in the asset accumulation functions. In the absence of growth, all saving is, of course, temporary in nature. The implied consumption function can be derived from the budget constraint

$$C = X - S = X - k(K^* - K) - b(D^* - D) - m(L^* - L). \quad (11.1.5)$$

Excess demand for any one asset thus has a negative effect on consumption. In the absence of cross effects, an increase in cash balances by $1, due to excess demand for money, would be exactly matched by a reduction in consumption; loosely speaking, the whole accumulation of cash would come out of consumption demand. This is clearly an extreme case. At the other extreme, the accumulation of cash would leave consumption unchanged, coming entirely out of other assets. Reality is probably somewhere in between. In the steady state the asset effects in the consumption function will disappear and consumption will equal disposable income.

11.2. The dynamic model

The dynamic model used in this chapter is derived from the static model of chapter 10 by adding the asset effects discussed in the preceding section and a few other dynamic relationships.

To incorporate the asset effects, (10.2.4)–(10.2.6) are reinterpreted as determining *desired* asset stocks (in real terms) K^*, D^*, and L^*. In view of applications to long-run monetary expansion, expected inflation, π, is added as an argument, though this will not be needed for small changes in the money supply. For the purpose of numerical simulation it is assumed that these functions are linear in the relevant range (which is relatively small). We thus obtain

$$K^* = K_X X + K_r r + K_i i + K_\pi \pi + k_0, \quad (11.2.1)$$

$$D^* = D_X X + D_r r + D_i i + D_\pi \pi + d_0, \quad (11.2.2)$$

$$L^* = L_X X + L_r r + L_i i + L_\pi \pi + l_0. \quad (11.2.3)$$

The complete macroeconomic accumulation functions are written as

$$dK/dt = \kappa_K(K^* - K) + \kappa_B(D^* - D) + \kappa_M(L^* - L), \quad (11.2.4)$$

$$d(B/ip)/dt = \beta_K(K^* - K) + \beta_B(D^* - D) + \beta_M(L^* - L)$$
$$+ (1/ip)dB/dt, \quad (11.2.5)$$

$$d(M/p)/dt = \lambda_K(K^* - K) + \lambda_B(D^* - D) + \lambda_M(L^* - L)$$
$$+ (1/p)dM/dt. \quad (11.2.6)$$

They thus consist of the sum of the asset effects described by (11.1.1)–(11.1.3) and the actual change in nominal assets supplied by the government. The term $(1/p)dM/dt$ in the accumulation function for cash balances expresses the idea that an increase in the nominal money supply is at first reflected in an instantaneous increase in real balances. It is only when the real balances are seen to be higher than desired that prices begin to react.[3] At any moment, the rate of change in real balances is the combined result of the adjustment of actual balances to desired balances and the new money supply. The term $(1/ip)dB/dt$ in (11.2.5) expresses the analogous idea for bonds.

Equation (11.2.6) can be solved for the rate of price change in terms of the excess demands for assets:

$$\frac{dp}{dt}\frac{1}{p} = -\frac{\lambda_K}{L}(K^* - K) - \frac{\lambda_B}{L}(D^* - D) - \frac{\lambda_M}{L}(L^* - L). \qquad (11.2.7)$$

An exogenous increase in real cash balances, resulting from an increase in the money supply, thus tends to initiate a rise in commodity prices. An exogenous increase in real bonds, however, resulting from an increase in the public debt tends to initiate a decline in prices, provided λ_B is different from zero. This is plausible, since an excess supply of bonds is likely to result in an increased demand for real cash balances, which, at given M, can only be provided by falling prices. It should be clear that this describes only the immediate effects and says nothing about the ultimate result of the adjustment process as a whole.

Equations (11.2.5) and (11.2.7) can be solved for the rate of change of the bond yield,

$$\frac{di}{dt}\frac{1}{i} = \left(\frac{\lambda_K}{L} - \frac{\beta_K}{D}\right)(K^* - K) + \left(\frac{\lambda_B}{L} - \frac{\beta_B}{D}\right)(D^* - D)$$

$$+ \left(\frac{\lambda_M}{L} - \frac{\beta_M}{D}\right)(L^* - L). \qquad (11.2.8)$$

An increase in L, resulting from an exogenous expansion in the money supply, thus has a double effect on the bond yield. On one hand, the excess supply of money "spills over" into the bond market as expressed by β_M, which causes bond prices to rise and yields to decline. In addition, the associated rise in commodity prices reduces the supply of real bonds, which produces an additional increase in the demand for nominal bonds and thus a further decline in their yield. Again, this describes only the immediate effect as long as K^*, D^*, K, and D have not had time to change.

It should be noted that this model does not require independent

---

3. In the dynamic consumption function (11.1.5), the subtraction of $(1/p)dM/dt$ means that there is an instantaneous fall in private consumption, but this is precisely matched by the additional government consumption financed by the new money. As a consequence, there is no instantaneous increase in total demand.

assumptions about the "sluggishness" of commodity prices and asset yields; the speed of their adjustment to changing market conditions is simply an implication of the speed with which people are willing and able to adjust their asset stocks. It should also be noted that the model makes it unnecessary to debate the question in what "market" each price or yield is determined, the answer being implied in the accumulation functions. The fruitful questions are about the adjustments of people, not of prices.

Another dynamic relationship concerns the labor market. In the static model it was assumed that the labor market always clears. We now wish to allow for the fact that wages seem to be quite inert, adjusting to changes in market conditions with a lag. However, since this is not a study on labor markets, we do not wish to derive the behavior of wages explicitly from the behavior of individuals. We thus assume, somewhat conventionally, that the excess of the percentage change in money wages over the expected rate of inflation, π, is proportionate to the excess of actual employment over equilibrium ("normal," "natural") employment, E^*:

$$\frac{dw}{dt}\frac{1}{w} = \omega(E - E^*) + \pi. \qquad \omega > 0 \qquad (11.2.9)$$

Graphically, this function is represented by a family of linear Phillips curves that, for a given state of expectations, express a trade-off between wage increases and employment, while each change in expectations produces a shift to a new curve (fig. 11.2.1). Inflation. in turn, is assumed to be subject to adaptive expectations:

$$\frac{d\pi}{dt} = \rho\left(\frac{dp}{dt}\frac{1}{p} - \pi\right). \qquad (11.2.10)$$

Once the changes in prices and wages are known, we can determine the change in employment by using the fact that firms hire workers up to the

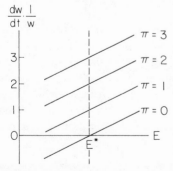

Figure **11.2.1**
The Wage Adjustment

point where their marginal product is equal to the real wage. Using a Cobb-Douglas production function, $Q = AK^\alpha E^{1-\alpha}$, we have $w/p = (1 - \alpha)AK^\alpha E^{-\alpha}$, from which we derive

$$\frac{dE}{dt}\frac{1}{E} = \frac{dK}{dt}\frac{1}{K} + \frac{1}{\alpha}\left(\frac{dp}{dt}\frac{1}{p} - \frac{dw}{dt}\frac{1}{w}\right). \qquad (11.2.11)$$

In addition to these dynamic relationships, the numerical simulation of the adjustment path requires an adaptation of the tax function. This will now be assumed to consist of three components. The first component is proportionate to national income Q with marginal tax rate t. The second component sees to it that income from the interest on the public debt is taxed away.[4] The third component is fixed at an amount that corresponds to the difference between government expenditure and proportional income taxes in the initial period. Thanks to this last component, changes in the tax rate from one simulation to another have no influence on the initial situation of the economy and thus do not impair the comparability of the results. The resulting tax function can be written

$$T = tQ + B/p + (G_0 - tQ_0). \qquad (11.2.12)$$

For the initial period this becomes

$$T_0 = B_0/p_0 + G_0,$$

and initial disposable personal income X_0 is thus independent of the tax rate,

$$X_0 = \left(Q_0 + \frac{B_0}{p_0}\right) - \left(\frac{B_0}{p_0} + G_0\right) = Q_0 - G_0.$$

With these extensions of the model, the paths of all variables are determined once the parameters of the functions, the initial conditions, and the paths of the exogenous variables M and B are specified.[5] In specifying the paths of the exogenous variables, we shall concentrate on the same policies that were analyzed in chapter 10. In the case of monetary expansion, the newly created money is used to finance additional expenditures, leaving debt constant. In the case of debt expansion, the government finances additional expenditures by selling bonds, leaving the money supply unchanged. In the case of open-market purchases, the government expands the money supply by buying bonds, while expenditures again adjust endogenously. This means that we shall not consider the case, discussed by Blinder and Solow (1973), in which government expenditures are held

4. See section 10.2.
5. For the numerical simulation of this differential-equation model we used the Runge-Kutta algorithm, which Kelly (1967) and Carnahan, Luther, and Wilkes (1969) consider one of the most stable and accurate numerical integration methods.

constant, while either the public debt adjusts endogenously to a given increase in the money supply, or the money supply adjusts endogenously to a given increase in the public debt.

11.3. The reference path

The main purpose is to show how the adjustment path of an economy is affected by different types of monetary policy and differences in parameters. This is a problem of comparative dynamics. As a basis for this investigation we need a reference or benchmark path that can serve as a standard of comparison. In addition, the reference path will give a representative example of the type of time profiles we may expect.

To construct such a reference path we use the initial conditions and parameters specified in the last section of chapter 10 and listed in tables 10.7.2 and 10.7.3. In addition, we have to specify the adjustment speeds in the dynamic relationships. Empirical knowledge about them is quite vague, and it will be more important to observe the consequences of high and low adjustment speeds than to search for the "correct" value. For the reference path we shall use the following values:

$$\kappa_K = 0.1 \qquad \kappa_B = 0 \qquad \kappa_M = 0 \qquad \omega = 0.1$$

$$\beta_K = 0 \qquad \beta_B = 0.2 \qquad \beta_M = 0 \qquad \rho = 0.1$$

$$\lambda_K = 0 \qquad \lambda_B = 0 \qquad \lambda_M = 0.2$$

Nonzero cross adjustment speeds will be introduced later. The numbers, which are meant to be quarterly adjustments, were chosen in such a way that they might well come from econometric estimates. It is plausible to assume that real capital adjusts to its own excess demand more slowly than financial assets.[6] Both for bonds and for money, some estimates have been higher than 0.2.[7] Other estimates for money, however, are much lower, and they cannot be dismissed as implausible. In particular, the perfect liquidity of cash balances is no compelling reason to expect a high adjustment speed, since the latter refers to a shift from money into other assets or consumption and thus the characteristics of those other assets are also relevant. In fact, it may well be that cash balances, being a typical "buffer stock" asset, are characterized by quite low adjustment speeds. Nevertheless, we did not want to assign bonds higher adjustment speeds than money in the reference set. The value for ω means that in the absence of expected inflation an

6. Jorgensen's estimates of the average lag of the capital stock (1971, table 11) correspond to quarterly adjustment coefficients between 0.09 and 0.17.

7. Hamburger's estimates (1968, p. 116) imply an adjustment speed for bonds of about 0.25–0.30 per quarter. For cash balances, Goldfeld (1973) obtained a quarterly speed of 0.283 for a partial adjustment model of this sort.

employment rate 1 percent above "normal" employment would produce an increase in wages by 0.1 percent per quarter or about 0.4 percent a year.[8] The assumption for ρ, finally, says that a 1 percent excess of actual (quarterly) inflation over expected inflation results in a rise of expected inflation by 0.1 percent per quarter.[9]

We also have to specify the initial change in monetary policy. It is assumed that the system, starting in full equilibrium, is disturbed in period 2 by an increase in the monetary base by 5 percent of its initial value, used to finance additional expenditures, while debt is constant. This is the case of money-financed expenditures. Thereafter the monetary base stays unchanged at the higher level. Since the change in the money supply is assumed to be small and temporary, we regard it as unnecessary to include expected inflation as an argument in the asset demand functions.

Government expenditures are endogenously determined as the sum of tax receipts and additions to the money supply, if any. This means that they do not remain constant at the higher level, but further vary as tax receipts change under the influence of changing incomes. It should be remembered that these simulations are for the case of zero growth, so that government deficits cannot be financed by new money or bonds in full equilibrium. In fact, in the reference simulation there is a deficit only in period 2 when the new money is issued, while in all other periods government expenditure for goods and services is equal to tax revenues.

The resulting adjustment paths are graphed in figure 11.3.1. There is an immediate decline in the bond yield as wealth holders shift their excess money balances into bonds. This is the phase that corresponds roughly to the instantaneous version of the static model.[10] However, after a few months the interest rate begins to rise again and approaches the new equilibrium level in mild, declining cycles, which agrees well with empirical work on

8. The wage equation for the United States estimated by Eckstein and Brinner (1972, p. 4) implies that at an unemployment level of 6 percent an increase in unemployment by 1 percent reduces the annual rate of wage increase by 0.31. For other estimates in the same range see Askin and Kraft (1974).

9. Using a series of expected inflation derived from a comparison of purchasing-power bonds and conventional bonds in Israel, Eileen Mauskopf (1976) estimated the following coefficients in an adaptive expectations model for 1968–74:

$$\pi_t = 0.917\,\pi_{t-1} + 0.059\,\dot{p}_{t-1} \qquad R^2 = 0.95$$

$$(0.024) \qquad (0.005) \qquad \text{D.W.} = 1.8$$

A sum of unity, as implied in (11.2.10) is within the standard error of the coefficients. A value for ρ of 0.059 per month corresponds to a little less than 0.2 per quarter. For a subperiod with relatively slow inflation, the corresponding figure was about 0.1 per quarter.

10. Such correspondences cannot be exact, since in each of the static versions of the model certain adjustment processes are artificially suppressed, while in the dynamic model they are proceeding simultaneously.

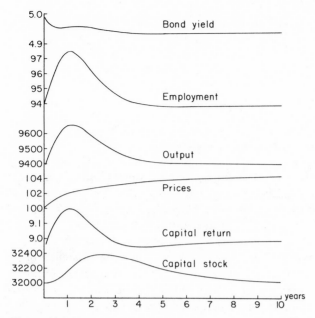

Figure **11.3.1**
Monetary Expansion: The Reference Path

interest rates.[11] The final equilibrium of the bond yield is clearly below the initial level, since an increase in the bond price is necessary to reconcile the fixed supply of bonds to the increased demand.

In the short run, the expansion in the money supply produces an increase in employment and output, which again is in agreement with the corresponding version of the static analysis. The employment rate rises for about a year, but after three to four years the positive effects are largely dissipated, and the employment rate thereafter approaches its initial level in hardly noticeable oscillations. Output follows a similar path, though somewhat more slowly. It is interesting to consider the real income multipliers of money-financed expenditures implied in the reference path. They are graphed in figure 11.3.2. No claim is made that the particular curve resulting from the reference set of parameters is a faithful picture of reality; in fact, little is known about the true adjustment path, and the quantitative differences between the paths implied in different econometric models are considerable. The graph shows, however, that our reference

11. The lag distributions of monetary effects on the rate of interest generated by the present model are similar to those found by Cagan and Gandolfi (1969, chart I), though they oscillate somewhat more rapidly. The size of the initial decline seems to depend largely on the adjustment speed of cash balances.

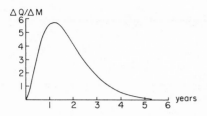

Figure **11.3.2**
Output Multiplier of Money-Financed Expenditures

path could well be one of a family of adjustment paths generated by macroeconometric models for the United States.[12]

Prices behave quite differently. They rise over a long period, taking more than a year to rise by half of their ultimate increase and continuing to rise, slowly but steadily, for many years thereafter. Ultimately, prices rise almost proportionately to the money supply, but the existence of bonds prevents the quantity theory from being fully valid. This corresponds to the long-term version of the static model. While the peak effect, measured in percent, is of the same order of magnitude for prices as for employment, prices continue to rise when the initial output gains have been lost.[13] "Stagflation" appears as a puzzle only to those who never learned to look beyond the intermediate run. In fact, it is one of the normal phases of the classical adjustment path. Myopic policy makers are thus forever tempted to use monetary policy for the short-term stimulation of output, while leaving it to their successors to deal with the long-run legacy of rising prices and falling employment. Indeed, the difference in the adjustment pattern for employment and prices may be regarded as the single most important fact about macroeconomics. It provides the main test for the competence and wisdom of economic advisors and of the leadership of governments in economic matters.

The rate of return on capital is in the short run more closely related to output than to the bond yield, increasing and decreasing with the rise and fall of capacity utilization. In the long run, the lower bond yield is associated with a slightly lower yield on capital goods, but the difference is very small.

The capital stock, finally, first increases, stimulated by higher income, higher rates of return, and lower bond yields. After about a year, however, investments begin to decline. Later they turn even negative, as the reactions of the bond yield, employment, and the rate of return to their initial

12. A family of such paths is graphed in Christ (1975, fig. 5). While they relate to an increase in the money supply achieved through a reduction in debt at constant expenditures, the simulations for fiscal policies show that the difference is relatively minor.
13. This is in agreement with simulations based on econometric models for the United States. See Fromm and Klein (1976, p. 17).

overshooting begin to have their effect. With the assumed slowness of capital adjustment, it will take an extremely long time until the capital stock is permanently close to its new, slightly higher, equilibrium level. This is where the dynamic adjustment path merges into the full-equilibrium phase of the static analysis.

The details of the adjustment path are evidently dependent on the particular choice of monetary policies, initial conditions, and parameters. The general outlines, however, are quite resistant to changes in parameters within a reasonable range. They are also compatible with the paths of adjustment to monetary policy generated by econometric models. It seems they can be taken as representative for the dynamic adjustment to money-financed expenditures. The specific influence of different parameters and different monetary policies will be the subject of the following sections.

11.4. The influence of specific parameters

The specific features of the reference path clearly depend on the selection of parameters representing the behavior of the economy. What we would like to know is the influence of individual parameters on the adjustment path. Is it true, for example, that the effect of monetary policy on output is highly dependent on the interest-elasticity of the demand for money, as has been argued so often? Is it true that wage flexibility reduces the effect of monetary policy on output? We can hope to answer such questions by computing the adjustment path for different values of a given parameter.[14] The following discussion will be restricted to the paths of prices and output.

The significance of the interest-elasticity of the demand for money is illustrated in figure 11.4.1 by comparing the reference path (with $\epsilon_{Li} = -0.50$) with two other paths obtained by varying this elasticity. This leads to the following observations:

1. The lower the interest-elasticity of the demand for money, the stronger is the expansionary effect of money-financed expenditure, both on prices and output, in the short run. This is not only economically plausible, as the low interest-elasticity of money increases the pressure for an expansion of money income, but also consistent with the results from Keynesian IS/LM diagrams.

2. The lower the interest-elasticity of the demand for money, the higher is the price increase in the long run, with the difference in output becoming negligible. In fact, with an elasticity as low (absolutely) as 0.1, prices increase almost in proportion to the quantity of money. A low interest-elasticity of the demand for money thus makes the economy

14. In principle, it would be desirable also to vary parameters 2,3, . . . at a time, as the influence of one parameter may depend on the particular value of the others. However, this produces rapidly an almost unmanageable mass of data.

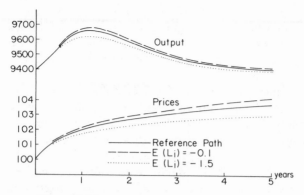

Figure **11.4.1**
Monetary Expansion: Different Interest Elasticities of Money

conform more closely to the quantity theory even in the presence of bonds.

A high elasticity of the demand for money with respect to the rate of return on capital seems to produce as its main effect a more rapid expansion in the early phases followed by a reaction in later years. In output this results in more pronounced cycles, while for prices a continuous increase is transformed into mild oscillations (see figure 11.4.2).

The elasticities of the demand for bonds with respect to the yields of bonds and capital goods both have negligible effects on output and prices, but a high value of the own-elasticity, not unexpectedly, helps to reduce the fluctuations in the bond yield. An analogous statement can be made for the interest elasticities of the demand for capital goods.

The influence of the marginal tax rate is more interesting. The higher the rate, the more rapid is the rise in prices and the stronger is the short-run expansion of employment following an expansion in the money supply.

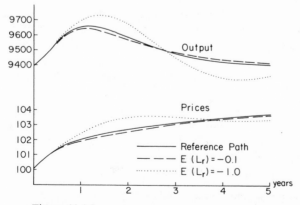

Figure **11.4.2**
Monetary Expansion: Different Capital Return Elasticities of Money

This is easy to understand, since the government is assumed to spend all additional taxes on goods and services. With higher marginal tax rates, a given dose of money-financed expenditures will thus give rise to a larger increase in total government expenditures, while private demand, in view of the propensity to save, will be reduced by a smaller amount. It is also true, however, that with higher tax rates the initial stimulus to output will be more short-lived, and in the long run tax rates make no appreciable difference for prices and employment.

The various adjustment speeds, while having no influence on the final equilibrium, may have strong effects on the intermediate phases. The effects of the adjustment speed of cash balances, λ_M, are summarized in figure 11.4.3. We are not surprised to find that a higher speed accelerates the initial price and employment effects of money-financed expenditures. For the course of prices during the first few months λ_M is indeed of decisive importance. It seems that the apparent rigidity of prices and the disappointing output effects of monetary policy in the early phases of adjustment, which since Keynes have played such an important role in macroeconomic controversies, depend to a large extent on the speed with which firms and households adjust their cash balances to changing conditions.[15]

The main effect of a higher adjustment speed of capital goods, κ_K, is a more pronounced overshooting in the stock of capital goods in the early periods, followed by a more pronounced downward correction. The early

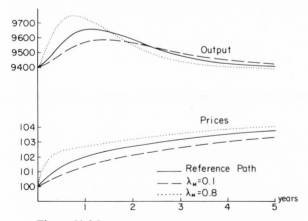

Figure **11.4.3**
Monetary Expansion: Different Adjustment Speeds of Money

15. It was pointed out in section 11.3 that the high liquidity of cash balances does not preclude a low adjustment speed, since the latter also depends on the characteristics of the things (like bonds, capital goods, consumer goods) that are substituted for cash balances in this adjustment. The fact that a dollar bill can always be exchanged against a dollar bill on short notice without a loss says nothing about the ease with which excess dollars can be transformed into other assets or consumption.

and excessive expansion of the capital stock helps to raise output and, by so doing, to dampen the initial price increase. However, the overall effect on output and prices is quite small. The adjustment speed of bonds, β_B, has no appreciable effect on anything, except that a high value helps interest rates to avoid oscillations in their downward adjustment. Instantaneous downward overshooting of the bond yield appears to be largely due to a slow adjustment speed of bonds.

The speed of wage adjustment, as figure 11.4.4 indicates, is again of considerable importance. If it is increased, prices approach their ultimate equilibrium more rapidly, the initial stimulus to employment and output is dissipated earlier, the rate of return on capital falls below the initial value sooner and there is less initial capital accumulation. If, on the other hand, the speed of wage adjustment is progressively reduced, we ultimately approach the case of rigid money wages. Prices are still not constant, to be sure. In particular, there is still some price increase in the early phase provided the adjustment speed of cash balances is high enough, followed by a long period of virtually stable, and sometimes actually falling, prices. There is a strong and long-lasting expansion of employment, capital returns improve, and there is extended capital accumulation. This is the Keynesian dream.

A high adjustment speed of price expectations, finally, helps to speed up the price reaction to monetary expansion, while the output effect is reduced. In the present model this influence is very weak, even for large variations in the adjustment speed. However, since the model is not built to analyze continuing inflation and expectations have been omitted in the asset demand functions, this observation should not be given too much weight.

In summary it may be said that the adjustment path of the economy

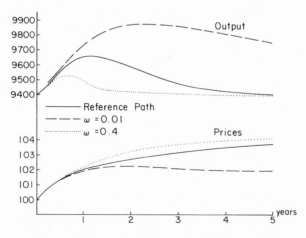

Figure **11.4.4**
Monetary Expansion: Different Wage Adjustment Speeds

following a dose of money-financed expenditures depends most strongly on the interest-elasticity of the demand for money, on the marginal tax rate, and on the adjustment speeds of money balances and wages.

11.5. A comparison of monetary policies: Does fiscal policy matter?

One of the central questions in the debate about monetarism is whether the money supply is all that matters or whether it also matters how it is brought about. The reference path describes the adjustment of the economy to money-financed expenditures. By comparing it with the alternative path resulting from a different monetary policy, but with the same initial conditions and parameters, we can obtain an answer to the above question. This answer will be the dynamic counterpart to the static comparisons in the preceding chapter.

In figure 11.5.1 the reference path is compared to the corresponding path for an open-market operation. In both cases there is a once-over increase in the money supply by 5 percent of its initial level, but in one case the new money is used to pay for government expenditures, while in the other case it is used to reduce the government debt. Government expenditures are not constant in either case, since in addition to exogenous changes in net financial assets they reflect the endogenous changes in tax revenues. It should be noted that this specification of money-financed expenditures and open-market purchases is only one of several possibilities. Alternatively it could be assumed, for example, that endogenous increases in tax revenues are used to reduce either the money supply or the public debt. It is clear that such variations may have a considerable effect on the adjustment path for each monetary policy. It may be suspected, however, that their effect on

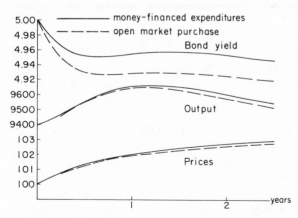

Figure **11.5.1**
A Comparison of Alternative Monetary Policies

the *difference* between two monetary policies is considerably smaller, and it is this difference that matters in the present context.

Qualitatively, the differences between the two paths conform to expectations and to the static results. Open-market purchases have a considerably stronger impact effect on the bond yield, and the long-run reduction in the latter is also stronger, but the long-run difference between the two curves is soon established and does not noticeably change thereafter. Money-financed expenditures, on the other hand, have a stronger (positive) short-run effect on output (and employment). This difference disappears in the course of time, however, and in later years open-market operations actually have an output advantage, though of almost imperceptible size and again only temporary.

While differences in employment, by virtue of the definition of normal employment, cannot be permanent in a stable system, money-financed expenditures have a permanently stronger effect on the price level. By using new money to buy goods and services instead of bonds, the government can provide a stronger temporary stimulus to output, but at the expense of a larger permanent increase in the price level. None of the simulation experiments produced the paradoxical case where open-market purchases actually lower the long-run price level (see sec. 10.6). Finally, the stimulating effect on the accumulation of real capital is weaker for open-market purchases in the short run, which can be explained by the weaker output effects, but it is stronger in the long run, as the lower bond yield induces wealth owners to shift into capital goods.

However, except for the bond yield, these differences are very small. While it certainly matters, in principle, how new money is created, at least for the reference set of parameters it does not matter a great deal. Since the effect of pure fiscal policy is simply the difference between those of money-financed expenditures and open-market purchases, this proposition implies that pure fiscal policy, while it matters in principle, does not matter very much relative to an increase in the money supply, however achieved. We first illustrate this implication for the reference set and shall then consider its validity for alternative sets of parameters.

The path of adjustment to a temporary dose of bond-financed expenditures is described by figure 11.5.2. In the short run, there is an expansionary effect on employment and output, which is reinforced by the demand for new capital goods generated by the rising income through the accelerator effect. The peak is reached after about six quarters. This expansion of output is associated with an increase in the bond yield, which, however, stabilizes rapidly at a higher level. The higher interest rate has, in turn, a negative influence on the demand for capital goods; public expenditures begin to "crowd out" private investment. Once output is slowing down, the accelerator works in reverse. Eventually, output begins to decline again, and after about four years employment and output are

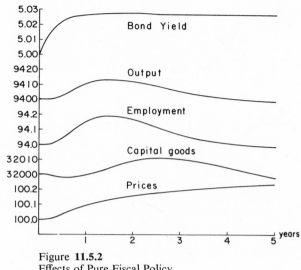

Figure **11.5.2**
Effects of Pure Fiscal Policy

close to their initial levels. Thereafter, output will be permanently lower as the higher interest rate results in a lower capital/labor ratio. Prices, however, will remain permanently higher, reflecting the increase in financial assets. In percentage terms, the permanent increase in the price level (and also in money income) is of about the same order of magnitude as the transitory employment gain at its peak. Qualitatively, this description of the adjustment to pure fiscal policy is quite similar to descriptions based on econometric models.[16]

It would be interesting to know whether this broad agreement also extends to the quantitative aspects of the process. The real output multipliers for debt-financed expenditures can be read off figure 11.5.2 if it is kept in mind that the simulation relates to an increase in expenditures by $45. The curve shows that output rises by about one-third of the additional expenditures within six quarters, but the whole effect has practically disappeared after four years. These dynamic multipliers cannot be directly compared with those derived from econometric models for the United States, since the latter relate to *sustained* increases in expenditures.[17]

Comparability can be improved by computing the adjustment path under the present model for a continuing increase in government debt. The result is plotted in figure 11.5.3. Except for the heavy curves, this graph is reproduced from Christ (1975, p. 70). It shows the dynamic multiplier

16. See Fromm and Klein (1976, pp. 16 ff.) and Modigliani and Ando (1976).
17. See Fromm and Klein (1976), Christ (1975, table 3, fig. 4), and Modigliani and Ando (1976, p. 25 ff.).

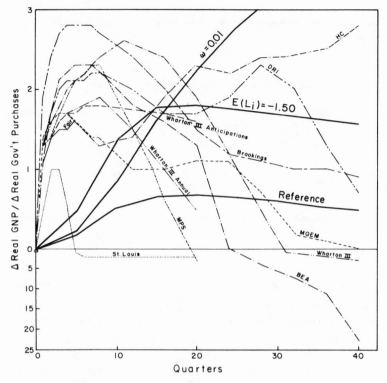

Figure **11.5.3**
Output Multipliers of Debt-Financed Expenditures

effects of a maintained increase in real government purchases upon real GNP (without accommodating monetary policy) implied in eleven econometric models of the U.S. economy, based on Fromm and Klein (1976). The heavy curves graph the corresponding multipliers for the reference set and two parameter variations on the assumption of a progressive increase in government debt used to finance expenditures. The reference set happens to result in a significantly lower peak of the multiplier curve than the econometric models for the United States. However, by just varying the interest elasticity of the demand for money and the adjustment speed of wages, it is easy to produce adjustment paths whose peaks span the whole range of the econometric model simulations. The most noticeable difference is the slower rise of output toward its peak implied in the present model. At the present time we are unable to say to what extent the almost instantaneous reaction of output to government expenditures implied in econometric models reflects an empirical observation and to what extent it reflects the specifications of these models. As a consequence, it is not clear whether the slower reaction of the present model is a virtue or a vice.[18] Overall, this comparison gives no reason to discard the reference path as manifestly unrealistic.

However, the comparison is still biased in two respects. First the reference path relates to increments that are constant in nominal terms, while the other multipliers are for increases in real expenditures. Since prices are rising, this means that the reference path is progressively biased downward. Second, what is held constant in the econometric simulations is the increase in government expenditures while the increment in government debt gradually declines as rising incomes provide higher tax revenues. In the present model, however, it is the increment in debt that is held constant over time while government expenditures gradually increase with the tax revenues. This imparts a progressive upward bias to the reference path in comparison to the econometric simulations. Since the two biases have opposite signs, the direction of their net effect is uncertain. On balance, it seems fair to say that the adjustment paths for fiscal policy derived from the present model exhibit characteristics similar to those of the adjustment paths derived from nonmonetarist econometric models.

Comparing the output effect of debt-financed expenditures, now again in the once-over sense, with those of money-financed expenditures and open-market operations, we note that it amounts to only a fraction of the latter. While the multiplier for monetary expansion rises to about 6 (see fig. 11.3.2), the multiplier of pure fiscal policy peaks at about one-third. For open-market operations the difference is not much less. One may be tempted to interpret this observation as highly "monetarist." In fact, the same conclusion is implied in simulations from econometric models, no matter how "nonmonetarist." Consider the dynamic multipliers for government expenditures and for an increase in the money supply graphed by Christ (1975) in figures 4 and 5. They cannot be directly compared, since the increase in unborrowed reserves (or, for the St. Louis model, M_1) is once over, while the additional expenditures are recurring. In order to make them comparable, we would need to know the multipliers for a once-over dose of expenditures, financed by new debt. While these are not available, it is clear that they can be only a fraction, say one-fourth or so, of those in Christ's figure 4. For every model except *BEA* and Wharton III (Anticipations) the peak of the money multipliers must be many times as high as the peak of the hypothetical fiscal multipliers, a typical ratio being perhaps 15 : 1. In this respect, too, the present model seems to reflect a rather broad consensus. The proposition that the quantity of money matters much more than the way it is created is evidently common to both monetarists and nonmonetarists.

18. A possible reason for slow adjustment may be the assumption that the capital stock is always fully utilized.

To what extent do the foregoing conclusions depend on the particular choice of reference parameters? This question can be answered by simulating the fiscal-policy path for different sets of parameters. Concentrating on output effects, it turns out that most of the parameters have hardly any influence on the result. These include, in particular, the elasticity of bonds with respect to the capital return, the elasticity of capital with respect to the bond yield, the adjustment speeds of capital goods and bonds, the adjustment speed of inflation expectations, and the marginal tax rate. What matters is the demand function for money and the wage adjustment speed.

Of these, by far the most important is the interest elasticity of the demand for money. As figure 11.5.4 shows, by raising this elasticity from -0.10 to -1.50, the peak output effect can be increased in about the same proportion. This agrees well with the employment effect of fiscal policy in the short-run static model, which was shown to be proportionate to L_i (see section 10.4). How much fiscal policy matters is largely a question of the interest-elasticity of the demand for money. The elasticity of money with respect to the rate of return on capital is much less important for the size of fiscal policy effects than for their cyclical character, which is plausible, as this elasticity links money to the accelerator effects in the capital stock.

We further observe that the peak output effect is positively related to the adjustment speed of money balances. The reverse is true, not surprisingly, for the speed of wage adjustment; the more rigid the wage rate, the more pronounced is the output effect of fiscal policy and the longer it lasts. Indeed, with relatively rigid wages fiscal policy has a significant effect for

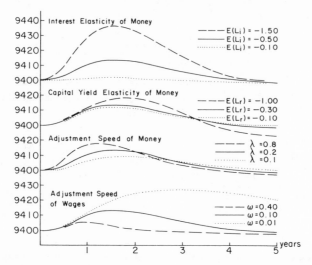

Figure **11.5.4**
Determinants of Fiscal Policy Effects on Output

years, but with flexible wages its effect is weak and ephemeral. Overall, by just varying the interest elasticity of the demand for money and the flexibility of wages, the "lump" in output resulting from fiscal policy can be varied from a fleeting ripple to a quasi-permanent tidal wave.

11.6. Progressive inflation and Phillips curves

The subject of the preceding discussion was the dynamic adjustment of the economy to a once-over dose of monetary expansion. Policy discussions, however, are often about the effects of a continuing increase in the money supply. We would like to know, for example, how unemployment, wage rates, and the rate of inflation adjust to a progressive increase in the money supply by a given percentage per quarter. This is the nature of the question considered in this section. The emphasis will be on prices, wages, and unemployment, while the associated movements of other variables are not made explicit.

In the recent macroeconomic literature the relationships between inflation and unemployment were usually formalized in Phillips curves (Phillips, 1958). Since these relationships and the associated policy problems were widely discussed long before Phillips, this terminology is historically misleading, but it will here be retained for convenience. The term "Phillips curve" is used in (at least) four different meanings. In its narrowest sense it denotes the partial relationship between the rate of change of money wages and the rate of unemployment, everything else remaining constant. In the present model this type of relationship is represented by one of the lines in figure 11.2.1, drawn for a given rate of expected inflation. For a constant speed of wage adjustment ω these are straight lines. In a somewhat wider interpretation, π is allowed to vary. We thus obtain an "expectations-augmented Phillips curve" or a "Phillips surface" as expressed in (11.2.9) and represented by the whole family of straight lines in figure 11.2.1.

Once it is known how π is related to $(E - E^*) = (U^* - U)$, the rate of wage change can again be expressed as a function of $(E - E^*)$ or $(U^* - U)$ only. The resulting curve may be called a "virtual Phillips curve." While the underlying Phillips surface is a behavior relationship, summarizing microeconomic information about labor markets, the virtual Phillips curve depends on all those characteristics of the macroeconomic system which may influence the association between employment and expected inflation. In particular, this curve may look very different for different types of economic policy. It is thus futile to describe or estimate its characteristics independently of the underlying macroeconomic process. Finally, in the widest sense of the term, a Phillips curve may be interpreted as describing the association of employment, not with the rate of wage change, but with the rate of price change. In this sense, it is even more clearly a relationship between two endogenous variables that may be expected to exhibit all sorts of patterns, depending on the macroeconomic system and the path of the exogenous variables.

The subject of the present section is the virtual Phillips curves, for both wages and prices, associated with a continuing increase in money-financed expenditures. These expenditures will be incorporated in the dynamic model in the form of a monetary expansion in an amount of 2 percent of the initial money supply per quarter. Since such a policy produces progressive inflation, expected inflation now has to be introduced as an argument in the asset demand functions. Expected inflation is like a negative yield on both cash balances and bonds. The reaction of desired asset stocks to a one-percent change in expected inflation should thus be the sum of their reactions to a one-percent change in the bond yield and a one-percent change in the rate of return on cash balances. For the purpose of this section it is assumed that the reaction of desired asset stocks to the yield on cash balances, R (not otherwise appearing in this model), would be as follows:

$$K_R = -40,000$$
$$D_R = -10,500$$
$$L_R = -63,000$$

Adding these reactions to the assumptions about the effects of the bond yield listed in table 10.7.3, we obtain the following reactions of desired asset stocks to expected inflation:

$$K_\pi = 104,000$$
$$D_\pi = -94,500$$
$$L_\pi = -54,000$$

These parameters are now incorporated into the reference set, which otherwise remains unchanged.[19] In particular, the cross adjustment speeds of one asset with respect to the excess demand for another asset are still set at zero at this stage.

The virtual Phillips curves for wages and prices resulting under these conditions are graphed in figure 11.6.1. At the present stage we concentrate on the rising branch of each arrow. In terms of inflation the process has three distinct phases of very unequal length. At first monetary expansion is reflected in a practically instantaneous rise in the rate of inflation. Despite the lagged adjustment in real cash balances, the excess supply of money results in some bidding-up of commodity prices. However, this effect is

19. It turned out to be convenient, however, to simulate only one value per quarter instead of two as in the preceding simulations.

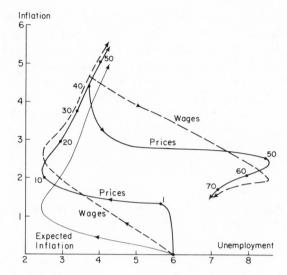

Figure **11.6.1**
Continued Monetary Expansion: Phillips Curves

small relative to the total inflation eventually generated by this policy, amounting to only a small fraction of the rate of monetary expansion. For moderate rates of monetary expansion it would hardly be noticed.

The second phase is a period of rapid decline in unemployment, accompanied by little further inflation. This is the Keynesian short run. During this period, unemployment is reduced by almost 3 percent to about half its normal level, while inflation increases by less than 1 percent. Toward the end of this period unemployment appears to become increasingly resistant to further reduction, while the rate of inflation accelerates. If this change of economic climate took place in a real economy, commentators would probably argue that a "full employment ceiling" has been reached, so that the "classical" quantity theory begins to assert itself. While to a Keynesian macroeconomist this interpretation may sound plausible, it would nevertheless be false, since (1) the present model has no "ceilings" around 3 percent unemployment, (2) the dynamic adjustment functions are perfectly linear, and (3) there is no dichotomy between two "regimes," one for underemployment and the other for full employment. The end of the Keynesian phase is simply due to the interplay of particular adjustment speeds, and it will turn out that with different adjustment speeds the imaginary ceiling will appear at very different employment levels.

The Keynesian phase is followed by a third phase, characterized by a parallel increase in both unemployment and inflation. For several years, an acceleration of inflation by one percent is accompanied by an increase in unemployment by about one-half of one percent. During this period, commentators would probably express puzzlement about the "paradoxes" of "stagflation;" they would claim to have discovered a "new inflation," unknown to "standard economic doctrine," and would send economists "back to the drawing boards." In fact, the present model produces the prolonged period of rising unemployment combined with accelerating inflation from perfectly traditional elements. "Stagflation" is the perfectly normal, if delayed, consequence of an increase in the rate of monetary expansion. This phase comes to an end when unemployment has again reached its normal level U^*, while prices continue to increase roughly in proportion to the money supply.[20] In the very long run, the virtual Phillips curve for prices is vertical.

For wages, the virtual Phillips curve shows a similar pattern, except that there is no instantaneous "jump." Even though the partial Phillips curve is linear by assumption, the virtual Phillips curve for wages rises at an increasing rate and is thus convex downward. This is simply due to the fact that the expected rate of inflation is slowly rising, so that the virtual Phillips curve climbs across the Phillips surface to progressively higher values of π. After about three years the wage curve, too, turns around and begins to slope upward in a positive direction, increasing unemployment being associated with rising wages. During this phase, casual observers would probably blame trade unions for "cost-push" inflation, even though the whole process, by virtue of the underlying assumptions, is entirely due to monetary expansion.

While the reference path has no claim to be regarded as an empirical model of the U.S. economy, it is nevertheless instructive to compare it, at least in its broad qualitative outlines, with the historical patterns of inflation and unemployment during an episode of accelerated monetary expansion. The 1960s, in fact, were such an episode. During that period the United States was still under a gold/exchange standard. As a consequence, both the money supply and the monetary base were endogenous variables, and the exogenous monetary variable was the domestic security portfolio of the Federal Reserve System. In the fall of 1961, this policy variable had been roughly constant for about 3 years. Federal Reserve Credit was then expanded rapidly, beginning in the second half of 1961, and the annual rate of expansion fluctuated without a clear-cut trend between 6 and 14 percent until 1969, when it was abruptly (though not permanently) reduced (Niehans, 1976). The radical change in Federal Reserve policy in the fall of 1961 was probably the most significant monetary event of the decade; it made world monetary history. It is also a reasonably good approximation to the assumption of a monetary expansion of 2 percent per quarter that underlies the reference path.

20. The qualifier "roughly" is necessary because with a fixed supply of bonds the quantity theory of money does not strictly apply.

The historical paths of unemployment and inflation from 1961 to 1971 are well known: They are indeed characterized by a prolonged improvement in employment with minor, and sometimes negative, inflation. After three to four years, however, inflation rates began to rise rapidly, while the employment gains vanished. At the end of 1969, the acceleration of inflation was (temporarily) arrested, but unemployment shot up rapidly. It is not claimed, of course, that the dynamic model used in this section, together with the reference parameters, are a valid representation of the U.S. economy in the 1960s. The point is rather that the main outlines of the actual development might well have resulted from a dynamic process similar to that crudely formalized in this model.

The next question is to what extent the characteristics of the reference path depend on the chosen parameters. In particular, we would like to know how sensitive they are to variations in the dynamic adjustment speeds. Some of the answers are relatively straightforward. First, a more rapid adjustment in wages, as expressed by a higher ω, reduces the temporary gain in employment (see fig. 11.6.2). With ω approaching 1, the virtual Phillips curves become almost vertical from the start. On the other hand, increased wage rigidity reinforces and extends the early employment gains from monetary expansion. The numerical simulation thus confirms what macroeconomics has taught, namely that the Keynesian short-run effects of monetary policy are due to sticky money wages. Second, the adjustment speeds of bonds and capital goods have no significant effect on the virtual Phillips curves, though a rapid adjustment of capital goods or bonds to the excess demand for capital goods may produce moderate ripples in employment. Even wide variations in these coefficients leave the path of output and prices essentially unchanged.

The influence of other parameters is more complex. In particular, even small variations in the adjustment speeds of cash balances can have a considerable effect on the virtual Phillips curves. Rapid adjustment of cash balances to the excess demand for money, as measured by λ_M, increases the instantaneous price adjustment and may produce an initial overshooting of

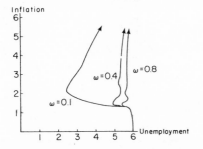

Figure **11.6.2**
Phillips Curves for Different Wage Adjustment Speeds

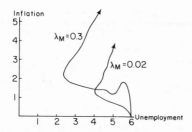

Figure **11.6.3**
Phillips Curves for Different Own-Adjustment Speeds of Money

inflation rates (see fig. 11.6.3). Slow own-adjustment of cash balances, on the other hand, reduces the instantaneous price effect. At the same time, however, it reduces the short-term employment gains. There is thus a direct relationship between the short-run employment gains from accelerated monetary expansion and the rapidity with which actual cash balances are adjusted to desired balances.

To the extent the accumulation of cash balances reacts (negatively) to the excess demand for bonds, this tends to produce cyclical oscillations in the virtual Phillips curve; the larger (absolutely) the cross adjustment speed, the more marked these oscillations become (fig. 11.6.4). We further note that the cross adjustment speed of cash balances with respect to the excess demand for capital goods can also produce complex oscillatory patterns in inflation and unemployment. Thus a simple permanent change in monetary expansion can result in a seemingly irregular adjustment path.

In reality, of course, a change in monetary policy will hardly ever be of such a simple nature. Changes in the rate of monetary expansion will often be made long before the economy has fully adjusted to the preceding policy. This means that new adjustments are superimposed on ongoing adjustments. If, under such conditions, an observer simply compared the rate of monetary expansion to the paths of output and prices, he would probably find that the latter react to the former with a lag that is not only rather long, but also variable (Friedman, 1948). Simple correlations

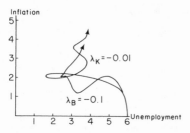

Figure **11.6.4**
Phillips Curves for Different Cross-Adjustment Speeds of Money

between the money supply and the value of output may turn out to be quite low. It would be premature to conclude from this observation that the behavior of the economy is constantly changing. In fact, the point is rather that in a dynamic system a succession of monetary impulses can create the impression of variable apparent lags even though the underlying adjustment speeds, defining the real lags in the economy, are unchanged.

So far the discussion concentrated on the rising branch of the virtual Phillips curves resulting from accelerated monetary expansion maintained forever. In fact, such expansion is unlikely to be maintained forever. It is therefore interesting to consider, finally, the reverse adjustment if the rate of monetary expansion is suddenly reduced again. It may be conjectured that the resulting Phillips curve is roughly the mirror image of the rising branch.[21] Simulation with the reference path confirms this conjecture. If the rate of monetary expansion is reduced to zero beginning with period 40, the economy follows the falling path in figure 11.6.1. This path is characterized by some early success in combating inflation. The "monetary medicine" is working. Soon, however, inflation seems to become more and more resistant to further reduction, while unemployment inexorably increases. This is the "Keynesian contraction." It is only after about three years of mounting unemployment that the path turns downward. There is now a "classical contraction," when inflation rates fall with little change in unemployment. The counterpart of stagflation, finally, is a "golden age" when, for a while, the economy seems to get the best of both worlds, receding inflation being accompanied by recovery of output, before it again reaches the neighborhood of normal unemployment and zero inflation, though at a much higher price level.

Taken together, the rising and the declining branch of the virtual Phillips curve form what may be called a "Phillips loop." Such loops, typically clockwise, would be generated by successive phases of expansionary and stationary monetary policy. It may thus be said that stop-go policy produces Phillips loops. The point is that the phases of these loops, though seemingly dominated by very different economic behavior, are produced by the same economic model without any change in assumptions except for the intermittent monetary expansion.

This concludes the analysis of the macrodynamic adjustment process to monetary policy. This analysis showed that, in pure logic, the same monetary policy can result in quite different paths of the economy depending on its specific characteristics. In particular, variations in the speed with which assets, wages, and expectations adjust to changing conditions may sometimes result in marked changes in the path of output, interest rates, or prices. As a consequence, general propositions are hard to establish, and

---

21. The word "roughly" allows for the fact that the reversal occurs before the economy has fully adjusted to monetary expansion.

most of the analysis had to be based on numerical simulation. By varying the parameters of the model between rather wide limits, it was nevertheless possible to derive conclusions that are likely to be valid for a wide range of circumstances. These conclusions may be summarized briefly as follows:

1. A once-over increase in the money supply results in an immediate fall in the bond yield, perhaps with overshooting, a short-term stimulation of output and employment followed by a reaction, a slow but lasting rise in the price level, and ultimately, after some cyclical fluctuations, some increase in the capital stock.

2. The adjustment of the economy to monetary policy depends significantly on the interest-elasticity of the demand for money, on the adjustment speed of cash balances, and on the degree of wage flexibility.

3. Money-financed expenditures have stronger output and price effects, dollar for dollar, than open-market purchases, but the difference is very small. While it matters how money is created, it does not matter a great deal.

4. By implication, the output and price effects of debt-financed expenditures, dollar for dollar, are only a small fraction of those of monetary expansion.

5. Continuing monetary expansion normally results in a Phillips curve characterized by the succession of a Keynesian phase with rapidly falling unemployment and little inflation, a classical phase with increasing prices and little net change in employment, and a stagflation phase with rising inflation and unemployment. Monetary contraction would develop in analogous stages.

6. The particular shape of the Phillips curve is again highly dependent on the demand function for money, the adjustment speed of money balances and the degree of wage flexibility.

It is not claimed that these propositions are novel. In fact, in spite of controversial verbiage, they seem to be consistent with received monetary doctrine and supported by a rather wide consensus. In particular, the weakness of the effects, dollar for dollar, of pure fiscal policy relative to monetary policy, while usually emphasized by monetarists, is, in fact, supported by nonmonetarist models of the U.S. economy. Due to the absence of a market-determined interest rate on government-supplied money (as Tobin pointed out), which is in turn related to the use of money as a medium of exchange, money plays indeed a dominant short-run role in the macroeconomic system.

Twelve

THE ART OF CENTRAL BANKING

Introduction

The macroeconomic discussion of the preceding chapters proceeded as if there were no central banks. In chapters 8 and 9 the monetary functions of the government were assumed to be restricted to the operation of a mint. The subject of chapters 10 and 11 was indeed the supply of fiat money by the government, but commercial banks were merged into the private sector and the central bank was assumed to be consolidated with the fiscal operations of the government. However, one of the most central, most interesting, and also most difficult problems of monetary theory concerns exactly the specific role of the central bank. This role will be the subject of this final chapter. Its main features are the separation of the banking sector from the rest of the private economy and the separation of the central bank from the treasury, shifting the focus to the interaction between the banking system and the central bank.

The economic functions of the central bank are described in qualitative terms in section 12.1. Section 12.2 analyzes the quantitative relationship between central bank money and the supply of bank deposits by commercial banks, first in terms of money multipliers and then in terms of general equilibrium. Section 12.3, finally, discusses the rules or principles that might guide central bank policy from the point of view of (1) long-run price stability, (2) short-run stabilization of employment, and (3) the ultrashort-run liquidity of the banking system.

In the monetary literature, central banking is usually considered in the context of particular national institutions. Indeed, the effects and the effectiveness of central bank policy depend to a large extent on technical and institutional details that vary from one country to another and in the course of time. In the present study it is neither possible nor desirable to go into such details.[1] As in the preceding chapters, a strong effort will be made, rather, to concentrate on points of general significance.

---

1. For an authoritative description of U.S. monetary policy instruments, see Young (1973).

12.1. The economic functions of the central bank

In a broad sense, the economic functions of central banks are the same as those of other financial intermediaries, including commercial banks. On one hand, they provide brokerage services that help to make the financial system more efficient than it would be in their absence. On the other hand, they provide asset transformation, lending funds of different risk, liquidity, and maturity from those they borrow. These functions are the subject of the present section.

12.1.1. ASSET TRANSFORMATION BY THE CENTRAL BANK. I begin with a description of the types of asset transformation provided by central banks. In a first step, we have to separate the monetary operations of the central bank from the fiscal operations of the government. A consolidated government budget constraint was specified in (10.2.11). For the present purpose it requires two modifications. First, since commercial banks are now assumed to be separated from the private nonbank sector, a new symbol (M_B) is used for central bank money, called "the monetary base" to distinguish it from the money supply (M) in the hands of the nonbank sector. Second, gold (A) is recognized as a financial asset of the government. In the open economies of the real world this item, together with foreign exchange holdings, mostly reflects international transactions. Under the present assumption of a closed economy, A reflects the extent to which the government buys and sells gold as a financial asset. Under a gold standard such transactions take place at a fixed price.

With these modifications the consolidated government budget constraint reads

$$G + \frac{B}{p} - T = \frac{1}{p} \Delta M_B + \frac{1}{ip} \Delta B - \frac{p_A}{p} \Delta A. \tag{12.1.1}$$

This is now partitioned into a treasury constraint

$$G + \frac{B}{p} - T = \frac{1}{ip} \Delta B^T, \tag{12.1.2}$$

where B^T denotes treasury bonds outstanding, and a central bank constraint

$$\frac{1}{i} (\Delta B^T - \Delta B) + p_A \Delta A = \Delta M_B, \tag{12.1.3}$$

where $\Delta B^T - \Delta B = \Delta S$ denotes the net change in domestic credit extended by the central bank in the form of discounts and security purchases. The first constraint postulates that the treasury finances all deficits by debt and never issues money. The second constraint states that the central bank supplies money by buying nonmonetary assets.[2] The fact that B, and not B^T, appears on the left-hand side of the treasury constraint implies that the central bank is assumed to pay its interest revenues over to the treasury. The following discussion will be concerned only with the central bank constraint.

The central bank constraint is easily recognized as the first-difference version of the central bank balance sheet. In the highly simplified form of (12.1.3) it says that the central bank transforms less liquid securities and gold holdings into more liquid cash balances. The aggregate amount of net financial assets of the private sector is determined by the treasury and the economics of gold mining, where the latter may be interpreted as a closed-economy proxy for the economics of foreign transactions. There is nothing the central bank can directly do about it. Central bank policy relates to the *composition* of these assets, usually in the direction of an increase in their liquidity. In the following discussion it will always be assumed that the aggregate supply of net financial assets to the private sector is exogenously given. The subject thus becomes the asset transformation by the central bank.

In reality, the central bank balance sheet is, of course, less simple. Typical assets and liabilities in an open economy would include the following:[3]

Assets		*Liabilities*	
Discounts (advances, acceptances)	(S)	Currency	(M_B)
Domestic securities		Deposits (bank reserves, nonbank)	
Gold	(A)	Foreign liabilities	
Foreign claims		Equity	

The monetary base can thus be regarded from two sides, namely, (1) as the sum of currency and demand deposits, or (2) as the sum of domestic credit, gold, and net foreign assets, minus equity. The following discussion will again abstract from foreign assets.

Since central bank deposits are convertible into currency at a price of unity, the central bank has no power over the division of the monetary base between currency and demand deposits. If, in addition, base money is convertible into gold at a fixed price as under a gold standard, the central bank also lacks direct control over the aggregate amount of gold, which means that it cannot control the monetary base either. However, with a variable price of gold (which is the closed-economy proxy for floating exchange rates) the central bank can indeed determine its gold holdings, which means that it can control the aggregate monetary base. The basic

2. For an analysis of this dual budget constraint, see Hansen (1973).
3. Float, treasury currency outstanding, treasury cash holdings, and treasury deposits are omitted.

task of central bank policy is the determination of purchases and sales of those assets which it is not obliged to buy and sell at an exogenously fixed price. In a closed fiat-money economy this implies control over the monetary base. Under a gold standard it implies control over domestic credit. It was one of the weaknesses of U.S. monetary analysis in the 1960s that the monetary base was so often regarded as being controlled by the central bank, while the Bretton Woods system made such control in fact impossible.

Equity, in the present context, is relevant only as an asset valuation adjustment. In particular, if the value of the security portfolio changes due to a variation in the bond yield, or if the value of the gold stock changes due to a variation in the gold price, these valuation changes are reflected in central bank equity, thus leaving the monetary base unchanged.

12.1.2. INSTRUMENTS AND INDICATORS OF CENTRAL BANK POLICY. What instruments of monetary policy the central bank has in its tool kit depends on its position in the various asset markets. If the central bank is a relatively small unit in a large market, all it can decide is the quantity it wishes to buy or sell; the asset price, and thus the yield, will remain virtually unaffected by its activities. In this case the monetary influence of the central bank is negligible. It can operate essentially like a profit-seeking commercial bank. This is very much the way the Bank of England operated during its early history.

Under present-day conditions, the position of the central bank in the markets for its principal assets (to the extent their price is not exogenously fixed) is likely to be such that it has considerable influence on the asset price. This is what makes the central bank a monetary power. In principle, policy makers have the choice of specifying either the price at which they are willing to trade an asset on a given day, or the quantity they wish to buy and sell (more will be said about this yield/quantity problem in sec. 12.3). In addition, market power may enable the central bank to practice quantitative credit rationing. I shall briefly review what this means in the principal asset markets.

Discount credit is usually characterized by interest rates that are set for considerable periods of time, combined with more or less formal credit rationing reaching from explicit quotas to the use of discretion in meeting individual credit applications. Aside from its potential role in the control of the overall domestic credit, discount credit seems well suited for the smoothening of temporary liquidity problems of individual banks or regions. The discount rate then appears as the penalty rate of theoretical banking models. This function of the central bank as a "lender of last resort" is particularly important if the market for interbank loans is highly imperfect. With a highly perfect interbank market, as exemplified by the federal funds market in the United States or by the Eurodollar market, it loses much of its importance.

Operations in government securities are in most cases relatively free of credit rationing, the central bank trading in the "open market," typically through security brokers. In the few countries in which the market for government securities is—to use the American terminology—sufficiently "wide," "deep," and "resilient," [4] open market operations become the paradigmatic instrument to provide central banking credit to the system as a whole. In the United States they are, indeed, the dominant instrument of monetary policy at the present time.

Except through domestic credit, the central bank can provide base money by buying gold, either at a fixed price as under the gold standard or at variable market prices. In the open economies of the real world, purchases and sales of foreign exchange are a closely similar instrument. It may be worth noting that for some highly developed economies gold and foreign exchange operations continue to be the dominant instrument of monetary policy even after the collapse of the gold standard.

The central bank may supplement its own operations with restrictions on the assets transformation by other financial intermediaries, especially banks. In particular, it may have authority to impose minimum requirements on bank reserves, quantitative restrictions on bank credit, or interest ceilings.

The question is often raised whether in a given period central bank policy has been expansionary or contractive and to what extent. This question can be answered by using an appropriate indicator of central bank policy. If the bank has used only one instrument, such an indicator is easy to define. For example, if monetary policy is restricted to open market operations in one type of securities, the size of the security portfolio is the appropriate indicator. Whenever the portfolio increases, monetary policy is expansionary, and vice versa. However, monetary policy usually employs several instruments. If some of them are used in an expansionary direction, while others are used in a restrictive sense, the overall direction of monetary policy ceases to be obvious. Even if all instruments are used in the same direction, their relative importance may vary from one period to another. It may therefore be difficult to decide whether the degree of tightness or ease of monetary policy has increased or declined. In such cases the definition of an appropriate indicator requires economic analysis; the so-called indicator problem raises its head. [5]

The indicator problem is basically a straightforward aggregation problem. In principle, the correct indicator is the weighted sum of the

---

4. "Width" is meant to denote a large volume and numerous investors, "depth" means that the schedule of existing orders at a given moment has considerable price elasticity, while "resilience" relates to the reaction of new orders to price variations.

5. On the indicator problem see Brunner and Meltzer (1967b), though that paper is not so much about valid indicators as about various (and more or less invalid) proxies for valid indicators. The following evaluation agrees with Benjamin Friedman (1975).

various instrument levels, where each weight is the marginal multiplier of the corresponding instrument with respect to a reference variable (see Brunner and Meltzer, 1967b, eq. 1). Suppose open market operations and changes in reserve requirements are the instruments, while the money supply to the private nonbank sector is used as the reference variable. The weights are then found by estimating the marginal effects of a change in the security portfolio and of a change in reserve requirements on the money supply. The resulting indicator value may, of course, be different for different reference variables. With reference to a narrow definition of the money supply a given policy may be expansionary, while with reference to a wider definition of the money supply or with reference to, say, unemployment it may conceivably be restrictive.[6]

In general, none of the customary macroeconomic series will provide an indicator of monetary policy. In particular, series like the money supply or interest rates, being endogenous variables of the economic system, are usually the combined result of both monetary policy and many other exogenous (and lagged endogenous) variables, thus providing misleading readings about monetary policy alone. Under a gold standard the monetary base is subject to the same qualification: Since one of its important components, namely gold, is an endogenous variable, it cannot provide a reliable policy indicator. In particular, the monetary base may underestimate the strength of monetary policy, since a given expansion of domestic credit results in a loss of gold, which reduces the effect on the monetary base, in extreme cases even to zero. The components of a valid indicator of monetary policy should thus be the actual policy variables.

The importance of the indicator problem, like that of other aggregation problems, should not be overestimated, though. Whenever there is disagreement about the appropriate aggregation procedure, we are free to analyze the problem in disaggregated terms. In monetary policy this means that we can always describe the use of each policy instrument separately without expressing an overall judgment on the "thrust" of monetary policy. Indicators are sometimes convenient, but never crucial.

12.1.3. THE ROLE OF THE CENTRAL BANK. Today central banks are a familiar part of the economic landscape. Their existence tends to be taken for granted without question. Actually, they are of relatively recent origin, having grown to their present role largely during the half-century before the First World War. They emerged in response to specific economic problems,

6. It makes little sense to use social welfare as the reference variable as suggested by Brunner and Meltzer, for the terms "contractive" and "expansionary" would then lose any monetary meaning and become synonymous with "good" and "bad." In the neighborhood of an optimal policy, no matter what it is, the value of the indicator would always be near zero provided the functions are smooth. Describing monetary policy should not be confused with judging it.

and it is possible that future changes in the economic system will make them obsolete or produce radical changes in their functions. What are the challenges to which central banks were the response? Why do most of us feel that the money supply and the composition of financial assets of the private nonbank sector cannot be left to the private banking system? These questions will here be answered, not from a historical perspective, but from an analytical point of view.

The general justification of the existence of central banks must be the belief—to express it in a familar phrase—that "money does not manage itself." Reasons for this belief can be found at different levels. If a country maintains a pure fiat money system, this provides perhaps the most un-disputable, but also the most trivial, reason; clearly the supply of fiat money cannot be left to competitive enterprise, but must be monopolized by the state (see sec. 9.3.3).

Reasons of a second, and more interesting, kind have to do with efficiency. Perhaps the most fundamental of these relates to transaction costs. If all transaction costs were proportional or increasing at the margin, free competition could be expected to result in optimal payments arrangements. However, as pointed out in earlier chapters, transaction costs are often characterized by increasing returns, both with respect to the scale of individual transactions and with respect to market scale. As a consequence, the competitive equilibrium cannot, in general, be relied upon to be efficient. Appropriate central bank intervention may then be able to improve the efficiency of the banking system by reducing the transaction costs for a given volume of transactions. Indeed, one of the basic objectives of central banks has traditionally been stated to be the improvement of the payments mechanism by things like the establishment of efficient clearing arrangements, the standardization of bank notes, and the maintenance of convertibility between different denominations of currency.

Another efficiency consideration relates to the short-term money market and, in particular, the interbank credit market. If this market is large relative to the size of individual banks and highly perfect, a bank experiencing unusually heavy deposit withdrawals for random causes can usually borrow from other banks at the going rate of interest. However, if the interbank money market is highly imperfect (because, say, the market is small relative to the size of individual banks), it may be impossible to obtain the required funds at the going rate. As a consequence, the bank in question may find itself in an acute liquidity squeeze. In this case, the central bank, since it is not guided by the same risk and profit calculus as commercial banks, may be able to correct the market deficiency by acting as a lender of last resort. As a by-product, the availability of a lender of last resort may be reflected in a reduction of the reserves commercial banks find it prudent to hold.

A third group of possible reasons for the existence of central banks relates to the possibility that the banking system may be inherently unstable. Of course, the mere fact that the money supply is a multiple of gold currency or central bank money does not make the system unstable. However, an old and imposing tradition in economics holds that the banking system, if left to itself, has an inherent tendency to impart cyclical fluctuations to the rest of the economy, punctuated by periodic banking crises.[7]

This general idea, while articulated in many different ways, seems to consist of two interrelated strands of ideas. On one hand, the money supply is seen to be positively related to the *level* of bank reserves (perhaps consisting of gold). This can be crudely formalized by writing

$$M_t = mR_t, \qquad m > 0 \tag{12.1.4}$$

where M is the money supply, R denotes bank reserves, and the subscript identifies the time period. On the other hand, the *change* in bank reserves is seen to depend negatively on the level of the money supply, though with a lag. This can be expressed by

$$R_t - R_{t-1} = bM_{t-2} + \beta. \qquad b < 0 \tag{12.1.5}$$

Under a gold standard, the latter relationship may reflect the fact that a higher money supply produces a rise in prices and wages, thus discouraging gold production and stimulating nonmonetary demand for gold. In an open economy under fixed exchange rates the effect of the domestic money supply on the balance of payments has an analogous result. Taken together, the two relationships constitute a (primitive) accelerator/multiplier model, though not of the Samuelsonian saving/investment variety but of a purely monetary character.

The model can be solved to give the money supply as a function of its own past values,

$$M_t = M_{t-1} + mbM_{t-2} + m\beta. \tag{12.1.6}$$

Depending on the parameters, the system may move either monotonically or in oscillations, and it may be either dampened or explosive. Of course, this simple formal exercise is not meant to be a theory of business fluctuations nor to do justice to the economic richness of the monetary approach to business cycles. The point is rather that extremely simple characteristics of the monetary system may be enough to produce cyclical oscillations, in extreme cases even of an explosive nature. Whoever subscribes to such a view of the monetary system may well call for a central bank to stabilize it. While the Keynesians, attributing business cycles to the interaction of saving and investment, visualized stabilization mainly in terms of active fiscal policy, the "monetarists" who preceded them, attributing business

---

7. The classical review of this tradition is Haberler (1958), particularly chapters 2, 3A.

cycles largely (if not exclusively) to the interaction of supply and demand for money, visualized stabilization mainly in terms of central bank policy.

The banking system may produce instability in another way. The preceding argument assumed that the parameters of the system remain constant. In fact, they may be subject to change. In particular, as will be shown in more detail in the following section, the money multiplier m in (12.1.4) may have a propensity to rise during expansions and to fall during contractions. Once a recession produces liquidity problems and default losses for some banks, confidence in other banks may be undermined. Bankers may react with an effort to increase their reserves drastically, thus producing a rapid, and perhaps catastrophic, contraction of the money supply. Again central banks, by vigorous open market purchases and liberal lending to banks, may be able to forestall such a contraction.

During the formative decades up to the First World War, central banks were considered mainly from the point of view of efficiency and banking stability. Central banks were regarded essentially as banks, though with a somewhat different purpose from commercial banks. While they were supposed to be operated, in principle, for the general interest, this was assumed to be in reasonable harmony with the interest of the banking community. This is probably the main reason why central banks were not simply set up as government agencies, but as semi-independent institutions in close contact with the banking community.

During the interwar period, however, a fourth type of arguments moved into the foreground. According to these, the banking system in itself is reasonably stable, but the private nonbank sector is inherently unstable. This was largely the view of Keynes as well as many of his contemporaries. From this point of view, central banks become one of the main command posts from which the stabilization policies of government are directed. This macroeconomic perspective seems to have dominated discussions about monetary policy during recent decades, overshadowing the earlier banking considerations. Today it seems doubtful whether this shift in perspective was warranted. It may be argued that the private nonbank sector is, in fact, reasonably stable, while the banking system, if left to itself, would still be subject to dangerous fluctuations. This does not mean, of course, that central banks do not have important stabilizing functions. It means, however, that these functions may relate more to the potential instability of the monetary system itself than to the instability of the nonmonetary sector.

12.2. The money supply in a two-stage banking system

The preceding section described the activities of the central bank. In the present section it will be shown how these activities, interacting with the banking system and the private nonbank sector, determine the money supply. This requires a model of a two-stage banking system, in which the money supplied by the central bank becomes the basis of the money supplied to the nonbank sector. Components of such a model were provided in chapters 9–11. They will now have to be combined. The main question concerns the quantity of bank deposits that are supplied to the private nonbank sector for any given amount of central bank money. For the purpose of this discussion it will be assumed that monetary policy is conducted exclusively by open market operations; extensions to other policy instruments are left to the reader.

The accounting framework is reduced to the bare essentials. The central bank balance sheet is assumed to look as follows:

Assets	*Liabilities*
Securities (S)	Currency (C)
	Bank reserves (R)

The monetary base is thus defined as

$$M_B = C + R = S. \tag{12.2.1}$$

This omits important items like discounts, advances, acceptances, treasury currency, treasury and other deposits with the central bank, float, and gold, as well as foreign claims and liabilities.

The consolidated balance sheet of the commercial banking system is similarly reduced to

Assets	*Liabilities*
Reserves (R)	Demand deposits (D)
Loans (L)	Time deposits (T)

or, in the form of an equation,

$$R + L = D + T. \tag{12.2.2}$$

The private nonbank sector, for the present purpose, is characterized by its holdings of currency, government bonds, demand and time deposits and its debt to banks. The money supply will be conventionally defined as the sum of currency and demand deposits,

$$M = C + D. \tag{12.2.3}$$

Successively wider definitions of money may be formed by adding time deposits and other liquid assets. What we seek is the level of M for any given M_B. Two approaches to this problem are described in the following subsections.

12.2.1. THE FIXED-COEFFICIENT APPROACH. During the half-century from 1920 to 1970, economic analysis of the money supply in a two-stage banking system was dominated by Phillips' (1920) fixed-coefficient or multiplier approach. From the point of view of credit transformation in an individual bank, this approach was described in section 9.2. It will now be applied to the banking system as a whole. Suppose the banks hold given proportions of their demand and time deposits in the form of reserves, so that $R = r_D D + r_T T$. Suppose also that the demand and time deposits of the private sector each amount to a given proportion of its cash balances, which can be written

$$D = sM, \tag{12.2.4}$$

$$T = tM. \tag{12.2.5}$$

Since the difference between total cash balances and demand deposits reflects the demand for currency, (12.2.4) can alternatively be written as a demand function for currency $C = (1 - s)M$, where $(1 - s)$ is the currency ratio.

It is simple to show that under these assumptions the money supply is a multiple of the monetary base, namely

$$M = \frac{1}{1 - s(1 - r_D) + tr_T} M_B, \tag{12.2.6}$$

with the multiplier depending positively on the demand deposit ratio and negatively on the two reserve ratios and the time deposit ratio. It has often been argued in elementary banking literature that a banking system can do what an individual bank cannot do, namely create money. It may thus be worth pointing out that, except for the inclusion of time deposits and the omission of equity, the above multiplier is formally identical to the deposit multiplier for an individual bank as derived in section 9.2.1, with the demand deposit ratio simply taking the place of the redeposit ratio. As Phillips knew well, there is no qualitative difference between an individual bank and the banking system. There may be, however, a large quantitative difference inasmuch as the demand deposit ratio for the system is typically much higher than the redeposit ratio for the individual bank. Expressed differently, the "leakages" for the individual bank are usually much larger than for the banking system as a whole. In most cases the base multiplier will be larger than one and possibly as high as three or four. This is the textbook case of multiple money creation by the banking system.

This elementary exercise can be varied, extended, and generalized in many ways (for examples see Sheppard and Barrett, 1965). Other assets can be added. Nonbank intermediaries can be included, resulting in a three-stage model of the banking system. In the place of M, other variables like bank loans or bank deposits can be linked to M_B. Different groups of banks with different reserve ratios can be distinguished, which makes the money supply dependent on the distribution of deposits among banks. Different groups of nonbank agents can be recognized to have different deposit (or currency) ratios and to do business with different groups of banks, which introduces still more distribution effects (about these distribution effects see Brunner, 1961).

While this fixed-coefficient approach, though perhaps pedestrian, is often useful and, for certain purposes, illuminating, it is also subject to serious limitations. Taken at face value it *seems* to say that money is very different from other things, inasmuch as demand has no influence on the quantity available; the quantity seems to be purely supply-determined. However, this is a superficial impression. It is well recognized that the coefficients appearing in the multiplier are not, in fact, technological constants, but depend, in turn, on interest rates (Brunner and Meltzer, 1968). If interest rates are independent of the monetary base, this does not impair the usefulness of the fixed-coefficient approach, and a shift in the demand for money would exert its influence on M through changes in the coefficients resulting from the associated shifts in interest rates. The multiplier, while variable, would still be independent of the multiplicand. However, to the extent that a change in M_B itself calls forth a change in interest rates, the approach loses its usefulness, since every change in the multiplicand then leads to a change in the multiplier, typically in the opposite direction. If this change in the multiplier is disregarded, the effect of a given change in the monetary base will usually be overstated.[8]

As Tobin has pointed out, the multiplier approach is designed for imperfect credit markets, where interest rates are rigid and thus fail to clear the market. The textbook model of multiple deposit creation by the banking system, far from being a general theory, was tailor-made for the American banking system with its regulations on interest rates and bank reserves. More perfect credit markets require a more perfect approach.

12.2.2. THE GENERAL EQUILIBRIUM APPROACH. The fixed-coefficient model of the two-stage money supply process will now be generalized to allow for the effects of endogenous variations in interest rates. This requires a general-equilibrium model in which interest rates are determined jointly with the money supply. When Tobin described this approach (1963; see also 1969), he had good reason to call it the "new view." Today it has become the dominant view, and its long ancestry in the pre-Phillips tradition of money supply theory has been recognized. The general-equilibrium approach, too, will be presented in its simplest possible form; it is

8. Instructive examples of this sort of error can be found in the recent literature on the Eurodollar market, where the low reserve ratios of Eurobanks, together with the neglect of the interest mechanism, have resulted in quite unrealistic estimates of the money-creating power of the Euromarket (as, for example, in Friedman, 1969b).

left to the reader to apply it to more complex situations. In particular, real capital will be disregarded.

The economy is again assumed to consist of the private nonbank sector, banks, and the central bank; the only function of the treasury is to supply a given amount of government securities. There are three assets, namely central bank money (consisting of currency and bank reserves), demand deposits with commercial banks, and bonds. Central bank money carries no interest. Demand deposits pay interest i_d, which is assumed to equalize the demand of the nonbank sector to the supply by banks. The bonds may be issued by the government or by nonbank units, but they are assumed to be perfectly homogeneous in all respects. As a consequence, no generality is lost by visualizing banks as holding all earning assets in the form of government bonds. To simplify the exposition, though at the expense of realism, it is assumed that the bonds always trade at par, but have a variable coupon corresponding to the interest rate i_b.

The private nonbank sector has demands for currency and deposits, each depending on both interest rates,

$$C = C(i_d, i_b), \qquad C_d < 0 \qquad C_b < 0 \tag{12.2.7}$$

$$D = D(i_d, i_b), \qquad D_d > 0 \qquad D_b < 0 \tag{12.2.8}$$

with the partial derivatives given on the right. It is safe to postulate $D_d + C_d > 0$, since an increase in the deposit rate will not lower the total demand for money.

The banks' demand for reserves and securities similarly depends on the interest rates,

$$R = R(i_d, i_b), \qquad R_d < 0 \qquad R_b < 0 \tag{12.2.9}$$

$$L = L(i_d, i_b). \qquad L_d < 0 \qquad L_b > 0 \tag{12.2.10}$$

The postulated signs are consistent with the discussion in 9.2.3. There it was shown, however, that the sign of R_b may conceivably be positive; $R_b < 0$ thus represents an additional, though plausible, restriction. There is no independent supply of bank deposits, as this can be derived from (12.2.9) and (12.2.10) together with the balance-sheet constraint $R + L = D$.

What we wish to determine is the money supply

$$M = C(i_d, i_b) + D(i_d, i_b). \tag{12.2.11}$$

It can be represented graphically as a family of "iso-money curves," each of which connects combinations of i_d and i_b resulting in the same demand for money (see fig. 12.2.1). Interest rates thus appear as the crucial link between the quantity of money and the monetary base. The M-curves have positive slope; to keep the demand for money constant, a higher bond yield must be neutralized by a higher yield on demand deposits. It is easily verified that an increase in i_d at a given i_b raises the demand for money.

The next step is to determine the set of interest rates resulting from a given supply of base money, M_B. This is a simple problem of two inter-dependent markets.[9] On one hand, the nonbank demand for demand deposits must equal the supply forthcoming from banks as implied in their demand for reserves and loans,

$$D(i_d, i_b) = R(i_d, i_b) + L(i_d, i_b). \tag{12.2.12}$$

In terms of i_d and i_b this defines a "deposit equilibrium curve." This D-curve is upward sloping, as an increase in i_d creates an excess demand for demand deposits, which must be neutralized by a rise in i_b. Stability requires, however, that the D-curve is less steep than the M-curves.

On the other hand, the aggregate demand for base money must equal the supply provided by the central bank,

$$C(i_d, i_b) + R(i_d, i_b) = M_B. \tag{12.2.13}$$

For a given base, this defines a "base-equilibrium curve" that is downward sloping, as represented in figure 12.2.1 by the M_B-curve. Full equilibrium is attained where both markets are simultaneously in equilibrium. In the graph this combination of interest rates is represented by the intersection of

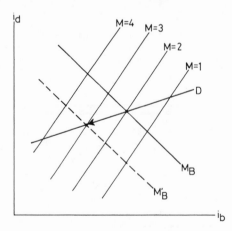

Figure **12.2.1**
General Equilibrium of the Money Supply

9. There is no independent equilibrium condition for bonds. If the central bank, commercial banks, and the nonbank sector all satisfy their respective balance-sheet constraints, and if two of the three markets are in equilibrium, then the third market is also in equilibrium.

the D-curve with the M_B-curve. The corresponding money supply can then be read off the M-curve going through this point.

If the monetary base is increased, the M_B-curve shifts downward and to the left, as indicated by M'_B. The equilibrium thus moves along the D-curve to lower interest rates. Since the M-curves are steeper than the D-curve, this implies an increase in the aggregate money supply. The multiplier is unambiguously positive. It is less clear that it also exceeds unity. Once the interest mechanism is allowed for, it is not absolutely certain that an increase in the monetary base by one dollar will produce an increase in the money supply by more than a dollar. To the extent that base money, in the form of currency, is a substitute for demand deposits, this ambiguity should not be surprising: If additional wheat is supplied from government stocks, the aggregate supply will increase by a lesser amount as the fall in wheat prices will reduce the private supply.

Further analysis shows that the multiplier, in the present model, is indeed likely to be less than unity. More precisely, $dM/dM_B < 1$ if, and only if,

$$L_d D_b < L_b D_d + (L_d R_b - L_b R_d). \tag{12.2.14}$$

The product of the cross interest effects on the left-hand side will normally be positive. It will usually be dominated, however, by the product of the direct interest effects appearing on the right-hand side. Since the bracketed terms involving bank reserves are also positive, the inequality is likely to be satisfied. The important point is that the money multiplier is highly dependent on the interest mechanism, and that, at the margin, it may conceivably turn out to be a "divisor."

We may finally inquire how this general-equilibrium model is related to the fixed-coefficient model that preceded it. To give a precise answer to this question I modify the general-equilibrium model in the following respects: (1) the interest rate on the demand deposits is assumed to be fixed exogenously, for example, by the central bank; (2) bank demand for reserves is assumed to be insensitive to the bond yield; (3) the proportion between demand deposits and currency is also assumed to be insensitive to the bond yield.

The first modification means that the deposit rate is no longer market clearing. The equilibrium condition for demand deposits thus disappears from the model, the banks simply accepting whatever demand deposits are forthcoming at the fixed deposit rate, and the quantity of these deposits becomes a determinant of reserve demand. Modification (1) thus results in the model

$$M = C(i_b) + D(i_b), \tag{12.2.15}$$

$$C(i_b) + R(i_b, D) = C(i_b) + R[i_b, D(i_b)] = M_B. \tag{12.2.16}$$

By taking differentials, the marginal base multiplier can be derived as

$$\frac{dM}{dM_B} = \frac{1}{1 - \dfrac{D_b}{C_b + D_b}\,(1 - R_D) + \dfrac{R_b}{C_b + D_b}}. \tag{12.2.17}$$

Modifications (2) and (3) mean that $R_b = 0$ and

$$\frac{D_b}{C_b + D_b} = \frac{D}{C + D} = \frac{D}{M} = s,$$

where s is again the deposit ratio. With these additional assumptions, the marginal multiplier further simplifies to

$$\frac{dM}{dM_B} = \frac{1}{1 - s(1 - R_D)}. \tag{12.2.18}$$

In the absence of time deposits, this is identical to the fixed-coefficient multiplier (12.2.6). This confirms that the distinctive features of the fixed-coefficient approach are, indeed, the assumptions expressed by modifications (1)–(3). In an institutional environment in which assumptions (1)–(3) are close to reality, the fixed-coefficient approach may offer a valuable shortcut to the truth. In other cases it may be seriously misleading. In particular, since $R_b/(C_b + D_b)$ is usually positive, the neglect of the interest-sensitivity of bank reserves will typically result in an overestimation of the multiplier. In fact, if R_b is high enough, the multiplier may conceivably fall below unity. In such an extreme case, a marginal dollar of base money produces an expansion of the money supply by less than a dollar.

12.2.3. THE BANKS' DEMAND FOR RESERVES. Whatever approach is used, the money supply in a two-stage banking system depends crucially on the banks' demand for reserves. If this demand shifts upward, the money supply contracts, and vice versa. For a given monetary base, marked fluctuations in reserve demand can thus produce large inverse fluctuations in the money supply. The model of the preceding section described the demand for bank reserves as a function of interest rates and, for an exogenously fixed deposit rate, of the volume of demand deposits. I shall now consider two additional sets of factors that may cause this function to shift.

One set of factors relates to the influence of the central bank. First, we have to consider bank borrowing from the central bank. If banks can obtain any amount of discount credit from the central bank at the posted rate, the exogenous discount rate, i_p, must be added to the determinants of bank reserves and bank loans in (12.2.9) and (12.2.10). We also have to add to the model a demand function for discount credit in terms of the same rates. The monetary base thus becomes an endogenous variable even in the absence of gold. With a rising discount rate banks will, *ceteris paribus*, reduce their borrowing, which means a reduction in the monetary base. As explained in section 9.2.3, banks will also find it profitable to reduce their loans and to increase reserves, which lowers the money supply for a given base.

However, bank borrowing from the central bank is usually characterized by various forms and degrees of credit rationing, reaching from explicit quotas to unwritten rules and traditions. In the United States, in particular, the "Riefler doctrine" (Riefler, 1930) was based on the proposition that banks have an ingrained aversion to continuous borrowing from the central bank, created by experience and maintained by central bank practices. As a consequence, borrowing banks can be expected, so the doctrine ran, to contract their loans. The level of bank borrowing thus became the main predictor for the behavior of the money market. The Riefler doctrine was an important contribution to the understanding of the money supply mechanism, but it neglected other important elements and was restricted to the very short run.

The second extension concerns legal reserve requirements. As in the case of discount credit, their effect depends to a large extent on the technical details. For example, it may make a considerable difference whether they are computed weekly, monthly, or quarterly; whether they relate to end-of-period figures or daily average; whether they are uniform or differentiated; whether they relate to levels or increments of balance-sheet items; and what the penalties are. These technicalities must be considered in the context of the respective banking system and cannot be discussed here. It is important, however, to note some general points.

In general, reserve requirements will have a stronger modifying effect on the volume of reserves the higher their level relative to the reserves that would have been held in their absence. With low reserve requirements, excess reserves will be high and banks will determine their actual reserves virtually as if reserve requirements did not exist. With relatively high reserve requirements, actual reserves may depend on little else, excess reserves will be low and transitory, and changes in required reserves will promptly be reflected in actual reserves.

In the United States, recognition of this fact led to the expansion of the Riefler doctrine to the "free reserve doctrine." [10] Until the early 1930s, excess reserves used to be low. It seemed that in a first approximation they could be disregarded. With rising excess reserves the doctrine was amended by the additional proposition that profit motives induce banks with excess reserves to expand loans. For the banking system as a whole, the basic predictor of money market behavior thus became the level of free reserves,

10. A concise summary can be found in Brunner and Meltzer (1964).

defined as the difference between excess reserves and bank borrowing or, equivalently, the difference between actual reserves and the sum of required reserves and bank borrowing. With relatively high free reserves, money market rates would be expected to fall, while with low free reserves they would be expected to rise. The high level of excess reserves later in the 1930s thus appeared as a huge inflationary potential that made "monetary control," as it was called, virtually impossible. It might have been more fruitful to inquire why banks so stubbornly refused to behave as the free reserve doctrine predicted. This would have led to the third consideration, now to be discussed.

The free reserve doctrine is conspicuous for its disregard of interest rates as a determinant of reserve demand. Except for very high reserve requirements and tight rationing of discount credit, this may be expected to result in erroneous predictions. Research since the early sixties can be interpreted as an effort to restore interest rates to their proper place. This led to the "desired reserve doctrine" (Meigs, 1962). It assigns the crucial role to the difference between actual free reserves and desired free reserves. Whenever this difference is positive, banks would be expected to expand their earning assets, thus lowering interest rates; whenever the difference is negative, banks would be expected to contract their earning assets, thereby raising interest rates. Bank behavior thus began to be interpreted in terms of a stock adjustment model similar to that used in the macrodynamic analysis of chapter 11.

Desired free reserves, in turn, were assumed to be negatively related to the yield on earning assets as postulated in the general-equilibrium model of the preceding subsection and in chapter 9. This implied that the *change* in interest rates became negatively dependent on the actual level of free reserves and the *level* of interest rates. In full equilibrium, free reserves would be negatively related to the loan rate. This approach thus made it possible to incorporate reserve requirements into a model of banks maximizing their profits for given interest rates. This became the prototype of banking models.

Cagan (1969) has noted (1) that fluctuations in free reserves are largely due to fluctuations in borrowing, and not in excess reserves, and (2) that the discount rate, representing the penalty rate, seems to have little influence on desired reserves. This means that observed fluctuations take place largely through increases in the loan rate inducing banks to increase their borrowings and vice versa. Cagan regarded this observation as evidence for short-run deviations from profit maximization, the banks borrowing at unprofitable penalty rates to accommodate old customers in a tight market. However, there are (at least) two alternative interpretations, both consistent with profit maximization. First, it was shown in chapter 9 that in view of the costs of bank operations the penalty rate may well be below the loan rate without giving the profit-maximizing bank an incentive for additional borrowing. If the loan rate increases, profit maximization then requires an expansion of borrowings and loans. Second, bank borrowings are usually not obtained at market-clearing discount rates but are subject to credit rationing by the central bank. In a tight market, characterized by high interest rates, more banks may qualify for borrowing, which is equivalent to a decline in the discount rate in a perfect market. Under easy credit conditions the reverse would be true. Cagan's observation can thus be fitted into a profit-maximizing model of banks.[11]

These considerations all related to the influence of the central bank. The other important source of shifts in the demand for reserves is the set of stochastic properties of deposits and loans. It was shown in section 9.2.3 how the demand for bank reserves depends on the mean and variance of deposit withdrawals and default losses. The demand function for reserves as expressed by (12.2.9) assumes that these parameters are given. In reality they are subject to variations. Since the parameters express the bankers' hopes and fears about the future behavior of deposits and loans, these variations may be rapid and severe. From the point of view of the central bank, this is probably the most important single fact about the banking system.

Not all variations in the distribution of deposit withdrawals and default losses for individual banks are of equal importance for the banking system. If the expectations of individual banks are subject to random variations due to many independent causes, the aggregate effect is likely to be negligible. Such variations are easily handled by temporary loans from surplus banks to deficit banks through the interbank loan market. The same is true if the variations, while not random, are compensating in nature. Thus a shift of deposits from one bank or region to another may affect the means of the respective withdrawal functions in a compensatory fashion. The same may be true for default losses if good and bad credit risks shift between banks.

Variations are more serious if the same forces affect all banks in a parallel fashion. Thus a higher mobility of deposits among banks would tend to increase the variance of withdrawals for all banks simultaneously. More importantly, a business downturn may raise both the means and the variances of deposit withdrawals and default losses for all banks, thus producing an increase in aggregate reserve demand and a contraction of loans per dollar of equity. It is clear that interbank loans do not help in such a case.

The most ominous variations are those which are self-reinforcing. Suppose a bank suffers heavy withdrawals. This may create concern about its liquidity that, in turn, causes more depositors to withdraw their funds,

11. For a recent attempt to interpret bank borrowing in terms of profit maximization, see Sutch and Thurston (1976).

producing a rapid increase in the mean and variance of expected withdrawals in this particular bank. If, as a consequence, the bank becomes actually illiquid, the externalities of confidence may undermine depositor confidence in other banks, thus leading to a chain reaction of rapidly increasing reserve demand. On the side of loans, failure of one debtor may cause other debtors to fail. Failure of one bank because of default losses, by making the deposits of its creditors illiquid, may cause defaults in loans from other banks. As a result, the means and variances of expected default losses may rise for the system as a whole.

The result of such variations in the means and variance of deposit withdrawals and default losses may be large and sudden shifts in desired reserves, associated with opposite shifts in the base multiplier and thus in the money supply. As a consequence, the banking system, if left to itself, may be quite unstable. In fact, throughout the century before the Great Depression business cycles used to be punctuated by "bank panics." It was these periodic financial collapses which seemed to transform business recessions into "crises."

The development of central banking and banking legislation during that period can largely be understood as the history of responses to the challenge of this apparent instability. By extending liberal discount credit to threatened banks as lenders of last resort, central banks tried to forestall and counteract cumulative contraction. The development of open-market operations was meant to make stabilizing monetary policy more powerful. Reserve requirements, by preventing desired reserves from falling below a certain minimum in times of high confidence, would mitigate the contraction in periods of failing confidence, and equity requirements would promise similar effects with respect to default losses. Deposit insurance was designed to reduce the externalities of depositor confidence.

Since the Great Depression there have been no "bank panics." The attention of economists has thus shifted away from the potential instability of the commercial banking system to other sources of monetary fluctuations, perhaps originating in mistaken central bank policy. There is, however, no convincing evidence that the banking system, in the absence of central bank action, would be much more stable today then it was in the nineteenth century. It can plausibly be argued that bank panics have disappeared precisely because the development of central banks and banking legislation was reasonably successful in meeting this particular challenge.

12.3. Guidelines for central bank policy

Much about the theory of monetary policy has been said, or implied, in the preceding chapters. It now remains to round off this discussion by considering the principles that should guide central bank decisions. This is a subject on which vast claims have been made, a few important points have been established, and most remains to be done. It will be impossible on a few pages to do justice to the many technical aspects of the problem. While most of this book consisted of analysis, the emphasis in this final section will thus be on judgment and perspective.

The recent debate on the principles of central bank policy has focused on three questions:

1. Should the decision-making process be one-stage, linking the ultimate instruments (like open market operations) directly to the ultimate targets (like output and the price level), or should it be two-stage, using "irrelevant" variables like the money supply or long-term interest rates as intermediate targets? I shall call this the "procedure problem."

2. Should policy be formulated in terms of quantities of assets (like the money supply or the open market portfolio) or in terms of yields (like the rates on interbank loans and treasury bills)? This may be called the "yield/quantity problem."

3. Once the instruments are chosen, which quantitative rules should guide their use? This is the "rules problem."

The debate arose mainly in response to a challenge thrown out by Milton Friedman (1959, 1968). This challenge took the form of a clear-cut and provocative answer to each of these questions, namely, that (1) the decision procedure should be two-stage; (2) policy should be formulated in terms of quantities, with the money supply, appropriately defined, as the intermediate target; and (3) the money supply should be expanded at a constant rate roughly equal to the long-term rate of economic growth.

Friedman's challenge, in important respects supported by other eminent critics of central bank policies like Brunner and Meltzer (1964), had some visible success inasmuch as the formulation of central bank policies shifted gradually, though hesitantly, in the postulated direction.[12] As in many similar cases, however, economic theory tended to lag behind intuition, and today most of the fundamental questions still await precise analysis. While the yield/quantity problem and the rules problem will be taken up in subsections 12.3.2–12.3.4, the following section is devoted to a discussion of the procedure problem. The analysis will throughout be limited to open market operations in a closed economy with a given supply of treasury assets.

12.3.1. A THREE-FREQUENCY DECISION PROCEDURE. Let us suppose the yield/quantity problem has been resolved in favor of quantities. Under a two-stage procedure, policy makers first decide about the optimal

---

12. An authoritative study of Federal Reserve open market strategy in transition is Guttentag (1966). Axilrod (1971) captures a somewhat later stage.

quantity of, say, the money supply in view of ultimate objectives like inflation or employment. In the second stage, they then determine the optimal amount of open market operations in view of the intermediate money target.

As a matter of history, the two-stage approach, though not with the money supply as the intermediate target, has characterized Federal Reserve policy formulation for decades. Most likely, this was not due to economic considerations but to institutional arrangements, providing for monthly meetings of the Federal Open Market Committee in Washington, while the day-to-day trading is done by the manager of the System Open Market Account in New York. With such a two-level command hierarchy, the tendency to develop a two-stage decision procedure will be almost irresistible, regardless of its economic merits.

Efforts to base the two-stage procedure on economic analysis came relatively late and are still incomplete. As usual, Friedman has been most articulate. From a long-term point of view, so his argument runs, the economy requires a steady growth of monetary aggregates. The lag with which money acts on output and employment is too long and too variable to make monetary policy a suitable instrument for short-run stabilization. Monetary policy should be used, however, to neutralize sharp and possibly critical disturbances in the day-to-day money supply process. A constant rate of growth of an intermediate target, namely the money supply, is seen as a simple and workable technique by which all three objectives can be attained in one stroke: Monetary aggregates will indeed show steady long-run growth, cyclical activism is precluded, and variations in the monetary base have to be used to neutralize disturbances in bank liquidity. However, this argument is open to (at least) two serious objections. First, the apparent simplicity of the intermediate-target rule may not be helpful, because large disturbances in the money supply process often make it impossible to translate it into operational rules for open market operations. Second, to contribute to the short-run stabilization of output is widely regarded, not as a temptation to be resisted, but as a job to be learned and done.

More general—but also less lucid—arguments for a two-stage approach have run in terms of informational efficiency. Since the behavior of the economy is imperfectly known and since, in particular, money supply figures become available more promptly than real income figures, it is efficient, so it is argued, to use the money supply as the intermediate target. While this argument looks superficially plausible, its correctness has never been demonstrated. Whatever analysis is available indicates, to the contrary, that a two-stage procedure is never superior to a one-stage procedure and is usually inferior. To be sure, endogenous variables that would be classified as "irrelevant" in the Tinbergen terminology can often supply valuable advance information about the behavior of the economy.

It is usually inefficient, however, to single out one particular irrelevant variable, namely the money supply, and elevate it to the rank of an intermediate target.[13] In the present state of knowledge, until the advocates of a two-stage approach have made a more convincing case for its informational efficiency, there seems to be little reason, therefore, to enter into a detailed discussion of its doctrines, and the monetary theorist is justified in relating the policy instruments directly to the ultimate targets. As a welcome corollary, the perennial question about the proper choice of a money supply variable becomes moot. It should be noted that this position is compatible with any degree of "monetarism," as this body of ideas was described in chapter 10. Fortunately, monetarists are not forced by the logic of their argument to advocate inefficient decision procedures.

Another aspect of the decision procedure is of more substantive interest. Monetary policy has three clearly distinct objectives:

1. The first objective is to keep the trend of prices roughly stable in the long run. There is little reason for concern about price fluctuations from quarter to quarter or even from year to year, even rather violent ones. Nor is there much reason to worry about long-term variations in the price level, provided they do not exceed, say, 1 percent per year; a doubling of the price level over a century would hardly present serious problems. What matters are price movements from, say, one decade to the next at substantial rates.

2. The second objective is to reduce the fluctuations of output and employment in the Keynesian short run. In the long run, as discussed in the preceding chapter, monetary policy has no appreciable effect on employment, and economists do not know how to stimulate long-run growth with monetary means. From quarter to quarter and from year to year, however, monetary policy has strong, though transitory, effects on output and employment. Monetary policy should thus be used in such a way that the fluctuations in output and employment are reduced rather than increased.

3. The third objective is to prevent critical fluctuations in bank liquidity from day to day and from week to week.

In a Tinbergen perspective, three objectives require (at least) three different instruments. In the present case, there is only one policy variable, namely, open-market operations. We can forge three instruments out of one policy variable by observing that the three objectives relate to disturbances with very different frequencies: The secular swings in prices relate to the trend over several output cycles, while each of the output cycles, in turn, spans numerous oscillations in the money supply process. By partitioning open market operations into components of corresponding frequencies, policy makers can thus obtain a distinct instrument for each objective: The long-run growth of the security portfolio is used to control the trend of

13. For an analytical survey of this issue, see Benjamin Friedman (1975).

prices, the short-run variations of the portfolio are used to stabilize output and employment, and day-to-day operations are used to forestall liquidity crises. This is what I propose to call the "three-frequency approach" to monetary policy. Its distinctive feature is the relative independence of the objectives and policies for the various frequencies; short-run policies are not used to implement long-run goals, but for economic purposes of their own.

The basic idea can best be visualized by imagining that the security portfolio of the central bank is actually divided into three distinct accounts, managed by separate departments according to different rules. The price department, managing the long-term trend account, is initially assigned the entire security portfolio. It is free to engage in any operation it regards as necessary to reach its objective.

The output department, managing the short-run stabilization account, starts out with a base portfolio of zero. It is free to buy any amount it deems advisable from the point of view of output stabilization, *provided that the account is again brought down to zero sometime in the next five years.* It is also free to sell any amount it wishes by borrowing securities from the trend account, provided the borrowed securities are returned sometime within the next five years. Whenever the zero base is reached again, be it after two months or four years, the five-year period begins to run anew. This arrangement is designed to give the output department a high degree of freedom for output stabilization over business cycles, while at the same time preventing it from affecting the long-run trend of prices. Whenever the account managers are tempted to stimulate output, they are on notice that they also assume responsibility for the offsetting restrictions at a later time.

The liquidity department, finally, managing the ultrashort-run banking account, also starts from a zero base and is free to buy and sell securities (possibly borrowed from the trend account) in any amount it considers desirable. In this case, however, *the account must again be brought to zero within no more than six months.* This constraint forces the department to reverse its actions after roughly one quarter, thus preventing it from affecting output and employment to a significant extent. Of course, the zero-base constraints on the output and liquidity departments are a crude way to limit their operations to certain frequencies. Clever technicians can easily invent much more ingenious, and thus more intellectually satisfying, schemes. This crude device seems to be good enough, however, to convey the basic idea.

I believe the three-frequency approach helps to disentangle several lines of argument that, in the discussion about the two-stage intermediate-target approach, became almost hopelessly intertwined. I hope the following three sections will bear this out.

12.3.2. STABILIZATION OF THE PRICE TREND. The price department, managing the trend account, would be assigned the objective of preventing secular inflation or deflation as measured by the movements of (non-overlapping) five-year averages of prices. It would be instructed to pursue this objective with a minimum of changes in the rate of growth of the trend account, without regard to cyclical fluctuations and credit market conditions.

If, in the long run, (1) the income velocity of money were roughly constant, (2) the base multiplier were roughly constant, and (3) the treasury were to expand the government debt roughly at the rate of growth of the economy, then the implementation of these instructions would require an expansion of the trend account at the long-term rate of growth of the economy. In reality, the three conditions will hardly ever be satisfied. Technological change in the payments system and structural change in the nonbank sector may affect the demand for money per dollar of output.[14] Innovation and structural change in the banking system may affect the long-run base multiplier. The treasury may expand government debt at a rate that is either higher or lower than the growth rate of the economy. At a constant growth rate of the trend portfolio, the price level will then drift slowly upward or downward. Such drifts would have to be offset by gradual adjustments in the rate of portfolio growth.[15] The trend account would thus be managed, by and large, according to the Friedman rule.

This means that the yield/quantity problem has been resolved in favor of quantities. For the trend account this choice follows from fundamental stability considerations. Assuming that government debt happens to expand at the rate of economic growth, it is true that in comparing balanced-growth paths of the economy there is a one-to-one relationship between rates of portfolio expansion and rates of interest, where higher expansion rates, through higher inflation rates, are associated with higher (nominal) interest rates.[16] One might thus be tempted to argue that the long-term rate of inflation could be lowered just as well by setting a lower rate of interest and letting the rate of monetary expansion adjust as by setting a lower rate of monetary expansion and letting the rate of interest adjust. In fact, as Wicksell was the first to show (1898/1936), this would be seriously wrong.

14. It is clear that the quantitatively more significant changes due to short- and medium-term fluctuations in the interest structure and to varying rates of inflation are not relevant in this context.

15. A rate of debt expansion different from the rate of growth would be associated, under these rules, with a long-term rise or fall of interest rates. Balanced growth at stable prices would be impossible. The proposed rule implies that unbalanced growth at stable prices is preferred to balanced growth with inflation or deflation at rates determined, not by the central bank, but by the treasury.

16. As Mundell (1963) has shown, an increase in the rate of monetary expansion by 1 percent is typically associated with an increase in the rate of interest by less than 1 percent.

The reason is that an inflationary equilibrium with an exogenous rate of interest is usually unstable, while an inflationary equilibrium with an exogenous monetary base is stable. Suppose the rate of monetary expansion has been 10 percent, the rate of inflation is 6 percent, and the (nominal) rate of interest is 8 percent. If the rate of monetary expansion is now lowered to 4 percent, the rate of interest will first shoot up, reflecting the increased tightness of money, but gradually the rate of inflation will decline, the rate of expected inflation will follow suit, and, as a consequence, the rate of interest will soon begin to decline. The system will gradually move toward a new balanced growth path without inflation and with a rate of interest of, say, 3 percent. If, instead, the central bank announces its willingness to buy any securities offered at a (nominal) yield of 3 percent (implying an initial real yield of minus 3 percent), the rate of portfolio expansion will rise above 10 percent and the rate of inflation will rise; this lowers the real rate of interest even below minus 3 percent, which pushes the rate of portfolio expansion still higher, and so forth. Inflation will accelerate, and the economy will move away from the new equilibrium path instead of toward it.

In order to accomplish by an interest policy what can be accomplished by simply fixing a lower rate of portfolio expansion, the trend account managers would have to move the rate of interest along a complicated trajectory, first raising it to slow down inflation, and then gradually lowering it as expected inflation subsides, always by exactly the right percentage. What a quantity policy can achieve by a simple rule would become extremely difficult to achieve under a yield policy.

This does not mean that secular inflation, if past errors have permitted it to build up, is best eliminated by reducing the rate of portfolio expansion to the zero-inflation level overnight. What will have to be determined is the "optimal rate of disinflation." This problem can be visualized in terms of the (virtual) Phillips curves of the preceding chapter (see fig. 11.6.1). Suppose the economy finds itself on a path of balanced inflation at a rate of 6 percent and with unemployment at the natural rate. It is then the task of the trend account managers to move it to a zero-inflation path with unemployment again at the natural rate. This can be done along infinitely many different paths, generally involving very different rates of temporary unemployment and in some cases displaying violent cycles. The problem is to select the best among these paths.

Economics has so far discovered no operational solution to this problem.[17] I would be inclined to conjecture that a gradual reduction in the rate of monetary expansion is usually preferable to an abrupt reduction and that a reduction from, say, 12 percent to 4 percent should be spread out

17. Prominent among the few contributions are those by Mundell (1965) and Stein-Infante (1973).

over two to three years. One appealing rule is to let the trend account expand at roughly the current rate of inflation or slightly below until its rate of expansion is again at the level of economic growth. Considering the long-run growth of the economy, this would be sure to exert a relatively gentle, but persistent downward pressure on the rate of inflation. But these conjectures are based on intuition and not on analysis. The optimal rate of disinflation is clearly an urgent topic for policy-oriented analysis.

12.3.3. STABILIZATION OF OUTPUT FLUCTUATIONS. The output department is assigned the task of reducing fluctuations in output and employment in the Keynesian short run. It would get a perfect score if employment were steady at the normal rate. Whenever there are deviations, the department would have to consider whether there is a sequence of future open market operations that promises a marked improvement in the future adjustment path of the economy. This makes it clear that the choice is not between different levels of variables but between different trajectories over time.[18]

Like the trend department, the output department first has to choose between an interest policy and a quantity policy. The main piece of analysis in this field has been provided by Poole (1970a). In a deterministic model, he pointed out, the two policies are equivalent: Whatever can be accomplished by setting the volume of open market purchases and letting the market decide the rate of interest can just as well be accomplished by setting the rate of interest and letting the market buy or sell the securities it wishes. This is different if the behavior functions of the system are subject to stochastic disturbances. In this case, the two policies will generally result in different disturbances in real income. In particular, a quantity policy turns out to be superior (in the sense of minimizing the variance of real output) if the disturbances are mainly concentrated in the demand for goods and services, while an interest policy is superior if the disturbances are mainly concentrated in the monetary sector. A "mixed" policy, whereby the central bank would fix neither the quantity nor the yield of its securities, but determine the quantity to be traded as a function of the yield, would usually be superior to both "pure" policies. This type of analysis can be, and has been, extended and generalized in many directions.[19]

While Poole's stochastic approach provided a rational solution to the short-run yield/quantity problem, I do not believe that it focuses on the really important factors. Stochastic disturbances in behavior functions would indeed be important if the output department had to decide on its operations for, say, a year at a time without the possibility of intermediate

18. It is natural, therefore, that this problem has recently been approached in terms of optimal control. For an excellent nontechnical survey of Federal Reserve efforts in this field, see Pierce (1976). Kalchbrenner and Tinsley (1976) report on recent experiments.

19. See, again, B. Friedman (1975).

adjustments. In this case, the disturbances could indeed be decisive. In fact, however, the output department can adjust its policies, if necessary, almost continuously. Once disturbances occur, adjustments can be made before the errors become large. I find it hard to believe, therefore, that the choice between quantity policies and interest policies should really be made on the basis of stochastic considerations.[20] While Poole's approach has dominated the analytical literature in recent years, central bankers have probably shown good common sense in not using it as the basis of their choice of policy.

Stability may again be a more important consideration. However, in a cyclical context, in the absence of inflationary expectations, Wicksell's argument no longer applies; it is no longer true that interest policies usually produce instability. Nor is it necessarily true, on the other hand, that a system that is stable under a money supply policy is also stable under an interest policy. Consider the macroeconomic models analyzed in chapter 10. In each case, the comparative-static model can be rearranged in such a way that the change in the bond yield appears as the exogenous variable, while the money supply is endogenous. Dynamic analysis shows, however, that the stability conditions differ between the two variants. As a consequence, the money supply variant may, in principle, be stable while the interest variant is unstable, or vice versa. I have so far not discovered any particular rule to the effect that one variant is more likely to be stable than the other, and in a wide range of cases both will be stable. Until more is known on this question, we are forced to conclude that from the point of view of stability the output department may legitimately formulate its policies either in terms of the quantity of its purchases and sales *or* in terms of interest rates.

Under the three-frequency approach there is still another criterion, though. While any number of departments may simultaneously follow a quantity policy, their operations simply being additive, at most one department can use an interest policy without producing conflicts. Anticipating the argument of the following section, it may be postulated that the liquidity department should have the main claim to using an interest policy. Indeed, if the output department formulated its policy in terms of the bond yield, the liquidity department would find it all but impossible to do its job. This implies that the output department, like the trend department, should use a quantity policy.

Once the output department has decided in favor of a quantity policy, what rules should guide its transactions? Three considerations will be

20. In an interesting note Kareken and Wallace (1972) have argued, however, that with more frequent adjustment the choice between a quantity policy and an interest policy may conceivably become more important, depending on the serial correlation of the disturbances in the goods and money markets.

relevant in this context. First, the operations of the price department will keep expected inflation within narrow bounds. As a consequence, the family of Phillips curves depicted in figure 11.2.1 is essentially reduced to the line for $\pi = 0$ going through E^*. While Keynesian economists had to learn during the last twenty years that, because of expectations, there is no simple trade-off between unemployment and the short-term rate of price change, the activities of the price department, if successful, would come close to establishing such a trade-off. However, short-run fluctuations in the rate of price change are economically quite harmless. The output department can thus disregard prices altogether and concentrate on real output. In addition, stabilization of the price trend means that the economy, once it finds itself above or below normal employment, has a built-in tendency to move back to normal, though perhaps not as quickly or directly as desired. Through the operations of the price department, the output department thus finds its task much simplified.

Second, any effort of the output department to keep unemployment permanently below normal, since it requires progressive security purchases, would violate its zero-base constraint. The operations of the output department are thus restricted to temporary measures. Furthermore, even temporary measures involve the risk that the zero-base constraint would force a reversal at a moment when this is economically or politically inopportune. In view of this risk, the output department will probably limit its interventions to severe disturbances.

Third, the output department will have to consider the lag with which open market operations affect real output (see sec. 11.3). There is broad agreement that this lag is several quarters long. Friedman emphasized that it is also highly variable, but it is not clear to what extent this variability is real, due to erratic changes in the economic structure, and to what extent it is only apparent, due to the use of an oversimplified dynamic model (see above, p. 260). While Friedman argued that the length and variability of the lag make it likely that short-run stabilization efforts turn out to be de-stabilizing, recent studies suggest that even simple feedback control rules are likely to produce a reduction in output fluctuations. In particular, Fischer and Cooper (1973) have shown that with a long and variable lag the potential gains from the use of proportional and derivative controls are indeed reduced and intervention should be more cautious, but careful use of such simple policies is still stabilizing relative to nonintervention.[21] Their simulation studies with different macroeconometric models for the United States also indicate that simple derivative control rules would have

21. It should be noted, however, that in the presence of lags, whether constant or variable. monetary policy can only be effective if the disturbances are serially correlated. If monetary policy in 1975 affects output only in 1976 and if disturbances in the two years are completely independent, then monetary policy can do nothing to reduce the variability of output (see Fischer and Cooper, p. 855).

been more stabilizing than constant monetary growth (Cooper and Fischer, 1972, 1974). With less mechanical policies, to the extent that they are based on actual knowledge of the economic system, one may hope to do considerably better.

With these considerations in mind, the output department will probably want to buy securities whenever it is reasonably certain that employment will be significantly below normal within about a year, while periods of high employment will be used to bring the account back to the zero base. In this way, the disturbances of employment away from the normal level could probably be reduced and the gravitation of employment toward the normal level could be accelerated. Clearly, if the output department misjudges the behavior of the economy, it may easily make matters worse. In the present, quite imperfect state of knowledge, the activities of the output department will thus have to be closer to cautious experimentation than to ambitious schemes of "fine tuning."

12.3.4. STABILIZATION OF BANK LIQUIDITY. The objective of the liquidity department in managing the banking account is the prevention of liquidity crises in the banking system. This is largely the purpose for which central banks came to be established. In practice, the open market operations of the liquidity department will be supported by other measures including, in particular, discount policy. For the present purpose these will be disregarded.

Other short-run objectives have often been added. Thus central banks were assigned the task of dampening seasonal fluctuations in interest rates by providing an "elastic currency" and of reducing interregional differences in credit market conditions. It was also regarded as desirable, or even necessary, to offset erratic fluctuations in treasury operations, international transactions, the check-clearing process, the currency ratio, the demand for money, and the distribution of deposits between different classes of deposits, banks, and individuals. In addition, by reducing the fluctuations of the yield on short-term government securities, the risk on these securities can be lowered, thus making them more attractive as an asset and reducing the interest at which a given treasury debt can be financed. In the United States, these "defensive" motives seem to have been responsible for an overwhelming proportion of annual open market transactions. In a highly imperfect credit market, a valid case can be made that they contribute to the efficiency of the economy. With a well-developed money market and, in particular, interbank credit market, these motives have little force, and often come close to the advocacy of special interests. What remains is the basic objective of preventing cumulative contractions in the money supply process of the sort described in the preceding section.

While the objectives of the price department and of the output department can each be summarized in terms of a single time series, this is not possible for bank liquidity. The liquidity department will thus wish to look at a number of indicators for possible signs of impending difficulties. Most of these indicators will be short-term interest rates, but if these rates are not market clearing, quantity series will also have to be used. Thus the volume of bank borrowings from the central bank may be relevant, since the discount rate, being set by the central bank, is often not a sensitive gauge of market conditions. The same can be true for excess reserves if transaction costs prevent their prompt adjustment through the money market. While the "money market strategy" (Guttentag, 1966), developed by the Federal Reserve to such a high degree of sophistication, is seriously deficient as an overall approach to central bank policy, it is a fair approximation of what the banking department may wish to consider.

With respect to the procedure problem, the liquidity department has an easy choice: It is clear that it will have to formulate its policy in terms of yields. What it wishes to prevent are dramatic changes in the terms at which banks can borrow, and this is most directly achieved by setting the terms at which credit can be obtained from the central bank. To try to formulate such policies in terms of the quantity of security purchases would expose them to large errors, because in the situation of a potential liquidity crisis, demand and supply functions and thus the relationship between quantities and yields may be subject to rapid shifts. What can be done with $10 million today may require $50 million tomorrow. This does not mean, of course, that the yield on government securities is held fixed; it only means that operating instructions are expressed in terms of yields, however changing these may be from day to day.

This leaves the rules problem: What trajectory should the yield on government securities be made to follow from day to day? As has often been pointed out, even large day-to-day fluctuations usually do little harm. International comparisons show that money markets without significant defensive operations may perform quite well. It is conceivable, therefore, that the liquidity department could discharge its obligation quite satisfactorily with only sporadic operations in times of acute disturbances, including those created by the operations of the other departments. As a tactical matter, however, the liquidity department may find it easier to perform its emergency function if it is continuously in the market, even in normal periods. Through this back door, a high volume of day-to-day defensive operations, though not necessary and perhaps not even desirable per se, may turn out to be an important contribution to the prevention of liquidity crises. As explained above, these operations are always subject to the constraint that the banking account will have to be brought back to zero within at most six months. By this device, prices and output are, for practical purposes, insulated against influences from the banking account.

On the preceding pages the three-frequency approach to central bank policy has been expounded by describing separately the objectives, procedures, and rules for each department or account. This is legitimate, at least in a first approximation, because the zero-base constraints effectively permit treatment of the three departments as independent agencies. It has been shown that many of the procedures, propositions, and postulates that have been debated in recent years, though often apparently conflicting, find their appropriate place in such a scheme. Overall central bank policy can be then described by simply adding the three accounts. The point is that it will often be extremely difficult, if not impossible, to formulate guidelines for the aggregate account, fluctuations of different frequencies being superimposed on each other in a complex way, while it may still be relatively easy to formulate guidelines for each separate account. It is in this sense I hope that the three-frequency approach may help to add clarity, and perhaps even some measure of consensus, to the debate on central bank policy.

However, economists should be under no illusion that central banking will ever become a science. Academic critics love to chide central bankers for their lack of a fully articulated doctrine of monetary policy, based on testable—and perhaps even tested—hypotheses. These critics mistake central bankers for what they are themselves, namely teachers and intellectuals. In fact, a good central banker is a doer and a politician, for whom even ambiguity and inconsistency may sometimes serve his purposes. His field of action is the ever-changing stream of economic history, where every day may pose new problems requiring new solutions. He will use economic science as a commander of armies uses military science, namely as collected pieces of information and wisdom that, though often useful and sometimes indispensable, can never provide a recipe for victory. In fact, such a recipe would be a contradiction in terms, because both opposing armies could use it, but only one can win. Similarly, a set of proven rules for monetary policy would be a contradiction in terms, because once its application is fully expected by everybody, it ceases to be effective. In monetary policy, as on the battlefield, it is the unexpected that counts most. This treatise may thus end on a note of humility: However far monetary theory may progress, central banking is likely to remain an art.

BIBLIOGRAPHY

Aliber, R. Z. 1967. Gresham's law, asset preferences, and the demand for international reserves. *Quarterly Journal of Economics* 81(4):628–38.

Allais, M. 1972. Forgetfulness and interest. *Journal of Money, Credit and Banking* 4(1):40–73.

Angell, J. W. 1937. The components of the circular velocity of money. *Quarterly Journal of Economics* 51(1):224–72.

Archibald, G. C., and Lipsey, R. G. 1958. Monetary and value theory: a critique of Lange and Patinkin. *Review of Economic Studies* 26(1):1–22.

Arrow, K. J., and Enthoven, A. C. 1961. Quasi-concave programming. *Econometrica* 29(4):779–800.

Askin, A. B., and Kraft, J. 1974. Similarities and differences among three models of the inflation process, with a preliminary evaluation of controls. *Southern Economic Journal* 41(1):62–77.

Axilrod, S. H. 1971. Monetary aggregates and money market conditions in open market policy. *Federal Reserve Bulletin* 57(1):79–104.

Balinski, M. L., and Baumol, W. J. 1968. The dual in nonlinear programming and its economic interpretation. *Review of Economic Studies* 35(3):237–56.

Baltensperger, E. 1972a. Economies of scale, firm size, and concentration in banking. *Journal of Money, Credit and Banking* 4(3):467–88.

———. 1972b. Costs of banking activities: interactions between risk and operating costs. *Journal of Money, Credit and Banking* 4(3):595–611.

Barone, E. 1919. *Principi di economia politica*. Rome. Athenaeum.

Barro, R. J. 1970. Inflation, the payments period, and the demand for money. *Journal of Political Economy* 78(6):1228–63.

———. 1972. Inflationary finance and the welfare cost of inflation. *Journal of Political Economy* 80(5):978–1001.

———. 1976. Integral constraints and aggregation in an inventory model of money demand. *Journal of Finance* 31(1):77–88.

Barro, R. J., and Grossman, H. I. 1971. Open-market operations and the medium of exchange. *Journal of Money, Credit and Banking* 3(2):304–11.

Barro, R. J., and Santomero, A. M. 1972. Household money holdings and the demand deposit rate. *Journal of Money, Credit and Banking* 4(2):397–413.

Baumol, W. J. 1952. The transactions demand for cash: an inventory theoretic approach. *Quarterly Journal of Economics* 66(4):545–56.

———. 1966. The escalated economy and the stimulating effects of inflation. In *Essays in Honor of Marco Fanno*, ed. T. Bagiotti, 2:96–104. Padua.

Becker, G. S., and Baumol, W. J. 1952. The classical monetary theory: the outcome of the discussion. *Economica N.S.* 19(76):355–76.

Benston, G. J. 1965. Economies of scale and marginal costs in banking operations. *National Banking Review* 2:507–49.

———. 1970. Cost of operations and economies of scale in savings and loan associations. In *Study of the Savings and Loan Industry*, ed. I. Friend, pp. 667–761. Washington, D.C.: Federal Home Loan Bank Board.

———. 1972. Economies of scale of financial institutions. *Journal of Money, Credit and Banking* 4(2):312–41.

Bernholz, P. 1965. Aufbewahrungs- und Transportkosten als Bestimmungsgründe der Geldnachfrage. *Schweizerische Zeitschrift für Volkswirtschaft und Statistik* Bd 101(1):1–15.

———. 1967. Erwerbskosten, Laufzeit und Charakter zinstragender Forderungen als Bestimmungsgründe der Geldnachfrage der Haushalte. *Zeitschrift für die Gesamte Staatswissenschaft* Bd. 123(1):9–24.

Bieri, H. G. 1963. Der Streit um die "klassische Dichotomie." *Schweizerische Zeitschrift für Volkswirtschaft und Statistik* 99(2):172–81.

Blinder, A. S., and Solow, R. M. 1973. Does fiscal policy matter? *Journal of Public Economics* 2(4):319–37.

Bloomfield, A. I. 1959. *Monetary policy under the international gold standard, 1880–1914*. New York: Federal Reserve Bank of New York.

———. 1963. *Short-term capital movements under the pre-1914 gold standard*. Princeton Studies in International Finance, no. 11.

Brown, W. A. 1940. *The international gold standard reinterpreted, 1914–1934*. New York: National Bureau of Economic Research.

Brunner, K. 1961. A schema for the supply theory of money. *International Economic Review* 2(1):79–109.

Brunner, K., and Meltzer, A. H. 1964. The Federal Reserve's attachment to the free reserve concept. Committee on Banking and Currency, House of Representatives, 88th Congress, 2nd Session. Washington, D.C.: Government Printing Office.

———. 1967a. Economies of scale in cash balances reconsidered. *Quarterly Journal of Economics* 81(3):422–36.

———. 1967b. The meaning of monetary indicators. In *Monetary Process and Policy: A Symposium*, ed. G. Horwich, pp. 187–217. Homewood, Ill.: Irwin.

———. 1968. Liquidity traps for money, bank credit, and interest rates. *Journal of Political Economy* 76(1):1–37.

———. 1971. The uses of money: money in the theory of an exchange economy. *American Economic Review* 61(5):784–805.

———. 1976. An aggregative theory for a closed economy. In *Monetarism*, ed. J. L. Stein, pp. 69–103. Amsterdam: North-Holland.

Bushaw, D. W., and Clower, R. W. 1957. *Introduction to mathematical economics*. Homewood, Ill.: Irwin.

Cagan, P. 1956. The monetary dynamics of hyperinflation. In *Studies in the Quantity*

Theory of Money, ed. M. Friedman, pp. 25–117. Chicago: University of Chicago Press.

———. 1969. Interest rates and bank reserves—a reinterpretation of the statistical association. In *Essays on Interest Rates*, ed. J. M. Guttentag and P. Cagan, 1:223–271. New York: National Bureau of Economic Research.

Cagan, P., and Gandolfi, A. 1969. The lag in monetary policy as implied by the time pattern of monetary effects on interest rates. *American Economic Review* 59(2):277–84.

Cannan, E. 1921. The application of the theoretical apparatus of supply and demand to units of currency. *Economic Journal* 31(4):453–61.

Carnahan, B., Luther, H. A., and Wilkes, J. O. 1969. *Applied numerical methods*. New York: Wiley.

Christ, C. F. 1973. Monetary and fiscal influences on U.S. money income, 1891–1970. *Journal of Money, Credit and Banking* 5(1), pt. 2: 279–300.

———. 1975. Judging the performance of econometric models of the U.S. economy. *International Economic Review* 16(1):54–74.

Christensen, L. R., and Jorgensen, D. W. 1973. U.S. income, saving and wealth, 1929–1969. *Review of Income and Wealth* 19(4):329–62.

Cooper, J. P., and Fischer, S. 1972. Simulation of monetary rules in the FRB–MIT–Penn model. *Journal of Money, Credit and Banking* 4(2):384–96.

———. 1974. Monetary and fiscal policy in the fully stochastic St. Louis econometric model. *Journal of Money, Credit and Banking* 6(1):1–22.

Despres, E.; Kindleberger, C. P.; and Salant, W. S. 1966. *The dollar and world liquidity; a minority view*. Washington, D.C.: Brookings.

Eagly, R. V. 1964. On the nature of constant value and the desirability of a constant price level. *Weltwirtschaftliches Archiv* 92(2):350–65.

Eckstein, O., and Brinner, R. 1972. *The inflation process in the United States*. Study prepared for use of the Joint Economic Committee, 92nd Congress, 2nd Session. Washington, D.C.

Edgeworth, F. Y. 1888. The mathematical theory of banking. *Journal of the Royal Statistical Society* 51:113–27.

Fabricant, S. 1971. Inflation and the lag in accounting practice. In *Accounting in Perspective: Contributions to Accounting Thought by Other Disciplines*, pp. 115–52. Cincinnati: South Western.

Feige, L., and Parkin, M. 1971. The optimal quantity of money, bonds, commodity inventories, and capital. *American Economic Review* 61(3), pt. 1:335–49.

Finch, D. 1956. *Purchasing power guarantees for deferred payments*. International Monetary Fund Staff Papers 5(1):1–22.

Fischer, S. 1972. Money, income, wealth and welfare. *Journal of Economic Theory* 4(2):289–311.

———. 1974. Money and the production function. *Economic Inquiry* 12(4):517–33.

———. 1975. The demand for index bonds. *Journal of Political Economy* 83(3): 509–34.

Fischer, S., and Cooper, J. P. 1973. Stabilization policy and lags. *Journal of Political Economy* 81(4):847–77.

Fisher, I. 1911. *The purchasing power of money; its determination and relation to credit, interest and crises*. New York: Macmillan.

————. 1930. *The theory of interest as determined by impatience to spend income and opportunity to invest it*. New York: Macmillan.

Foley, D. 1970. Economic equilibrium with costly marketing. *Journal of Economic Theory* 2(3):276–91.

Friedman, B. M. 1975. Targets, instruments and indicators of monetary policy. *Journal of Monetary Economics* 1(4):443–73.

Friedman, M. 1948. A monetary and fiscal framework for economic stability. *American Economic Review* 38(3):245–64.

————. 1951. Commodity-reserve currency. *Journal of Political Economy* 59(3): 203–32.

————. 1953. Discussion of the inflationary gap. In *Essàys in Positive Economics*, pp. 251–62. Chicago: University of Chicago Press.

————. 1956. The quantity theory of money—a restatement. In *Studies in the Quantity Theory of Money*, pp. 3–24. Chicago: University of Chicago Press.

————. 1959. *A program for monetary stability*. New York: Fordham University Press.

————. 1968. The role of monetary policy. *American Economic Review* 58(1):1–17.

————. 1969a. *The optimal quantity of money and other essays*. Chicago: Aldine.

————. 1969b. The Eurodollar market: some first principles. *Morgan Guarantee Survey*, pp. 4–14.

————. 1974. *Monetary correction: a proposal for escalation clauses to reduce the cost of ending inflation*. With appendix by B. Griffiths, "English classical political economy and the debate on indexation" (with bibliography). London: Institute of Economic Affairs.

Fromm, G., and Klein, L. R. 1976. The NBER/NSF model comparison seminar: an analysis of results. *Annals of Economic and Social Measurement* 5(1):1–28.

Geary, R. C. 1950. A note on "a constant-utility index of the cost of living." *Review of Economic Studies* 18(1):65–66.

Goldfeld, S. M. 1973. The demand for money revisited. *Brookings Papers on Economic Activity*, no. 3, pp. 577–646.

Graham, B. 1937. *Storage and stability*. New York: McGraw-Hill.

————. 1944. *World commodities and world currency*. New York: McGraw-Hill.

Graham, F. D. 1942. *Social goals and economic institutions*. Princeton: Princeton University Press.

Grandmont, J. M., and Younes, Y. 1973. On the efficiency of a monetary equilibrium. *Review of Economic Studies* 40(2):149–65.

Greenbaum, S. I. 1967. A study of bank costs. *National Banking Review* 4:415–34.

Gurley, J. G., and Shaw, E. S. 1960. *Money in a theory of finance*. Washington, D.C.: Brookings.

Guttentag, J. M. 1966. The strategy of open market operations. *Quarterly Journal of Economics* 80(2):1–30.

Haberler, G. 1958. *Prosperity and depression*. 4th ed. Cambridge, Mass.: Harvard University Press.

Hahn, F. H. 1971a. Professor Friedman's views on money. *Economica* 38(149): 61–80.

————. 1971b. Equilibrium with transaction costs. *Econometrica* 39(3):417–39.

————. 1973. On transaction costs, inessential sequence economies and money. *Review of Economic Studies* 40(4):449–61.

Hamburger, M. J. 1968. Household demand for financial assets. *Econometrica* 36(1):97–118.

Hanke, S.; Carver, P. H.; and Bugg, P. 1975. Project evaluation during inflation. *Water Resources Research* 11(4):511–14.

Hansen, B. 1973. On the effects of fiscal and monetary policy: a taxonomic discussion. *American Economic Review* 63(4):546–71.

Heller, W. P. 1972. Transactions with set-up costs. *Journal of Economic Theory* 4(3):465–78.

———. 1974. The holding of money balances in general equilibrium. *Journal of Economic Theory* 7(1):93–108.

Hicks, J. R. 1933. Gleichgewicht und Konjunktur. *Zeitschrift für Nationalökonomie* 4(4):441–55.

———. 1935. A suggestion for simplifying the theory of money. *Economica* N.S. 2(1):1–19.

———. 1967. *Critical essays in monetary theory*. Oxford: Clarendon Press.

Horsefield, J. K., and de Vries, M. G. 1969. *The international monetary fund, 1945–1965*. Washington, D.C.: International Monetary Fund.

Jevons, W. S. 1875. *Money and the mechanism of exchange*. London: King.

Johnson, H. G. 1962. Monetary theory and policy. *American Economic Review* 52(3):335–84.

———. 1963. Equilibrium under fixed exchanges. *American Economic Review* 53(2):112–19.

———. 1967. Theoretical problems of the international monetary system. *Pakistan Development Revue* 7(1):1–28.

———. 1968. Problems of efficiency in monetary management. *Journal of Political Economy* 76(5):971–90.

———. 1969. Inside money, outside money, income, wealth, and welfare in monetary theory. *Journal of Money, Credit and Banking* 11(1):30–45.

Jorgensen, D. W. 1971. Econometric studies of investment behavior: a survey. *Journal of Economic Literature* 9(4):1111–47.

Kalchbrenner, J. H., and Tinsley, P. A. 1976. On the use of feedback control in the design of aggregate monetary policy. *American Economic Review* 66(2):349–55.

Kareken, J. H., and Wallace, N. 1972. The monetary instrument variable choice: how important? *Journal of Money, Credit and Banking* 4(3):723–29.

Karni, E. 1972. Inflation and real interest rate: a long-term analysis. *Journal of Political Economy* 80(2):365–74.

———. 1973. Transactions costs and the demand for media exchange. *Western Economic Journal* 11(1):71–80.

Kelly, L. G. 1967. *Handbook of numerical methods and applications*. Reading, Mass.: Addison-Wesley.

Keynes, J. M. 1923. *A tract on monetary reform*. London: Macmillan.

———. 1930. *A treatise on money*. 2 vols. London: Macmillan.

———. 1936. *The general theory of employment, interest, and money*. London: Macmillan.

Kinley, D. 1904. *Money; a study of the theory of exchange*. London: Macmillan.

Klein, B. 1974. The competitive supply of money. *Journal of Money, Credit and Banking* 6(4):423–53.

Klein, M. A. 1971. A theory of the banking firm. *Journal of Money, Credit and Banking* 3(2):205–18.

Kurz, M. 1974. Equilibrium with transaction cost and money in a single market exchange economy. *Journal of Economic Theory* 7(4):418–52.

Landry, A. 1905. La rapidité de la circulation monétaire. *Revue d'économie politique* 19:155–74.

Lange, O. 1942. Say's law: a restatement and criticism. In *Studies in Mathematical Economics and Econometrics*, ed. O. Lange, et al. pp. 49–68. Chicago: University of Chicago Press.

Leavens, D. H. 1939. *Silver Money*. Cowles Commission for Research in Economics, no. 4. Bloomington, Ind.: Principia Press.

Leontief, W. 1948. Postulates: Keynes' general theory and the classicists. In *The New Economics*, ed. S. Harris. New York: Knopf.

Lerner, A. 1947. Money as a creature of the State. *American Economic Review* 37(2):312–17.

Levhari, D., and Patinkin, D. 1968. The role of money in a simple growth model. *American Economic Review* 58(4):713–53.

Longbrake, W. A., and Haslem, J. A. 1975. Productive efficiency in commercial banking. *Journal of Money, Credit and Banking* 7(3):317–30.

McNelis, P. D. 1974. A simulation analysis of monetary policy and macroeconomic adjustments. Ph.D. diss., Johns Hopkins University.

Mangoletsis, I. D. 1975. The microeconomics of indirect finance. *Journal of Finance* 30(4):1055–63.

Marget, A. W. 1938. *The theory of prices*, vol. 1. London:King.

Markowitz, H. 1952. Portfolio selection. *Journal of Finance* 7(1):77–91.

———. 1959. *Portfolio selection—efficient diversification of investments*. New York: Wiley.

Marschak, J. 1950. The rationale of the demand for money and of "money illusion." *Metroeconomica* 2:71–100.

Marshall, A. 1923. *Money, credit and commerce*. London: Macmillan.

———. 1925. Remedies for fluctuations of general prices. In *Memorials of Alfred Marshall*, ed. A. C. Pigou, pp. 188–211. London: Macmillan.

———. 1926. *Official papers*. London: Macmillan.

Marty, A. L. 1968. The optimal rate of growth of money. *Journal of Political Economy* 76(4), pt. 2:860–73.

Mauer, L. J. 1966. The Patinkin controversy: a review. *Kyklos* 19(2):299–314.

Mauskopf, E. 1976. Inflation expectations in Israel: direct estimates from purchasing-power bonds. Ph.D. diss., Johns Hopkins University.

Meigs, A. J. 1962. *Free reserves and the money supply*. Chicago: Chicago University Press.

Menger, C. 1871. *Grundsätze der Volkswirtschaftslehre*. Vienna: Braumüller.

Metzler, L. A. 1945. Stability of multiple markets: the Hicks conditions. *Econometrica* 13:277–92.

———. 1951. Wealth, saving, and the rate of interest. *Journal of Political Economy* 59(2):93–116.

Mill, J. S. 1857. *Principles of political economy*. 4th ed. 2 vols. London: Parker.

Miller, M. H., and Orr, D. 1966. A model of the demand for money by firms. *Quarterly Journal of Economics* 80(3):413–35.

————. 1968. The demand for money by firms: extensions of analytic results. *Journal of Finance* 23(5):735–59.

Mises, L. 1924. *Theorie des Geldes und der Umlaufsmittel.* 2nd ed. Munich/Leipzig: Duncker & Humblot.

Modigliani, F., and Ando, A. 1976. Impacts of fiscal actions on aggregate income and the monetarist controversy: theory and evidence. In *Monetarism*, ed. J. L. Stein, pp. 17–42. Amsterdam: North-Holland.

Mundell, R. 1963. Inflation and real interest. *Journal of Political Economy* 71(3): 280–83.

————. 1965. Growth, stability, and inflationary finance. *Journal of Political Economy* 73(2):97–109.

Newlyn, W. T. 1962. *Theory of money.* Oxford: Clarendon Press.

Niehans, J. 1962. The effects of post-war inflation on the distribution of income. In *Inflation—proceedings of a conference held by the International Economic Association*, ed. D. C. Hague, pp. 73–92. London: Macmillan.

————. 1969a. Money in a static theory of optimal payment arrangements. *Journal of Money, Credit and Banking* 1(4):706–26.

————. 1969b. The neoclassical dichotomy as a controlled experiment. *Journal of Political Economy* 77(4), pt. 1:504–11.

————. 1970. Die Geldnachfrage in einer dynamischen Optimierungstheorie des Zahlungssystems. *Schweizerische Zeitschrift für Volkswirtschaft und Statistik* 106(2):129–48.

————. 1971. Money and barter in general equilibrium with transactions costs. *American Economic Review* 61(5):773–83.

————. 1973. The flexibility of the gold-exchange standard and its limits. In *The Economics of Common Currencies*, ed. H. G. Johnson and A. K. Swoboda, pp. 46–64. London: Allen & Unwin.

————. 1974a. Monetary policy with full stock adjustment. *Zeitschrift für Wirtschafts- und Sozialwissenschaften*, no. 1, pp. 17–43.

————. 1974b. Reserve composition as a source of independence for national monetary policies. In *National Monetary Policies and the International Financial System*, ed. R. Z. Aliber, pp. 273–880. Chicago: University of Chicago Press.

————. 1975. Interest and credit in general equilibrium with transactions costs. *American Economic Review* 65(4):548–66.

————. 1976. How to fill an empty shell. *American Economic Review* 66(2):177–83.

Niehans, J., and Hewson, J. 1967. The euro-dollar market and monetary theory. *Journal of Money, Credit and Banking* 7(1):1–27.

Nordhaus, W. D. 1973. The effects of inflation on the distribution of economic welfare. *Journal of Money, Credit and Banking* 5(1), pt. 2:465–504.

Orr, D. 1970. *Cash management and the demand for money.* New York: Praeger.

Orr, D., and Mellon, W. G. 1961. Stochastic reserve losses and expansion of bank credit. *American Economic Review* 51(4):614–23.

Ostroy, J. M. 1973. The informational efficiency of monetary exchange. *American Economic Review* 63(4):597–610.

Pantaleoni, M. 1898. *Pure economics*, trans. T. B. Bruce. London: Macmillan.

Patinkin, D. 1948. Relative prices, Say's law, and the demand for money. *Econometrica* 16(2):135–54.

————. 1965. *Money, interest, and prices.* 2nd ed., New York: Harper & Row.

———. 1969. Money and wealth: a review article. *Journal of Economic Literature* 7(4):1140–60.

———. 1972. Samuelson on the neoclassical dichotomy: a comment. *Canadian Journal of Economics* 5(2):279–83.

Pesek, B. P., and Saving, T. R. 1967. *Money, wealth, and economic theory*. New York: Macmillan.

Phillips, A. W. 1958. The relation between unemployment and the rate of change of money wage rates in the United Kingdom, 1861–1957. *Economica* N.S. 25(100):283–99.

Phillips, C. A. 1920. *Bank Credit*. New York: Macmillan.

Pierce, J. L. 1976. Quantitative analysis for decisions of the Federal Reserve, *The Impact of the Federal Reserve's Money Policies on the Economy*, pp. 157–62. Hearings before the subcommittee on domestic monetary policy, 94th Congress, 2nd Session. Washington, D.C.: Government Printing Office.

Pigou, A. C. 1917. The value of money. *Quarterly Journal of Economics* 32(4):38–65.

Poole, W. M. 1970a. Optimal choice of monetary policy instruments in a simple stochastic macromodel. *Quarterly Journal of Economics* 84(2):197–216.

———. 1970b. Gradualism: a mid-course view. *Brookings Papers on Economic Activity*, no. 2, pp. 271–295.

Pyle, D. H. 1971. On the theory of financial intermediation. *Journal of Finance* 26(3):737–47.

Riefler, W. W. 1930. *Money rates and money markets in the United States*. New York: Harper.

Roscher, W. 1880. *Grundlagen der Nationalökonomie*. System der Volkswirtschaft 1, 15th ed. Stuttgart.

Rosenstein-Rodan, P. N. 1936. The coordination of the general theories of money and price. *Economica* N.S. 3(11):257–80.

Samuelson, P. A. 1947. *Foundations of economic analysis*. Cambridge, Mass.: Harvard University Press.

———. 1963. D. H. Robertson (1890–1963). *Quarterly Journal of Economics* 77(4):517–36.

———. 1968. What classical and neoclassical monetary theory really was. *Canadian Journal of Economics* 1(1):1–15.

———. 1969. Nonoptimality of money holding under "laissez faire." *Canadian Journal of Economics* 2(2):303–308.

Santomero, A. M. 1974. A model of the demand for money by households. *Journal of Finance* 29(1):89–102.

Sarnat, M. 1973. Purchasing power risk, portfolio analysis, and the case for index-linked bonds. *Journal of Money, Credit and Banking* 5(3):836–45.

Schumpeter, J. A. 1934. Robinson's economics of imperfect competition. *Journal of Political Economy* 42(2):249–57.

Selden, R. T. 1956. Monetary velocity in the United States. In *Studies in the Quantity Theory of Money*, ed. M. Friedman, pp. 179–257. Chicago: University of Chicago Press.

Shanahan, E. (ed.) 1974. *Indexing and inflation*, American Enterprise Institute Roundtable. Washington, D.C. (contr. by W. Fellner, M. Friedman, R. J. Gordon, Ch. Walker).

Sheppard, D. K., and Barrett, C. R. 1965. Financial credit multipliers and the availability of funds. *Economica* N.S. 32(126):198–214.

Smith, A. 1776/1904. *An inquiry into the nature and causes of the wealth of nations*, ed. Cannan. Vol. 1. London: Methuen.

Sontheimer, K. 1972. On the determination of money prices. *Journal of Money, Credit and Banking* 4(3):489–508.

Starr, R. M. 1970. Equilibrium and demand for media of exchange in a pure exchange economy with transactions costs. Cowles Foundation Discussion Paper no. 300.

———. 1972. Exchange in barter and monetary economies. *Quarterly Journal of Economics* 86(2):290–302.

———. 1974. The price of money in a pure exchange monetary economy with taxation. *Econometrica* 42(1):45–54.

Starrett, D. 1973. Inefficiency and the demand for "money" in a sequence economy. *Review of Economic Studies* 40(4):437–48.

Stein, J. L. 1971. *Money and capacity growth*. New York: Columbia University Press.

———. 1976. Inside the monetarist black box. In *Monetarism*, ed. J. L. Stein, pp. 183–232. Amsterdam: North-Holland.

Stein, J. L., and Infante, E. F. 1973. Optimal Stabilization Paths. *Journal of Money, Credit and Banking* 5(1), pt. 2:525–562.

Sutch, R. C., and Thurston, T. B. 1976. Member bank borrowing from the Federal Reserve System and the impact of discount policy. *Quarterly Review of Economics and Business* 16(3):7–23.

Talley, R. J. 1975. *The relative importance of the speculative and precautionary motives for holding money*. Ph.D. diss., Johns Hopkins University.

Thornton, H. 1802/1939. *An enquiry into the nature and effects of the paper credit of Great Britain*, ed. F. A. v. Hayek. London: Allen & Unwin.

Tobin, J. 1956. The interest-elasticity of transactions demand for cash. *Review of Economics and Statistics* 3(38):241–47.

———. 1958. Liquidity preference as behavior towards risk. *Review of Economic Studies* 25(1):65–86.

———. 1963. Commercial banks as creators of "money." In *Banking and Monetary Studies*, ed. D. Carson. Homewood, Ill.: Irwin.

———. 1965. The theory of portfolio selection. In *The Theory of Interest Rates*, ed. F. Hahn and F. P. R. Brechling. London: Macmillan.

———. 1969. A general equilibrium approach to monetary theory. *Journal of Money, Credit and Banking* 1(1):15–29.

Tobin, J., and Brainard, W. C. 1963. Financial intermediaries and the effectiveness of monetary controls. *American Economic Review* 53(2):383–400.

Tobin, J., and Buiter, W. 1976. Long-run effects of fiscal and monetary policy on aggregate demand. In *Monetarism*, ed. J. L. Stein, pp. 273–309. Amsterdam: North-Holland.

Tolley, G. S. 1957. Providing for growth of the money supply. *Journal of Political Economy* 65(6):465–85.

Tsiang, S. C. 1969. The precautionary demand for money: an inventory theoretical analysis. *Journal of Political Economy* 77(1):99–117.

Viner, J. 1923. Taxation and changes in price levels. *Journal of Political Economy* 31(4):494–520.

———. 1937. *Studies in the theory of international trade*. New York: Harper.

Walras, L. 1886. *Théorie de la monnaie*. Lausanne: Corbaz.

———. 1900. *Eléments d'économie politique pure, ou théorie de la richesse sociale.* 4th ed. Lausanne: Rouge; Paris: Pichon.

Whalen, E. L. 1966. A rationalization of the precautionary demand for cash. *Quarterly Journal of Economics* 80(2):314–24.

Wicksell, K. 1934/35. *Lectures on political economy*, trans. E. Classen. 2 vol. London: Routledge.

———. 1898/1936. *Interest and prices*, trans. R. F. Kahn. London: Macmillan.

Young, R. A. 1973. *Instruments of monetary policy in the United States—the role of the Federal Reserve System*. Washington, D.C.: International Monetary Fund.

NAME INDEX

Aliber, R. Z., 159
Allais, M., 39
Ando, A., 251
Angell, J. W., 23
Archibald, G. C., 10, 67, 206, 234
Arrow, K. J., 26
Axilrod, S. H., 283

Balinski, M. L., 27
Baltensperger, E., 176, 181
Barone, E., 154
Barrett, C. R., 273
Barro, R. J., 19–20, 39–40, 51, 232
Baumol, W. J., 10, 17, 27, 42, 45, 49, 132
Becker, G. S., 10
Benston, G. J., 181
Bernholz, P., 19, 68
Bieri, H. G., 10
Blinder, A. S., 202, 206, 208, 234, 240–41
Brainard, W. C., 203
Brunner, K., 51, 63, 209, 267–68, 274, 279, 283
Bugg, P., 126
Buiter, W., 203, 206, 215
Bushaw, D. W., 235

Cagan, P., 39, 243, 280–81
Cannan, E., 13
Carver, P. H., 126
Carver, T. N., 4
Cassel, G., 13
Christ, C. F., 244, 251, 253
Clower, R. W., 235
Cooper, J. P., 291–92

Despres, E., 160

Eagly, R. V., 118
Edgeworth, F. Y., 175
Enthoven, A. C., 26

Fabricant, S., 137
Feige, L., 51
Fellner, W., 136–37
Finch, D., 132
Fischer, S., 15, 134, 185, 192, 291–92
Fisher, I., 5, 12, 133, 201
Foley, D., 19
Friedman, B., 267, 285, 289
Friedman, M.: on commodity money, 150, 154; on constant money supply rule, 283–84, 287; on escalator clauses, 136–37; on eurodollar multiplier, 274; on inflation tax, 36; on money demand, 82; on money as producer good, 15; on optimal money supply, 6, 79, 93; on policy lags, 260, 291; on quantity theory, 5, 202; on transaction costs, 27, 95; on utility of money, 27, 36, 77–78
Fromm, G., 244, 251–52

Gandolfi, A., 243
Geary, R. C., 130
Gesell, S., 92
Graham, B., 153
Graham, F. D., 153
Grandmont, J. M., 79, 92–93, 96
Greenbaum, S. J., 181
Grossman, H. I., 232
Gurley, J. G., 166, 172, 192, 204, 220, 234
Guttentag, J. M., 283, 293

305

SUBJECT INDEX

Accounting costs, 119–24

Adjustment path, 233–62; sensitivity of, 245–49; stages of, 200–201, 209–31, 242–45, 256–61

Asset demand, macroeconomic: adjustment speeds of, 209–10, 235–36, 247–48; functions of, specified, 204–05, 237–38; significance of interest elasticities of, 214–16, 219, 223–24, 245–46

Asset diversification. *See* Portfolio diversification

Asset prices, 200–201, 204, 209–12

Asset transformation, 167–82, 264–66

Automatic stabilizers: fiscal, under inflation, 137; monetary, under gold standard, 146, 150, 152

Balance of payments, 149, 162, 264

Bank: borrowing, 173–75, 177–78, 189, 278–79; deposits, 168–84, 186–91, 193–97, 272–78; equity, 170–72, 176–81, 194, 266; loans, 168–82, 186–91, 272–81; redeposit ratio, 171, 273; regulation, 198, 267, 269–71, 282; panics, 199, 271, 282; service charges, 197. *See also* Reserves, bank

Banking system: economic effects of, 168–70, 191–93; efficiency of, 196–98; imperfect competition in, 182, 192, 194–96, 198; structure of, 182, 198

Banking theory: with fixed coefficients, 170–73, 272–74; for general equilibrium, 185–91, 274–78; optimizing, 173–82; 188–90

Barter, 99–117; inefficiency of, 2–5, 111

Bimetallism, 153–58

Bond demand: aggregate, 82, 91, 96–97, 204–5, 235–38; individual, 41–59, 64, 67

Bretton Woods, 158, 266

Broker, function of, 42, 62, 104, 166–67, 173–75, 264

Budget constraints: government, 83, 89, 151, 207, 240, 264–65; individual, 6, 9, 26, 66; multiple, 26, 65–66, 107, 115

Business cycles, 199, 242–49, 256–61, 270–71, 281–82, 289–94

Capital gains, 61, 84, 200–201, 209–12

Capitalism, 125–26

Capital stock: capacity effects of, 220–25; demand for, 204–5, 235–38; dynamic adjustment of, 244–45; effect of monetary policy on, 220–26; prices of, 200–201, 204, 209–12; in transaction cost model, 98

Cash balance approach, 5, 17

Central banks: functions of, 264–71, 282; policy guidelines of, 282–94; portfolios, of, 258, 265, 285–94

Chicago Rule (of money supply), 93–97

Commodity flows: endogenous, 24–29, 60–79, 105–13; exogenous, 24, 100–105

Commodity money: in general equilibrium, 103–5, 111–13, 116; under gold standard, 140–65; under inflation, 127; nonneutrality of, 9, 113, 147–48, 193; as numéraire, 129

Commodity stocks, 14, 60–79, 115–16

308

Library of Congress Cataloging
in Publication Data

Niehans, Jürg.
    The theory of money.

    Bibliography: pp. 295–304
    Includes index.
    1. Money.   I.   Title.
HG221.N66   332.4'01   77–17247
ISBN 0–8018–2055–3 (hardcover)
ISBN 0–8018–2372–2 (paperback)